DOCUMENTS SET

Raymond Hylton

THE WORLD'S HISTORY

Volume I

HOWARD SPODEK

PRENTICE HALL, *Upper Saddle River, New Jersey 07458*

© 1998 by PRENTICE-HALL, INC.
Simon & Schuster / A Viacom Company
Upper Saddle River, New Jersey 07458

10 9 8 7 6 5 4 3 2 1

ISBN 0-13-679078-X
Printed in the United States of America

Table of Contents

PART III: EMPIRE AND IMPERIALIZATION

PART IV: THE RISE OF WORLD RELIGIONS

CHAPTER 1

1–1
"Nihongi": the ancient Japanese perspective on the World's creation.

The "Nihongi" or "Japanese Chronicles," along with the "Kujiki" and "Kojiki," forms the oldest extant written basis of Shinto (or, more accurately, "Kami-no Michi," the "Way of the Gods"), the indigenous faith of Japan. It was compiled by an unknown author (or authors) around 720 C.E., but draws on much older archives, legends, and traditions.

Source: Raymond Van Over, ed., *Sun Songs: Creation Myths from Around the World* (New York: Mentor, 1980), p. 353–361.

Of old, Heaven and Earth were not yet separated, and the Yin (female) and Yang (male) principles not yet divided. They formed a chaotic mass like an egg which was of obscurely defined limits and contained germs (life principle).

The purer and clearer part was thinly drawn out, ascended and formed Heaven, while the heavier and grosser element settled down and became Earth. The finer element easily became a united body, but the consolidation of the heavy and gross element was accomplished with difficulty. Heaven was therefore formed first, and Earth was established subsequently. Thereafter Divine Beings were produced between them.

Hence, it is said that when the world began to be created, the soil of which lands were composed floated about in a manner which might be compared to the floating of a fish sporting on the surface of the water.

At this time a certain thing was produced between Heaven and Earth. It was in form like a reed-shoot. Now this became transformed into a God, and was called Land-eternal-stand-of-august-thing.

Next there was Land-of-right-soil-of-augustness, and next Rich-form-plain-of-augustness—in all three deities.

These were pure males spontaneously developed by the operation of the principle of Heaven (Yang).

In one writing it is said: "Before Heaven and Earth were produced, there was something which might be compared to a cloud floating over the sea. It had no place of attachment for its root. In the midst of this a thing was generated which resembled a reed-shoot when it is first produced in the mud. This became straightway transformed into human (deity) shape and was called Kuni no toko-tachi no Mikoto (Land-eternal-of-august-thing).

Thereupon they thrust down the jewel-spear of Heaven, and groping about therewith found the ocean. The brine which dripped from the point of the spear coagulated and became an island which received the name of Ono-goro-jima (Spontaneously-congeal-island).

The two Deities thereupon descended and dwelt in this island. Accordingly they wished to become husband and wife together, and to produce countries.

So they made Spontaneous-island, or Ahaji, the pillar of the center of the land.

Two Kami, He-who-invites and She-who-invites, stood on the floating bridge of Heaven and held counsel together, saying: "Is there not a country beneath?"

Then the eight-great-islands country was produced by the coagulation of the foam of the saltwater."

It is also stated that they were produced by the coagulation of the foam of fresh water,

In one writing it is said: "The Gods of Heaven addressed He-who-invites and She-who-invites, saying: "There is the country Abundant-reed-plain. Do ye proceed and bring it into order?" They then gave them the jewel-spear of Heaven. Hereupon the two Gods stood on the floating bridge of Heaven, and plunging down the spear, sought for land. Then upon stirring the ocean with it, and bringing it up again, the brine which dripped from the spear-point coagulated and became an island, which was called Ono-goro-jima (Spontaneously-congeal-island). The two gods descended, dwelt in this island, and erected there an eight-fathom place. They also set up the pillar of Heaven."

Then the male Deity asked the female Deity, saying: "Is there anything formed in thy body?"

She answered and said: "My body has a place completely formed, and called the source of femininity."

The male god said: "My body again has a place completely formed, and called the source of masculinity. I desire to unite my source of masculinity to thy source of femininity."

Having thus spoken, they prepared to go around the pillar of Heaven, and made a promise, saying: "Do thou, my younger sister, go around from the left, while I will go around from the right." Having done so, they went around separately and met, when the female Deity spoke first, "How pretty! a lovely youth!"

The male Deity then answered and said: "How pretty! a lovely maiden!"

Finally they became husband and wife. Their first child was the leech, whom they straightway placed in a reed boat and sent adrift. Their next was the Island of Ahaji. This also was not included in the number of their children. Wherefore they returned up again to Heaven, and fully reported the circumstances. Then the Heavenly Gods divined this by the greater divination. Upon which they instructed them, saying: "It was by reason of the woman's having spoken first; ye had best return thither again." Thereupon having divined a time, they went down.

They next produced the sea, then the rivers, and then the mountains. Then they produced the ancestor of the trees, and next the ancestor of herbs.

After this He-who-invites and She-who-invites consulted together, saying: "We have now produced the Great-eight-island country, with the mountains, rivers, herbs, and trees. Why should we not produce someone who shall be lord of the universe?" They then together produced the Sun-Goddess, who was called Great-noon-female-of-possessor.

The resplendent luster of this child shone throughout all the six quarters. Therefore the two Deities rejoiced, saying: "We have had many children, but none of them have been equal to this wondrous infant. She ought not to be kept long in this land, but we ought of our own accord to send her at once to Heaven, and entrust to her the affairs of Heaven."

At this time, Heaven and Earth were still not far separated, and therefore they sent her up to Heaven by the ladder of Heaven.

They next produced the Moon-god, or the Bow-of-darkness.

His radiance was next to that of the Sun in splendor. This God was to be the consort of the Sun-Goddess, and to share in her government. They therefore sent him also to Heaven.

Next they produced the leech-child, which even at the age of three years could not stand upright. They therefore placed it in the rock-camphor-wood boat of Heaven, and abandoned it to the winds.

Their next child was Impetuous Male.

This God had a fierce temper and was given to cruel acts, Moreover he made a practice of continually weeping and wailing. So he brought many of the people of the land to an untimely end. Again he caused green mountains to become withered. Therefore the two Gods, his parents, addressed Impetuous Male, saying: "Thou art exceedingly wicked, and it is not meet that thou shouldst reign over the world. Certainly thou must depart far away to the Nether Land." So they at length expelled him.

In one writing it is said: "After the sun and moon, the next child which was born was the leech-child. When this child had completed his third year, he was nevertheless still unable to stand upright. The reason why the leech-child was born was that in the beginning, when He-who-invites and She-who-invites went around the pillar, the female Deity was the first to utter an exclamation of pleasure, and the law of male and female was therefore broken. They next procreated Impetuous Male. This God was of a wicked nature, and was always fond of wailing and wrath. Many of the people of the land died, and the

green mountains withered. Therefore his parents addressed him, saying: "Supposing that thou wert to rule this country, much destruction of life would surely ensue. Thou must govern the far-distant Nether Land." Their next child was the bird-rock-camphor-wood boat of Heaven. They forthwith took this boat and, placing the leech-child in it, abandoned it to the current. Their next child was Kaqu tsuchi" (God of Fire).

Now She-who-invites was burned by Kagu tsuchi, so that she died. When she was lying down to die, she gave birth to the Earth-Goddess (Hani-yama-hime) and the Water-Goddess (Midzu-ha-no-me). Upon this, Kagu tsuchi took to wife Hani-yama-hime, and they had a child. On the crown of this Deity's head were produced the silkworm and the mulberry tree, and in her navel the five kinds of grain.

In one writing it is said: "The Sun-Goddess, aware from the beginning of the fierce and relentless purpose of Impetuous Male said (to herself) when he ascended: "The coming of my younger brother is not for a good object. He surely means to rob me of my Plain of Heaven." So she made manly warlike preparation, girding upon her a ten-span sword, a nine-span sword, and an eight-span sword. Moreover, on her back she slung a quiver, and on her forearm drew a dread loud-sounding elbow-pad. In her hand she took a bow and arrow, and going forth to meet him in person, stood on her defense. The Impetuous Male declared to her, saying: "From the beginning I have had no evil intentions. All that I wished was to see thee, my elder sister, face to face. It is only for a brief space that I have come." Thereupon the Sun-Goddess, standing opposite to Impetuous Male, swore an oath, saying: "If thy heart is pure, and thou hast no purpose of relentless robbery, the children born to thee will surely be males." When she had finished speaking, she ate first the ten-span sword which she had girded on, and produced a child. Moreover, she ate the nine-span sword, and produced another child. Moreover she ate the eight-span sword, and produced another child—in all three female Deities. After this Impetuous Male took the string of five hundred august jewels which hung upon his neck, and having rinsed them in the Nuna (True) well of Heaven, another name for which is the true-well of Isa, and ate them. So he produced a child, in all five male Deities. Therefore, as Impetuous Male had thus acquired proof of his victory, the Sun-Goddess learned exactly that his intentions were wholly free from guilt. The three female Deities which the Sun-Goddess had produced were accordingly sent down to the Land of Tsukushi. She therefore instructed them, saying: "Do you, three Deities, go down and dwell in the center of the province, where you will assist the descendants of Heaven, and receive worship from them.'"

In one writing it is said: "The Sun-Goddess stood opposite to impetuous Male, separated from him by the Tranquil River of Heaven, and established a covenant with him, saying, "If thou hast not a traitorous heart, the children which thou wilt produce will surely be males, and if they are males, I will consider them my children, and will cause them to govern the Plain of Heaven." Hereupon the Sun-Goddess first ate her ten-span sword, which became converted into a child, the Goddess Oki-tsu-shima. Next she ate her nine-span sword, which became converted into a child, the Goddess Tagi-tsu hime. Again she ate her eight-span sword, which became converted into a child, the Goddess Ta-giri hime. Upon this, Impetuous Male took in his mouth the string of 500 jewels which was entwined in the left knot of his hair, and placed it on the palm of his left hand, whereupon it became converted into a male child. He then said: "Truly I have won."

In one writing it is said: "The august Sun-Goddess took an enclosed rice field and made it her Imperial rice field. Now Impetuous Male, in spring, filled up the channels and broke down the divisions, and in autumn, when the grain was formed, he forthwith stretched around them division ropes. Again when the Sun-Goddess was in her Weaving-Hall, he flayed alive a piebald colt and flung it into the Hall. In all these various matters his conduct was rude in the highest degree. Nevertheless, the Sun-Goddess, out of her friendship for him, was not indignant or resentful, but took everything calmly and with forbearance.

When the time came for the Sun-Goddess to celebrate the feast of first-fruits, Impetuous Male secretly voided excrement under her august seat in the New Palace. The Sun-Goddess, not knowing this, went straight there and took her seat. Accordingly the Sun-Goddess drew herself up, and was sickened. She therefore was enraged, and straightaway took up her abode in the Rock-cave of Heaven, and fastened its Rockdoor.

Then all the Gods were grieved at this, and forthwith caused Ama no nuka-do, the ancestor of the Be of mirror-makers, to make a mirror, Futo-dama, the ancestor of the Imibe, to make offerings, and Toyo-tama, the ancestor of the Be of jewel-makers, to make jewels. They also caused Mountain God to procure eighty precious combs of the five-hundred-branched true sakaki tree, and Moor God to produce eighty precious combs of the five-hundred-branched suzuki grass. When all these various objects were collected, Ama no Koyane, the ancestor of the Nakatomi, recited a liturgy in honor of the Deity. Then the Sun-Goddess opened the Rockdoor and came out. At this time, when the mirror was put into the Rock-cave, it struck against the door and received a slight flaw, which remains until this day. This is the great

Deity worshiped at Ise. After this, Impetuous Male was convicted, and fined in the articles required for the ceremony of purification. Hereupon these were the things abhorrent of luck of the tips of his fingers, and the things abhorrent of calamity of the tips of his toes. Again, of his spittle he made white soft offerings, and of his nose-mucus he made blue soft offerings, with which the purification service was performed. Finally he was banished according to the law of Divine banishment."

In one writing it is said: "After this the Sun-Goddess had three rice fields, which were called the Easy Rice field of Heaven, the Level Rice field of Heaven, and the Village-join Rice field of Heaven. All these were good rice fields, and never suffered even after continuous rain or drought. Now Impetuous Male had also three rice fields, which were called the Pile-field of Heaven, the River-border Field of Heaven, and the Mouth-Sharp Field of Heaven. All these were barren places. In the rains, the soil was swept away, and in droughts it was parked up. Therefore, Impetuous Male was jealous and destroyed his elder sister's rice fields. In spring, he knocked away the pipes and troughs, filled up the channels, and broke down the divisions. He also sowed seed over again. In autumn, he set up combs, and made horses lie down in the rice fields. Notwithstanding all these wicked doings, which went on incessantly, the Sun-Goddess was not indignant, but treated him always with calmness and forbearance, etc., etc.

When the Sun-Goddess came to shut herself up in the Rock-cave of Heaven, all the Gods sent the child of Kogoto Musubi, Ama no Koyane, and made him recite a liturgy. Hereupon Ama no Koyane rooted up a true Sakaki tree of the Heavenly Mount Kagu and hung upon its upper branches a mirror of eight hands, made by the ancestor of the mirror-makers; on the middle branches he hung curved jewels of Yasaka gem made by the ancestor of the jewel-makers.

Futo-dama was thereupon made to take these things in his hand, and, with lavish and earnest words of praise, to recite a liturgy.

When the Sun-Goddess heard this, she said: "Though of late many prayers have been addressed to me, of none has the language been so beautiful as this." So she opened a little the Rock-door and peeped out. Thereupon the God Ama no Tajikara-wo no Kami, who was waiting beside the Rock-door, forthwith pulled it open, and the radiance of the Sun-Goddess filled the universe. Therefore all the Gods rejoiced greatly, and imposed on Impetuous Male a fine of a thousand articles of purification.

Questions

(1) To what extent and in what particular instances might geographical factors play a role in the Shinto Creation story?

(2) What passages in "Nihongi" tend to stress the alleged Shinto emphasis on proper ceremony and ritual?

(3) What might "Nihongi" reveal about the moral and gender values of ancient Japan?

"Theogony" of Hesiod: the ancient Greek Creation Myth in poetic form.

Hesiod (fl. 8th century B.C.E.) is generally considered to be Greece's earliest non-epic poet. Some scholars, indeed, believe him to have been a contemporary of Homer, and to have lived towards the end of the so-called Greek "Dark Age." His monumental poem "Theogony," which may be translated: "Origin of the gods," draws upon centuries-old folklore and priestly tradition to put together the first known comprehensive account of the emergence of Greek gods and goddesses and their respective roles in fashioning the universe.

Source: Raymond Van Over, *Sun Songs: Creation Myths from Around the World* (New York: Mentor, 1980), pp. 198–209.

Hail! daughters of Jove; and give the lovely song. And sing the sacred race of immortals ever-existing, who sprang from Earth and starry Heaven, and murky Night, whom the briny Deep nourished. Say, too, how at the first the gods and earth were born, and rivers and boundless deep, rushing with swollen stream, and shining stars, and the broad Heaven above; and the gods who were sprung from these, givers of good gifts; and say how they divided their wealth, and how they apportioned their honors, and how at the first they occupied Olympus with-its-many-ravines. Tell me these things, ye Muses, abiding in Olympian homes from the beginning, and say ye what was the first of them that rose.

In truth then foremost sprang Chaos, and next broad-bosomed Earth, ever secure seat of all the immortals, who inhabit the peaks of snow-capped Olympus, and dark dim Tartarus in a recess of Earth having-broadways, and Love, who is most beautiful among immortal gods. Love that relaxes the limbs, and in the breasts of all gods and all men, subdues their reason and prudent counsel. But from Chaos were born Erebus and black Night; and from Night again sprang forth Ether and Day, whom she bore after having conceived, by union with Erebus in love. And Earth, in sooth, bore first indeed like to herself (in size) starry Heaven, that he might shelter her around on all sides, that so she might be ever a secure seat for the blessed gods; and she brought forth vast mountains, lovely haunts of deities, the Nymphs who dwell along the woodland hills. She too bore also the barren Sea, rushing with swollen stream, the Deep, I mean, without delightsome love; but afterward, having bedded with Heaven, she bore deep-eddying Ocean, Caeus and Crius, Hyperion and Iapetus, Thea and Rhea, Themis, Mnemosyne, and Phoebe with golden coronet, and lovely Tethys. And after these was born, youngest, wily Cronus, most savage of their children; and he hated his vigor-giving sire. Then brought she forth next the Cyclops, having an overbearing spirit, Brontes, and Steropes, and stout-hearted Arges, who both gave to Jove his thunder, and forged his lightnings. Now these, in sooth, were in other respects, it is true, like to gods, but a single eye was fixed in their mid-foreheads. And they from immortals grew up speaking mortals, and Cyclops was their appropriate name, because, I wot, in their foreheads one circular eye was fixed. Strength, force, and contrivances were in their works. But again,

from Earth and Heaven sprung other three sons, great and mighty, scarce to be mentioned, Cottus and Briareus and Gyas, children exceeding proud. From the shoulders of these moved actively a hundred hands, not brooking approach, and to each above sturdy limbs there grew fifty heads from their shoulders. Now monstrous strength is powerful, joined with vast size. For of as many sons as were born of Earth and Heaven, they were the fiercest, and were hated by their sire from the very first: as soon as any of these was born, he would hide them all, and not send them up to the light, in a cave of the earth, and Heaven exulted over the work of mischief, while huge Earth inly groaned, straitened as she was; and she devised a subtle and evil scheme. For quickly having produced a stock of white iron, she forged a large sickle, and gave the word to her children, and said encouragingly, though troubled in her heart: "Children of me and of a sire madly violent, if ye would obey me, we shall avenge the baneful injury of your father; for he was the first that devised acts of indignity." So spake she, but fear seized on them all, I wot, nor did any of them speak; till, having gathered courage, great and wily Cronus bespake his dear mother thus in reply:

"Mother this deed at any rate I will undertake and accomplish, since for our sire, in sooth, of-detested-name, I care not; for he was the first that devised acts of indignity."

Thus spake he, and huge Earth rejoiced much at heart, sad hid and planted him in ambush: in his hand she placed a sickle with jagged teeth, and suggested to him all the stratagem.

Then came vast Heaven bringing Night with him, and, eager for love, brooded around Earth, and lay stretched, I wot, on all sides: but his son from out his ambush grasped at him with his left hand, while in his right he took the huge sickle, long and jagged-toothed, and hastily mowed off the genitals of his sire, and threw them back to be carried away behind him. In nowise vainly slipped they from his hand; for as many gory drops as ran thence, Earth received them all; and when the years rolled around, she gave birth to stern Furies, and mighty giants, gleaming in arms, with long spears in hand, and Nymphs whom men call Ashnymphs, (Meliae), over the boundless earth. But the genitals, as after first severing them with the steel he had cast them into the heaving sea from the continent, so kept drifting along time up and down the deep, and all around kept rising a white foam from the immortal flesh; and in it a maiden was nourished; first she drew nigh divine Cythera, and thence came next to wave-washed Cyprus. Then forth stepped an awful, beauteous goddess; and beneath her delicate feet the verdure throve around: her gods and men name Aphrodite, the foam-sprung goddess, and fair-wreathed Cytherea—the first because she was nursed in foam, but Cytherea, because she touched at Cythera; and Cyprus-born, because she was born in wave-dashed Cyprus.

And her Eros accompanied and fair Desire followed, when first she was born, and came into the host of the gods. And from the beginning this honor hath she, and this part hath she obtained by lot among men and immortal gods, the amorous converse of maidens, their smiles and wiles, their sweet delights, their love, and blandishment. Now those sons, their fathers, mighty Heaven, called by surname Titans, upbraiding those whom he had himself begotten; and he was wont to say that, outstretching their hands in infatuation, they had wrought a grave act, but that for it there should be vengeance hereafter.

Night bore also hateful Destiny, and black Fate, and Death: she bore Sleep likewise, she bore the tribe of dreams; these did the goddess, gloomy Night, bear after union with none. Next again Momus, and Care full-of-woes, and the Hesperides, whose care are the fair golden apples beyond the famous ocean, and trees yielding fruit; and she produced the Destinies, and ruthlessly punishing Fates, Clotho, Lachesis, and Atropos, who assign to men at their births to have good and evil; who also pursue transgressions both of men and gods, nor do the goddesses ever cease from dread wrath, before that, I wot, they have repaid sore vengeance to him, whosoever shall have sinned. Then bore pernicious Night Nemesis also, a woe to mortal men: and after her she brought forth Fraud, and Wanton-love, and mischievous Old Age, and stubborn-hearted Strife. But odious Strife gave birth to grievous Trouble, and Oblivion, and Famine, and tearful Woes.

Now these were born eldest daughters of Oceanus and Tethys; there are, however, many others also: for thrice a thousand are the tapering-ankled Ocean-nymphs, who truly spreading far and near, bright children of the gods, haunt everywhere alike earth and the depths of the lake. And again, as many other rivers flowing with a ringing noise, sons of Ocean, whom august Tethys bore: of all of whom 'twere difficult for mortal man to tell the names, but each individual knows them, of as many as dwell around them. And Thia, overcome in the embrace of Hyperion, brought forth the great Sun, and bright Moon, and Morn, that shines for all that-dwell-on-the-earth, and for immortal gods, who occupy broad heaven. Eurybia too, a goddess among goddesses, bore to Crius, after union in love, huge Astraeus, and Pallas, and Perses, who was transcendent in all sciences.

And to Astraeus Morn brought forth the strong-spirited winds, Argestes, Zephyr, swift-speeding Boreas, and Notus, when she, a goddess, had mingled in love with a god. And after them the goddess of morning produced the star Lucifer, and the brilliant stars wherewith the heaven is crowned.

And Styx, daughter of Ocean, after union with Pallas, bore within the house Zelus and beautous-ankled Victory; and she gave birth to Strength and Force, illustrious children, whose mansion is not apart from love, nor is there any seat, or any way, where the god does not go before them; but ever sit they beside deep-thundering Jupiter. For thus counseled Styx, imperishable Ocean-nymph, what time the Olympian Lightener summoned all the immortal gods to broad Olympus, and said that whoso of the gods would fight with him against the Titans; none of them would he rob of his rewards, but each should have the honor, to wit, that which he had aforetime among the immortal gods. And he said that him, who was unhonored or ungifted by Cronus, he would stablish in honor, and rewards, according to justice. Then first I wot came imperishable Styx to Olympus along with her children through the counsels of her sire. And Jove honored her, and gave her exceeding gifts.

For her he ordained to be the great Oath-witness of the gods, and her children to be dwellers-with-her all their days. An even in such wise as he promised, he performed to them all forever: for he hath power and reigns mightily.

And next Phoebe came to the much-beloved couch of Coeus: then in truth having conceived, a goddess by love of a god, she bore dark-robed Latona, ever mild, gentle to mortals and immortal gods, mild from the beginning, most kindly within Olympus. And she bore renowned Asteria, whom erst Perses led to an ample palace to be called his bride. And she becoming pregnant, brought forth Hecate, whom Jove, the son of Cronus, honored beyond all: and provided for her splendid gifts, to wit, to hold a share of earth and of barren sea. But she has obtained honor also from starry Heaven, and has been honored chiefly by immortal gods. For even now when anywhere some one of men upon-the-earth duly propitiates them by doing worthy sacrifice, he calls on Hecate: and abundant honor very speedily attends him, whose vows the goddess shall receive, that is to say, graciously, yea, and to him she presents wealth, for she has the power. For as many as were born of Earth and Heaven, and received a share of honor, of all these she has the lot, neither did the son of Cronus force any portion from her, nor did he take away as many honors as she had obtained by lot, among the elder gods, the Titans, but she hath them, as at the first the distribution was from the beginning Nor, because she is sole-begotten, has the goddess obtained less of honor, and her prerogative on earth, and in heaven, and sea, but even still much more, seeing that Jove honors her. And to whom she wills, she is greatly present, and benefits him, and he is distinguished, whom she may will, in the form among the people; and when men arm for mortal-destroying war, then the goddess draws nigh to whom she will, kindly to proffer victory and to extend renown to them; and in judgment she sits beside august kings; and propitiously again, when men contend in the games, there the goddess stands near these also, and helps them.

And when he has conquered by strength and might, a man carries with ease a noble prize, and rejoicingly presents glory to his parents. Propitious is she also to be present with horsemen, whom she will; and to them who ply the rough silvery main; and they pray to Hecate and the loud-sounding Earth-shaker. Easily too the glorious goddess presents an ample spoil, and easily is she wont to withdraw it when it is shown, that is, if she is so disposed in her mind. And (propitious along with Mercury to increase the flock in the folds) the herds of cattle, and the droves, and broad herds of goats, and flocks of fleecy sheep, if she choose in her heart, she makes great from small and is wont to make less from being many. Thus, in truth though being sole-begotten from her mother, she has been honored with rewards amidst all the immortals. And the son of Cronus made her the nursing-mother-of-children, who after her have beheld with their eyes the light of far-seeing Morn. Thus is she from the beginning nursing-mother, and such are her honors.

Rhea too, embraced by Cronus, bare renowned children, Vesta, Demeter, and Here of-the-golden-sandals, and mighty Hades, who inhabits halls beneath the earth, having a ruthless heart; and loud-resounding Neptune, and counseling Jupiter, father of gods as well as men, by whose thunder also the broad earth quakes. And then indeed did huge Cronus devour, namely, every one who came to the mother's knees from her holy womb, with this intent, that none other of the illustrious heaven-born might hold royal honor among the immortals. For he had heart from Earth and starry Heaven that it was fated for him, strong though he was, to be subdued by his own child, through the counsels of mighty Jove: wherefore he did not keep a careless watch, but lying in wait for them, kept devouring his own sons; while a grief not-to-be-forgotten possessed Rhea. But when at length she was about to bear Jove, the sire of gods as well as men, then it was that she essayed to supplicate her parents dear, Earth and starry Heaven, to contrive a plan how she might without observation bring forth her son, and take vengeance on the furies of their sin; against his children, whom great and wily Cronus devoured.

But they duly heard and complied with their dear daughter, and explained to her as much as it had been fated should come to pass concerning king Cronus, and his strong-hearted son. And they sent her to Lyctus, to the fertile tract of Crete, when I wot she was about to bear the youngest of her sons, mighty Jove: whom indeed vast Earth received from her to rear and nurture in broad Crete. Thereupon indeed came she, bearing him through the swift dark night, to Lyctus first, and took

him in her hands and hid him in a deep cave 'neath the recesses of the divine earth, in the dense and wooded Aegean mount. But to the great prince, the son of Heaven, former sovereign of the gods, she gave a huge stone, having wrapped it in swathes: which he then took in his hands, and stowed away into his belly, wretch as he was, nor did he consider in his mind that against him for the future his own invincible and untroubled son was left instead of a stone, who was shortly about to subdue him by strength of hand, and to drive him from his honors, and himself to reign among the immortals.

Quickly then, I ween, throve the spirit and beauteous limbs of the king, and, as years came around, having been beguiled by the wise counsels of Earth, huge Cronus, wily counselor, let loose again his offspring, having been conquered by the arts and strength of his son. And first he disgorged the stone, since he swallowed it last. This stone Jove fixed down upon the earth with-its-broad-ways, in divine Pytho, beneath the clefts of Parnassus, to be a monument thereafter, a marvel to mortal men. Then he loosed from destructive bonds his father's brethren, the sons of Heaven, whom his sire had bound in his folly. Who showed gratitude to him for his kindnesses, and gave him the thunder, and the smoking bolt, and lightning; but aforetime huge Earth had hidden them: trusting on these, he rules over mortals and immortals.

Iapetus, moreover, wedded the damsel Clymene, a fair-ankled Oceanid, and ascended into a common bed. And she bore him Atlas, a stout-hearted son, and brought forth exceeding-famous Menaetius, and artful Prometheus, full of various wiles, and Epimetheus of-erring-mind, who was from the first an evil to gain-seeking men: for he first, I wot, received from Jove the clay-formed woman, a virgin. But the insolent Menaetius wide-seeing Jove thrust down to Erebus, having stricken him with flaming lightning, on account of his arrogance, and overweening strength.

But Atlas upholds broad Heaven by strong necessity, before the clear-voiced Hesperides, standing on earth's verge, with head and unwearied hands. For this lot counseling Jove apportioned to him. And wily-minded Prometheus he bound in indissoluble bonds, with painful chains, having thrust them through the middle of a column. And he urged against him an eagle with-wings-outspread: but it kept feeding on his immortal liver, while it would increase to a like size all-around by night, to what the eagle with-wings-outspread had eaten during the whole day before. This bird indeed, I wot, Hercules, valiant son of fair-ankled Alemene, slew, and repelled from the son of Iapetus the baneful pest, and released him from his anxieties, not against the wishes of high-reigning Olympian Jove, that so the renown of Thebes-sprung Hercules might be yet more than aforetime over the many-feeding earth. Thus, I ween, he honors his very famous son, through veneration for him: and though incensed, ceased from the wrath which he was before cherishing, because he strove in plans against the almighty son of Cronus. For when gods and mortal men were contending at Mecone, then did he set before him a huge ox, having divided it with ready mind, studying to deceive the wisdom of Jove. For here, on the one hand, he deposited the flesh and entrails with rich fat on the hide, having covered it with the belly of the ox; and there, on the other hand, he laid down, having well disposed them with subtle art, the white bones of the ox, covering them with white fat. Then it was that the sire of gods and men addressed him, "Son of Iapetus, far-famed among all kings, how unfairly, good friend, you have divided the portions." Thus spake rebukingly Jupiter, skilled in imperishable counsels. And him in his turn wily Prometheus addressed, laughing low, but he was not forgetful of subtle art: "Most glorious Jove greatest of ever-living gods, choose which of these your inclination within your breast bids you." He spake, I ween, in subtlety: but Jove knowing imperishable counsels was aware, in sooth, and not ignorant of his guile; and was boding in his heart evils to mortal men, which also were about to find accomplishment. Then with both hands lifted he up the white fat. But he was incensed in mind, and wrath came around him in spirit, when he saw the white bones of the ox arranged with guileful art. And thenceforth the tribes of men on the earth burn to the immortals white bones on fragrant altars. Then cloud-compeling Jove addressed him, greatly displeased: "Son of Iapetus, skilled in wise plans beyond all, you do not, good sir, I wot, yet forget subtle art." Thus spake in his wrath Jove knowing imperishable counsels: from that time forward in truth, ever mindful of the fraud, he did not give the strength of untiring fire to wretched mortal men, who dwell upon the earth.

But the good son of Iapetus cheated him, and stole the far-seen splendor of untiring fire in a hollow fennel stalk; but it stung high-thundering Jove to his heart's core, and incensed his spirit, when he saw the radiance of fire conspicuous among men. Forthwith then wrought he evil for men in requital for the fire bestowed.

Thus it is not possible to deceive or overreach the mind of Jove, for neither did Prometheus, guileless son of Iapetus, escape from beneath his severe wrath; but a great chain, by necessity, constrains him, very knowing though he is.

But when first their sire become wroth in spirit against Briareus, Cottus, and Gyes, he bound them with a strong bond, admiring their overweening courage, and also their form and bulk; and he made them dwell beneath the roomy earth: then they in sooth in grief dwelling 'neath the earth, sat at the verge, on the extremities of vast Earth, very long, afflicted, having a great woe at heart; but them the son of Cronus, and other immortal gods, whom fair-haired Rhea bore in the embrace of Cronus, by the counsels of Earth brought up again to light: for she recounted to them at large everything, how that they should along with those (Titans)

gain victory and splendid glory. Long time then they fought, incurring soulvexing toil, the Titan gods and as many as were born from Cronus, in opposition to each other in stout conflicts; the one side, the glorious Titans from lofty Othrys, and the other, I wot, the gods, givers of good things, whom Rhea the fair-haired had borne to Cronus, in union with him, from Olympus. They then, I ween, in soul-distressing battle, one party with the other, were fighting continuously more than ten years. Nor was there any riddance or end of severe contention to either party, and the completion of the war was extended equally to either. But when at length Jove set before them all things agreeable, to wit, nectar and ambrosia, on which the gods themselves feed, a noble spirit grew in the breasts of all. And when they had tasted the nectar and delightful ambrosia, then at length the sire of gods and men addressed them: "Hear me, illustrious children of Earth and Heaven, that I may speak what my spirit within my breast prompts me to speak. For now a very long space are we fighting, each in opposition to other, concerning victory and power, all our days, the Titan gods and as many of us as are sprung from Cronus. Now do ye show against the Titans in deadly fight both mighty force and hands invincible, in gratitude for our mild loving-kindness, namely after how many sufferings ye came back again to the light, from afflictive bondage, through our counsels, from the murky gloom." Thus he spake; and him again the blameless Cottus addressed in answer: "Excellent Lord, thou dost not tell things unlearned by us: but we too are aware that thy wisdom is excellent, and excellent shine intellect, and that thou hast been to the immortals an averter of terrible destruction. And back again, from harsh bonds, have we come from the murky darkness, through thy thoughtful care, O royal son of Cronus, having experienced treatment unhoped for. Wherefore also now with steadfast purpose and prudent counsel we will protect thy might in dread conflict, fighting with the Titans in stout battles." Thus spake he: and the gods, givers of good, applauded, when they had heard his speech: and their spirit was eager for battle still more than before, and they stirred up unhappy strife all of them, female as well as male, on that day, both Titan gods, and as many as had sprung from Cronus, and they whom Jove sent up to light from Erebus, beneath the earth, terrible and strong, having overweening force. From the shoulders of these a hundred hands outsprung to all alike, and to each fifty heads grew from their shoulders over their sturdy limbs. They then were pitted against the Titans in deadly combat, holding huge rocks in their sturdy hands. But the Titans on the other side made strong their squadrons with alacrity, and both parties were showing work of hand and force at the same time, and the boundless sea re-echoed terribly, and earth resounded loudly, and broad heaven groaned, being shaken, and vast Olympus was convulsed from its base under the violence of the immortals, and a severe quaking came to murky

Tartarus, namely, a hollow sound of countless chase of feet, and of strong battle-strokes: to such an extent, I ween did they hurl groan-causing weapons. And the voice of both parties reached to starry heaven, as they cheered: for they came together with a great war cry.

Nor longer, in truth, did Jove restrain his fury, but then forthwith his heart was filled with fierceness, and he began also to exhibit all his force: then, I wot, from heaven and from Olympus together he went forth lightening continually: and the bolts close together with thunder and lightning flew duly from his sturdy hand, whirling a sacred flash, in frequent succession, while all-around life-giving Earth was crashing in conflagration, and the immense forests on all sides crackled loudly with fire. All land was boiling, and Ocean's streams, and the barren sea: warm vapor was circling the earth-born Titan and the incessant blaze reached the divine dense-atmosphere while flashing radiance of thunderbolt and lightning was bereaving their eyes of sight, strong heroes though they were. Fearful heat likewise possessed Chaos: and it seemed, to look at, face to face, with the eye, and to hear the sound with the ear, just as if earth and broad heaven from above were threatening to meet: (for such an exceeding crash would have arisen from earth falling in ruins, and heaven dashing it down from above). Such a din there rose when the gods clashed in strife. The winds too at the same time were stirring up quaking and dust together, thunder and lightning and smoking bolt shafts of the mighty Jove; and they were bearing shout and battle cry into the midst, one of another, then a terrible noise of dreadful strife was roused, strength of prowess was put forth, and the battle was inclined: but before that time assailing one another, they were fighting incessantly in stern conflict. Now the others, I wot, among the first ranks roused the keen fight, Cottus, Briareus, and Gyes insatiable in war, who truly were hurling from sturdy hands three hundred rocks close upon each other, and they had overshadowed the Titans with missiles, sent them 'neath the broad-wayed earth, and bound them in irksome bonds, (having conquered them with their hands, overhaughty though they were), as far beneath under earth as heaven is from the earth, for equal is the space from earth to murky Tartarus. For nine nights and days also would a brazen anvil be descending from the heaven, and come on the tenth to the earth: and nine days as well as nights again would a brazen anvil be descending from the earth, to reach on the tenth to Tartarus. Around it moreover a brazen fence has been forged: and about it Night is poured in three rows around the neck; but above spring the roots of Earth and barren Sea. There, under murky darkness, the Titan gods lie hidden by the counsels of cloud-compeling Jupiter in a dark, drear place, where are the extremities of vast Earth. These may not go forth, for Neptune has placed above them brazen gates, and a wall goes around them on both sides. There dwell Gyes, and Cottus, and high-spirited Briareus, faithful guards of aegis-bearing Jove. And there are the sources and boundaries of dusky Earth, of murky Tartarus, of barren Sea, and starry Heaven, all in their order: boundaries oppressive and gloomy, which also even gods abhor, a vast chasm, not even for a whole round of a year would one reach the pavement, after having first been within the gates: but hurricane to hurricane would bear him onward hither and thither, distressing him, and dreadful even to immortal gods is this prodigy, and there the dread abodes of gloomy Night stand shrouded in dark clouds. In front of these the son of Iapetus stands and holds broad Heaven, with his head and unwearied hands, unmovedly, where Night and Day also drawing nigh are wont to salute each other, as they cross the vast brazen threshold. The one is about to go down within, while the other comes forth abroad, nor ever doth the abode constrain both within; but constantly one at any rate being outside the dwelling, wanders over the earth, while the other again being within the abode, awaits the season of her journey, until it come; the one having a far-seeing light for men-on-the-earth, and the other, destructive Night, having Sleep, the brother of Death, in its hands, being shrouded in hazy mist.

And there the sons of obscure Night hold their habitation, Sleep and Death, dread gods: nor ever cloth the bright sun look upon them with his rays, as he ascends the heaven, or descends from the heaven. Of whom indeed the one tarries on the earth and the broad surface of the sea, silently and soothingly to men; but of the other, iron is the heart, and brazen is his ruthless soul within his breast; and whomsoever of men he may have first caught, he holdeth: and he is hostile even to immortal gods. There in the front stand the resounding mansions of the infernal god, of mighty Hades, and awful Persephone besides; and a fierce dog keeps guard in front, a ruthless dog; and he has an evil trick: those who enter he fawns upon with his tail and both ears alike, yet he suffers them not to go forth back again, but lies in wait and devours whomsoever he may have caught going forth without the gates of strong Hades and dread Persephone.

Questions

(1) What does the Creation Myth in "Theogony" reveal as to the nature and most significant values attributed to their gods by the Greeks?

(2) For what flaws/crimes were Heaven and Cronus punished, and deposed from their positions of rulership over the gods?

(3) What were the crimes of Atlas and Prometheus, and the nature of their punishments?

1–3

The myth of the Incas: a case of double creation?

The implication of the Inca creation story is that, in the original version, the Incas conceived of creation mainly in terms of their own ethnic group, which was allegedly favored as adoptive offspring of the Sun. However, as the Inca themselves subdued neighboring peoples in forging their vast Andean Empire, they appear to have taken on a more Universalist view of creation; wherein the whole world was the handiwork of a highly activist deity, Viracocha.

Source: Padraic Colum, *Myths of the World* (New York: MacMillan & Co., 1952), cited in Van Over, *Sun Songs*, pp. 112–116.

In other days we who are of the race of the Incas worshipped the Sun; we held that he was the greatest and most benignant of all beings, and we named ourselves the children of the Sun. We had traditions that told of the pitiable ways that we and the rest of the human race lived in before the Sun, having had compassion upon us, decided to lead us towards better ways of living…Lo, now! Our Lord, the Sun, put his two children, a son and a daughter, in a boat upon Lake Titicaca. He told them they were to float upon the water until they came to where men lived. He put his golden staff into the hands of his son. He told him he was to lead men into a place where that staff, dropped upon the earth, sank deep down into it.

So the children of our Lord the Sun went upon the waters of Lake Titicaca. They came to where our fathers lived in those far days…Where we live now we see villages and cities; we see streams flowing down from the mountains, and being led this way and that way to water our crops and our trees; we see flocks of llamas feeding on good grass with their lambs—countless flocks. But in those days we lived where there were thickets and barren rocks; we had no llamas; we had no crops, we knew not how to make the waters flow this way and that way; we had no villages, no cities, no temples. We lived in clefts of the rocks and holes in the ground. The covering of our bodies was of bark or of leaves, or else we went naked in the day and without covering to put over us at night. We ate roots that we pulled up out of the ground, or fought with the foxes for the dead things they were carrying away. No one bore rule amongst us, and we knew nothing of duty or kindness of one to another.

Out of their boat on Lake Titicaca came the children of our Lord to us. They brought us together; they had rule over us, and they showed us how to live as husband and wife and children, and how to know those who were leaders amongst us and how to obey those leaders. And having showed us these things they led us from the land they had found us in.

And often did he who was the son of our Lord the Sun drop the golden staff upon the ground as we went on. Sometimes the staff sank a little way into the earth, sometimes it sank to half its length in the earth. We came to a place where the golden staff, dropped by him who was the son of our Lord the Sun, sank into the earth until only its top was to be seen. And there we stayed, or,

rather, there our fathers stayed, for we are many generations from the men and women who came into this place with the two who were the children of the Sun.

They showed us how to sow crops in that rich ground, and how to lead water down from the hills to water the crops and the trees. They showed us how to tame the llamas, and how to herd them and tend them as tamed beasts. They showed us how to take the wool from them and weave the wool into garments for ourselves; also, they showed us how to dye our garments so that we went brightly clad in the light of the sun. They showed us how to work in gold and silver, and how to make vessels of clay, and how to put shapes and figures upon these vessels. They showed us how to build houses, and how to build villages, and cities, and temples. And they showed us, too, how to obey the rule of those who were left to rule over us, the Incas.

Then the two who were the son and daughter of the Sun left us. Before they went from us they told us that the Sun, their father, would adopt us as his children. And so we of the Inca race became the children of the Sun. They said to us, too, "Our father, the Sun, does good to the whole world; he gives light that men may see and follow their pursuits; he makes men warm when they had been cold; he ripens their crops; he increases their flocks of llamas; he brings dew upon the ground. The Sun, our father, goes round the earth each day that he may know of man's necessities and help him to provide for them. Be like the Sun, then, far-seeing, regular in all your occupations. And bring the worship of the Sun amongst the tribes who live in darkness and ignorance."

And so these two, his son and daughter who were sent to us by the Sun, were seen no more by us. But we knew ourselves now as the children of the Sun. We subdued the tribes in his name, and brought the knowledge of his beneficence amongst them. We built a great temple to him. And the daughters of the Incas in hundreds served him as Virgins of the Sun.

Yes, but there were those amongst us who came to have other thoughts about Heaven and the ways of Heaven. "Does not the Sun go as another being directs him to go?" one of the Incas said to his councillors. "Is he not like an arrow shot onward by a man? Is he not like a llama tethered by the will of a man rather than like one who has freedom? Does he not let a little cloud obscure his splendour? Is it not plain that he may never take rest from his tasks?"

So men amongst us have said, and they who have said them have mentioned a name. Viracocha that name is. And then they would say words from rites that were known to the people of this land before the Incas came into it. They would say, "O conquering Viracocha! Thou gavest life and valour to men, saying, 'let this be a man,' and to women saying, 'let this be a woman.' Thou madest them and gavest them being! Watch over them that they may live in health and peace! Thou who art in the high heavens, and among the clouds of the tempest, grant this with long life, and accept this sacrifice, O Creator!" So those who were priests in the land before our fathers came into it prayed.

And they said that it was Viracocha who created the Sun, and created the Moon also. They said that at the beginning the Sun was not brighter than the Moon, and that in his jealousy he flung ashes upon the face of the Moon and dimmed the Moon's primal brightness. And they said that Viracocha could make great terraces of rock and clay rear themselves up with crops upon them, and that he could bring the watercourses to freshen terraces and gardens merely by striking with a hollow cane that he carried.

Now although Viracocha was so great, he obscured himself, and came back to live amongst the Gods in the guise of a beggar. None knew him for Viracocha, the Creator of all things. And he saw the Goddess Cavillaca as she sat amongst llama lambs under a lucma-tree, weaving the wool of the white llama. He saw her and he approached her. He left a ripe fruit beside her. She ate the fruit and she became with child by him.

And when her child was born her parents and her friends said to her, "You must find out who is the father of this child. Let all who live near come to this lucma-tree, and let the child crawl amongst them. The man he crawls to and touches with his hand we will know is his father."

So under the lucma-tree Cavillaca sat, and her child was with her. All who lived near came to that place, and amongst them came Viracocha, still in his beggar's dress. All came near to Cavillaca and her child. The child crawled where they stood. He came to Viracocha. He put his hand up and touched the man who was in the beggar's garb.

Then was Cavillaca made ashamed before all the Gods. She snatched up her child and held him to her. She fled away from that place. She fled towards the ocean with her child. Viracocha put on his robes of splendour and hastened after her. And as he went he cried out, "O Goddess, turn; look back at me! See how splendid I am!" But the Goddess, without turning, fled with her child from before him.

Viracocha went seeking them. As he crossed the peaks he met a condor, and the condor flew with him, and consoled him. Viracocha blessed the condor, and gave him long life and the power to traverse the wilderness and go over the highest peaks; also he gave him the right to prey upon creatures. Afterwards he met a fox; but the fox derided him, telling him that his quest was vain. He cursed the fox, saying to him that he would have to hunt at night, and that men would slay him. He met a puma, and the puma went with him and consoled him. He blessed the puma, saying that he would receive honour from men. As he went down the other side of the mountain, he came upon parrots flying from the trees of their forest. And the parrots cried out words that were of ill-omen. He cursed the parrots, saying that they would never have honour from men. But he blessed the falcon that flew with him down to the sea.

And when he came to the sea he found that Cavillaca and her child had plunged themselves into the water and had been transformed into rocks. Then Viracocha in his grief remained beside the sea.

Now beside the sea there were two virgins who were Urpihuachac's daughters. They were guarded by a serpent. Viracocha charmed the serpent with his wisdom, and the serpent permitted him to approach Urpihuachac's daughters. One flew away and became a dove. But the other lived there with Viracocha. And this Virgin of the Sea showed Viracocha where her mother kept all the fishes of the world. They were in a pond and they could not go through the waters of the world. Viracocha broke down the walls of their pond, and let them go through the streams and the lakes and the sea. And thus he let men have fishes to eat.

He lived amongst men, and he taught them many arts. He it was, as the priests of those who were here before the Incas say, showed men how to bring streams of water to their crops, and taught them how to build terraces upon the mountains where crops would grow. He set up a great cross upon the mountain Caravay. And when the bird that cries out four times at dawn cried out, and the light came upon the cross he had set up, Viracocha went from amongst men. He went down to the sea, and he walked across it towards the west. But he told those whom he had left behind that he would send messengers back who would protect them and give them renewed knowledge of all he had taught them. He left them, but men still remember the chants that those whom he left on the mountain, by the cross, cried out their longing:

> Oh, hear me!
> From the sky above,
> In which thou mayst be,
> From the sea beneath,
> In which thou mayst be,
> Creator of the world,
> Maker of all men;
> Lord of all Lords,
> My eyes fail me
> For longing to see thee;
> For the sole desire to know thee.

Questions
(1) In what ways does Viracocha compare to and contrast with the gods in "Nihongi" and "Theogony" (Documents 1 and 2)?
(2) What appears to have been the most significant attribute, in the eyes of the Incas of the Sun? Of Viracocha?
(3) Do the dual myths and roles of the Sun and Viracocha seem to be more contradictory, or complementary? How so?

1–4
The Seven Days and the Garden: the Judaic account of creation.

Within the Judeo-Christian belief system the creation story is to be found in the opening chapters of Genesis, the first book of the Hebrew Torah, traditionally ascribed to Moses. Chapter 1 through Chapter 2, verse 3 describes a general global creation process, while Chapter 2, verse 4 through Chapter 3, verse 24 refers to the specific (and, some scholars allege, separate) creation and early history of the first two human individuals.

Source:*The New English Bible, with the Apocrypha* (Oxford & Cambridge University Presses, 1970), pp. 1–4.

THE CREATION OF THE WORLD

IN THE BEGINNING OF CREATION, when God made heaven and earth, the earth was without form and void, with darkness over the face of the abyss, and a mighty wind that swept over the surface of the waters. God said, 'Let there be light', and there was light and God saw that the light was good, and he separated light from darkness He called the light day, and the darkness night. So evening came, and morning came, the first day.

God said, 'Let there be a vault between the waters, to separate water from water.' So God made the vault, and separated the water under the vault from the water above it, and so it was; and God called the vault heaven. Evening came, and morning came, a second day.

God said, 'Let the waters under heaven be gathered into one place, so that dry land may appear'; and so it was. God called the dry land earth, and the gathering of the waters he called seas; and God saw that it was good. Then God said, 'Let the earth produce fresh growth, let there be on the earth plants bearing seed, fruit-trees bearing fruit each with seed according to its kind.' So it was; the earth yielded fresh growth, plants bearing seed according to their kind and trees bearing fruit each with seed according to its kind; and God saw that it was good. Evening came, and morning came, a third day.

God said, 'Let there be lights in the vault of heaven to separate day from night, and let them serve as signs both for festivals and for seasons and years. Let them also shine in the vault of heaven to give light on earth.' So it was; God made the two great lights, the greater to govern the day and the lesser to govern the night; and with them he made the stars. God put these lights in the vault of heaven to give light on earth, to govern day and night, and to separate light from darkness; and God saw that it was good. Evening came, and morning came, a fourth day.

God said, 'Let the waters teem with countless living creatures, and let birds fly above the earth across the vault of heaven.' God then created the great sea-monsters and all living creatures that move and swarm in the waters, according to their kind, and every kind of bird; and God saw that it was good. So he blessed them and said, 'Be fruitful and increase, fill the waters of the seas; and let the birds increase on land.' Evening came, and morning came, a fifth day.

God said, 'Let the earth bring forth living creatures, according to their kind: cattle, reptiles, and wild animals, all according to their kind.' So it was; God made wild animals, cattle, and all reptiles, each according to its kind; and he saw that it was good. Then God said, 'Let us make man in our image and likeness to rule the fish in the sea, the birds of heaven, the cattle, all wild animals on earth, and all reptiles that crawl upon the earth.' So God created man in his own image; in the image of God he created him; male and female he created them. God blessed them and said to them, 'Be fruitful and increase, fill the earth and subdue it, rule over the fish in the sea, the birds of heaven, and every living thing that moves upon the earth.' God also said, 'I give you all plants that bear seed everywhere on earth, and every tree bearing fruit which yields seed: they shall be yours for food. All green plants I give for food to the wild animals, to all the birds of heaven, and to all reptiles on earth, every living creature.' So it was; and God saw all that he had made, and it was very good. Evening came, and morning came, a sixth day.

Thus heaven and earth were completed with all their mighty throng. On the sixth day God completed all the work he had been doing, and on the seventh day he ceased from all his work. God blessed the seventh day and made it holy, because on that day he ceased from all the work he had set himself to do.

This is the story of the making of heaven and earth when they were created.

THE BEGINNINGS OF HISTORY

WHEN THE LORD GOD MADE EARTH AND HEAVEN, there was neither shrub nor plant growing wild upon the earth, because the LORD God had sent no rain on the earth; nor was there any man to till the ground. A flood used to rise out of the earth and water all the surface of the ground. Then the LORD God formed a man from the dust of the ground and breathed into his nostrils the breath of life. Thus the man became a living creature. Then the LORD God planted a garden in Eden away to the east, and there he put the man whom he had formed. The LORD God made trees spring from the ground, all trees pleasant to look at and good for food; and in the middle of the garden he set the tree of life and the tree of the knowledge of good and evil.

There was a river flowing from Eden to water the garden, and when it left the garden it branched into four streams. The name of the first is Pishon; that is the river which encircles all the land of Havilah, where the gold is. The gold of that land is good; bdellium and cornelians are also to be found there. The name of the second river is Gihon; this is the one which encircles all the land of Cush. The name of the third is Tigris; this is the river which runs east of Asshur. The fourth river is the Euphrates.

The LORD God took the man and put him in the garden of Eden to till it and care for it. He told the man, 'You may eat from every tree in the garden, but not from the tree of the knowledge of good and evil; for on the day that you eat from it, you will certainly die.' Then the LORD God said, 'It is not good for the man to be alone. I will provide a partner for him.' So God formed out of the ground all the wild animals and all the birds of heaven. He brought them to the man to see what he would call them, and whatever the man called each living creature, that was its name. Thus the man gave names to all cattle, to the birds of heaven, and to every wild animal; but for the man himself no partner had yet been found. And so the LORD God put the man into a trance, and while he slept, he took one of his ribs and closed the flesh over the place. The LORD God then built up the rib, which he had taken out of the man, into a woman. He brought her to the man, and the man said:

'Now this, at last—
bone from my bones,
flesh from my flesh!—
this shall be called woman,
for from man was this taken.'

That is why a man leaves his father and mother and is united to his wife, and the two become one flesh. Now they were both naked, the man and his wife, but they had no feeling of shame towards one another.

THE SERPENT WAS MORE CRAFTY than any wild creature that the LORD God had made. He said to the woman, 'Is it true that God has forbidden you to eat from any tree in the garden ?' The woman answered the serpent, 'We may eat the fruit of any tree in the garden, except for the tree in the middle of the garden; God has forbidden us either to eat or to touch the fruit of that; if we do, we shall die.' The serpent said, 'Of course you will not die. God knows that as soon as you eat it, your eyes will be opened and you will be like gods knowing both good and evil.' When the woman saw that the fruit of the tree was good to eat, and that it was pleasing to the eye and tempting to contemplate, she took some and ate it. She also gave her husband some and he ate it. Then the eyes of both of them were opened and they discovered that they were naked; so they stitched fig-leaves together and made themselves loincloths.

The man and his wife heard the sound of the LORD God walking in the garden at the time of the evening breeze and hid from the LORD God among the trees of the garden. But the LORD God called to the man and said to him, 'Where are you?' He replied, 'I heard the sound as you were walking in the garden, and I was afraid because I was naked, and I hid myself.' God answered, 'Who told you that you were naked? Have you eaten from the tree which I forbade you?' The man said, 'The woman you gave me for a companion, she gave me fruit from the tree and I ate it.' Then the LORD God said to the woman, 'What is this that you have done?' The woman said, 'The serpent tricked me, and I ate.' then the LORD God said to the serpent:

'Because you have done this you are accursed
  more than all cattle and all wild creatures.
On your belly you shall crawl, and dust you shall eat
  all the days of your life.
I will put enmity between you and the woman,
  between your brood and hers.
They shall strike at your head,
  and you shall strike at their heel.'

To the woman he said:

'I will increase your labour and your groaning,
  and in labour you shall bear children.
You shall be eager for your husband,
  and he shall be your master.'

And to the man he said:

'Because you have listened to your wife
  and have eaten from the tree which I forbade you,
  accursed shall be the ground on your account.

With labour you shall win your food from it
  all the days of your life.
It will grow thorns and thistles for you,
  none but wild plants for you to eat.
You shall gain your bread by the sweat of your brow
  until you return to the ground;
    for from it you were taken.
Dust you are, to dust you shall return.'

The man called his wife Eve because she was the mother of all who live. The LORD God made tunics of skins for Adam and his wife and clothed them. He said, 'The man has become like one of us, knowing good and evil; what if he now reaches out his hand and takes fruit from the tree of life also, eats it and lives for ever?' So the LORD God drove him out of the garden of Eden to till the ground from which he had been taken. He cast him out, and to the east of the garden of Eden he stationed the cherubim and a sword whirling and flashing to guard the way to the tree of life.

Questions

(1) Does the place assigned to Mankind in Genesis compare/contrast to that assigned in Documents 1–1, 1–2, and 1,–3? How, or how not?

(2) Are there major similarities or differences between the Genesis Creator and his role as opposed to that of the creator(s) in Documents 1–1, 1–2, and 1–3? Explain.

(3) How effectively might each of the Creation stories depicted here fulfill the purposes of explaining origins and establishing purpose for human existence? Explain.

(4) What message can be derived from each of these Creation narratives as to the status and role of women in the overall scheme of existence?

1–5

A controversial theorist takes his ideas to their ultimate conclusion.

Although Charles Darwin (1809–1882) had thoroughly shaken the Victorian world with the publication of On the Origin of Species, *he had hesitated to specifically apply the evolutionary theory to human beings, being perhaps of the opinion that the time was not right. In 1871, however, at the age of 62, he felt assured that his ideas had gained sufficient acceptance for him to take this step by publishing* The Descent of Man. *As controversial as this was in and of itself, Darwin's work opened new avenues of contention in his statements concerning both mankind's possible geographic origins and religion.*

Source: Herbert Thomas, *Human Origins: The Search for Our Beginnings* (New York: Harry N. Abrams, Inc. 1995), pp. 130–133.

We have now seen that man is variable in body and mind; and that the variations are induced, either directly or indirectly, by the same general causes, and obey the same general laws, as with the lower animals. Man has spread widely over the face of the earth, and must have been exposed, during his incessant migrations, to the most diversified conditions....The early progenitors of man must also have tended, like all other animals, to have increased beyond their means of subsistence; they must therefore occasionally have been exposed to a struggle for existence, and consequently to the rigid law of natural selection. Beneficial variations of all kinds will thus, either occasionally or habitually, have been preserved, and injurious ones eliminated. I do not refer to strongly-marked deviations of structure, which occur only at long intervals of time, but to mere individual differences....

Man in the rudest state in which he now exists is the most dominant animal that has ever appeared on the earth. He has spread more widely than any other highly organised form; and all others have yielded before him. He manifestly owes this immense superiority to his intellectual faculties, his social habits, which lead him to aid and defend his fellows, and to his corporeal structure. The supreme importance of these characters has been proved by the final arbitrament of the battle for life....

We are naturally led to enquire where was the birthplace of man at that stage of descent when our progenitors diverged from the Catarhine [monkey] stock. The fact that they belonged to this stock clearly shews that they inhabited the Old World; but not Australia nor any oceanic island, as we may infer from the laws of geographical distribution. In each great region of the world the living mammals are closely related to the extinct species of the same region. It is therefore probable that Africa was formerly inhabited by extinct apes closely allied to the gorilla and chimpanzee; and as these two species are now man's nearest allies, it is somewhat more probable that our earliest progenitors lived on the African continent than elsewhere....

The main conclusion arrived at in this work, and now held by many naturalists who are well competent to form a sound judgment, is that man is descended from some less highly organised form. The grounds upon which this conclusion rests will never be shaken, for the close similarity between man and the lower animals in embryonic development, as well as in innumerable points of structure and constitution, both of high and of the most trifling importance,— the rudiments which he retains and the abnormal reversions to which he is occasionally liable,—are facts which cannot be disputed. They have long been known, but until recently they told us nothing with respect to the origin of man.

Now when viewed by the light of our knowledge of the whole organic world their meaning is unmistakable. The great principle of evolution stands up clear and firm, when these groups of facts are considered in connection with others, such as the mutual affinities of the members of the same group, their geographical distribution in past and present times, and their geological succession. It is incredible that all these facts should speak falsely. He who is not content to look, like a savage, at the phenomena of nature as disconnected, cannot any longer believe that man is the work of a separate act of creation. He will be forced to admit that the close resemblance of the embryo of man to that, for instance, of a dog—the construction of his skull, limbs, and whole frame, independently of the uses to which the parts may be put, on the same plan with that of other mammals—the occasional reappearance of various structure, for instance of several distinct muscles, which man does not normally possess, but which are common to the Quadrumana—and a crowd of analogous facts—all point in the plainest manner to the conclusion that man is the co-descendant with other mammals of a common progenitor.

We have seen that man incessantly presents individual differences in all parts of his body and in his mental faculties. These differences or variations seem to be induced by the same general causes, and to obey the same laws as with the lower animals. In both cases similar laws of inheritance prevail. Man tends to increase at a greater rate than his means of subsistence; consequently he is occasionally subjected to a severe struggle for existence, and natural selection will have effected whatever lies within its scope. A succession of strongly-marked variations of a similar nature are by no means requisite; slight fluctuating differences in the individual suffice for the work of natural selection. We may feel assured that the inherited effects of the long-continued use or disuse of parts will have done much in the same direction with natural selection. Modifications formerly of importance, though no longer of any special use, will be long inherited. When

one part is modified, other parts will change through the principle of correlation, of which we have instances in many curious cases of correlated monstrosities. Something may be attributed to the direct and definite action of the surrounding conditions of life, such as abundant food, heat, or moisture; and lastly, many characters of slight physiological importance, some indeed of considerable importance, have been gained through sexual selection....

By considering the embryological structure of man— the homologies which he presents with the lower animals,—the rudiments which he retains,—and the reversions to which he is liable, we can partly recall in imagination the former condition of our early progenitors; and can approximately place them in their proper position in the zoological series. We thus learn that man is descended from a hairy quadruped, furnished with a tail and pointed ears, probably arboreal in its habits, and an inhabitant of the Old World....

The greatest difficulty which presents itself, when we are driven to the above conclusion on the origin of man, is the high standard of intellectual power and of moral disposition which he has attained. But every one who admits the general principle of evolution, must see that the mental powers of the higher animals, which are the same in kind with those of mankind, though so different in degree, are capable of advancement. Thus the interval between the mental powers of one of the higher apes and of a fish, or between those of an ant and scale-insect, is immense. The development of these powers in animals does not offer any special difficulty; for with our domesticated animals, the mental faculties are certainly variable, and the variations are inherited. No one doubts that these faculties are of the utmost importance to animals in a state of nature. Therefore the conditions are favourable for their development through natural selection. The same conclusion may be extended to man; the intellect must have been all-important to him, even at a very remote period, enabling him to use language, to invent and make weapons, tools, traps, etc.; by which means, in combination with his social habits, he long ago became the most dominant of all living creatures.

A great stride in the development of the intellect will have followed, as soon as, through a previous considerable advance, the half-art and half-instinct of language came into use; for the continued use of language will have reacted on the brain, and produced an inherited effect; and this again will have reacted on the improvement of language....

The belief in God has often been advanced as not only the greatest, but the most complete of all the distinctions between man and the lower animals. It is however impossible, as we have seen, to maintain that this belief is innate or instinctive in man. On the other hand a belief in all-pervading spiritual agencies seems to be universal; and apparently follows from a considerable advance in the reasoning powers of man, and from a still greater advance in his faculties of imagination, curiosity and wonder.

I am aware that the assumed instinctive belief in God has been used by many persons as an argument for His existence. But this is a rash argument, as we should thus be compelled to believe in the existence of many cruel and malignant spirits, possessing only a little more power than man; for the belief in them is far more general than of a beneficent Deity. The idea of a universal and beneficent Creator of the universe does not seem to arise in the mind of man, until he has been elevated by long-continued culture.

He who believes in the advancement of man from some lowly-organised form, will naturally ask how does this bear on the belief in the immortality of the soul....Few persons feel any anxiety from the impossibility of determining at what precise period in the development of the individual, from the first trace of the minute germinal vesicle to the child either before or after birth, man becomes an immortal being; and there is no greater cause for anxiety because the period in the gradually ascending organic scale cannot possibly be determined.

I am aware that the conclusions arrived at in this work will be denounced by some as highly irreligious; but he who thus denounces them is bound to shew why
it is more irreligious to explain the origin of man as a distinct species by descent from some lower form, through the laws of variation and natural selection, than to explain the birth of the individual through the laws of ordinary reproduction. The birth both of the species and of the individual are equally parts of the grand sequence of events, which our minds refuse to accept as the result of blind chance. The understanding revolts at such a conclusion, whether or not we are able to believe that every slight variation of structure,—the union of each pair in marriage,—the dissemination of each seed,—and other such events, have all been ordained for some special purpose.

The main conclusion arrived at in this work, namely that man is descended from some lowly-organised form will, I regret to think, be highly distasteful to many persons. But there can hardly be a doubt that we are descended from barbarians....

Man may be excused for feeling some pride at having risen, though not through his own exertions, to the very summit of the organic scale; and the fact of his having thus risen, instead of having been aboriginally placed there, may give him hopes for a still higher destiny in the distant future. But we are not here concerned with hopes or fears, only with the truth as far as our reason allows us to discover it. I have given the evidence to the best of my ability; and we must acknowledge, as it seems to me, that man with all his noble qualities, with sympathy which feels for the most debased, with benevolence which extends not only to other men but to the humblest living creature, with his god-like intellect which has penetrated into the movements and constitution of the solar system— with all these exalted powers—Man still bears in his bodily frame the indelible stamp of his lowly origin.

Questions
(1) Where does Darwin theorize that Mankind originated? On what basis of evidence?
(2) Does Darwin appear to suggest that religion and science are incompatible? How or how not?
(3) How does Darwin account for the development of human intellect?

1–6
The lingering debate: how, and from whence, did human beings populate the globe?

The controversy over origins did not begin and end with Darwin, nor has the fact that scientific evolutionists have divorced themselves from religious considerations prevented the emergence of contending evolutionary viewpoints and sub-theories. One thorny question revolves around the relationship between Europe's Neanderthals and Homo sapiens.

Source: Christopher Stringer and Clive Gamble, *In Search of the Neanderthals* (London: Thames & Hudson, 1993), cited in Thomas *Human Origins*, pp. 146–147.

Today there are two main competing scientific camps, each believing it holds the solution. Both accept that there was a migration out of Africa by *Homo erectus* populations beginning around 1 million years ago ("Out of Africa 1" as we shall call it). One camp, however, argues that there was at least one other major wave of migration ("Out of Africa 2") around 100,000 years ago, this time of anatomically modern humans—*Homo sapiens*—people who had evolved in Africa from *Homo erectus* stock and subsequently replaced all other populations in the world including the Neanderthals. Against this model of *population replacement,* the rival camp sets its model of *regional continuity.* For the followers of this latter school, there was no pronounced Out of Africa 2 migration. Instead, modern humans evolved semi-independently in different regions of the world from independent populations of Ancients (Neanderthals in Eurasia, *Homo erectus* in China and Java), with continual gene flow or interbreeding between geographically contiguous groups so that a single but racially diverse modern human species was the result.

It becomes clear that the Neanderthals—for whom we have a wealth of evidence greater than for any of our other fossil relatives—are central to this argument. Did they evolve into people like us, as the multiregionalists would have us believe, or were they an evolutionary dead end, as the proponents of population replacement would argue?…

According to current scientific thinking, speciation—the process by which new species are formed—is most commonly a product of the geographic isolation of an interbreeding group or population. Set out by Ernest Mayr, this geographical model of speciation is known as allopatry, and in the case of human evolution may draw on genetic, anatomical and archaeological evidence. Isolation can be produced either by geographical barriers, such as mountain formation or a rise in sea levels, or by new behavioural or morphological obstacles to interbreeding within a previously continuous population. The multiregional and replacement models for speciation disagree over the extent of isolation present in widely dispersed early human populations.

Multiregional evolution emphasizes continuity in both time and space. According to this model, isolation was never sufficient to allow allopatric speciation, since genes (the basic units of heredity) were circulated and exchanged between all the human populations of the Pleistocene. There could be no speciation because throughout the last 1 million years there was really only one species: *Homo sapiens.* This judgment implies that since the first dispersal of hominids out of Africa a million years or more ago, all the observable variation is within this one species. Multiregionalists argue that the mechanism of change was predominantly behavioural, with anatomy eventually evolving to accommodate progressive changes in behaviour that usually involved improvements in technology. These changes, like the genes, circulated around the inhabited world. The different regional lineages responded in similar ways to these universal forces, directing change globally towards modern-looking humans. Nevertheless, certain local differences were, at the same time, being maintained. Selection for specific features in particular environments kept them in local populations as they gradually became more modern, e.g. the large noses of Neanderthals were maintained throughout the transition to modern Europeans, probably in response to the European climate, and the strong cheek bones of Javanese *Homo erectus* were maintained in the transition to modern native Australians, perhaps due to behavioural or dietary factors. The mechanism of inter-regional gene flow is all-important in multiregional evolution, to continually introduce new characteristics which can be worked on by local selection, and to counterbalance the tendency to local specializations which would increase divergence between geographically remote populations.

The population replacement camp has not so far produced a comparable theoretical dogma to account for evolutionary change.…The differences between the Neanderthals and modern humans…lay in their society and culture as well as in their anatomy.…The two communities were supported by different capacities for communication—verbal, visual and symbolic—and…this in turn affected their organization of camp-sites, their exploitation of the landscape, and their colonization of new habitats. But to conclude that the Neanderthals were different from us is not to condemn them in the same way that earlier popularizers and scientists did.… The Neanderthals were not ape-men, nor missing links—they were as human as us, but they represented a different brand of humanity, one with a distinctive blend of primitive and advanced characteristics. There was nothing inevitable about the triumph of the Moderns, and a twist of Pleistocene fate could have left the Neanderthals occupying Europe to this day. The 30,000 years by which we have missed them represent only a few ticks of the Ice Age clock.

Questions

(1) In brief, how do the two scientific camps differ in their views of the eventual fate of the Neanderthals?

(2) What possible role could geographical isolation have played in human evolution/development?

(3) To what degree and in what particular respects might the Neanderthals have differed from modern humans?

CHAPTER 2

2–1
Lugal Sulgi: role model for Mesopotamian royalty.

The Sumerians often endowed the original lugals (priest-kings) of their city-states with extra-human power and semi-divine ancestry. In the case of the legendary Sulgi of Nippur, his parentage included the deities Ninsun and Lugalbanda. In the cuneiform tablet that relates the story of his reign, "Sulgi, the Ideal King," he is held up as being what the perfect lugal should be; modesty certainly not being one of his flaws.

Source: Jacob Klein, "The Royal Hymns of Sulgi, King of Ur," in *Transactions of the American Philosophical Society*, v. 71, pt. 7 (1981), Philadelphia; pp. 13, 15, 17, 19.

The hero avenged his city,
Whatever had been destroyed in Sumer, he destroyed
in the foreign land,
He made the god of its city withdraw from it.
Its spirit (of) the good eye, (and) its angel (of) the
good eye he caused to stand aside,
In its cultivated fields of lustrous barley, he
caused weeds to grow,
He destroyed its wide and large trees (with) the axe,
He tore down its date-palms by their crown,
He uprooted its small trees,
In its orchards and gardens, where the 'honey' of
fig-trees had been produced, he made weeds grow,
So that *thistles* and *thorns* broke through the ground.
The king—after he destroyed the cities, ruined
the walls,
Terrified the evil land (like) a flood,
Dispersed the seed of the Gutians like seed-grain,
The pure lapis-lazuli of the foreign land he loaded
into leather-sacks and leather-bags,
Heaped up all its treasures,
Amassed all the wealth of the foreign land.
Upon its fattened oxen (and) fattened sheep,
He invokes the name of Enlil,
He invokes the name of Ninlil (ŠD 334–353.)

***

Let me extoll all my achievements!
The fame of my power has reached very far,
My wisdom is full of subtleties,
What of mine is not a *mistery?*

***

That the king might let known his enduring name into
distant days,
That Šulgi, the king of Ur—
The hymn of his power, the song of his might,
That the wise one—the everlasting name of his
preeminence,
Unto the offspring of future days might hand down,

For the mighty one, the son of Ninsun,
The Wisdom of the future was brought to the fore.
He praises his (own) power in a song,
He exalts his own intelligence, the good that he has
acquired from birth (lines 1–9).

***

As a youth, I studied the scribal art in the e d u b b a,
from the tablets of Sumer and Akkad,
Of the nobility, no one was able to write a tablet like
me,
In the place *where* the people *attend* to learn the
scribal art,
Adding, subtracting, counting and accounting—
I completed all (their courses);
The fair Nanibgal, Nisaba,
Endowed me generously with wisdom and
intelligence (lines 13–19).

***

(Then) I arose like a hawk, (like) a falcon,
(And) returned to Nippur in my vigor.
On that day, the storm shrieked, the west wind
whirled,
The north wind and the south wind howled at each
other,
Lightning together with the 'seven winds' devoured
each other in heaven,
The thundering storm made the earth quake.
Iškur roared in the broad heavens,
The clouds of heaven mingled with the waters of the
earth,
Their small (hail-)stones and their large (hail-)stones
Were striking on my back.
I, the king, I feared not, nor was I terrified.
Like a fierce lion I gnashed my teeth.
Like a wild ass I galloped.
With my heart full of joy, I ran onward.
Racing like a solitary wild-donkey,

(Before) Utu set his face toward his 'house',
I traversed a distance of fifteen 'miles'.
My sag-ur-sag priests gazed at me (with
  astonishment):
In Nippur and Ur, in one day, I celebrated their
  e š e š- festival!
With my 'brother (and) companion', the hero Utu,
I drank beer in the palace, founded by An,
My singers sang for me to the (accompaniment of)
the 'seven' t i g i-drums,
(And) my consort, holy Inanna, the lady, the joy of
  heaven and earth,
Sat there with me at the banquet.

***

My shining like fine silver,
My (having a perfect) 'ear', and being an expert in
  song and speech,
I, the shepherd, my attaining a perfect control of
  anything,
In my kingship, let all these be seemly recited!
As many lines as there may be in my songs,
None of them is false, (all of them) are verily true!
My songs, be they royal prayers or supplications,

Be they long-ballads, the praises of kingship,
Be they psalms, love-poems or love dialogues,
Be they flute-songs or drum-songs—
In order that they shall never pass from memory, and
  that they shall never depart from (man's) lips,
Let no one neglect them in the cult-places!
Let them never cease (to be sung) in the lustrous
  Ekur!
Let them be played for Enlil, in his New-Moon
  shrine!
In its *monthly-festivals,* where sparkling beer is
  copiously libated like water,
Let them be firmly established for Enlil and Ninlil,
  who dwell there together!

***

I, the upright, the benefactor of the land—
Let my songs be (placed) in every mouth,
Let my poems never pass from memory!
That these, my paeans, spoken in praise,
These (laudatory) words, which Enki established for
  me,
These, the joyfully *deliberated wisdom* of Geštinanna,
Should not be forgotten for distant days—

Questions

(1) What was involved in carrying out a successful military campaign of retaliation?

(2) In what ways does Sulgi's prowess go beyond the military realm?

(3) Using Sulgi's reputed words as a clue, what virtues did the Sumerians consider most important in their rulers?

2–2

Suffering, resignation, and explanation: two Mesopotamian outlooks.

Sumeria and its successor-cultures in Mesopotamia were largely pessimistic in their ultimate view of the present and future. Human beings were totally at the mercy of the rather capricious whims of the gods, and destined for death and an unfulfilling afterlife (though suffering could sometimes be assuaged, and death postponed). Mesopotamia's unpredictable weather patterns, natural disasters, and invariable raids and invasions by the inhabitants of the Zagros Mountains may have contributed to this fatalistic state of mind, which would find its most cogent expression in the Gilgamesh epics. However, the attitude itself predated, and was independent of, the Gilgamesh legend, as evidenced in these two lamentations, the first a Sumerian poem (Document A) and the other an Akkadian world-view (Document B).

Sources: Samuel Noah Kramer, *From the Tablets of Sumer,* (Indian Hills, Co.: Falcon's Wing Press, 1956), pp. 148–151; James B. Pritchard, *Ancient Near Eastern Texts Relating to the Old Testament* (Princeton, N.J.: Princeton University Press, 1969), pp. 596–598.

DOCUMENT A

"I am a man, a discerning one, yet who respects me
  prospers not,
My righteous word has been turned into a lie,

The man of deceit has covered me with the
  Southwind, I am forced to serve him,
Who respects me not has shamed me before you.

"You have doled out to me suffering ever anew,

I entered the house, heavy is the spirit,
I, the man, went out to the streets, oppressed is the
   heart,
With me, the valiant, my righteous shepherd has
become angry, has looked upon me inimically.

"My herdsman has sought out evil forces against me
   who am not his enemy,
My companion says not a true word to me,
My friend gives the lie to my righteous word,
The man of deceit has conspired against me,
And you, my god, do not thwart him.…

"I, the wise, why am I bound to the ignorant youths?
I, the discerning, why am I counted among the
   ignorant?
Food is all about, yet my food is hunger,
On the day shares were allotted to all, my allotted
   share was suffering.

"My god, (I would stand) before you,
Would speak to you,…, my word is a groan,
I would tell you about it, would bemoan the bitterness
   of my path,
(Would bewail) the confusion of.…

"Lo, let not my mother who bore me cease my lament
   before you.
Let not my sister utter the happy song and chant.
Let her utter tearfully my misfortunes before you,
Let my wife voice mournfully my suffering,
Let the expert singer bemoan my bitter fate.

"My god, the day shines bright over the land, for me
   the day is black.
The bright day, the good day has…like the…
Tears, lament, anguish, and depression are lodged
   within me,
Suffering overwhelms me like one chosen for nothing
   but tears,
Evil fate holds me in its hand, carries off my breath of
   life,
Malignant sickness bathes my body…

"My god, you who are my father who begot me, lift
up my face.
Like an innocent cow, in pity…the groan,
How long will you neglect me, leave me unprotected?
Like an ox,…,
How long will you leave me unguided?

"They say—valiant sages —a word righteous and
   straightforward:
'Never has a sinless child been born to its mother,
…a sinless youth has not existed from of old.'"

                        ***

The man—his god harkened to his bitter tears and
   weeping,
The young man—his lamentation and wailing soothed
   the heart of his god.
The righteous words, the pure words uttered by him,
   his god accepted.
The words which the man prayerfully confessed,
Pleased the…, the flesh of his god, and his god with-
   drew his hand from the evil word,
…which oppresses the heart,…he embraces,
The encompassing sickness-demon, which had spread
   wide it wings, he swept away.
The (disease) which had smitten him like a…,
   he dissipated,
The evil fate which had been decreed for him in
   accordance with his sentence, he turned aside,
He turned the man's suffering into joy,
Set by him the kindly genii as a watch and guardian,
Gave him…angels with gracious mien.

DOCUMENT B

Tablet I

I will praise the lord of wisdom, the [*deliberative*]
   god,
Who lays hold of the night, but frees the day,
Marduk, the lord of wisdom, the [*deliberative*] god,
Who lays hold of the night, but frees the day,
Whose fury surrounds him like a storm wind,
But whose breeze is as pleasant as a morning zephyr,
Whose anger is irresistible, whose rage is a
   devastating flood,
But whose heart is merciful, whose mind forgiving,
The…of whose hands the heavens cannot hold back,
But whose gentle hand sustains the dying,
Marduk, the…of whose hands the heavens cannot
   hold back,
But whose gentle hand sustains the dying,…

The lord […] the *confusion*
And the warrior *Enlil* […] his…
My god has forsaken me and *disappeared*,
My goddess has cut me off and stayed removed from me.
The benevolent spirit who was (always) beside [me]
   has departed,
My protective spirit has flown away and seeks
   someone else.
My dignity has been taken away, my manly good
   looks jeopardized,
My pride has been cut off, my protection has skipped
   off.
Terrifying omens have been brought upon me,
I was put out of my house and wandered about
   outside.
The omens concerning me are confused, daily there *is*
   inflammation.

I cannot stop going to the diviner and dream
  interpreter.
What is said in the street portends ill for me.
When I lie down at night my dream is terrifying.
The king, the very flesh of the gods, the sun of his
  peoples,
His heart is enraged (with me) and cannot be
  appeased.
Even though I stand *praying* they…against me.
They gather together telling things that ought not be
  said.
Thus the first, "I have made him want to end his life."
The second says, "I made him vacate his post."
Likewise the third, "I shall take over his position."
"I will take over his house," says the fourth.
The fifth…
The sixth and seventh will pursue his…
The group of seven has assembled their forces,
Merciless as a storm demon, they are like…
They are one in flesh, united in purpose.
Their hearts rage against me and they are ablaze like
  fire.
They agree on slander and lies about me.
They have sought to muzzle my respectful mouth.
I, whose lips always prattled, have become like a
  mute.
My hearty shout is [reduced] to silence,
My proud head is bowed to the ground,
Fear has weakened my brave heart.
Even a youngster has turned back my broad chest.
My arms, (though once) strong, are…
I, who used to walk like a proud man, have learned to
  slip by unnoticed.
Though I was a respectable man, I have become a
  slave.
To my *many relations* I have become like a recluse.
If I walk the street, fingers are pointed at me;
If I enter the palace, eyes blink.
My own town looks on me as an enemy;
Even my land is savage and hostile.
My friend has become a stranger,
My companion has become an evil person and a
  demon.
In his rage my comrade denounces me,
Constantly my associate *furbishes* his weapons.
My close friend has brought my life into danger;
My slave has publicly cursed me in the assembly.
…the crowd has defamed me.
When someone who knows me sees me, he *passes by
  on the other side.*
My family treats me as if I were not related to them,
The grave is ready for anyone who speaks well of me,
But he who speaks ill of me is promoted.
The one who slanders me has the god's help;
The…who says "god have mercy" when death is
  imminent
Without delay becomes well through his protective god.

I have no one to go at my side, nor have I found any
  one understanding.
They divided all my possessions among foreign
  riffraff.
They stopped up the source of my canal with silt.
They have stopped the joyous harvest song in my
  fields,
And silenced my city like an enemy city.
They have let another take over my duties,
They appointed someone else to be present at the rites
  (where I should be).
By day there is sighing, by night lamentation,
The month is wailing, the year is gloom.
I moan like a dove all day long.
[Instead of singing a] song I *groan loudly.*
My eyes are…[through] constant weeping,
My lower eyelids are swollen [from *ceaseless*] tears.
[…]before me the fears of my heart
[…] panic and fear.
            (The rest of the tablet is badly damaged.)

Tablet II

I survived to the next year; the appointed time passed.
I turn around, but it is bad, very bad;
My *ill luck* increases and I cannot find what is right.
I called to my god, but he did not show his face,
I prayed to my goddess, but she did not raise her
head.
Even the diviner with his divination could not make
  prediction,
And the interpreter of dreams with his libation could,
  not elucidate my case.
I sought the favor of the *zaqīqu*-spirit, but he would
  not enlighten me;
The exorcist with his ritual could not appease the
  divine wrath against me.
What strange conditions everywhere!
When I look behind (me), there is persecution,
  trouble.
Like one who has not made libations to his god,
Nor invoked his goddess when he ate,
Does not *make* prostrations nor recognize (the
  necessity of) bowing down,
In whose mouth supplication and prayer are lacking,
Who has even *neglected* holy days, and ignored
  festivals,
Who was negligent and did not observe the gods' rites,
Did not teach his people reverence and worship,
But has eaten his food without invoking his god,
And abandoned his goddess by not bringing a flour
  offering,
Like one who has gone crazy and forgotten his lord,
Has frivolously sworn a solemn oath by his god, (like
  such a one) do I *appear.*
For myself, I gave attention to supplication and
  prayer:

My prayer was discretion, sacrifice my rule.
The day for worshipping the god was a joy to my
 heart;
The day of the goddess's procession was profit and
 gain to me.
The king's blessing—that was my joy,
And the accompanying music became a delight for
 me.
I had my land keep the god's rites,
And brought my people to value the goddess's name.
I made the praise for the king like a god's,
And taught the people respect for the palace.
I wish I knew that these things would be pleasing to
 one's god!
What is good for oneself may be offense to one's god,
What in one's own heart seems despicable may be
 proper to one's god.
Who can know the will of the gods in heaven?
Who can understand the plans of the underworld
 gods?
Where have humans learned the way of a god?
He who was alive yesterday is dead today.
One moment he is worried, the next he is boisterous.
One moment he is singing a joyful song,
A moment later he wails like a professional mourner.
Their condition changes (as quickly as) opening and
 shutting (the *eyes*).
When starving they become like corpses,
When full they oppose their god.
In good times they speak of scaling heaven,
When they are troubled they talk of going down to hell.
I am *perplexed* at these things; I have not been able to
 understand their significance.
As for me, exhausted, a windstorm is driving me on!
Debilitating Disease is let loose upon me:
An Evil Wind has blown [from the] horizon,
Headache has sprung up from the surface of the
 underworld,
An Evil Cough has left its *Apsu*,
The Irresistible Demon has left *Ekur,*
[The Lamashtu-demon came] clown from the
 Mountain,
Cramp set out [with…] the flood,
Weakness breaks through the ground along with the
 plants.
[They all joined in] and came on me together.
[They *struck*] my head, they enveloped my skull;
[My] face is gloomy, my eyes flow.
They have wrenched my neck muscles and made (my)
 neck limp.
They struck [my chest,] beat my breast.
They affected my flesh and made me shake,
[In] my epigastrium they kindled a fire.
They churned up my bowels,…[they]…my…
Causing the discharge of phlegm, they tired out my
 [lungs].
They tired out my limbs and made my *fat* quake.

My upright stance they knocked down like a wall,
My robust figure they laid down like a rush,
I am thrown down like a…and cast on my face.
The *alû*-demon has clothed himself in my body as
 with a garment;
Sleep covers me like a net.
My eyes stare straight ahead, but cannot see,
My ears are open, but cannot hear.
Feebleness has overcome my whole body,
An attack of illness has fallen upon my flesh.
Stiffness has taken over my arms,
Weakness has come upon my knees,
My feet forget their motion.
[A stroke] has got me; I choke like someone prostrate.
Death has [*approached*] and has covered my face.
If someone is concerned about me, I am not even able
 to answer the one who inquires.
[My…] weep, but I cannot control myself.
A snare is laid on my mouth,
And a bolt keeps my lips barred.
My "gate" is barred, my "drinking place" blocked,
My hunger is…, my windpipe constricted.
I eat grain as though it were a vile thing,
Beer, the sustenance of mankind, is distasteful to me.
My malady is indeed protracted.
Through not eating, my looks have become strange,
My flesh is flaccid, and my blood has ebbed away.
My bones look separated, and are covered (only) with
 my skin.
My flesh is inflamed, and the…-disease has afflicted me.
I have taken to a bed of *bondage;* going out is a pain;
My house has become my prison.
My arms are powerless—my own flesh is a manacle,
My feet are fallen flat—my own person is a fetter.
My afflictions are grievous, my wound is severe.
A whip full of needles has struck me,
The goad that pricked me was covered with barbs
All day long the tormentor torments [me],
And at night he does not let me breathe easily for a
 minute.
Through twisting my joints are parted,
My limbs are splayed and knocked apart.
I spent the night in my dung like an ox,
And wallowed in my excrement like a sheep.
My symptoms are beyond the exorcist,
And my omens have confused the diviner.
The exorcist could not diagnose the nature of my
 sickness,
Nor could the diviner set a time limit on my illness.
My god has not come to the rescue nor taken me by
 the hand;
My goddess has not shown pity on me nor gone by
 my side.
My grave was waiting, and my funerary paraphernalia
 ready,
Before I was even dead lamentation for me was
 finished.

All my country said, "How he is crushed!"
The face of him who gloats lit up when he heard,
The news reached her who gloats, and her heart
  rejoiced.
I know the day for my whole family,
When, among my friends, their Sun-god will have
  mercy.

Tablet III

His hand was heavy upon me, I could not bear it.

My dread of him was alarming, it [...me]
His fierce wind [*brought on*] a destructive flood.
His stride was..., it... [...]
...the severe illness does not [leave] my person,
I forget wakefulness, it makes [my mind] stray.
Both day and night I groan,
Whether awake or dreaming I am equally miserable.
A remarkable young man of outstanding physique,
Splendid in body, clothed in new garments—
Since in waking moments...
Clad in splendor, robed in dread,...

Questions

(1) What specific complaints are voiced by the young sufferer in the first document and what might this reveal about his society and culture?

(2) What conclusions might one come to regarding the nature of the young sufferer's god?

(3) What particular aspects of misfortune seem to most concern the sufferer in the second (Akkadian) document?

(4) What contrasts/comparisons could be made between the two documents?

2–3
The Nippur Murder Trial and the "Silent Wife."

One of the earliest known examples of a criminal justice proceedings was the trial of men accused of murdering a temple servant (nishakku) at Nippur. The Assembly of Nippur whose responsibility it was to render a verdict also had to make a ruling on the situation of the victim's wife, who had been informed of the murder (by the murderers) after the crime had been committed, but had chosen to remain silent on the matter, and was therefore prosecuted as an accessory to murder.

Source: Samuel Noah Kramer, *From the Tablets of Sumer* (Indian Hills, Co: Falcon's Wing Press, 1956), pp. 53–54.

Nanna-sig, the son of Lu-Sin, Ku-Enlil, the son of Ku-Nanna, the barber, and Enlil-ennam, the slave of Adda-kalla, the gardener, killed Lu-lnanna, the son of Lugal-apindu, the *nishakku-official.*

After Lu-Inanna, the son of Lugal-apindu, had been put to death, they told Nin-dada, the daughter of Lu-Ninurta, the wife of Lu-Inanna, that her husband Lu-Inanna had been killed.

Nin-dada, the daughter of Lu-Ninurta, opened not her mouth, (her) lips remained sealed.

Their case was (then) brought to (the city) Isin before the king, (and) the King Ur-Ninurta ordered their case to be taken up in the Assembly of Nippur.

(There) Ur-gula, son of Lugal-.., Dudu, the bird-hunter, Ali-ellati, the dependent, Buzu, the son of Lu-Sin, Eluti, the son of..-Ea, Shesh-Kalla, the porter (?), Lugal-Kan, the gardener, Lugal-azida, the son of Sin-andul, (and) Shesh-kalla, the son of Shara-.., faced (the Assembly) and said:

"They who have killed a man are not (worthy) of life. Those three males and that woman should be killed in front of the chair of Lu-Inanna, the son of Lugal-apindu, the *nishakku*-official."

(Then) Shu..-lilum, the..-official of Ninurta, (and) Ubar-Sin, the gardener, faced (the Assembly) and said:

"Granted that the husband of Nin-dada, the daughter of Lu-Ninurta, had been killed, (but) what had (?) the woman done (?) that she should be killed?"

(Then) the (members of the) Assembly of Nippur faced (them) and said:

"A woman whose husband did not support (?) her—granted that she knew her husband's enemies, and that (after) her husband had been killed she heard that her husband had been killed—why should she not remain silent (?) about (?) him? Is it she (?) who killed her husband? The punishment of those (?) who (actually) killed should suffice."

In accordance with the decision (?) of the Assembly of Nippur, Nanna-sig, the son of Lu-Sin,

Ku-Enlil, the son of Ku-Nanna, the barber, and Enlil-ennam, the slave of Adda-kalla, the gardener, were handed over (to the executioner) to be killed.

(This is) a case taken up by the Assembly of Nippur.

Questions
(1) What possible motive is suggested for the wife's "silence"?
(2) Summarize briefly the argument presented, and accepted by the Assembly, for sparing the wife's life.
(3) What appears to have been the standard legal procedure in Sumerian criminal cases, and how might it compare/contrast to contemporary procedure in the U.S. legal system?

2–4
Beloved but deadly: the goddess Inanna of Ur.

The Mesopotamian gods were generally a selfish, quarrelsome, unpredictable lot—more likely to elicit dread than sincere reverence. If there was an exception to the rule it was Inanna (Ishtar), goddess of fertility, whose function was of such vital importance in assuring the community's continued survival, and whose portfolio covered both the regenerative pleasures of love and the destructive power of warfare. The prayer of Enheduanna, priestess of Ur and daughter of Emperor Sargon the Great of Akkad (c. 2200 B.C.E.), reveals the dual aspects of this divinity. "Me" in the poem might be defined as the powers, tasks, and duties of the universal order.

Source: James B. Pritchard, *Ancient Near Eastern Texts Relating to the Old Testament* (Princeton, N.J.: Princeton University Press, 1969), pp. 579–582.

Queen of all the *me,* radiant light,
Life-giving woman, beloved of An (and) Urash,
Hierodule of An, much bejewelled,
Who loves the life-giving tiara, fit for *en*-ship,
Who grasps in (her) hand, the seven *me,*
My queen, you who are the guardian of all the great
  me,
You have lifted the *me,* have tied the *me* to your
  hands,
Have gathered the *me,* pressed the *me* to your breast.

You have filled the land with venom, like a dragon.
Vegetation ceases, when you thunder like Ishkur,
You who bring down the Flood from the mountain,
Supreme one, who are the Inanna of heaven (and)
  earth,
Who rain flaming fire over the land,
Who have been given the *me* by An, queen who rides
  the beasts,
Who at the holy command of An, utters the (divine)
  words,
Who can fathom your great rites!

Destroyer of the foreign lands, you have given wings
  to the storm,

Beloved of Enlil you made it (the storm) blow over
  the land,
You carried out the instructions of An.
My queen, the foreign lands cower at your cry,
In dread (and) fear of the South Wind, mankind
Brought you their anguished clamor,
Took before you their anguished *outcry*
Opened before you wailing and weeping,
Brought before you the "great" lamentations in the
city streets.

In the van of battle, everything was struck down
  before you,
My queen, you are all devouring in your power,
You kept on attacking like an attacking storm,
Kept on blowing (louder) than the howling storm,
Kept on thundering (louder) than Ishkur,
Kept on moaning (louder) than the evil winds,
Your feet grew not weary,
You caused wailing to be uttered on the "lyre of
lament."

My queen, the Anunna, the great gods,
Fled before you like fluttering bats,
Could not stand before your awesome face,

Could not approach your awesome forehead.
Who can soothe your angry heart!
Your baleful heart is beyond soothing!
Queen, happy of "liver," joyful of heart,
(But) whose anger cannot be soothed, daughter of
Sin,
Queen, paramount in the land, who has (ever) paid
you (enough) homage!

The mountain who kept from paying homage to
 you—vegetation became "tabu" for it,
You burnt down its great gates,
Its rivers ran with blood because of you, its people
had nothing to drink,
Its troops were led off willingly (into captivity)
before you,
Its forces disbanded themselves willingly before you,
Its strong men paraded willingly before you,
The amusement places of its cities were filled with
 turbulence,
Its adult males were driven off as captives before you.

Against the city that said not "yours is the land,"
That said not "It belongs to the father who begot
 you,"
You promised your holy word, turned away from it,
Kept your distance from its womb,
Its woman spoke not of love with her husband,
In the deep night she whispered not (tenderly) with
 him,
Revealed not to him the "holiness" of her heart.

Rampant wild cow, elder daughter of Sin,
Queen, greater than An, who has (ever) paid you
(enough) homage!
You who in accordance with the life giving *me*, great
 queen of queens,
Have become greater than your mother who gave
birth to you, (as soon as) you came forth from the
holy womb,
Knowing, wise, queen of all the lands,
Who multiplies (all) living creatures (and) peoples—I
 have uttered your holy song.
Life-giving goddess, fit for the *me,* whose acclama-
tion is exalted,
Merciful, life-giving woman, radiant of heart, I have
 uttered it before you in accordance with the *me.*

I have entered before you in my holy *gipar,*
I the *en,* Enheduanna,
Carrying the *masab*-basket, I uttered a joyous chant,
(But now) I no longer dwell in the goodly place you
 established.
Came the day, the sun scorched me
Came the shade (of night), the South Wind
 overwhelmed me,
My honey-sweet voice has become *strident,*

Whatever gave me pleasure has turned into dust.

Oh Sin, king of heaven, my (bitter) fate,
To An declare, An will deliver me,
Pray declare it to An, he will deliver me.

The kingship of heaven has been seized by the
 woman (Inanna),
At whose feet lies the flood-land.
That woman (Inanna) so exalted, who has made
 me tremble together the city (Ur),
Stay *her,* let her heart be soothed by me.
I, Enheduanna will offer supplications to her,
My tears, like sweet drinks.
Will I proffer to the holy Inanna, I will greet her
 in peace,
Let not Ashimbabbar (Sin) be troubled.

She (Inanna) has changed altogether the rites of
 holy An,
Has seized the Eanna from An,
Feared not the great An,
That house (the Eanna) whose charm was irresistible,
 whose allure was unending,
That house she has turned over to destruction,
Her...that she brought there has...
My wild cow (Inanna) assaults there its men, makes
 them captive.

I, what am I among the living creatures!
May An give over (to punishment) the rebellious
lands that hate your (Inanna's) Nanna,
May An split its cities asunder,
May Enlil curse it,
May not its tear-destined child be soothed by
 her mother,

Oh queen who established lamentations,
Your "boat of lamentations," has *landed* in an
 inimical land,
There will I die, while singing the holy song.

As for me, my Nanna watched not over me,
I have been attacked most cruelly.
Ashimbabbar has not spoken my verdict.
But what matter, whether he spoke it or not!
I, accustomed to triumph, have been driven forth from
 (my) house,
Was forced to flee the cote like a swallow, my life
 is devoured,
Was made to walk among the mountain thorns,
The life-giving tiara of *en*-ship was taken from me,
Eunuchs were assigned to me—"These are becoming
 to you," it was told me.

Dearest queen, beloved of An,
Let your holy heart, the noble, return to me,

Beloved wife of Ushumgalanna (Dumuzi),
Great queen of the horizon and zenith,
The Anunna have prostrated themselves before you.
Although at birth you were the younger *sister*,
How much greater you have become than the
Anunna, the great gods!
The Anunna kiss the ground before you.

It is not my verdict that has been completed, it is a
  strange verdict that has been *turned* into my verdict,
The fruitful bed has been abolished,
(So that) I have not interpreted to man the commands
  of Ningal.
For me, the radiant *en* of Nanna,
May your heart be soothed, you who are the queen
  beloved of An.
"You are known, you are known"—it is not of Nanna
  that I have recited it, it is of you that I have
  recited it.
You are known by your heaven-like height,
You are known by your earth-like breadth,
You are known by your destruction of rebel-lands,
You are known by your massacring (their people),
You are known by your devouring (their) dead like
  a dog,
You are known by your fierce countenance.
You are known by the raising of your fierce
  countenance,
You are known by your flashing eyes.
You are known by your *contentiousness* (and)

disobedience,
You are known by your many triumphs—
It is not of Nanna that I have recited it, it is of you
  that I have recited it.
My queen, I have extolled you, who alone are exalted,
Queen beloved of An, I have *erected* your daises,
Have heaped up the coals, have conducted the rites,
Have set up the nuptial chamber for you, may your
  heart be soothed for me,
Enough, more than enough innovations, great queen,
  have I made for you.
What I have recited to you in the deep night,
The *gala*-singer will repeat for you in midday.
It is because of your captive spouse, your captive son,
That your wrath is so great, your heart so unappeased.
The foremost queen, the prop of the *assembly*,
Accepted her prayer.
The heart of Inanna was restored,
The day was favorable for her, she was clothed with
  beauty, was filled with joyous allure,
How she carried (her) beauty—like the rising moon
  light!
Nanna who came forth in wonder true,
  (and) her mother Ningal, proffered prayers to her,
Greeted her at the doorsill (of the temple).

To the hierodule whose command is noble,
The destroyer of foreign lands, presented by An
  with the *me*,
My queen garbed in allure, O Inanna, praise!

Questions
(1) What endearing qualities of Inanna does Enheduanna seem to be most eager to emphasize?
(2) What negative aspects of Inanna are most strongly brought out by the priestess?
(3) Does Enheduanna appear to have a specific agenda? What passages might tend to indicate this?
(4) Does the priestess express fear/apprehension? If so, how?

2–5
Law and legality in early Sumeria and Babylonia.

Though the Code of King Hammurabi is unquestionably the best known, most complete, and most wide-ly quoted legal document of Mesopotamia, it was by no means unique, nor was it the earliest. In fact, the law in Mesopotamia approached the proportion of being a national obsession as numerous lugals and local worthies wrestled with the dilemma of how to temper strong government with justice. The first example (Document A) is a portion of the code of the Sumerian lugal, Ur-Nammu (c. 2100 BC.E.); and the second (Document B) is a code in the form of an edict of the Amorite (Old Babylonian) King Ammisaduqa (c. 1646–1626 B.C.E.).

Source: James B. Pritchard, *Ancient Near Eastern Texts Relating to the Old Testament* (Princeton, N.J.: Princeton University Press, 1969), pp. 523–525, 526–528.

DOCUMENT A

After An and Enlil had turned over the Kingship of Ur to Nanna, (36–40) at that time did Ur-Nammu, son born of (the goddess) Ninsun, for his beloved mother who bore him, (41–42) in accordance with his (i.e., of the god Nanna) principles of equity and truth,…(lines 43–72 destroyed or fragmentary).

(col. ii 73-74) He set up the seven…(75–78) Nam-mahni, the *ensi* of Lagash he slew. (79–84) By the might of Nanna, lord of the city (of Ur), he returned the Magan-boat of Nanna to the *boundary(-canal)*, (85–86) (and) made it famous in Ur.

(87–96) At that time, the field(s) had been subject to the *nisqum*-official, the maritime trade was subject to the seafarers' overseer, (col. iii) the herdsman was subject to the "oxen-taker," the "sheep-taker," and the "donkey-taker."

(lines 97–103 destroyed) (104–113) Then did Ur-Nam-mu, the mighty warrior, king of Ur, king of Sumer and Akkad, by the might of Nanna, lord of the city (of Ur), and in accordance with the true word of Utu, establish equity in the land (114–116) (and) he banished malediction, violence and strife. (117–122) *By granting immunity in Akkad to* the maritime trade from the seafarers' over-seer, to the herdsman from the "oxen-taker," the "sheep-taker," and the "donkey-taker," he (123–124) set Sumer and Akkad *free*.

(125–129) At that time, the…*of* Mar[ad] (and) Kazal[lu] he…(130–134) [By the might [of Nanna] (his) lord…, he…(135–142) The copper…, the (wooden)…(three lines missing), the copper…, the wooden…, [these] seven…, he standardized. (143–144) He fashioned the bronze *silá*-measure, (145–149) he standardized the one *mina* weight, (and) standardized the stone-weight of a shekel of silver *in relation to* one mina.

(150–152) At that time, the bank of the Tigris, the bank of the Euphrates…(153–160 destroyed)… (161) the king (or "owner") provided a head gardener.

(162–168) The orphan was not delivered up to the rich man; the widow was not delivered up to the mighty man; the man of one shekel was not delivered up to the man of one mina.

2: (206–215)…he shall plant for him, his…the planted…apple trees and cedars…[he…] without the owner's knowledge,…he shall bring in.

3: (216–221, destroyed)

4: (222–231 = B § I). If the wife of a man, *by employing her charms,* followed after another man and he slept with her, they (i.e., the authorities) shall slay that woman, but that male (i.e., the other man) shall be set free.

5:(232–239 = B § 2). If a man proceeded by force, and deflowered the virgin (lit.: "undeflowered") slave-woman of another man, that man must pay five shekels of silver.

6: (app. 240–244 = B § 3). If a man divorces his primary wife, he must pay (her) one mina of silver.

7: (app. 245–249 = B § 4). If it is a (former) widow (whom) he divorces, he must pay (her) one-half mina of silver.

8:(250–255 = B § 5). If (however) the man had slept with the widow without there having been any marriage contract, he need not pay (her) any silver.

9: (= 256–269 mostly destroyed)

10: (270–280). If a man had accused a(nother) man of …and he (i.e., the accuser) had him (i.e., the accused) brought to the river-ordeal, and the river-ordeal proved him innocent, then the man who had brought him (i.e., the accuser) must pay him three shekels of silver.

11: (281–290 = B § 10). If a man accused the wife of a man of fornication, and the river(-ordeal) proved her innocent, then the man who had accused her must pay one-third of a mina of silver.

12: (291–301) = B § 11). If a (prospective) son-in-law entered the house of his (prospective) father-in-law, but his father-in-law later gave [his daughter (i.e., the prospective bride) to] another man, he (the father-in-law) shall return to him (i.e., the rejected son-in-law) *two*-fold the amount of bridal presents he had brought.

13: (302–312 = B § 12). (Only traces remain.)

14: (313–323, omitted in B). If […] a slave-woman [*or a male slave fled from the master's house*] and crossed beyond the territory of the city, and (another) man brought her/him back, the owner of the slave shall pay to the one who brought him back *two* shekels of silver.

15: (324–330 = B § 13 + § 21). If a [man…] cut off the foot (var.: limb) of [another man *with his…*], he shall pay ten shekels of silver.

16: (331–338, omitted in B). If a man, in the course of a scuffle, smashed the limb of another man with a club, he shall pay one mina of silver.

17: (339–344 = B § 22). If someone severed the nose of another man with a *copper knife*, he must pay two-thirds of a mina of silver.

18: (A 345–? = B § 23). If a man cut off the […] of [another man] with a […] he shall pay [x shekels (?) of silv]er.

19: (B § 24 + § 16). If he [*knocked out*] his *to[oth]* with [a…] he shall pay two shekels of silver.

20: (missing). (There is a gap of close to 30 lines, which contained not more than three sections, including § 20, § 21, and the beginning of § 21′.)

21′: (B § 28)…he shall surely bring. If he has no slave-woman, he must surely pay ten shekels of silver. If he has no silver, *he shall pay him (with) whatever possessions he (owns).*

22′: (B § 29). If a man's slave-woman, comparing herself to her mistress, speaks insolently to her (or: him), her mouth shall be scoured with 1 quart of salt.

23′: (B § 30). If a man's slave-woman, comparing herself to her mistress, struck her…(rest missing).

24′: (almost completely missing, possibly more than one section in the gap.)

25′: (B § 34). If a man appeared as a witness (in a lawsuit), and was shown to be a perjurer, he must pay fifteen shekels of silver.

26′: (B § 35). If a man appeared as a witness (in a lawsuit), but declined to testify on oath, he must make good as much as is involved in that lawsuit.

27′: (B § 36). If a man proceeded by force, and plowed the arable field of a(nother) man, and he (i.e., the latter) brought a lawsuit (against him), but he (i.e., the squatter) reacts in contempt, that man will forfeit his expenses.

28′: (B § 37). If a man flooded the field of a(nother) man with water, he shall measure out (for him) three *kōr* of barley per *ikū* of field.

29′: (B § 38). If a man had leased an arable field to a(nother) man for cultivation, but he (the lessee) did not plow it, so that it turned into wasteland, he shall measure out (to the lessor) three *kōr* of barley per *ikū* of field.

DOCUMENT B

1: (Text C). The tablet [of the decree which the land was ordered] to hear at the time that the king invoked a *misharum* for the land.

2: (5) The arrears of the farming agents, the shepherds, the *Šusikku*-(agents) of the provinces, and (other) crown tributaries—the...of their firm *agreements* and the *promissory notes*...of their payments are herewith remitted. (10) The collecting officer may not sue the crown tributary for payment.

3: The "market" of Babylon, the "markets" of the country(side), the *ra'ibānum*-officer, which in the...tablet, are...*to* the collecting officer—(15) their arrears dating from the "Year in which King Ammiditana remitted the debts which the land had contracted (= year 21 of Ammiditana)" until the month of Nisan of the "Year: Ammisaduqa the king, Enlil having (20) magnified his noble lordship, like Shamash (Text A) he rose forth in steadfastness over his country, and instituted justice for the whole of his people (= year 1 of Ammisaduqa)"—because the king has invoked the *misharum* for the land, (25) the collecting officer may not sue the [...] for payment.

4: Whoever has given barley or silver to an Akkadian or an Amorite as an interest-bearing loan, or on the *melqētum* basis (30) [*or...*], and had a document executed—because the king has invoked the *misharum* for the land, his document is voided; (35) (Text C) he may not collect the barley or silver on the basis of his document.

5: But if, commencing with the month of Addar II of the "Year in which King Ammiditana destroyed the wall of Udinim constructed by Damqiilishu" (= Year 37 of Ammiditana), (40) he collected by constraint, he

shall refund whatever he had received through collection.

He who does not (thus) make a refund (45) in accordance with the royal decree, shall die.

6: Whoever has given barley or silver to an Akkadian or an Arnorite as an interest-bearing loan or on the *melqētum* basis, and in the document which he executed (50) perpetrated a deception by having it drawn up as a sale or a bailment and then persisted in taking interest, he (i.e., the debtor) shall produce his witnesses, and they shall indict him (i.e., the creditor) for taking interest; because he had distorted his document, his document shall be voided.

(55) A creditor may not sue against the house of an Akkadian or an Amorite for whatever he had loaned him; should he sue for payment, he shall die.

7: (Text A) If anyone had given barley or silver as an interest-bearing loan and had a document executed, (ii 3o) retaining the document in his own possession, and then stated: "I have certainly not given it to you as an interest-bearing loan or on the "*melqētum* basis; the barley or silver which I have given you, I have given (as an advance) for purchases, or for the production of profit, or for some other objective," the person who had received the barley or silver from the creditor shall produce his witnesses to the wording of the document which the lender had denied, and they shall speak (their testimony) before god. (ii 4o) Because he (i.e., the creditor) had distorted his document and denied the (truth of the) matter, he must pay (to the borrower) six-fold (the amount he had lent him). If he (the creditor) cannot make good his liability, he must die.

8: (iii) An Akkadian or an Arnorite who has received barley, silver, or (other) goods either as merchandise for a commercial journey, or as a joint enterprise for the production of profit, (5) his document is not voided (by the *misharum* act); he must repay in accordance with the stipulations of his agreements.

9: Whoever has given barley, silver, or (other) goods to an Akkadian or an Amorite either (as an advance) for purchases, for a commercial journey, or as a joint enterprise for the production of profit, (10) and had a document executed, (but) in the document he had executed, the creditor stipulated in writing that at the expiration of the term (of the contract) the money would accrue interest (15) or if he made any (other) additional stipulations, he (i.e., the obligee) shall not repay on the terms of the (added) stipulations, but shall repay (only) the barley or silver [on the terms of the (basic) document]. The (obligations of the supplementary) stipulations upon the Akkadian (20) or the Amorite are remitted.

10: [...]...*to* Babylon, [the market of ...], the market of Borsippa, [the market of...], the market of Isin, [the market of...], the market of Larsa, (25) [the market of...], the market of Malgium, [the market of Manki]sum, the market of Shitullum, [...] half (their) investment capital was given [them] (in the form of) merchandise out of the palace—the (other) half to be made up by them (i.e., the market associations of the named cities)—(30) any such merchandise shall be disbursed to them from the palace at the going price of the respective city.

11: If a (state) trading merchant, who customarily disposes of merchandise of the palace, made out a document in favor of the palace against the (collectable) arrears of crown tributaries as if he actually received (such) merchandise from the palace, and received (in turn) the (payable) document of the palace-tributary—thus no merchandise was actually given him from the palace in accordance with his document, nor did he receive (any funds) from the palace tributary—(40) because the king has remitted the arrears of the palace-tributary, (iv) that merchant shall declare on divine oath: "(I swear that) I have not received anything in payment from the palace-tributaries as stated in this document." After having (thus) declared, (5) he shall produce the document of the palace-tributary, they (i.e., the authorities and the principals) shall settle the accounts jointly, and out of the merchandise stipulated in the document made out by the merchant in favor of the palace they shall remit in behalf of the merchant as much as was stipulated by the document made out by the palace-tributary (10) in favor of the merchant.

12: The šusikku-agent of the land who (15) customarily receives [the carcasses] from the palace cattle-herdsmen, shepherds, and goatherds under divine oath, (and) who (21) customarily renders to the palace: For every cow carcass: one (quantity) of sin[ews] together with the skin; for every ewe-carcass: one-sixth...barley, together with the skin, plus 1¾ minas of wool; for every goat-carcass: one-sixth of [a shekel] of silver plus ⅔ of a mina of goat-wool,—because the king has instituted the misharum for the land, their arrears will not be collected. The...(of) the šusikku-agent of the land (25) (the quotas)...will not be filled.

13: The arrears of the porter(s) which had been assigned to the collecting-agent for collection are remitted; they will not be collected.

14:(30) The arrears of the Suhu country consisting of šibṣum-rents and/(or) half-share rents—because the king has instituted the misharum for the land, it is remitted; it will not be collected. (35) He (i.e., the collecting-agent) shall not sue for collection against the houses of Suhu (var.: the Suhian population).

15: The crop impost officer who customarily receives impost proportions of fields (planted to) [barley,] sesame, or minor crops belonging to the palace-tributaries, the..., the crown dependents, the infantrymen, the sergeants, or other special feudatories—(v) because the king has instituted the misharum for the land, it is remitted; it will not be proportioned (i.e., the impost shares of each crop will not be collected). (However,) the barley destined for sale or profit will be proportioned according to the customary ratio(s).

16: (5) The taverness(es) of the provinces who customarily pay silver (and/or) barley to the palace—because the king has instituted the misharum in the land, the collecting agent (10) will not sue for payment of their arrears.

17: A taverness who has given beer or barley as a loan may not collect any of what she had given as a loan.

18: A taverness or a merchant who [...] (15) dishonest weight shall die.

19: The infantryman or the sergeant who has leased [a...field] for three years does not perform the [...] service. (20) In the present [year], because the king has instituted the misharum in the land, the infantryman or the sergeant pays according to the (prevailing) ratio of his city..., a third or half (of the crop).

20: (25) If an obligation has resulted in foreclosure against a citizen of Numhia, a citizen of Emutbalum, a citizen of Idamaras, a citizen of Uruk, a citizen of Isin, a citizen of Kisurra, or a citizen of Malgium, (in consequence of which) he [placed] his own person, his wife (30) or his [children] in debt servitude for silver, or as a pledge—because the king has instituted the misharum in the land, he is released; his freedom (35) is in effect.

21: If a house-born slavewoman or male slave, citizen of Numhia, a citizen of Emutbalum, a citizen of Idamaras, a citizen of Uruk, a citizen of Isin, a citizen of Kisurra, (vi) or a citizen of Malgium...whose price..., has been sold for money, or was (5) given over for debt servitude, or was left as a pledge, his freedom will not be effected.

22: (10) The ra'ibānum or regional governor gives barley, silver, or wool to the "house" of an infantryman or a sergeant for harvest labor, or for the performance of (other) labor, (15) as the result of force, shall die. (That) infantryman or sergeant may (at the time) keep (lit.: "carry off") whatever had been given him.

Questions

(1) What assumptions might one make from these documents) concerning gender relationships, marriage, and the status of women in early Mesopotamian society?

(2) Does Ammisaduqa's policy favor either debtors, or creditors? In what ways?

(3) Scrutinizing both sets of laws, what do they reveal about the major problems and issues in early Mesopotamia, and of that civilization's set of priorities?

2–6

Shuruppak's instructions to his son: transmitting the knowledge of a lifetime's experience.

Proverbial/wisdom literature seems to have been a favored instructional vehicle in most ancient cultures, from the Nile to the Yellow River Valley, and an efficient means (by employing the cutting-edge technology of the times) for handing down data and practical, common-sense knowledge through the generations. The following instructional manual, allegedly addressed by the mythical flood-survivor Shuruppak to his son, is indeed quite old, dating to a period prior to 2500 B.C.E.

Source: James B. Pritchard, *Ancient Near Eastern Texts Relating to the Old Testament* (Princeton, N.J.; Princeton University Press, 1969), pp. 594–595.

Shuruppak [son of Uburtutu gave instructions],
To Utnepushtu [his son he gave instructions, saying],
"My son, [I will give you instructions, take my instructions];
Utnapushtu, [I will give you instructions],
[Do not neglect] my instructions.
[Do not disobey] the words [I have spoken to you].
[One should not buy an] ass who [brays (too much)].
[One should not locate] a cultivated field on a road[way].
Do not...] your field.
In your cultivated field [do not...].
Do not harm the daughter of a free man, for the *courtyard* will find out about it."

COUNSELS OF WISDOM

Do not talk [with a tale]bearer,
Do not consult [with a...]...who is an idler;
Because of your good qualities, you will be made into an *example* for them.
Then you will reduce your own work, forsake your path,
And will let your wise, modest opinion be perverted.
Let your mouth be restrained and your speech guarded;
(That) is a man's pride—let what you say be very precious.
Let insolence and blasphemy be an abomination for you;
Speak nothing profane nor any unjust report.
A talebearer is looked down upon.

Do not set out to stand around in the assembly.
Do not loiter where there is a dispute,
For in the dispute they will have you as an *observer.*
Then you will be made a witness for them, and
They will involve you in a lawsuit to affirm some thing that does not concern you.
In case of a dispute, get away from it, disregard it.
If a dispute involving you should flare up, calm it down.
A dispute is a *covered* pit,
A...wall which can *cover over* its foes;

It brings to mind what one has forgotten and makes an accusation against a man.
Do not return evil to your adversary;
Requite with kindness the one who does evil to you,
Maintain justice for your enemy,
Be friendly to your enemy.
(a number of lines damaged)

Give food to eat, beer to drink,
Grant what is requested, provide for and treat with honor.
At this one's god takes pleasure.
It is pleasing to Shamash, who will repay him with favor.
Do good things, be kind all your days.

Do not honor a slave girl in your house;
She should not rule [your] bedroom like a wife.
..., do not give yourself over [to] slave girls.
If she goes up your...you will not go down.
Let this be said [among] your people:
"The household which a slave girl rules, she disrupts."
Do not marry a prostitute, whose husbands are legion,
An *ishtarītu*-woman who is dedicated to a god,
A *kulmashītu*-woman whose...is much.
When you have trouble, she will not support you,
When you have a dispute she will be a mocker.
There is no reverence or submissiveness in her.
Even if she is powerful in the household, get rid of her,
For she pricks up her ears for the footsteps of another man.
Variant: Whatever household she enters (as wife) will be scattered and the one who marries her will not be stable.

My son, if it be the wish of a ruler that you belong to him,
If you are entrusted with his closely guarded seal
Open his treasure house (and) enter it,
For no one but you may do it.
Uncounted wealth you will find inside,

But do not covet any of that,
Nor set your mind on a secret crime,
For afterwards the matter wall be investigated
And the secret crime which you committed will
  be exposed.
The ruler will hear of it (and) will […],
His happy face will […],
        (a number of lines damaged)

Do not speak ill, speak (only) good.
Do not say evil things, speak well of people.
He who speaks ill and says evil—
People will waylay him because of his debt
  to Shamash.
Do not talk too freely, watch what you say.

Do not express your innermost thoughts even when
  you are alone.
What you say in haste you may *regret* later.
Exert yourself to restrain your speech.

Worship your god every day.
Sacrifice and (pious) utterance are the proper
  accompaniment of incense.
Have a freewill offering for your god,
For this is proper toward a god.
Prayer, supplication, and prostration
Offer him daily, then your prayer *will be granted,*
And you will be in harmony with your god.
Since you are learned, read in the tablet:
"Reverence begets favor…

Questions

(1) What one quality does the father appear to stress above all others, in his advice to the son?

(2) What qualities does the father admonish the son to look for in a woman? What is his advice on what not to look for?

(3) In what ways does the instruction in this document jibe with the laws in Document 2–5? What are the possible points of agreement, or contradiction?

2–7

An alumnus reminisces about scribal school in ancient Sumeria.

This is certainly one of the most humorous texts written in cuneiform, and it has all the hallmarks of a personal recollection of the author's, who was one of those young men set aside for special instruction and training for inclusion into what was the first educational/administrative elite, the profession of the scribe. Achieving this coveted status was obviously not always a pleasant undertaking.

Source: Samuel Noah Kramer, *The Sumerians,* (Chicago: University of Chicago Press, 1963), pp. 237–240.

I recited my tablet, ate my lunch, prepared my (new) tablet, wrote it, finished it; then my model tablets were brought to me; and in the afternoon my exercise tablets were brought to me. When school was dismissed, I went home, entered the house, and found my father sitting there. I explained (?) my exercise-tablets to my father, (?) recited my tablet to him, and he was delighted, (so much so) that I attended him (with joy).

***

I am thirsty, give me water to drink; I am hungry, give me bread to eat; wash my feet, set up (my) bed, I want to go to sleep. Wake me early in the morning, I must not be late lest my teacher cane me.

***

When I arose early in the morning, I faced my mother and said to her: "Give me my lunch, I want to go to school!" My mother gave me two rolls, and I set out; my mother gave me two rolls, and I went to school. In school the fellow in charge of punctuality said: "Why are you late?" Afraid and with pounding heart, I entered before my teacher and made a respectful curtsy.

***

My headmaster read my tablet, said:
"There is something missing," caned me…
The fellow in charge of neatness (?) said:
"You loitered in the street and did not straighten up (?) your clothes (?)," caned me…
The fellow in charge of silence said:
"Why did you talk without permission," caned me.
The fellow in charge of the assembly (?) said:
"Why did you 'stand at ease (?)' without permission," caned me.

The fellow in charge of good behavior said:
"Why did you rise without permission," caned me.
The fellow in charge of the gate said:
"Why did you go out from (the gate) without permission," caned me.
The fellow in charge of the whip said:
"Why did you take…without permission," caned me.
The fellow in charge of Sumerian said:
"Why didn't you speak Sumerian," caned me.
My teacher (*ummia*) said:
"Your hand is unsatisfactory,'" caned me.
(And so) I (began to) hate the scribe] art, (began to) neglect the scribal art.
My teacher took no delight in me; (even) [stopped teaching (?)] me his skill in the scribal art; in no way prepared me in the matters (essential) to the art (of being) a "young scribe," (or) the art (of being) a "big brother."

***

Give him a bit extra salary, (and) let him become more kindly (?); let him be free (for a time) from arithmetic; (when) he counts up all the school affairs of the students, let him count me (too among them; that is, perhaps, let him not neglect me any longer).

***

To that which the schoolboy said, his father gave heed. The teacher was brought from school, and after entering in the house, he was seated on the "big chair." The schoolboy attended and served him, and whatever he learned of the scribal art, he unfolded to his father. Then did the father in the joy of his heart say joyfully to the headmaster of the school: "My little fellow has

opened (wide) his hand, (and) you made wisdom enter there; you showed him all the fine points of the scribal art; you made him see the solutions of the mathematical and arithmetical (problems), you (taught him how) to make deep (?) the cuneiform script (?)

***

Pour for him *irda*-oil, bring it to the table for him. Make fragrant oil flow like water on his stomach (and) back; I want to dress him in a garment, give him some extra salary, put a ring on his hand.

***

Young fellow, (because) you hated not my words, neglected them not, (may you) complete the scribal art from beginning to end. Because you gave me everything without stint, paid me a salary larger than my effort (deserve), (and) have honored me, may Nidaba, the queen of guardian angels, be your guardian angel; may your pointed stylus write well for you; may your exercises contain no faults. Of your brothers, may you be their leader; of your friends may you be their chief; may you rank the highest among the school graduates, satisfy (?) all who walk (?) to and from in (?) the palaces. Little fellow, you "know" (your) father, I am second to him; that homage be paid to you, that you be blessed—may the god of your father bring this about with firm hand; he will bring prayer and supplication to Nidaba, your queen, as if it were a matter for your god. Thus, when you put a kindly hand on the…of the teacher, (and) on the forehead of the "big brother," then (?) your young comrades will show you favor. You have carried out well the school's activities, you are a man of learning. You have exalted Nidaba, the queen of learning; O Nidaba, praise!

Questions

(1) What seems to have been the student's attitude towards scribal education? That of his father?
(2) What qualities did the school headmaster, teacher, and staff attempt to instill in the day-to-day instructional routine?
(3) How does the father "make things right" between the teacher and his son?

2–8

Ua-aua: A Sumerian mother's lullaby to her ailing son.

This document is unique among those of ancient civilization, both in its form and in the human insights it affords us across more than four millenia. It purports to be the song of Queen Abisimti, wife of King Shulgi of Ur, to her son, who is obviously feverish, and in need of rest.

Source: James B. Pritchard, *Ancient Near Eastern Texts Pertaining to the Old Testament* (Princeton, N.J.: Princeton University Press, 1969), p. 652.

ua! aua!
In my song of joy—he will grow stout,

In my song of joy— he will grow big,
Like the *irina*-tree he will grow stout of root,

Like the *šakir* plant he will grow broad of crown.

Lord, from… you know…
Among those burgeoning apple trees by the river arrayed,
Who… will spread his hand on you,
Who lies there will lift his hand on you,
My son, sleep is about to overtake you,
Sleep is about to settle on you.

Come Sleep, come Sleep,
Come to my son,
Hurry Sleep to my son,
Put to sleep his restless eyes,
Put your hand on his (kohl)-painted eyes,
And (as for) his babbling tongue,
Let not the babbling hold back (his) sleep.

He will fill your lap with *emmer.*
I—I will make sweet for you the little cheeses,
Those little cheeses that are the healer of man,
The healer of man, the son of the Lord,
The son of the Lord Shulgi.

My garden is lettuce well-watered,
It is *gakkul* lettuce…,
The Lord will eat that lettuce.
In my song of joy—I will give him a wife,
[I will] give him [a wife], I will give him a [son],
The nursemaid, joyous of heart, will converse with him,
The nursemaid, joyous of heart, will suckle him;
I—I will [take] a wife for my son
She will [bear] him a son so sweet,
The wife will lie on his burning lap,
The son will lie in his outstretched arms
The wife will be happy with him,
The son will be happy with him.

The young wife will rejoice in his lap,
The son will grow big on his sweet knee.
You are in pain,
I am troubled,
I am struck dumb, I gaze at the stars,
The new moon *shines* down on my face,
Your bones will be arrayed on the wall,
The "man of the wall" will shed tears for you,
The *keeners* will pluck the harps for you,
The gekko will gash the cheek for you,
The fly will pluck the beard for you,
The lizard will *bite* his tongue for you,
Who "makes sprout" woe, will make it sprout all about you,
Who spreads woe, will spread it all about you.

(lines 51–56 fragmentary)

May the wife be your support,
May the son be your lot,
May the winnowed barley be your bride,
May Ashnan, the *kusu*-goddess be your ally,
May you have an eloquent guardian-angel,
May you *achieve* a reign of happy days,
May your feasts make bright the fore[head].

(lines 64–91 fragmentary)

And you, lie you in sleep!
Array the branches (of) your palm-tree,
It will fill you with joy like…
Stand at the side of Ur as a *huldubba-demon*
Stand at the side of Erech as a…-demon
Seize the mouth of the dog as a …-demon,
Pinion his "arms as with a net of reeds,
Make the dog cower before you,
Lest he will rip your back like a sack.

Questions
(1) What specific things does the Queen mention as possible cures for her son?
(2) Which of these emotions is dominant in the mother's song: hope, or fear?
(3) What does the Queen's lullaby indicate about the Sumerian concept of a happy/fulfilling life? How might it parallel or contrast to contemporary concepts?

CHAPTER 3

3–1

A humble farmer pleads his own case: the workings of Ma'at.

The "Tale of the Eloquent Peasant" is among the most accomplished works of the middle Kingdom, and underscores the basic concept of Ma'at (roughly translated as "the spirit of truth and righteousness") and the role of pharaoh as the paternal judge who sits at the court of last resort. The work also pays tribute to the power and beauty of the spoken word, even from such an unlikely source as the lips of the lowly peasant Khun-Anup.

Source: Miriam Lichtheim, *Ancient Egyptian Literature* (Berkeley, CA: University of California Press, 1975) v.1, pp. 170–184.

There was a man named Khun-Anup, a peasant of Salt-Field. He had a wife whose name was [Ma]rye. This peasant said to his wife: "Look here, I am going down to Egypt to bring food from there for my children. Go, measure for me the barley which is in the barn, what is left of [last year's] barley." Then she measured for him [twenty-six] gallons of barley. This peasant said to his wife: "Look, you have twenty gallons of barley as food for you and your children. Now make for me these six gallons of barley into bread and beer for every day in which [I shall travel]."

This peasant went down to Egypt. He had loaded his donkeys with rushes, *rdmt*-grass, natron, salt, sticks of ——, staves from Cattle-Country, leopard skins, wolf skins, *ns3*-plants, *'nw*-stones, *tnm*-plants, *hprwr*-plants, *s3hwt, s3skwt, miswt*-plants, *snt*-stones, *'b3w*-stones, *ibs3*-plants, *inbi*-plants, pidgeons, *n'rw*-birds, *wgs*-birds, *wbn*-plants, *tbsw*-plants, *gngnt,* earth-hair, and *inst;* in sum, all the good products of Salt-Field. This peasant went south toward Hnes. He arrived in the district of Perfefi, north of Medenyt. There he met a man standing on the riverbank whose name was Nemtynakht. He was the son of a man named Isri and a subordinate of the high steward Rensi, the son of Meru.

This Nemtynakht said, when he saw this peasant's donkeys which tempted his heart: "If only I had a potent divine image through which I could seize this peasant's goods!" Now the house of this Nemtynakht was at the beginning of a path which was narrow, not so wide as to exceed the width of a shawl. And one side of it was under water, the other under barley. This Nemtynakht said to his servant: "Go, bring me a sheet from my house." It was brought to him straightway. He spread it out on the beginning of the path, so that its fringe touched the water, its hem the barley.

Now this peasant came along the public road. Then this Nemtynakht said: "Be careful, peasant; don't step on my clothes!" This peasant said: "I'll do as you wish, my course is a good one." So he went up higher. This Nemtynakht said: "Will you have my barley for a path?" This peasant said: "My course is a good one. The riverbank is steep and our way is under barley, for you block the path with your clothes. Will you then not let us pass on the road?"

Just then one of the donkeys filled its mouth with a wisp of barley. This Nemtynakht said: "Now I shall seize your donkey, peasant, for eating my barley. It shall tread out grain for its offense!" This peasant said: "My course is a good one. Only one (wisp) is destroyed. Could I buy my donkey for its value, if you seize it for filling its mouth with a wisp of barley? But I know the lord of this domain; it belongs to the high steward Rensi, the son of Meru. He punishes every robber in this whole land. Shall I be robbed in his domain?" This Nemtynakht said: "Is this the saying people say: 'A poor man's name is pronounced for his master's sake.' It is I who speak to you, and you invoke the high steward!"

Then he took a stick of green tamarisk to him and thrashed all his limbs with it, seized his donkeys, drove them to his domain. Then this peasant wept very loudly for the pain of that which was done to him. This Nemtynakht said: "Don't raise your voice, peasant. Look, you are bound for the abode of the Lord of Silence!") This peasant said: "You beat me, you steal my goods, and now you take the complaint from my mouth! O Lord of Silence, give me back my things, so that I can stop crying to your dreadedness!"

This peasant spent the time of ten days appealing to this Nemtynakht who paid no attention to it. So this peasant proceeded southward to Hnes, in order to appeal to the high steward Rensi, the son of Meru. He found him coming out of the door of his house, to go down to his courthouse barge. This peasant said: "May I be allowed to acquaint you with this complaint? Might a servant of your choice be sent to me, through whom I could inform you of it?" So the high steward Rensi, the son of Meru, sent a servant of his choice ahead of him, and this peasant informed him of the matter in all its aspects.

Then the high steward Rensi, the son of Meru,

denounced this Nemtynakht to the magistrates who were with him. Then they said to him: "Surely it is a peasant of his who has gone to someone else beside him. That is what they do to peasants of theirs who go to others beside them. That is what they do. Is there cause for punishing this Nemtynakht for a trifle of natron and a trifle of salt? If he is ordered to replace it, he will replace it." Then the high steward Rensi, the son of Meru, fell silent. He did not reply to these magistrates, nor did he reply to this peasant.

Now this peasant came to appeal to the high steward Rensi, the son of Meru. He said: "O high steward, my lord, greatest of the great, leader of all!

> When you go down to the sea of justice
> And sail on it with a fair wind,
> No squall shall strip away your sail,
> Nor will your boat be idle.
> No accident will affect your mast,
> Your yards will not break.
> You will not founder when you touch land,
> No flood will carry you away.
> You will not taste the river's evils,
> You will not see a frightened face.
> Fish will come darting to you,
> Fatted fowl surround you.
> For you are father to the orphan,
> Husband to the widow,
> Brother to the rejected woman,
> Apron to the motherless.

Let me make your name in this land according to all the good rules:

> Leader free of greed,
> Great man free of baseness,
> Destroyer of falsehood,
> Creator of rightness,
> Who comes at the voice of the caller!
> When I speak, may you hear!
> Do justice, O praised one,
> Who is praised by the praised;
> Remove my grief, I am burdened,
> Examine me, I am in need!

Now this peasant made this speech in the time of the majesty of King Nebkaure, the justified. Then the high steward Rensi, the son of Meru, went before his majesty and said: "My lord, I have found one among those peasants whose speech is truly beautiful. Robbed of his goods by a man who is in my service, he has come to petition me about it." Said his majesty: "As truly as you wish to see me in health, you shall detain him here, without answering whatever he says. In order to keep him talking, be silent. Then have it brought to us in writing, that we may hear it. But provide for his wife and his children. For one of those peasants comes

here (only) just before his house is empty. Provide also for this peasant himself. You shall let food be given him without letting him know that it is you who gives it to him."

So they gave him ten loaves of bread and two jugs of beer every day. It was the high steward Rensi, the son of Meru, who gave it. He gave it to a friend of his, and he gave it to him. Then the high steward Rensi, the son of Meru, wrote to the mayor of Salt-Field about providing food for this peasant's wife, a total of three bushels of grain every day.

***

Now this peasant came to petition him a second time. He said: "O high steward, my lord, greatest of the great, richest of the rich, truly greater that his great ones, richer than his rich ones!

> Rudder of heaven, beam of earth,
> Plumb-line that carries the weight!
> Rudder, drift not,
> Beam, tilt not,
> Plumb-line, swing not awry!

A great lord taking a share of that which is (now) ownerless; stealing from a lonely man? Your portion is in your house: a jug of beer and three loaves. What is that you expend to satisfy your clients? A mortal man dies along with his underlings; shall you be a man of eternity?

> Is it not wrong, a balance that tilts,
> A plummet that strays,
> The straight becoming crooked?
> Lo, justice flees from you,
> Expelled from its seat!
> The magistrates do wrong,
> Right-dealing is bent sideways,
> The judges snatch what has been stolen.
> He who trims a matter's rightness makes it swing
>   awry:
> The breath-giver chokes him who is down,
> He who should refresh makes pant.
> The arbitrator is a robber,
> The remover of need orders its creation.
> The town is a floodwater,
> The punisher of evil commits crimes!"

Said the high steward Rensi, the son of Meru: "Are your belongings a greater concern to you than that my servant might seize you? This peasant said:

> "The measurer of grain-heaps trims for himself,
> He who fills for another shaves the other's share;
> He who should rule by law commands theft,
> Who then will punish crime?

The straightener of another's crookedness
Supports another's crime.
Do you find here something for you?
Redress is short, misfortune long,
A good deed is remembered.
This is the precept:
Do to the doer to make him do.
It is thanking a man for what he does,
Parrying a blow before it strikes,
Giving a commission to one who is skillful.

Oh for a moment of destruction, havoc in your vineyard, loss among your birds, damage to your water birds!

A man who saw has turned blind,
A hearer deaf,
A leader now leads astray!

......You are strong and mighty. Your arm is active, your heart greedy, mercy has passed you by. How miserable is the wretch whom you have destroyed! You are like a messenger of the Crocodile; you surpass the Lady of Pestilence! If you have nothing, she has nothing. If there's nothing against her, there's nothing against you. If you don't act, she does not act. The wealthy should be merciful; violence is for the criminal; robbing suits him who has nothing. The stealing done by the robber is the misdeed of one who is poor. One can't reproach him; he merely seeks for himself. But you are sated with your bread, drunken with your beer, rich in all kinds of [treasures].

Though the face of the steersman is forward, the boat drifts as it pleases. Though the king is in the palace, though the rudder is in your hand, wrong is done around you. Long is my plea, heavy my task. "What is the matter with him?" people ask.

Be a shelter, make safe your shore,
See how your quay is infested with crocodiles!
Straighten your tongue, let it not stray,
A serpent is this limb of man.
Don't tell lies, warn the magistrates,
Greasy baskets are the judges,
Telling lies is their herbage,
It weighs lightly on them.
Knower of all men's ways:
Do you ignore my case?
Savior from all water's harm:
See I have a course without a ship!
Guider to port of all who founder:
Rescue the drowning!
......"

***

Then this peasant came to petition him a third time; he said:

"High steward, my lord,
You are Re, lord of sky, with your courtiers,
Men's sustenance is from you as from the flood,
You are Hapy who makes green the fields,
Revives the wastelands.
Punish the robber, save the sufferer,
Be not a flood against the pleader!
Heed eternity's coming,
Desire to last, as is said:
Doing justice is breath for the nose.
Punish him who should be punished,
And none will equal your rectitude.
Does the hand-balance deflect?
Does the stand-balance tilt?
Does Thoth show favor
So that you may do wrong?
Be the equal of these three:
If the three show favor,
Then may you show favor!
Answer not good with evil,
Put not one in place of another!

My speech grows more than *snmyt*-weed, to assault the smell with its answers. Misfortune pours water till cloth will grow! Three times now to make him act!

By the sail-wind should you steer,
Control the waves to sail aright;
Guard from landing by the helm-rope,
Earth's rightness lies in justice!
Speak not falsely—you are great,
Act not lightly—you are weighty;
Speak not falsely—you are the balance,
Do not swerve—you are the norm!
You are one with the balance,
If it tilts you may tilt.
Do not drift, steer, hold the helm-rope!
Rob not, act against the robber,
Not great is one who is great in greed.
Your tongue is the plummet,
Your heart the weight,
Your two lips are its arms.
If you avert your face from violence,
Who then shall punish wrongdoing?
Lo, you are a wretch of a washerman,
A greedy one who harms a friend,
One who forsakes his friend for his client,
His brother is he who comes with gifts.
Lo, you are a ferryman who ferries him who pays,
A straight one whose straightness is splintered,
A storekeeper who does not let a poor man pass,
Lo, you are a hawk to the little people,
One who lives on the poorest of the birds.
Lo, you are a butcher whose joy is slaughter,
The carnage is nothing to him.
You are a herdsman......

......

Hearer, you hear not! Why do you not hear? Now I have subdued the savage; the crocodile retreats! What is your gain? When the secret of truth is found, falsehood is thrown on its back on the ground. Trust not the morrow before it has come; none knows the trouble in it."

Now this peasant had made this speech to the high steward Rensi, the son of Meru, at the entrance to the courthouse. Then he had two guards go to him with whips, and they thrashed all his limbs.

This peasant said: "The son of Meru goes on erring. His face is blind to what he sees, deaf to what he hears; his heart strays from what is recalled to him.

> You are like a town without a mayor,
> Like a troop without a leader,
> Like a ship without a captain,
> A company without a chief.
> You are a sheriff who steals,
> A mayor who pockets,
> A district prosecutor of crime
> Who is the model for the (evil)-doer!"

***

Now this peasant came to petition him a fourth time. Finding him coming out of the gate of the temple of Harsaphes, he said: "O praised one, may Harsaphes praise you, from whose temple you have come!

> Goodness is destroyed, none adhere to it,
> To fling falsehood's back to the ground.
> If the ferry is grounded, wherewith does one
>   cross?…...

Is crossing the river on sandals a good crossing? No! Who now sleeps till daybreak? Gone is walking by night, travel by day, and letting a man defend his own good cause. But it is no use to tell you this; mercy has passed you by. How miserable is the wretch whom you have destroyed!

> Lo, you are a hunter who takes his fill,
> Bent on doing what he pleases;
> Spearing hippopotami, shooting bulls,
> Catching fish, snaring birds.
> (But) none quick to speak is free from haste,
> None light of heart is weighty in conduct.
> Be patient so as to learn justice,
> Restrain your [anger] for the good of the humble
>   seeker.
> No hasty man attains excellence,
> No impatient man is leaned upon.

Let the eyes see, let the heart take notice. Be not harsh in your power lest trouble befall you. Pass over a matter, it becomes two. He who eats tastes; one addressed answers. It is the sleeper who sees the dream; and a judge who deserves punishment is a model for the (evil)doer. Fool, you are attacked! Ignorant man, you are questioned! Spouter of water, you are attained!

> Steersman, let not drift your boat,
> Life-sustainer, let not die,
> Provider, let not perish,
> Shade, let one not dry out,
> Shelter, let not the crocodile snatch!
> The fourth time I petition you!
> Shall I go on all day?"

***

Now this peasant came to petition him a fifth time; he said:

"O high steward, my lord! The fisher of *hwdw*-fish, ------, the --- slays the *iy*-fish; the spearer of fish pierces the `wbb*-fish; the *d3hbw*-fisher attacks the *p`kr*-fish; and the catcher of *wh`*-fish ravages the river. Now you are like them! Rob not a poor man of his goods, a humble man whom you know! Breath to the poor are his belongings; he who takes them stops up his nose. It is to hear cases that you were installed, to judge between two, to punish the robber. But what you do is to uphold the thief! One puts one's trust in you, but you have become a transgressor! You were placed as a dam for the poor lest he drown, but you have become a swift current to him!

***

Now this peasant came to petition him a sixth time; he said: "O high steward my lord!

> He who lessens falsehood fosters truth,
> He who fosters the good reduces ⟨evil⟩,
> As satiety's coming removes hunger,
> Clothing removes nakedness;
> As the sky is serene after a storm,
> Warming all who shiver;
> As fire cooks what is raw,
> As water quenches thirst.
> Now see for yourself:
> The arbitrator is a robber,
> The peacemaker makes grief,
> He who should soothe makes sore.
> But he who cheats diminishes justice!
> Rightly filled justice either falls short nor brims over.

If you acquire, give to your fellow; gobbling up is dishonest. But my grief will lead to parting; my accusation brings departure. The heart's intent cannot be known. Don't delay! Act on the charge! If you sever, who shall join? The sounding pole is in your hand; sound! The water is shallow! If the boat enters and is grounded, its cargo perishes on the shore.

You are learned, skilled, accomplished,
But not in order to plunder!
You should be the model for all men,
But your affairs are crooked!
The standard for all men cheats the whole land!
The vintner of evil waters his plot with crimes,
Until his plot sprouts falsehood,
His estate flows with crimes!"

***

Now this peasant came to petition him a seventh time; he said: "O high steward, my lord!

You are the whole land's rudder,
The land sails by your bidding;
You are the peer of Thoth,
The judge who is not partial.

My lord, be patient, so that a man may invoke you about his rightful cause. Don't be angry; it is not for you. The long-faced becomes short-tempered. Don't brood on what has not yet come, nor rejoice at what has not yet happened. The patient man prolongs friendship; he who destroys a case will not be trusted. If law is laid waste and order destroyed, no poor man can survive: when he is robbed, justice does not address him.

My body was full, my heart burdened. Now therefore it has come from my body. As a dam is breached and water escapes, so my mouth opened to speak. I plied my sounding pole, I bailed out my water; I have emptied what was in my body; I have washed my soiled linen. My speech is done. My grief is all before you. What do you want? But your laziness leads you astray; your greed makes you dumb; your gluttony makes enemies for you. But will you find another peasant like me? Is there an idler at whose house door a petitioner will stand?

There is no silent man whom you gave speech,
No sleeper whom you have wakened,
None downcast whom you have roused,
None whose shut mouth you have opened,
None ignorant whom you gave knowledge,
None foolish whom you have taught.
(Yet) magistrates are dispellers of evil,
Masters of the good,
Craftsmen who create what is,
Joiners of the severed head!"

***

Now this peasant came to petition him an eighth time; he said: "O high steward, my lord! Men fall low through greed. The rapacious man lacks success; his success is loss. Though you are greedy it does nothing for you. Though you steal you do not profit. Let a man defend his rightful cause!

Your portion is in your house; your belly is full. The grain-bin brims over; shake it, its overflow spoils on the ground. Thief, robber, plunderer! Magistrates are appointed to suppress crime. Magistrates are shelters against the aggressor. Magistrates are appointed to fight falsehood!

No fear of you makes me petition you; you do not know my heart. A humble man who comes back to reproach you is not afraid of him with whom he pleads. The like of him will not be brought you from the street!

You have your plot of ground in the country, your estate in the district, your income in the storehouse. Yet the magistrates give to you and you take! Are you then a robber? Does one give to you and the troop with you at the division of plots?

Do justice for the Lord of Justice
The justice of whose justice is real!
Pen, papyrus, palette of Thoth,
Keep away from wrongdoing!
When goodness is good it is truly good,
For justice is for eternity:
It enters the graveyard with its doer.
When he is buried and earth enfolds him,
His name does not pass from the earth;
He is remembered because of goodness,
That is the rule of god's command.

The hand-balance—it tilts not; the stand-balance—it leans not to one side. Whether I come, whether another comes, speak! Do not answer with the answer of silence! Do not attack one who does not attack you. You have no pity, you are not troubled, you are not disturbed! You do not repay my good speech which comes from the mouth of Re himself!

Speak justice, do justice,
For it is mighty;
It is great, it endures,
Its worth is tried,
It leads one to reveredness.

Does the hand-balance tilt? Then it is its scales which carry things. The standard has no fault. Crime does not attain its goal; he who is helpful reaches land."

***

Now this peasant came to petition him a ninth time; he said: "O high steward, my lord! The tongue is men's stand-balance. It is the balance that detects deficiency. Punish him who should be punished, and ⟨none⟩ shall equal your rectitude.---...When falsehood walks it goes astray. It does not cross in the ferry; it does not progress. He who is enriched by it has no children, has no heirs on earth. He who sails with it does not reach land; his boat. does not moor at its landing place.

> Be not heavy, nor yet light,
> Do not tarry, nor yet hurry,
> Be not partial, nor listen to desire.
> Do not avert your face from one you know,
> Be not blind to one you have seen,
> Do not rebuff one who beseeches you.
> Abandon this slackness,
> Let your speech be heard.
> Act for him who would act for you,
> Do not listen to everyone,
> Summon a man to his rightful cause!

A sluggard has no yesterday, one deaf to justice has no friend; the greedy has no holiday. When the accuser is a wretch, and the wretch becomes a pleader, his opponent is a killer. Here I have been pleading with you, and you have not listened to it. I shall go and plead about you to Anubis!"

***

Then the high steward Rensi, the son of Meru, sent two guards to bring him back. Then this peasant was fearful, thinking it was done so as to punish him for this speech he had made. This peasant said: "A thirsty man's approach to water, an infant's mouth reaching for milk, thus is a longed-for death seen coming, thus does his death arrive at last." Said the high steward Rensi, the son of Meru: "Don't be afraid, peasant; be ready to deal with me!" Said this peasant: "By my life! Shall I eat your bread and drink your beer forever?" Said the high steward Rensi, the son of Meru: "Now wait here and hear your petitions!" Then he had them read from a new papyrus roll, each petition in its turn. The high steward Rensi, the son of Meru, presented them to the majesty of King Nebkaure, the justified. They pleased his majesty's heart more than anything in the whole land. His majesty said: "Give judgment yourself, son of Meru!"

Then the high steward Rensi, the son of Meru, sent two guards [to bring Nemtynakht]. He was brought and a report was made of [all his property] ------ his wheat, his barley, his donkeys, ---, his pigs, his small cattle ------. --- of this Nemtynakht [was given] to this peasant ------.

Colophon: It is finished ------.

Questions

(1) What products did Khun-Aup bring with him on his journey to Egypt to trade for food?
(2) What legal pretext/ruse did Nemtynakht employ to confiscate Khun-Anup's donkey?
(3) What "appeals process" did Khun-Anup have to go through in order to receive pharaoh's ruling?
(4) What does the story of Khun-Anup reveal about the Egyptian concept of justice and legality?

3–2

The prestige and privileges of education in ancient Egypt.

A recurring theme in Egyptian papyri is the exhaltation of the scribe's profession, and the attribution of almost godlike abilities to the practitioners of the written word. Though this pride in profession could sometimes be carried to ridiculous levels of arrogance, the two New Kingdom papyri presented here (Papyrus Lansing and Papyrus Chester Beatty IV, respectively) clearly indicate the esteem in which scholarship and learning were held.

Source: Miriam Lichtheim, *Ancient Egyptian Literature* (Berkeley: University of California Press, 1975), v. 2, pp. 168–175.

PAPYRUS LANSING: A SCHOOLBOOK (TWENTIETH DYNASTY)

1. Title

(1,1) [Beginning of the instruction in letter-writing made by the royal scribe and chief overseer of the cattle of Amen-Re, King of Gotts, Nebmare-nakht] for his apprentice, the scribe Wenemdiamun.

2. Praise of the scribe's profession

[The royal scribe] and chief overseer of the cattle of Amen-[Re, King of Gods, Nebmare-nakht speaks to the scribe Wenemdiamun].[Apply yourself to this] noble profession. "Follower of Thoth" is the good name of him who exercises it. ------. He makes friends with those greater than he. Joyful ------. Write with your hand, read with your mouth. Act according to my words. ------, my heart is not disgusted. ------. ------ to my instructing you. You will find it useful. ------ [with bread and] beer. You will be advanced by your superiors. You will be sent on a mission ------. Love writing, shun dancing; then you become a worthy official. Do not long for the marsh thicket. Turn your back on throw stick and chase. By day write with your fingers; recite by night. Befriend the scroll, the palette. It pleases more than wine. Writing for him who knows it is better than all other professions. It pleases more than bread and beer, more than clothing and ointment. It is worth more than an inheritance in Egypt, than a tomb in the west.

3. Advice to the unwilling pupil

Young fellow, how conceited you are! You do not listen when I speak. Your heart is denser than a great obelisk, a hundred cubits high, ten cubits thick. When it is finished and ready for loading, many work gangs draw it. It hears the words of men; it is loaded on a barge. Departing from Yebu it is conveyed, until it comes to rest on its place in Thebes.

So also a cow is bought this year, and it plows the following year. It learns to listen to the herdsman; it only lacks words. Horses brought from the field, they forget their mothers. Yoked they go up and down on all his majesty's errands. They become like those that bore them, that stand in the stable. They do their utmost for fear of a beating.

But though 1 beat you with every kind of stick, you do not listen. If I knew another way of doing it, I would do it for you, that you might listen. You are a person fit for writing, though you have not yet known a woman. Your heart discerns, your fingers are skilled, your mouth is apt for reciting.

Writing is more enjoyable than enjoying a basket of *b3y* and beans: more enjoyable than a mother's giving birth, when her heart knows no distaste. She is constant in nursing her son; her breast is in his mouth every day. Happy is the heart (of) him who writes; he is young each day.

4. The idle scribe is worthless

The royal scribe and chief overseer of the cattle of Amen-Re, King of Gods, Nebmare-nakht, speaks to the scribe Wenemdiamun, as follows. You are busy coming and going, and don't think of writing. You resist listening to me; you neglect my teachings.

You are worse than the goose of the shore, that is busy with mischief. It spends the summer destroying the dates, the winter destroying the seed-grain. It spends the balance of the year in pursuit of the cultivators. It does not let seed be cast to the ground without snatching it ⌈in its fall⌉. One cannot catch it by snaring. One does not offer it in the temple. The evil, sharpeyed bird that does no work!

You are worse than the desert antelope that lives by running. It spends no day in plowing. Never at all does it tread on the threshing-floor. It lives on the oxen's labor, without entering among them. But though I spend the day telling you "Write," it seems like a plague to you. Writing is very pleasant! ------.

5. All occupations are bad except that of the scribe

See for yourself with your own eye. The occupations lie before you.

The washerman's day is going up, going down. All his limbs are weak, (from) whitening his neighbors' clothes every day, from washing their linen.

The maker of pots is smeared with soil, like one whose relations have died. His hands, his feet are full of clay; he is like one who lives in the bog.

The cobbler mingles with vats. His odor is penetrating. His hands are red with madder, like one who is smeared with blood. He looks behind him for the kite, like one whose flesh is exposed.

The watchman prepares garlands and polishes vase-stands. He spends a night of toil just as one on whom the sun shines.

The merchants travel downstream and upstream. They are as busy as can be, carrying goods from one town to another. They supply him who has wants. But the tax collectors carry off the gold, that most precious of metals.

The ships' crews from every house (of commerce), they receive their loads. They depart from Egypt for Syria, and each man's god is with him. (But) not one of them says: "We shall see Egypt again!"

The carpenter who is in the shipyard carries the timber and stacks it. If he gives today the output of yesterday, woe to his limbs! The shipwright stands behind him to tell him evil things.

His outworker who is in the fields, his is the toughest of all the jobs. He spends the day loaded with his tools, tied to his tool-box. When he returns home at night, he is loaded with the tool-box and the timbers, his drinking mug, and his whetstones.

The scribe, he alone, records the output of all of them. Take note of it!

6. The misfortunes of the peasant

Let me also expound to you the situation of the peasant, that other tough occupation. [Comes] the inundation and soaks him ---, he attends to his equipment. By day he cuts his farming tools; by night he twists rope. Even his midday hour he spends on farm labor. He equips himself to go to the field as if he were a warrior. The dried field lies before him; he goes out to get his team. When he has been after the herdsman for many days, he gets his team and comes back with it. He makes for it a place in the field. Comes dawn, he goes to make a start and does not find it in its place. He spends three days searching for it; he finds it in the bog. He finds no hides on them; the jackals have chewed them. He comes out, his garment in his hand, to beg for himself a team.

When he reaches his field he finds ⟨it⟩ ⌜broken up⌝. He spends time cultivating, and the snake is after him. It finishes off the seed as it is cast to the ground. He does not see a green blade. He does three plowings with borrowed grain. His wife has gone down to the merchants and found nothing for [barter.] Now the scribe lands on the shore. He surveys the harvest. Attendants are behind him with staffs, Nubians with clubs. One says (to him): "Give grain." "There is none." He is beaten savagely. He is bound, thrown in the well, submerged head down. His wife is bound in his presence. His children are in fetters. His neighbors abandon them and flee. When it's over, there's no grain.

If you have any sense, be a scribe. If you have learned about the peasant, you will not be able to be one. Take note of it!

7. Be a scribe

The scribe of the army and commander of the cattle of the house of Amun, Nebmare-nakht, speaks to the scribe Wenemdiamun, as follows. Be a scribe! Your body will be sleek; your hand will be soft. You will not flicker like a flame, like one whose body is feeble. For there is not the bone of a man in you. You are tall and thin. If you lifted a load to carry it, you would stagger, your legs would tremble. You are lacking in strength; you are weak in all your limbs; you are poor in body.

Set your sight on being a scribe; a fine profession that suits you. You call for one; a thousand answer you. You stride freely on the road. You will not be like a hired ox. You are in front of others.

I spend the day instructing you. You do not listen! Your heart is like an ⟨empty⟩ room. My teachings are not in it. Take their ⟨⌜meaning⌝⟩ to yourself!

The marsh thicket is before you each day, as a nestling is after its mother. You follow the path of pleasure; you make friends with revellers. You have made your home in the brewery, as one who thirsts for beer. You sit in the parlor with an idler. You hold the writings in contempt. You visit the whore. Do not do these things! What are they for? They are of no use. Take note of it!

8. The scribe does not suffer like the soldier

Furthermore. Look, I instruct you to make you sound; to make you hold the palette freely. To make you become one whom the king trusts; to make you gain entrance to treasury and granary. To make you receive the ship-load at the gate of the granary. To make you issue the offerings on feast days. You are dressed in fine clothes; you own horses. Your boat is on the river; you are supplied with attendants. You stride about inspecting. A mansion is built in your town. You have a powerful office, given you by the king. Male and female slaves are

about you. Those who are in the fields grasp your hand, on plots that you have made. Look, I make you into a staff of life! Put the writings in your heart, and you will be protected from all kinds of toil. You will become a worthy official.

Do you not recall the (fate of) the unskilled man? His name is not known. He is ever burdened (like an ass carrying) in front of the scribe who knows what he is about.

Come, ⟨let me tell⟩ you the woes of the soldier, and how many are his superiors: the general, the troop-commander, the officer who leads, the standard-bearer, the lieutenant, the scribe, the commander of fifty, and the garrison-captain. They go in and out in the halls of the palace, saying: "Get laborers!" He is awakened at any hour. One is after him as (after) a donkey. He toils until the Aten sets in his darkness of night. He is hungry, his belly hurts; he is dead while yet alive. When he receives the grain-ration, having been released from duty, it is not good for grinding.

He is called up for Syria. He may not rest. There are no clothes, no sandals. The weapons of war are assembled at the fortress of Sile. His march is uphill through mountains. He drinks water every third day; it is smelly and tastes of salt. His body is ravaged by illness. The enemy comes, surrounds him with missiles, and life recedes from him. He is told: "Quick, forward, valiant soldier! Win for yourself a good name!" He does not know what he is about. His body is weak, his legs fail him. When victory is won, the captives are handed over to his majesty, to be taken to Egypt. The foreign woman faints on the march; she hangs herself (on) the soldier's neck. His knapsack drops, another grabs it while he is burdened with the woman. His wife and children are in their village; he dies and does not reach it. If he comes out alive, he is worn out from marching. Be he at large, be he detained, the soldier suffers. If he leaps and joins the deserters, all his people are imprisoned. He dies on the edge of the desert, and there is none to perpetuate his name. He suffers in death as in life. A big sack is brought for him; he does not know his resting place.

Be a scribe, and be spared from soldiering! You call and one says: "Here I am." You are safe from torments. Every man seeks to raise himself up. Take note of it!

9. The pupil wishes to build a mansion for his teacher

Furthermore. (To) the royal scribe and chief overseer of the cattle of Amen-Re, King of Gods, Nebmare-nakht. The scribe Wenemdiamun greets his lord: In life, prosperity, and health! This letter is to inform my lord. Another message to my lord. I grew into a youth at your side. You beat my back; your teaching entered my ear. I am like a pawing horse. Sleep does not enter my heart by day; nor is it upon me at night. (For I say): I will serve my lord just as a slave serves his master.

I shall build a new mansion for you ⟨on⟩ the ground of your town, with trees (planted) on all its sides. There are stables within it. Its barns are full of barley and emmer, wheat, ⌈cumin,⌉ dates, *hrw-bik, gmnn,* beans, lentils, coriander, peas, seed-grain, *`dn,* flax, herbs, reeds, rushes, *ybr, istpn,* dung for the winter, alfa grass, reeds, *rdmt*-grass, produced by the basketful. Your herds abound in draft animals, your cows are pregnant. I will make for you five aruras of cucumber beds to the south.

10. The teacher has built a mansion

Raia has built a beautiful mansion; it lies opposite Edjo. He has built it on the border. It is [constructed] like a work of eternity. It is planted with trees on all sides. A channel was dug in front of it. The lapping of waves sounds in one's sleep. One does not tire of looking at it. One is gay at its door and drunk in its halls. Handsome doorposts of limestone, carved and chiseled. Beautiful doors, freshly carved. Walls inlaid with lapis lazuli.

Its barns are supplied with grain, are bulging with abundance. Fowl yard and aviary are filled with geese; byres filled with cattle. A bird pool full of geese; horses in the stable. Barges, ferryboats, and new cattle boats are moored at its quay. Young and old, the poor have come to live around it. Your provisions last; there is abundance for all who come to you.

You walk about on new lands and high lands without limit. Their grain is more abundant than the pond water that was there before. Crews land at the quay to make festive the barns with countless heaps for the Lord of Thebes. Its west side is a pond for snaring geese of all kinds, a resort of hunters from the very beginning. One of its ponds has more fish than a lake. Its *`h*birds are like marsh birds.

Happiness dwells within. No one says, "If only!" Many stables are around it, and grazing fields for cattle. Goats abound, kids caper; the many shorthorns are lowing. There are glens rich in green plants in summer and in winter. Fish abound in their basins: bulti-fish, *sn'*-fish, *d̠ss*-fish. The fish are more plentiful than the sands of the shore; one cannot reach the end of them.

Amun himself established it. The plantations are his in truth. You sit in their shade; you eat their fruit. Garlands are made for you of their branches; you are drunken with their wines. Boats are built for you of their pines, a chariot of their *t̠3g3*-trees. You flourish and prosper every day. The sustenance of Amun is with you, O Raia, chief overseer of the cattle of Amun!

11. An encomium of the teacher

You are nimble-handed with the censer, before the Lord of Gods at his every appearance.

You are father of the god in command of the mysteries, with censer in your right, byssus in your left; the censer in your fist blesses your lord.

You are a noble priest in the House of Ptah, versed in all the mysteries in the House of the Prince.

You are the burial priest of Kamutef, chief seer of Re in Thebes, offerer of his oblations.

You are swift-footed at the Sokar-feast, drawing Egypt's people to your lord with the flail.

You are graceful with the libation vase, pouring, censing, and calling the praises.

You are nimble-handed when you circulate the offerings, foremost in calling the daily praises.

You are he who holds the Eye of Mut, mistress of heaven, on the first day of her procession in Ashru.

You are the water-pourer of Khons in Thebes, on the day of circulating offerings in the House of the Prince.

You are wise in planning, skilled in speech; farseeing at all times; what you do succeeds.

You are a judge of hearts; you resemble the Ibis; wise in all ways like the Eye and the Ear.

You are the good champion of your people; your great meals overflow like Hapy.

You are rich in food, you know how to proffer it, to all whom you love, like a surging sea.

You are a magistrate who is calm, a son of praised ones; loved by all, and praised by the king.

You are a man of high standing since birth; your house overflows with foods.

You are rich in fields, your barns are full; grain clung to you on the day you were born.

You are rich in teams, your sails are bright; your barges on the deep are like jasper.

You are rich in crews skilled in rowing; their shouts please as they carry and load.

You are one weighty of counsel who weighs his answer: since birth you have loathed coarse language.

You are handsome in body, gracious in manner, beloved of all people as much as Hapy.

You are a man of choice words, who is skilled in saying them; all you say is right, you abhor falsehood.

You are one who sits grandly in your house; your servants answer speedily; beer is poured copiously; all who see you rejoice in good cheer.

You serve your lord, you nourish your people; whatever you say soothes the heart.

You are one who offers the beer-jug and fills the bowl; one beloved of the herdsman when the offering is made.

You are one who directs the jubilees (for) his lord, one who lays the Nine Bows under his feet, one who provides for his army.

THE IMMORTALITY OF WRITERS (P. CHESTER BEATTY IV = P. BRITISH MUSEUM 10684)

If you but do this, you are versed in writings.
As to those learned scribes,

Of the time that came after the gods,
They who foretold the future,
Their names have become everlasting,
While they departed, having finished their lives,
And all their kin are forgotten.

They did not make for themselves tombs of copper,
With stelae of metal from heaven.
They knew not how to leave heirs,
Children [of theirs] to pronounce their names;
They made heirs for themselves of books,
Of Instructions they had composed.

They gave themselves [the scroll as lector]-priest,
The writing-board as loving-son.
Instructions are their tombs,
The reed pen is their child,
The stone-surface their wife.
People great and small
Are given them as children,
For the scribe, he is their leader.

Their portals and mansions have crumbled,
Their ka-servants are [gone];
Their tombstones are covered with soil,
Their graves are forgotten.
Their name is pronounced over their books,
Which they made while they had being;
Good is the memory of their makers,
It is for ever and all time!
Be a scribe, take it to heart,
That your name become as theirs.
Better is a book than a graven stela,

Than a solid ⌈tomb-enclosure⌉.
They act as chapels and tombs
In the heart of him who speaks their name;
Surely useful in the graveyard
Is a name in people's mouth!

Man decays, his corpse is dust,
All his kin have perished;
But a book makes him remembered
Through the mouth of its reciter.
Better is a book than a well-built house,
Than tomb-chapels in the west;
Better than a solid mansion,
Than a stela in the temple!

Is there one here like Hardedef?
Is there another like Imhotep?
None of our kin is like Neferti,
Or Khety, the foremost among them.
I give you the name of Ptah-emdjehuty,
Of Khakheperre-sonb.
Is there another like Ptahhotep,
Or the equal of Kaires?
Those sages who foretold the future,
What came from their mouth occurred;
It is found as their pronouncement,
It is written in their books.
The children of others are given to them
To be heirs as their own children.
They hid their magic from the masses,
It is read in their Instructions.
Death made their names forgotten
But books made them remembered!

Questions

(1) From what is stated in the papyri, whose occupation is designated as being "the toughest of all the job," and why?
(2) What are the disadvantages suffered by the peasant?
(3) What disadvantages and discomforts attend those in the military?
(4) In what sense(s) does a scribe attain immortality?

3–3

Advice on statecraft: Pharaoh Amenemhet to his son Senusert.

The chaos, breakdown of order, and feudal warfare that characterized the First Intermediate period in Egypt (c. 2181-1991 B.C.E.) was brought to an end by Amenemhet I (Mentuhotep), Prince of Thebes, who had ruthlessly suppressed local warlords and established himself as the first pharaoh of the Middle Kingdom. In the process, he had made enemies and had survived assassination attempts; hence the cynical and suspicious tone of the advice he gives here to his son and heir Senusert. Amenemhet's pre-Machiavellian mindset was apparently well-founded, as he ultimately did fall victim to an assassin.

Source: Donald A. MacKenzie, *Egyptian Myths and Legends* (Avernal, N.J.: Crown Publishers, 1978), pp. 218–220.

Be thou in splendour like the god, my son…
Hearken and hear my words, if thou wouldst reign
In Egypt and be ruler of the world,
Excelling in thy greatness…Live apart
In stern seclusion, for the people heed
The man who makes them tremble; mingle not
Alone among them; have no bosom friend,
Nor intimate, nor favourite in thy train—
These serve no goodly purpose.

                    Ere to sleep
Thou liest down, prepare to guard thy life—
A man is friendless in the hour of trial…
I to the needy gave, the orphan nourished,
Esteemed alike the lowly and the great;
But he who ate my bread made insurrection,
And those my hands raised up, occasion seized
Rebellion to create…They went about
All uniformed in garments that I gave
And deemed me but a shadow…Those who shared
My perfumes for anointment, rose betimes
And broke into my harem.

                Through the land
Beholden are my statues, and men laud
The deeds I have accomplished…yet I made
A tale heroic that hath ne'er been told,
And triumphed in a conflict no man saw…
Surely these yearned for bondage when they smote
The king who set them free…Methinks, my son,
Of no avail is liberty to men
Grown blind to their good fortune.

                  I had dined
At eve and darkness fell. I sought to rest
For I was weary. On my bed I lay
And gave my thoughts release, and so I slept…
The rebels 'gan to whisper and take arms
With treacherous intent…I woke and heard
And like the desert serpent waited there
All motionless but watchful.

                Then I sprang
To fight and I alone…A warrior fell,
And lo! he was the captain of my guard.
Ah! had I but his weapons in that hour
I should have scattered all the rebel band—
Mighty my blows and swift!…but he, alas!
Was like a coward there…Nor in the dark,
And unprepared, could I achieve renown.

Hateful their purpose!…I was put to shame.
Thou wert not nigh to save…Announced I then
That thou didst reign, and I had left the throne.
And gave commands according to thy will…
Ah! as they feared me not, 't was well to speak

With courtesy before them…Would I could
Forget the weakness of my underlings!

My son, Senusert, say—Are women wont
To plot against their lords? Lo! mine have reared
A brood of traitors and assembled round
A rebel band forsworn. They did deceive
My servants with command to pierce the ground
For speedy entry.

                  Yet to me from birth
Misfortune hath a stranger been. I ne'er
Have met mine equal among valiant men…
Lo! I have set in order all the land.
From Elephantine adown the Nile
I swept in triumph: so my feet have trod
The outposts of my kingdom…Mighty deeds
Must now be measured by the deeds I've done.

I loved the corn god…I have grown the grain
In every golden valley where the Nile
Entreated me; none hungered in my day,
None thirsted, and all men were well content—
They praised me, saying: "Wise are his commands."

I fought the lion and the crocodile,
I smote the dusky Nubians, and put
The Asian dogs to flight.

                Mine house I built.
Gold-decked with azure ceilings, and its walls
Have deep foundations; doors of copper are,
The bolts of bronze…It shall endure all time.
Eternity regards it with dismay!
I know each measurement, O Lord of All!

Men came to see its beauties, and I heard
In silence while they praised it. No man knew
The treasure that it lacked…I wanted thee,
My son, Senusert…Health and strength be thine!
I lean upon thee, O my heart's delight;
For thee I look on all things…Spirits sang
In that glad hour when thou wert born to me.

All things I've done, now know, were done for thee;
For thee must I complete what I began
Until the end draws nigh…O be my heart
The isle of thy desire…The white crown now
Is given thee, O wise son of the god—
I'll hymn thy praises in the bark of Ra…
Thy kingdom at Creation was. 'T is thine
As it was mine—how mighty were my deeds!
Rear thou thy statues and adorn thy tomb…
I struck thy rival down…'T would not be wise
To leave him nigh thee…Health and strength be thine!

Questions

(1) What advantages does Amenemhet see in a ruler's isolating himself from friendship and from his own subjects?

(2) Who was the chief assassin in the failed plot mentioned by Amenemhet?

(3) What is the pharaoh's answer to his son's apparent question about the trustworthiness of women?

(4) What legacy does the pharaoh wish to leave to his son?

3–4

The "heretic" pharaoh's hymn to a fellow-god.

No pharaoh was as controversial as Akhenaten, who originally reigned as Amenhotep IV. For reasons which are unclear, he and his wife Nefertiti attempted a religious reform in which worship of the traditional Egyptian deities would be supplanted by two-god cult of the Solar Disk, Aten, and pharaoh himself. Though Atenism collapsed after Akhenaten's reign, some of the religious hymns survive, such as the "Great Hymn to the Aten" inscribed in the tomb of Ay.

Source: Miriam Lichtheim, *Ancient Egyptian Literature* (Berkeley: University of California Press, 1975), v. 2, pp. 96–99.

Adoration of *Re-Harakhti-who-rejoices-in-lightland In-his-name-Shu-who-is-Aten,* living forever; the great living Aten who is in jubilee, the lord of all that the Disk encircles, lord of sky, lord of earth, lord of the house-of-Aten in Akhet-Aten; (and of) the King of Upper and Lower Egypt, who lives by Maat, the Lord of the Two Lands, *Neferkheprure, Sole-one-of-Re;* the Son of Re who lives by Maat, the Lord of Crowns, *Akhenaten,* great in his lifetime; and his beloved great Queen, the Lady of the Two Lands, *Nefer-nefru-Aten Nefertiti,* who lives in health and youth forever. The Vizier, the Fanbearer on the right of the King...[Ay]; he says:

> Splendid you rise in heaven's lightland,
> O living Aten, creator of life!
> When you have dawned in eastern lightland,
> You fill every land with your beauty.
> You are beauteous, great, radiant,
> High over every land;
> Your rays embrace the lands,
> To the limit of all that you made.
> Being Re, you reach their limits,
> You bend them ⟨for⟩ the son whom you love;
> Though you are far, your rays are on earth,
> Though one sees you, your strides are unseen.
>
> When you set in western lightland,
> Earth is in darkness as if in death;
> One sleeps in chambers, heads covered,
> One eye does not see another.
> Were they robbed of their goods,
> That are under their heads,
> People would not remark it.
> Every lion comes from its den,

> All the serpents bite;
> Darkness hovers, earth is silent,
> As their maker rests in lightland.
>
> Earth brightens when you dawn in lightland,
> When you shine as Aten of daytime;
> As you dispel the dark,
> As you cast your rays,
> The Two Lands are in festivity.
> Awake they stand on their feet,
> You have roused them;
> Bodies cleansed, clothed,
> Their arms adore your appearance.
> The entire land sets out to work,
> All beasts browse on their herbs;
> Trees, herbs are sprouting,
> Birds fly from their nests,
> Their wings greeting your *ka.*
> All flocks frisk on their feet,
> All that fly up and alight,
> They live when you dawn for them.
> Ships fare north, fare south as well,
> Roads lie open when you rise;
> The fish in the river dart before you,
> Your rays are in the midst of the sea.
>
> Who makes seed grow in women,
> Who creates people from sperm;
> Who feeds the son in his mother's womb,
> Who soothes him to still his tears.
> Nurse in the womb,
> Giver of breath,
> To nourish all that he made.
> When he comes from the womb to breathe,
> On the day of his birth,

You open wide his mouth,
You supply his needs.
When the chick in the egg speaks in the shell,
You give him breath within to sustain him;
When you have made him complete,
To break out from the egg,
He comes out from the egg,
To announce his completion,
Walking on his legs he comes from it.

How many are your deeds,
Though hidden from sight,
O Sole God beside whom there is none!
You made the earth as you wished, you alone,
All peoples, herds, and flocks;
All upon earth that walk on legs,
All on high that fly on wings,
The lands of Khor and Kush,
The land of Egypt.
You set every man in his place,
You supply their needs;
Everyone has his food,
His lifetime is counted.
Their tongues differ in speech,
Their characters likewise;
Their skins are distinct,
For you distinguished the peoples.

You made Hapy in *dat,*
You bring him when you will,
To nourish the people,
For you made them for yourself.
Lord of all who toils for them,
Lord of all lands who shines for them,
Aten of daytime, great in glory!
All distant lands, you make them live,
You made a heavenly Hapy descend for them;
He makes waves on the mountains like the sea,
To drench their fields and their towns.
How excellent are your ways, O Lord of eternity!
A Hapy from heaven for foreign peoples,
And all lands' creatures that walk on legs,

For Egypt the Hapy who comes from *dat.*

Your rays nurse all fields,
When you shine they live, they grow for you;
You made the seasons to foster all that you made,
Winter to cool them, heat that they taste you.
You made the far sky to shine therein,
To behold all that you made;
You alone, shining in your form of living Aten,
Risen, radiant, distant, near.
You made millions of forms from yourself alone,
Towns, villages, fields, the river's course;
All eyes observe you upon them,
For you are the Aten of daytime on high.
.....------...

You are in my heart,
There is no other who knows you,
Only your son, *Neferkheprure, Sole-one-of-Re,*
Whom you have taught your ways and your might.
(Those on) earth come from your hand as you made
   them,
When you have dawned they live,
When you set they die;
You yourself are lifetime, one lives by you.
All eyes are on ⟨your⟩ beauty until you set,
All labor ceases when you rest in the west;
When you rise you stir [everyone] for the King,
Every leg is on the move since you founded the
   earth.
You rouse them for your son who came from your
   body,
The King who lives by Maat, the lord of the Two
   Lands,
Neferkheprure, Sole-one-of-Re,
The Son of Re who lives by Maat, the Lord of
   crowns,
Akhenaten, great in his lifetime;
(And) the great Queen whom he loves, the Lady of
   the Two Lands,
Nefer-nefru-Aten Nefertiti, living forever.

Questions
(1) What specific powers/attributes are ascribed to Aten?
(2) What position does Ay hold in the pharaoh's household?
(3) What properties does the hymn attach to the absence of Aten during the night?

3–5
Some common-sense advice from the scribe Any to his son.

As in Mesopotamia, instruction manuals were a popular form of imparting knowledge of the type that experience, rather than academic studies, could provide. In the "Instruction of Any," which dates back to the New Kingdom reign of Pharaoh Ahmose (c. 1550 B.C.E.), the intended beneficiary is not, as the usual case, royalty, but Any's own son, a member of the educated, emerging middle class.

Source: Miriam Lichtheim, *Ancient Egyptian Literature* (Berkeley: University of California Press, 1975), v. 2, pp. 136–145.

Take a wife while you're young,
That she make a son for you;
She should bear for you while you're youthful,
It is proper to make people.
Happy the man whose people are many,
He is saluted on account of his progeny.

Observe the feast of your god,
And repeat its season,
God is angry if it is neglected.
Put up witnesses when you offer,
The first time that you do it.
When one comes to seek your record,
Have them enter you in the roll;
When time comes to seek your purchase,
It will extol the might of the god.
Song, dance, incense are his foods,
Receiving prostrations is his wealth;
The god does it to magnify his name,
But man it is who is inebriated.

Do not enter the house of anyone,
Until he admits you and greets you;
Do not snoop around in his house,
Let your eye observe in silence.
Do not speak of him to another outside,
Who was not with you;
A great deadly crime
......

Beware of a woman who is a stranger,
One not known in her town;
Don't stare at her when she goes by,
Do not know her carnally.
A deep water whose course is unknown,
Such is it woman away from her husband.
"I am pretty," she tells you daily,
When she has no witnesses;
She is ready to ensnare you,
A great deadly crime when it is heard.
......

Do not leave when the chiefs enter,
Lest your name stink;
In a quarrel do not speak,
Your silence will serve you well.

Do not raise your voice in the house of god.
He abhors shouting;
Pray by yourself with a loving heart,
Whose every word is hidden.
He will grant your needs.
He will hear your words,

He will accept your offerings.
Libate for your father and mother,
Who are resting in the valley;
When the gods witness your action,
They will say: "Accepted."
Do not forget the one outside.
Your son will act for you likewise.

Don't indulge in drinking beer,
Lest you utter evil speech.
And don't know what you're saying.
If you fall and hurt your body.
None holds out a hand to you;
Your companions in the drinking
Stand up saying: "Out with the drunk!"
If one comes to seek you and talk with you,
One finds you lying on the ground.
As if you were a little child.

Do not go out of your house,
Without knowing your place of rest.
Let your chosen place be known,
Remember it and know it.
Set it before you as the path to take,
If you are straight you find it.
Furnish your station in the valley,
The grave that shall conceal your corpse;
Set it before you as your concern,
A thing that matters in your eyes.
Emulate the great departed,
Who are at rest within their tombs.
No blame accrues to him who does it,
It is well that you be ready too.
When your envoy comes to fetch you
He shall find you ready to come
To your place of rest and saying:
"Here comes one prepared before you."
Do not say, "I am young to be taken,"
For you do not know your death.
When death comes he steals the infant
Who is in his mother's arms,
Just like him who reached old age.

Behold, I give you these useful counsels,
For you to ponder in your heart;
Do it and you will be happy,
All evils will be far from you.
Guard against the crime of fraud,
Against words that are not ⟨true⟩;
Conquer malice in your self,
A quarrelsome man does not rest on the morrow.
Keep away from a hostile man,
Do not let him be your comrade;

Befriend one who is straight and true,
One whose actions you have seen.
If your rightness matches his,
The friendship will be balanced.
Let your hand preserve what is in your house,
Wealth accrues to him who guards it;
Let your hand not scatter it to strangers,
Lest it turn to loss for you.
If wealth is placed where it bears interest,
It comes back to you redoubled;
Make a storehouse for your own wealth,
Your people will find it on your way.
What is given small returns augmented,
⌈What is replaced brings abundance.⌉
The wise lives off the house of the fool,
Protect what is yours and you find it;
Keep your eye on what you own,
Lest you end as a beggar.
He who is slack amounts to nothing,
Honored is the man who's active.

…

Learn about the way of a man
Who undertakes to found his household.
Make a garden, enclose a patch,
In addition to your plowland;
Set out trees within it,
As shelter about your house.
Fill your hand with all the flowers
That your eye can see;
One has need of all of them,
It is good fortune not to lose them.

Do not rely on another's goods,
Guard what you acquire yourself;
Do not depend on another's wealth.
Lest he become master in your house.
Build a house or find and buy one,
Shun [contention.]
Don't say: "My mother's father has a house,
⌈'A house that lasts,'⌉ one calls it;"
When you come to share with your brothers,
Your portion may be a storeroom.
If your god lets you have children,
They'll say: "We are in our father's house."
Be a man hungry or sated in his house,
It is his walls that enclose him.
Do not be a mindless person,
Then your god will give you wealth.

Do not sit when another is standing,
One who is older than you,
Or greater than you in his rank.
No good character is reproached,
An evil character is blamed.
Walk the accustomed path each day,
Stand according to your rank.

"Who's there?" So one always says,
Rank creates its rules;
A woman is asked about her husband,
A man is asked about his rank.

Do not speak rudely to a brawler,
When you are attacked hold yourself back;
You will find this good when your relations are
   friendly,
When trouble has come it will help you bear up,
And the aggressor will desist.
Deeds that are effective toward a stranger
Are very noxious to a brother.
Your people will hail you when you are joyful,
They will weep freely ⌈⟨when you are sad⟩⌉;
When you are happy the brave look to you,
When you are lonely you find your relations.

One will do all you say
If you are versed in writings;
Study the writings, put them in your heart,
Then all your words will be effective.
Whatever office a scribe is given,
He should consult the writings;
The head of the treasury has no son,
The master of the seal has no heir.
The scribe is chosen for his hand,
His office has no children;
His pronouncements are his freemen,
His functions are his masters.

Do not reveal your heart to a stranger,
He might use your words against you;
The noxious speech that came from your mouth,
He repeats it and you make enemies.
A man may be ruined by his tongue,
Beware and you will do well.
A man's belly is wider than a granary,
And full of all kinds of answers;
Choose the good one and say it,
While the bad is shut in your belly.
A rude answer brings a beating,
Speak sweetly and you will be loved.
Don't ever talk back to your attacker,
⌈⟨Do not set a trap for him⟩⌉;
It is the god who judges the righteous,
His fate comes and takes him away.

Offer to your god,
Beware of offending him.
Do not question his images,
Do not accost him when he appears.
Do not jostle him in order to carry him,
Do not disturb the oracles.
Be careful, help to protect him,
Let your eye watch out for his wrath,
And kiss the ground in his name.

He gives power in a million forms,
He who magnifies him is magnified.
God of this earth is the sun in the sky,
While his images are on earth;
When incense is given them as daily food,
The lord of risings is satisfied.

Double the food your mother gave you,
Support her as she supported you;
She had a heavy load in you,
But she did not abandon you.
When you were born after your months,
She was yet yoked ⟨to you⟩,
Her breast in your mouth for three years.
As you grew and your excrement disgusted,
She was not disgusted, saying: "What shall I do!"
When she sent you to school,
And you were taught to write,
She kept watching over you daily,
With bread and beer in her house.
When as a youth you take a wife,
And you are settled in your house,
Pay attention to your offspring,
Bring him up as did your mother.
Do not give her cause to blame you,
Lest she raise her hands to god,
And he hears her cries.

Do not eat bread while another stands by
Without extending your hand to him.
As to food, it is here always,
It is man who does not last;
One man is rich, another is poor,
But food remains for him ⌈who shares it.⌉
As to him who was rich last year,
He is a vagabond this year;
Don't be greedy to fill your belly,
You don't know your end at all.
Should you come to be in want,
Another may do good to you.
When last year's watercourse is gone,
Another river is here today;
Great lakes become dry places,
Sandbanks turn into depths.
Man does not have a single way,
The lord of life confounds him.

Attend to your position,
Be it low or high;
It is not good to press forward,
Step according to rank.
Do not intrude on a man in his house,
Enter when you have been called;
He may say "Welcome" with his mouth,
Yet deride you in his thoughts.
One gives food to one who is hated,
Supplies to one who enters uninvited.

Don't rush to attack your attacker,
Leave him to the god;
Report him daily to the god,
Tomorrow being like today,
And you will see what the god does,
When he injures him who injured you.

Do not enter into a crowd,
If you find it in an uproar
And about to come to blows.
Don't pass anywhere near by,
Keep away from their tumult,
Lest you be brought before the court,
When an inquiry is made.
Stay away from hostile people,
Keep your heart quiet among fighters;
An outsider is not brought to court,
One who knows nothing is not bound in fetters.

It is useful to help one whom one loves,
⌈So as to cleanse him of his faults;⌉
⌈You will be safe from his errors.⌉
......
The first of the herd leads to the field,
......

Do not control your wife in her house,
When you know she is efficient;
Don't say to her: "Where is it? Get it!"
When she has put it in the right place.
Let your eye observe in silence,
Then you recognize her skill;
It is joy when your hand is with her,
There are many who don't know this.
If a man desists from strife at home,
He will not encounter its beginning.
Every man who founds a household
Should hold back the hasty heart.
Do not go after a woman,
Let her not steal your heart.

Do not talk back to an angry superior,
Let him have his way;
Speak sweetly when he speaks sourly,
It's the remedy that calms the heart.
Fighting answers carry sticks,
And your strength collapses;
......
Do not vex your heart.
He will return to praise you soon,
When his hour of rage has passed.
If your words please the heart,
The heart tends to accept them;
Choose silence for yourself,
Submit to what he does.

Befriend the herald of your quarter,

Do not make him angry with you.
Give him food from your house,
Do not slight his requests;
Say to him, "Welcome, welcome here,"
No blame accrues to him who does it.
......

Epilogue

The scribe Khonshotep answered his father,
  the scribe Any:
I wish I were like (you),
As learned as you!
Then I would carry out your teachings,
And the son would be brought to his father's place.
Each man is led by his nature,
You are a man who is a master,
Whose strivings are exalted,
Whose every word is chosen.
The son, he understands little
When he recites the words in the books.
But when your words please the heart,
The heart tends to accept them with joy.
Don't make your virtues too numerous,
That one may raise one's thoughts to you;
A boy does not follow the moral instructions,
Though the writings are on his tongue!

The scribe Any answered his son, the scribe
  Khonshotep:
Do not rely on such worthless thoughts,
Beware of what you do to yourself!
I judge your complaints to be wrong,
I shall set you right about them.
There's nothing [superfluous in] our words,
Which you say you wished were reduced.
The fighting bull who kills in the stable,
He forgets and abandons the arena;
He conquers his nature,
Remembers what he's learned,
And becomes the like of a fattened ox.
The savage lion abandons his wrath,
And comes to resemble the timid donkey.
The horse slips into its harness,
Obedient it goes outdoors.
The dog obeys the word,
And walks behind its master.

The monkey carries the stick,
Though its mother did not carry it.
The goose returns from the pond,
When one comes to shut it in the yard.
One teaches the Nubian to speak Egyptian,
The Syrian and other strangers too.
Say: "I shall do like all the beasts,"
Listen and learn what they do.

The scribe Khonshotep answered his father,
  the scribe Any:
Do not proclaim your powers,
So as to force me to your ways;
⌈Does it not happen to a man to slacken his hand,⌉
So as to hear an answer in its place?
Man resembles the god in his way
If he listens to a man's answer.
⌈One (man) cannot know his fellow,⌉
If the masses are beasts;
⌈One (man) cannot know his teachings,⌉
And alone possess a mind,
If the multitudes are foolish.
All your sayings are excellent,
But doing them ⌈requires virtues;⌉
Tell the god who gave you wisdom:
"Set them on your path!"

The scribe Any answered his son,
  the scribe Khonshotep:
Turn your back to these many words,
That are ⌈not worth⌉ being heard.
The crooked stick left on the ground,
With sun and shade attacking it,
If the carpenter takes it, he straightens it,
Makes of it a noble's staff,
And a straight stick makes a collar.
You foolish heart,
Do you wish us to teach,
Or have you been corrupted?

"Look," said he, "you ⌈my father,⌉
You who are wise and strong of hand:
The infant in his mother's arms,
His wish is for what nurses him."
"Look," said he, "when he finds his speech,
He says: "Give me bread.""

Questions

(1) What value does Any ascribe to the virtue of silence?

(2) To what extent does Any advocate a course of "self-reliance," and why?

(3) What is the gist of the conversational exchange between Any and Khonshotep at the end of the document?

(4) What practical advice does the father give regarding marriage?

3–6

Tutankhamen overturns the Atenist reform.

No sooner was Pharaoh Akhenaten out of the way than the priests of the traditional Egyptian gods, led by the powerful priesthood of Amen-Re, caused succeeding pharaohs to suppress Atenism and reaffirm their advocacy of the older forms of worship. Akhnaten's second successor was 9-year-old Tutankhamen (c. 1347-1339 B.C.E.) who, eager to demonstrate his commitment to restoring traditional forms, had the following declaration inscribed on one of his stela.

Source: James B. Pritchard, *Ancient Near Eastern Texts Pertaining to the Old Testament* (Princeton: Princeton University Press, 1969), pp. 251–252.

...The good ruler, performing benefactions for his father (Amon) and all the gods, for he has made what was ruined to endure as a monument for the ages of eternity and he has expelled deceit throughout the Two Lands, and justice was set up [*so that*] *it might make lying to be an abomination of the land, as (in) its first time.*

Now when his majesty appeared as king, the temples of the gods and goddesses from Elephantine [down] to the marshes of the Delta [had...and] gone to pieces. Their shrines had become desolate, had become *mounds* overgrown with [*weeds*]. Their sanctuaries were as if they had never been. Their halls were a footpath. The land was topsy-turvy, and the gods turned their backs upon this land. If [*the army* was] sent to Djahi to extend the frontiers of Egypt, no success of theirs came at all. If one prayed to a god to seek counsel from him, he would never come [at all]. If one made supplication to a goddess similarly, she would never come at all. Their hearts *were hurt* in their bodies, (so that) they did damage to that which had been made.

Now after days had passed by this, [his majesty] appeared [upon] the throne of his father. He ruled the regions of Horus; the Black Land and the Red Land were under his authority, and every land was bowing down to the glory of him.

Now when his majesty was in his palace which is in the House of Aa-kheper-ka-Re, like Re in the heavens, then his majesty was conducting the affairs of this land and the daily needs of the Two Banks. So his majesty deliberated plans with his heart, searching for any beneficial deed, seeking out acts of service for his father Amon, and fashioning his august image of genuine fine gold. He surpassed what had been done previously. He fashioned his father Amon upon thirteen carrying-poles, his holy image being of fine gold, lapis lazuli, [turquoise], and every august costly stone, whereas the majesty of this august god had formerly been upon eleven carrying-poles. He fashioned Ptah, South-of-His-Wall, Lord of Life of the Two Lands, his august image being of fine gold, [upon] eleven [carrying-poles], his holy image being of fine gold, lapis lazuli, turquoise, and every august costly stone, whereas the majesty of this august god had formerly been on [x +]3 carrying-poles.

Then his majesty made monuments for the gods, [fashioning] their cult-statues of genuine fine gold from the highlands, building their sanctuaries anew as monuments for the ages of eternity, established with possessions forever, setting for them divine offerings as a regular daily observance, and provisioning their food-offerings upon earth. He surpassed what had been previously, [he] went beyond what had [been done] since the time of the ancestors. He has inducted priests and prophets from the children of the nobles of their towns, (each) the son of a known man, whose (own) name is known. He has increased their [property] in gold, silver, bronze, and copper, without limit in [any respect]. He has filled their workhouses with male and female slaves, the product of his majesty's capturing [*in every foreign country*]. All the [property] of the temples has been doubled, tripled, and quadrupled in silver, [gold], lapis lazuli, turquoise, every (kind of) august costly stone, royal linen, white linen, fine linen, olive oil, gum, fat, (20)...incense, *benzoin,* and myrrh, without limit to any good thing. His majesty—life, prosperity, health!—has built their barques upon the river of new cedar from the terraces, of the choicest (wood) of Negau worked with gold from the highlands. They make the river shine.

His majesty—life, prosperity, health !—has consecrated male and female slaves, women singers and dancers, who had been maidservants in the palace. Their work is charged against the palace and against the...of the Lord of the Two Lands. I cause that they be privileged and protected to (the benefit of) my fathers, all the gods, through a desire to satisfy them by doing what their *ka* wishes, so that they may protect Egypt.

The hearts of the gods and goddesses who are in this land are in joy; the possessors of shrines are rejoicing; the regions are in jubilee and exultation throughout the [entire] land:—the good [*times*] have come! The Ennead of gods who are in the Great House (raise) their arms in praise; their hands are filled with jubilees [for] ever and ever; all life and satisfaction are with them for the nose of the Horus who repeats births, the beloved son [of Amon],....for He fashioned him in order that He (Himself) might be fashioned. ...

Questions

(1) What was the reputed state of temples and temple-worship prior to the accession of Tutankhamen to the throne?

(2) What reforms did the pharaoh allegedly undertake?

(3) How might the priestly establishment have tangibly benefited from the pharaoh's reforms?

3–7

The most intense struggle; the soul's triumph over death.

Victory over one's own mortality is the most powerfully-asserted themes of ancient Egypt. While descriptions of the afterlife and of the soul's precise path through it vary, the carvings and papyri of all epochs take up the common theme of the certainty of continued existence and the bliss of Paradise awaiting all the departed souls who live up to the standards of Ma'at.

Source: James B. Pritchard, *Ancient Near Eastern Texts Pertaining to the Old Testament* (Princeton: Princeton University Press, 1969), pp. 32–33.

THE CONQUEST OF DEATH

a

O King Unis, thou-hast not at all departed dead, the hast departed living! For thou sittest upon the throne, of Osiris, with thy scepter in thy hand, that thou mightest give command to the living, and with the *grip* of thy wand in thy hand, that thou mightest give command to those secret of place. Thy arm is Atum, thy shoulders are Atum, thy belly is Atum, thy back is Atum, thy rear is Atum, thy legs are Atum, and thy face is Anubis. The regions of Horus serve thee, and the regions of Seth serve thee.

b

O Atum, the one here is that son of thine, Osiris, whom thou hast caused to survive and to live on. He lives—(so also) this King Unis lives. He does not die—(so also) this King Unis does not die. He does not perish—(so also) this King Unis does not perish. He *is* not *judged.*—(so also) this King Unis *is* not *judged.* (But) he *judges*—(so also) this King Unis *judges....*

What thou hast eaten is an eye. Thy belly is rounded out with it. Thy son Horus leaves it for thee, that thou mayest live on it. He lives—this King Unis lives. He does not die—this King Unis does not die. He does not perish—this King Unis does not perish. He *is* not *judged*—this King Unis *is* not *judged.* He *judges*—this King Unis *judges.*

Thy body is the body of this King Unis. Thy flesh is the flesh of this King Unis. Thy bones are the bones of this King Unis. When thou departest, this King Unis departs. When this King Unis departs, thou departest.

THE FIELDS OF PARADISE

Title

GOING IN AND OUT OF THE EASTERN DOORS OF HEAVEN AMONG THE FOLLOWERS OF RE. I KNOW THE EASTERN SOULS.

The Place of Rebirth

I know that central door from which Re issues in the east. Its south is the pool of *kha*-birds, in the place where Re sails with the breeze; its north is the water of *ro*-fowl, in the place where Re sails with rowing. I am the keeper of the halyard in the boat of the god; I am the oarsman who does not weary in the barque of Re.

I know those two sycamores of turquoise(-green) between which Re comes forth, the two which came from the sowing of Shu at every eastern door at which Re rises.

I know that Field of Reeds of Re. The wall which is around it is of metal. The height of its barley is four cubits; its beard is one cubit, and its stalk is three cubits. Its emmer is seven cubits; its beard is two cubits, and its stalk is five cubits. It is the horizon-dwellers, nine cubits in height, who reap it, by the side of the Eastern Souls.

Conclusion

I KNOW THE EASTERN SOULS. THEY ARE HAR-AKHTI, THE KHURER-CALF AND THE MORNING STAR.

THE GOOD FORTUNE OF THE DEAD

The Singer with the Harp of the God's Father of Amon, Nefer-hotep, the triumphant, said:

All ye excellent nobles, the Ennead of the Mistress of
  Life,
Hear ye how praises are made to the God's Father,
With homage paid to the excellent noble's efficacious
  soul,
Now that he is a god living forever,
Magnified in the West.
May they become a remembrance for the future,
For all who come to pass by.

I have heard those songs which are in the ancient
  tombs
And what they tell in magnifying (life) on earth
And in belittling the necropolis.
Why is it that such is done to the land of eternity,
The right and true, without terrors?

Quarreling is its abomination,
And there is no one who arrays himself against his
  fellow.
This land which has no opponent—
All our kinsfolk rest in it since the first day of time.
They who are to be, for millions of millions,
Will all have come to it.
There exists none who may tarry in the land of
  Egypt;
There is not one who fails to reach yon place.

As for the duration of what is done on earth,
It is a kind of a dream;
(But) they say: "Welcome, safe and sound!"
To him who reaches the West.

Questions

(1) Which gods are instrumental in assuring King Unis' perpetual survival?

(2) How are the Fields of Paradise described in the second document?

(3) What alluring qualities are ascribed to the Paradise referred to in the third document?

CHAPTER 4

4–1
"Shih ching": a glimpse into the mind of China during its legendary phase.

The "Shih ching" or "Book of Songs" was one of the "Six Classics" of ancient China, allegedly compiled by Confucius (c. 551–478 B.C.E.), though much of it dates back far earlier, to the early Zhou, Shang, or even Xia periods (c. 2357–627 B.C.E.). The contents run the gamut from love ballads and ritual hymns to lyric and semi-narrative verse.

Source: Cyril Birch, ed., *Anthology of Chinese Literature* (N.Y.: Grove Press, 1967), pp. 5–7, 10–11, 18, 24–25.

1

She who in the beginning gave birth to the people,
This was Chiang Yüan.
How did she give birth to the people?
Well she sacrificed and prayed
That she might no longer be childless.
She trod on the big toe of God's footprint,
Was accepted and got what she desired.
Then in reverence, then in awe
She gave birth, she nurtured;
And this was Hou Chi.

Indeed, she had fulfilled her months,
And her first-born came like a lamb
With no bursting or rending,
With no hurt or harm.
To make manifest His magic power
God on high gave her ease.
So blessed were her sacrifice and prayer
That easily she bore her child.

Indeed, they put it in a narrow lane;
But oxen and sheep tenderly cherished it.
Indeed, they put it in a far-off wood;
But it chanced that woodcutters came to this wood.
Indeed, they put it on the cold ice;
But the birds covered it with their wings.
The birds at last went away,
And Hou Chi began to wail.

Truly far and wide
His voice was very loud.
Then sure enough he began to crawl;
Well he straddled, well he reared,
To reach food for his mouth.
He planted large beans;
His beans grew fat and tall.
His paddy-lines were close set,
His hemp and wheat grew thick,
His young gourds teemed.

Truly Hou Chi's husbandry

Followed the way that had been shown.
He cleared away the thick grass,
He planted the yellow crop.
It failed nowhere, it grew thick,
It was heavy, it was tall,
It sprouted, it eared,
It was firm and good,
It nodded, it hung—
He made house and home in T'ai.

Indeed, the lucky grains were sent down to us,
The black millet, the double-kernelled,
Millet pink-sprouted and white.
Far and wide the black and the double-kernelled
He reaped and acred;
Far and wide the millet pink and white
He carried in his arms, he bore on his back,
Brought them home, and created the sacrifice.

Indeed, what are they, our sacrifices?
We pound the grain, we bale it out,
We sift, we tread,
We wash it—soak, soak;
We boil it all steamy.
Then with due care, due thought
We gather southernwood, make offering of fat,
Take lambs for the rite of expiation,
We roast, we broil,
To give a start to the coming year.

High we load the stands,
The stands of wood and of earthenware.
As soon as the smell rises
God on high is very pleased:
'What smell is this, so strong and good?'
Hou Chi founded the sacrifices,
And without blemish or flaw
They have gone on till now.

9

He's to the war
for the duration;

Hens to wall-hole,
beasts to stall,
shall I not remember
him at night-fall?

He's to the war
for the duration,
fowl to their perches,
cattle to byre;
is there food enough
drink enough
by their camp fire?

10

Yellow, withered all flowers, no day without its march,
who is not alerted?
Web of agenda over the whole four coigns.

Black dead the flowers,
no man unpitiable.
Woe to the levies,
are we not human?

Rhinos and tigers might do it, drag it out
over these desolate fields, over the sun-baked waste.
Woe to the levies,
morning and evening no rest.

Fox hath his fur, he hath shelter in valley grass,
Going the Chou Road, our wagons our hearses, we pass.

20

Tall stands that pear-tree;
Its leaves are fresh and fair.
But alone I walk, in utter solitude.
True indeed, there are other men;
But they are not like children of one's own father.
Heigh, you that walk upon the road,
Why do you not join me?
A man that has no brothers,
Why do you not help him?

Tall stands that pear-tree;
Its leaves grow very thick.
Alone I walk and unbefriended.
True indeed, there are other men;
But they are not like people of one's own clan.
Heigh, you that walk upon the road,
Why do you not join me?
A man that has no brothers,
Why do you not help him?

28

In the seventh month the Fire ebbs;

In the ninth month I hand out the coats.
In the days of the First, sharp frosts;
In the days of the Second, keen winds.
Without coats, without serge,
How should they finish the year?
In the days of the Third they plough;
In the days of the Fourth out I step
With my wife and children,
Bringing hampers to the southern acre
Where the field-hands come to take good cheer.

In the seventh month the Fire ebbs;
In the ninth month I hand out the coats.
But when the spring days grow warm
And the oriole sings
The girls take their deep baskets
And follow the path under the wall
To gather the soft mulberry-leaves:
'The spring days are drawing out;
They gather the white aster in crowds.
A girl's heart is sick and sad
Till with her lord she can go home.'

In the seventh month the Fire ebbs;
In the eighth month they pluck the rushes,
In the silk-worm month they gather the mulberry-
   leaves,
Take that chopper and bill
To lop the far boughs and high,
Pull towards them the tender leaves.
In the seventh month the shrike cries;
In the eighth month they twist thread,
The black thread and the yellow:
'With my red dye so bright
I make a robe for my lord.'

In the fourth month the milkwort is in spike,
In the fifth month the cicada cries.
In the eighth month the harvest is gathered,
In the tenth month the boughs fall.
In the days of the First we hunt the racoon,
And take those foxes and wild-cats
To make furs for our Lord.
In the days of the Second is the great Meet;
Practice for deeds of war.
The one-year-old boar we keep;
The three-year-old we offer to our Lord.

In the fifth month the locust moves its leg,
In the sixth month the grasshopper shakes its wing,
In the seventh month, out in the wilds;
In the eighth month, in the farm,
In the ninth month, at the door.
In the tenth month the cricket goes under my bed.
I stop up every hole to smoke out the rats,
Plugging the windows, burying the doors:
'Come, wife and children,

The change of the year is at hand.
Come and live in this house.'

In the sixth month we eat wild plums and cherries,
In the seventh month we boil mallows and beans.
In the eighth month we dry the dates,
In the tenth month we take the rice

To make with it the spring wine,
So that we may be granted long life.
In the seventh month we eat melons,
In the eighth month we cut the gourds,
In the ninth month we take the seeding hemp,
We gather bitter herbs, we cut the ailanto for firewood,
That our husbandmen may eat.

Questions

(1) How does the Song # 1 compare to creation narratives in Chapter 1? To who might Chiang Yuan and Hou Chi be compared?

(2) What do Songs # 9, 10, and 20 indicate about the status and condition of soldiers and vagabonds in ancient Chinese society?

(3) What does Song # 28 reveal concerning agriculture, diet, work, and potential dangers in ancient China?

4–2
Might makes right: the "Shu ching" sets forth the Mandate of Heaven.

The earliest of the six Confucian classics is the "Shu ching" or "Book of Historical Documents." Its semi-mythical chronologies and events notwithstanding, the "Shu ching" remains the prime source of knowledge for the history and policies of the Xia, Shang, and early Zhou rulers. Here, the "Books of Yu" describes ideal government under the Xia ("Hea") Dynasty; the "Books of Hea", is a punitive imperial expedition against corrupt administrators; and the "Books of Shang" sets forward the justification for that Dynasty's overthrow of Xia—the "Mandate of Heaven."

Source: James Legge, trans., *The Chinese Classics, Vol. III: Shoo King* (originally published by Oxford University Press, 1935; N.Y.: distributed by Paragon Book Gallery, 1960), pp. 52–67, 162–169, 173–89.

THE BOOKS OF YU

Book II. The counsels of the great Yu.

I. On examining into antiquity, we find that the great Yu was called Wăn-ming. Having arranged and divided *the empire,* all to the four seas, in reverent response to the *inquiries of the former* emperor, he said, "If the sovereign can realize the difficulty of his sovereignship, and the minister can realize the difficulty of his ministry, government will be well ordered, and the people will sedulously seek to be virtuous." The emperor said, "Yes; let this really be the case, and good words will nowhere lie hidden; no men of virtue and talents will be neglected away from court: and the myriad States will all enjoy repose. *But* to ascertain the views of all; to give up one's own opinion and follow that of others; to refrain from oppressing the helpless; and not to neglect the straitened and poor:—it was only the emperor *Yaou* who could attain to "this." Yih said, "Oh! your virtue, O emperor, is vast and incessant. It is sagely, spiritual, awe-inspiring, and adorned with all accomplishments. Great Heaven regarded you with its favoring decree, and suddenly you obtained all within

the four seas, and became sovereign of the empire."

Yu said, "Accordance with the right is good fortune; the following of evil is bad:—the shadow and the echo." Yih said, "Alas! be cautious! Admonish yourself to caution when there seems to be no reason for anxiety. Do not fail in due attention to the laws and ordinances. Do not find your enjoyment in indulgent ease. Do not go to excess in pleasure. In your employment of men of worth, let none come between you and them. Put away evil without hesitation. Do not try to carry out doubtful plans. Study that all your purposes may be with the light of reason. Do not go against what is right to get the praise of the people. Do not oppose the people to follow your own desires. *Attend to these things* without idleness or omission, and from the four quarters the barbarous tribes will come and acknowledge your sovereignty."

Yu said, "Oh! think *of these things,* O emperor. Virtue is seen in the goodness of the government, and the government is tested by its nourishing of the people. There are water, fire, metal, wood, earth, and grain,—these must be duly regulated; there are the rectification of *the people's* virtue, the conveniences of life, and the securing abundant means of sustentation,—these must be harmoniously attended to. When the nine services *thus indicated* have been orderly accomplished, let that accomplishment be celebrated by songs. Caution the people with gentle words; correct them with the majesty of *law*; stimulate them with the songs on those nine subjects,—in order that your success may never suffer diminution."

The emperor said, "Yes. The earth is *now* reduced to order, and *the influences of* heaven operate with effect; those six magazines and three businesses are all truly regulated, so that a myriad generations may perpetually depend on them:—this is your merit."

II. The emperor said, "Come, you, Yu. I have occupied the imperial throne for thirty and three years. I am between ninety and a hundred years old, and the laborious duties weary me. Do you, eschewing all indolence, take the leadership of my people." Yu said, "My virtue is not equal *to the position; the people will not repose in me. But there is* Kauo-yauo, with vigorous activity sowing abroad his virtue, which has descended on the black-haired people, till they cherish him in their hearts. O emperor, think of him! When I think of him, my mind rests on him, *as the man for this office;* when I would put him out of my thoughts, they still rest on him; when I name and speak of him, my mind rests on him *for this;* the sincere outgoing of my thoughts about him is that he is the man. O emperor, think of his merits!"

The emperor said, "Kaou-yaou, that of these my ministers and people, hardly one is found to offend against the regulations of my government, is owing to your being the minister of Crime, and intelligent in the use of the five punishments to assist the *inculcation of the* five duties, with a view to the perfection of my government, and that through punishment there may come to be no punishments, but the people accord with the *path of the* Mean. *Continue to* be strenuous." Kauo-yauo said, "Your virtue, O emperor, is faultless. You condescend to your ministers with a liberal ease; you preside over the multitude with a generous forbearance. Punishments do not extend to the criminal's heirs; while rewards reach to after generations. You pardon inadvertent faults, however great; and punish purposed crimes, however, small. In cases of doubtful crimes, you deal with them lightly; in cases of doubtful merit, you prefer the high estimation. Rather than put to death an innocent person, you will run the risk of irregularity and error. This life-loving virtue has penetrated the minds of the people, and this is why they do not render themselves liable to be punished by your officers." The emperor said, "To enable me to follow after and obtain what I desire in my government, the people everywhere responding as if I moved by the wind;—this is your excellence."

The emperor said, "Come, Yu. The innundating waters filled me with dread, when you realized all that you represented, and accomplished your task,—thus showing your superiority to other men. Full of toilsome earnestness in the service of the State, and sparing in your expenditure on your family; and this without being full of yourself or elated; you *again* show your superiority to other men. Without any prideful presumption, there is no one in the empire to contest with you the palm of ability; without any boasting, there is no one in the empire to contest with you the claim of merit. I see how great is your virtue, how admirable your vast achievements. The determinate appointment of Heaven rests on your person; you must eventually ascend *the throne of* the great sovereign. The mind of man is restless—prone *to err;* its affinity for the *right* way is small. Be discriminating, be undivided, that you may sincerely hold fast the Mean. Do not listen to unsubstantiated words; do not follow undeliberated plans. Of all who are to be loved, is not the sovereign the chief? Of all who are to be feared, are not the people the chief? If the multitude were *without* the sovereign, whom should they sustain aloft? If the sovereign had not the multitude, there would be none to guard the country for him. Be reverent. Carefully demean yourself on the throne which you will occupy, respectfully cultivating *the virtues* which are to be desired in you. If within the four seas there be distress and poverty, your Heaven-conferred revenues will come to a perpetual end. It is the mouth which sends forth what is good, and gives rise to war. My words I will not repeat."

Yu said, "Submit the meritorious ministers one by one to the trial of divination, and let the fortunate indication be followed." The emperor said, "Yu, the officer of divination, when the mind has been made up on a subject, then refers it to the great tortoise. *Now, in this matter,* my mind was determined in the first place. I consulted and deliberated with all *my ministers and people,* and they were of one accord with me. The spirits signified their assent, the tortoise and grass having both concurred. Divination, when fortunate, may not be repeated." Yu did obeisance, with his head to the ground, and firmly declined the throne. The emperor said, "Do not do so. It is you who can *occupy my place.*" On the first morning of the first month, *Yu* received the appointment in the *temple of the* spiritual Ancestor, and took the leading of all the officers, as had been done at the commencement of the emperor's *government.*

III. The emperor said, "Alas! O Yu, there is only the prince of the Meaou, who refuses obedience;—do you go and correct him." Yu on this assembled all the princes, and made a speech to the host, saying, "Ye multitudes, listen all to my orders. Stupid is this prince of Meaou, ignorant, erring, and disrespectful. Despiteful and insolent to others, he thinks that all ability and virtue are with himself. A rebel to the right, he destroys *all the obligations of* virtue. Superior men are kept by him in obscurity, and mean men fill all the offices. The people reject and will not protect him.

Heaven is sending calamities down upon him. On this account I have assembled you, my multitude of gallant men, and bear the instructions *of the emperor* to punish his crimes. Do you proceed with united heart and strength, so shall our enterprize be crowned with success."

At the end of three decades, the people of Meaou continued rebellious against the *emperor's* commands, when Yih came to the help of Yu, saying, "It is virtue which moves Heaven; there is no distance to which it does not reach. Pride brings loss, and humility receives increase:—this is the way of Heaven. In the early time of the emperor, when he was living by mount Leih, he went into the fields, and daily cried with tears to compassionate Heaven, and to his parents, taking to himself and bearing all guilt and evil. *At the same time,* with respectful service, he appeared before Koo-sow, looking grave and awe-struck, till Koo also became truly transformed by his example. Entire sincerity moves spiritual beings;—how much more will it move this prince of Meaou!" Yu did homage to the excellent words and said, "Yes." *Thereupon* he led back his army, having drawn off the troops. The emperor *also* set about diffusing his accomplishments and virtue more widely. They danced with shields and feathers between the two staircases of *the court.* In seventy days the prince of Meaou came to make his submission.

THE BOOKS OF HEA

Book IV. The punitive expedition of Yin

I. When Chung-k'ang commenced his reign over all within the four seas, the prince of Yin was commissioned to take charge of the imperial armies. *At this time,* He and Ho had neglected the duties of their office, and were sunk in wine in their *private* cities, and the prince of Yin received the imperial charge to go and punish them.

II. He made an announcement to his hosts saying, "Ah! ye, all my troops, there are the well-counselled instructions of' the sage *founder of our dynasty,* clearly verified in their power to give stability and security *to the State*—'The former kings were carefully attentive to the warnings of Heaven, and their ministers observed the regular laws of *their offices.* All the officers, *moreover,* watchfully did their duty to assist *the government,* and the sovereign became entirely intelligent.' Every year in the first *month* of spring, the herald with his wooden-tongued bell goes along the roads, *proclaiming,* 'Ye officers able to direct, be prepared with your admonitions. Ye workmen engaged in mechanical affairs, remonstrate on the subject of your business! If any of you disrespectfully *neglect this requirement,* the country has regular punishments for you.'

"Now here are He and Ho. They have entirely subverted their virtue, and are sunk and lost in wine. They have violated the duties of their office, and left their posts. They have been the first to allow the regulations of heaven to get into disorder, putting far from them their proper business. On the first day of the last month of autumn, the sun and moon did not meet harmoniously in Fang. The blind *musicians* beat their drums; the inferior officers and common people bustled and ran about. He and Ho, however, as if they were mere personators of the dead in their offices, heard nothing and knew nothing;—so stupidly went they astray *from their duty* in the matter of the heavenly appearances, and rendering themselves liable to the death appointed by the former kings. The statutes of government say, 'When they anticipate the time, let them be put to death without mercy; when they are behind the time, let them be put to death without mercy.'

"Now I, with you all, am entrusted with the execution of the punishment appointed by Heaven. Unite your strength, all of you warriors, for the imperial House. Lend me your help, I pray you, reverently to carry out the dread charge of the son of Heaven."

"When the fire blazes over the ridge of Kwǎn, gems and stones are burned together; *but* when a minister of Heaven exceeds in doing his duty, the consequences are fiercer than raging fire. I will so destroy *only* the chief criminals, and not punish their forced followers, while those who have long been stained by their filthy manners will be allowed to renovate themselves."

"Oh! when sternness overcomes compassion, then things are surely conducted to a successful issue. When compassion overcomes sternness, no merit can be achieved. All ye, my warriors, exert yourselves, and be cautious."

PART IV. THE BOOKS OF SHANG

Book I. The speech of Tang.

I. The king said, "Come, ye multitude of the people, listen to my words. It is not I, the little child, who dare to undertake *what may seem to be* a religious enterprize; but for the many crimes of the sovereign of Hea Heaven has given the charge to destroy him.

"Now, ye multitudes, you are saying, 'Our prince does not compassionate us, but is calling us away from our husbandry to attack and punish *the ruler* of Hea.' I have indeed heard *these* words of you all: *but* the sovereign of Hea is an offender, and, *as* I fear God, I dare not but punish him.

"Now you are saying, 'What are the crimes of Hea to us? The king of Hea does nothing but exhaust the strength of his people, and exercise oppression in the cities of Hea. His people have all become idle *in his service,* and will not assist him. They are saying, 'When will this sun expire? We will all perish with thee.' Such is the course *of the sovereign of* Hea, and now I must go *and punish him.*

II. Assist, I pray you, me, the one man, to carry out the punishment appointed by Heaven. I will greatly reward you. On no account disbelieve me;—I will not eat my words. If you do not obey the words which I have spoken to you, I will put your children with you to death;—you will find no forgiveness."

Book II. The announcement of Chung-Hwuy.

I. When T'ang, the Successful, was keeping Kĕĕ in banishment in Nan-ch'aou, lie had a feeling of shame on account of his conduct, and said, "I am afraid that in future ages men will fill their mouths with me."

II. On this Chung-hwuy made the following announcement:—"Oh! Heaven gives birth to the people with *such* desires, that without a ruler they must fall into all disorders and Heaven *again* gives birth to the man of intelligence whose business it is to regulate them. The sovereign of Hea had his virtue all-obscured, and the people were *as if they were* fallen amid mire and charcoal. Heaven hereupon gifted *our* king with valour and wisdom, to serve as a mark and director to the myriad States, and to continue the old ways of Yu. You are now only following the standard course, honouring and obeying the appointment of Heaven. The king of Hea was an offender, falsely pretending to the sanction of supreme Heaven, to spread abroad his commands among the people. On this account God viewed him with disapprobation, caused *our* Shang to receive His appointment, and employed you to enlighten the multitudes of the people.

III. "Contemners of the worthy and parasites of the powerful,—many such followers he had indeed, *but* from the first our country was to the sovereign of Hea like weeds among the springing corn, and blasted grains among the good. *Our people,* great and small, were in constant apprehension, fearful though they were guilty of no crime. How much more was this the case, when our *prince's* virtues made them a theme *eagerly* listened to! *Our* king did not approach to *dissolute* music and women; he did not seek to accumulate property and money. To great virtue he gave great offices; to great merit he gave great rewards. He employed others as *if their abilities were* his own; he was not slow to change his errors. Rightly indulgent and rightly benevolent, from the display *of such virtue* confidence was reposed in him by the millions of the people.

"When the chief of Kŏ showed his enmity to the provision-carriers, the work of punishment began with Kŏ. When it went on in the east, the wild tribes of the west murmured; when it went on in the south, those of the north murmured :—they said, "Why does he make

us alone the last?' To whatever people he went, they congratulated one another in their chambers, saying, 'We have waited for our prince;—our prince is come, and we revive.' The people's honouring our Shang is a thing of long existence.

IV. "Show favour to the able and right-principled *among the princes,* and aid the virtuous; distinguish the loyal, and let the good have free course. Absorb the weak, and punish the wilfully blind; take their States from the disorderly, and deal summarily with those going to ruin. Thus overthrowing the perishing and strengthening what is being preserved, how will the States all flourish!

"When a *sovereign's* virtue is daily being renewed, he is cherished throughout the myriad States; when he is full of his own will, he is abandoned by the nine classes of his kindred. Exert yourself, O king, to make your great virtue illustrious, and set up the *pattern of the* Mean before the people. Order your affairs by righteousness; order your heart by propriety:—so shall you transmit a grand example to posterity. I have heard the saying:—'He who finds instructors for himself, comes to the supreme dominion; he who says that others are not equal to himself, comes to ruin. He who likes to ask becomes enlarged; he who uses *only* himself becomes small.'

Oh! he who would take care for his end must be attentive to his beginning. There is establishment for the observers of propriety, and overthrow for the blinded and wantonly indifferent. To revere and honour the way of Heaven is the way ever to preserve the favouring regard of Heaven."

Book III. The announcement of T'ang.

I. The king returned from vanquishing Hea, and came to Pŏ. There he made a grand announcement to the myriad regions.

II. The king said, "Ah! ye multitudes of the myriad regions, listen clearly to the announcement of me, the one man. The great God has conferred *even* on the inferior people a moral sense, compliance with which would show their nature invariably right. *But* to cause them tranquilly to pursue the course which it would indicate, is the work of the sovereign.

"The king of Hea extinguished his virtue and played the tyrant, extending his oppression over you, the people of the myriad regions. Suffering from his cruel injuries, and unable to endure the wormwood and poison, you protested with one accord your innocence to the spirits of heaven and earth. The way of Heaven is to bless the good and to punish the bad. It sent down calamities on *the House of* Hea, to make manifest its crimes.

"Therefore, I, the little child, charged with the decree of Heaven and its bright terrors, did not dare to forgive *the criminal.* I presumed to use a dark coloured victim, and making clear announcement to the spiritual Sovereign of the high heavens, requested leave to deal with the ruler of Hea as a criminal. Then I sought for the great sage, with whom I might unite my strength, to request the favour *of Heaven* on behalf of you, my multitudes. High Heaven truly showed its favour to the inferior people, and the criminal has been degraded and subjected. Heaven's appointment is without error;—brilliantly *now* like the blossoming of flowers and trees, the millions of the people show a true reviving.

III. "It is given to me, the one man, to give harmony and tranquillity to your States and Families; and now I know not whether may not offend *the powers* above and below. I am fearful and trembling, as if I should fall into a deep abyss.

"Throughout all the States that enter on a new life under me, do not, *ye princes,* follow lawless ways; make no approach to insolent dissoluteness: let everyone observe to keep his statutes:—that so we may receive the favour of Heaven. The good in you, I will not dare to conceal; and for the evil in me, I will not dare to forgive myself;—I will examine these things in harmony with the mind of God. When guilt is found anywhere in you who occupy the myriad regions, it must rest on me. When guilt is found in me, the one man, it will not attach to you who occupy the myriad regions."

Questions

(1) In what ways might the "Book of Yu" stress the Chinese ideal of harmony?

(2) In the excerpt from the "Book of Hea," what seems to have been the cause(s) for the downfall of He and Ho?

(3) In the "Book of Shang" ascertain the rationale for why Hea deserved to be driven from power; and how Shang merited the throne.

4–3
Ch'u Yuan and Sung Yu: individual voices in a chaotic era.

The later Zhou period ("Era of Warring States") was a time of intrigue, uncertainty, and confusion—a time when the individual could very easily be lost from view. Politics, ethics, warfare, and religion, underlined by that supreme piece of logical irrationality, the "Mandate of Heaven," cast a generally depressing shadow over the years before the Qin period. The mandarins Ch'u Yuan (332–295 B.C.E.) and his nephew Sung Yu, in their enthusiastic, distinct styles and down-to-earth descriptions, provide a refreshing contrast.

Source: Arthur Waley, trans. *170 Chinese Poems*, (London: Constable & Co., 1945), pp. 23–26.

BATTLE

"We grasp our battle-spears: we don our breast-plates
  of hide.
The axles of our chariots touch: our short swords
  meet.
Standards obscure the sun: the foe roll up like clouds.
Arrows fall thick: the warriors press forward.
They menace our ranks: they break our line.
The left-hand trace-horse is dead: the one on the right
  is smitten.
The fallen horses block our wheels: they impede the
  yoke-horses!"

They grasp their jade drum-sticks: they beat the
  sounding drums.
Heaven decrees their fall: the dread Powers are angry.

The warriors are all dead: they lie on the moor-field.

They issued but shall not enter: they went but shall
  not return.
The plains are flat and wide: the way home is long.
Their swords lie beside them: their black bows, in
  their hand.
Though their limbs were torn, their hearts could not
  be repressed.
They were more than brave: they were inspired with
  the spirit of "Wu."
Steadfast to the end, they could not be daunted.
Their bodies were stricken, but their souls have taken
  Immortality—
Captains among the ghosts, heroes among the dead.

THE MAN-WIND AND THE WOMAN-WIND

HSIANG, king of Ch'u, was feasting in the Orchid-tower, Palace, with Sung Yü, and Ching Ch'ai to wait upon him. A gust of wind blew in and the king bared his breast to meet it, saying: "How pleasant a thing is this wind which I share with the common people." Sung Yü answered: "This is the Great King's wind. The common people cannot share it." The king said: "Wind is a spirit of Heaven and Earth. It comes wide spread and does not choose between noble and base or between high and low. How can you say 'This is the king's wind'?" Sung answered: "I have heard it taught that in the crooked lemon-tree birds make their nests and to empty spaces winds fly. But the wind-spirit that comes to different things is not the same." The king said: "Where is the wind born?" and Sung answered, "The wind is born in the ground. It rises in the extremities of the green p'ing-flower. It pours into the river-valleys and rages at the mouth of the pass. It follows the rolling flanks of Mount T'ai and dances beneath pine-trees and cypresses. In gusty bouts it whirls. It rushes in fiery anger. It rumbles low with a noise like thunder, tearing down rocks and trees, smiting forests and grasses.

"But at last abating, it spreads abroad, seeks empty places and crosses the threshold of rooms. And so growing gentler and clearer, it changes and is dispersed and dies.

"It is this cool clear Man-Wind that, freeing itself, falls and rises till it climbs the high walls of the Castle and enters the gardens of the Inner Palace. It bends the flowers and leaves with its breath. It wanders among the osmanthus and pepper-trees. It lingers over the fretted face of the pond, to steal the soul of the hibiscus. It touches the willow leaves and scatters the fragrant herbs. Then it pauses in the courtyard and turning to the North goes up to the Jade Hall, shakes the hanging curtains and lightly passes into the inner room.

"And so it becomes the Great King's wind."

"Now such a wind is fresh and sweet to breathe and its gentle murmuring cures the diseases of men, blows away the stupor of wine, sharpens sight and hearing and refreshes the body. This is what is called the Great King's wind."

The king said: "You have well described it. Now tell me of the common people's wind." Sung said: "The common people's wind rises from narrow lanes and streets, carrying clouds of dust. Rushing to empty spaces it attacks the gateway, scatters the dust-heap, sends the cinders flying, pokes among foul and rotting things, till at last it enters the tiled windows and reaches the rooms of the cottage. Now this wind is heavy and turgid, oppressing man's heart. It brings fever to his body, ulcers to his lips and dimness to his eyes. It shakes him with coughing; it kills him before his time.

"Such is the Woman-wind of the common people."

Questions

(1) What view does Ch'u Yuan apparently have of war? Of the afterlife?

(2) To what extent do you think that Ch'u Yuan might actually have participated in military campaigns? On what might you base your assumptions?

(3) What does Sung Yu's prose poem about the winds tell us about social and gender-based attitudes in Zhou China?

4–4

"Wagadu": the Soninke epic of ancient Ghana.

The West African historical tradition has, until recently, been a totally oral tradition with generations of griots (signifying a combination of "bard" and "minstrel") preserving the early history of long-vanished kings and their empires. "Wagadu" is among the oldest of the griot epics. The theme is the rise and fall the ancient empire of Ghana (c. 900-1100 C.E.),which had its capital at Kumbi, and was ruled by kings of the Soninke nation. The versions of the griots Diarra Sylla and Jiri Silla are combined here.

Source:John William Johnson, Thomas A Hale, & Stephen Belcher, *Oral Epics of Africa* (Bloomington & Indianapolis: Indiana University Press, 1997), pp. 4–7.

[Diarra Syila first tells his listeners about Dinga Khoré, ancestor of the descendants of the Ghana empire. In this version, they came from India via Yemen and Israel to an unidentified place in Africa approximately 1,000 miles east of present-day Mauritania. Toward the end of his life, Dinga left a message for a vulture to convey to his descendants:]

…I have a message 1 would like to entrust to you.
The vulture replied, "We are at your service."
Dinga spoke again: "After my death, when all the
   sacrifices have been made, you will tell my
   descendants to go toward the West.
"There is a place there called Kumbi, there is a well
   at that place, and there is something in the well,

people talk with that creature, for it is not an
ordinary creature, they only settle down there after
they have reached an understanding with the
creature in question."

[The vulture transmitted the message to one of Dinga's
sons, Djabé Cissé.]

Djabé Cissé asked, "How can one find this place?"
The vulture replied, "You will kill forty fillies for us,
one a day."
"The lungs and the liver are for me, the vulture, and
the remainder of the meat you will give to the
hyena"

[After the sacrifices were made, the vulture explained
what the descendants of Dinga would find at Kumbi.]

…after their arrival at Kumbi, they will find there a
well and inside the well a monster.
They will be called upon to make a contract with this
creature.

[Djabé Cissé and his people set off with the hyena and
the vulture for Kumbi.]

They walked for forty days before reaching Kumbi.
At their arrival the hyena stopped at the edge of a
well and the vulture perched at the top of a tree
near the well.
The vulture said then to the children of Dinga, "Here
is Kumbi, here is the well."
Then a loud noise arose from the well.
The voice asked who was there, and the vulture
replied that they were the children of Dinga and that
they had come to settle there.
At these words, an enormous snake rose out of the
well. He was very black, he had a crest on his head
like that of a rooster, and the crest was very red.
He said, "No one will settle here."
Djabé replied, "We will settle here, for our father at
the end of his life ordered us to come to Kumbi.
And this is certainly Kumbi, here is the well! We
shall settle here."
"Agreed!" said the snake called Bida. "But there are
conditions for that."
Djabé declared then, "We are ready to listen to these
conditions."
"Fine!" replied Bida.
"Each year," he said, "in the seventh month, on the
seventh day of the seventh month, you will offer
me 100 heifers, 100 fillies, and 100 girls."
"Agreed," said Djabé, "but each year, the loss of 100
heifers, 100 fillies, and 100 girls will amount to the
ruin of the country."
They bargained and finally agreed on one filly and
one girl—but the filly will be the best in the entire

country and the girl the most beautiful in the entire
country.

[Djabé won the title of King of Wagadu as the result
of a competition lift four heavy drums. The snake then
gave him conditional power rule.]

When Djabé was installed as ruler, Bida declared to
him that he would be supplied with people and
goods as long as he honors the contract that linked
them together.

[The Jiri Silla version follows from here on. When the
time for the sacrifice came next year, the people prepared themselves.]

At the end of the rainy season, in the seventh month
and on the seventh day, all the people gathered and
the sacrifice was carried out.
The morning of the sacrifice, the morning of the
solemn day, everyone turned up before the door of
the ruler, drummers as well citizens, all gathered in
this spot.

As for the girl, she was already dressed, dressed in
such an extraordinary way that you had to see it to
appreciate it.
The filly was so fat that it was beyond commentary.

When they arrived near the well, the cortege divided
in two.
The griots were always in front of the ruler, competing with each other in turn until they arrived at the
edge of the well.

Before the griots could return to the ruler with their
songs, Bida the snake suddenly surged out of the
well and made a terrifying loud noise.

[After coming out and going back into the well twice,
the snake appeared again for a final time.]

He wrapped himself around the girl and the filly; he
carried them into his lair.
The ruler and his people returned to the town.

[The snake kept his promise. Gold rained down on the
country and the people prospered. But during the annu-
al sacrifice to Bida another year, after the third appearance of the snake from the well, a man attacked it.]

Mahamadu the Taciturn cut off his head with his
saber.
At the very moment his head fell away, the serpent
cried out: "Seven stars, seven luminous stars,"
"Seven famines, seven great famines,"
"Seven rainy seasons, seven entire rainy seasons,"

"No rain will fall in the country of Wagadu." "And even less gold."

"People will say that Mahamadu the Taciturn ruined Wagadu!"

[After the flight of the Wagadu people from the land, some of them returned home to see what was left.]

They found that everyone was dead.
Wagadu emigrated.
It divided into three groups.

One went along the banks of the river.
One group headed toward the Sahel.
And the third left by the middle way.
The one that left by the middle maintained the use of the Soninké language.

[Today, all that remains at Kumbi are some ruins. But the Soninké people live on in many parts of the Sahel from Senegal to Niger. An archaic form of their language has become the occult tongue of Songhay sorcerers and griots.]

Questions

(1) What was the deal that Djabé Cissé struck with the Bida Snake?
(2) From whence did Djabé Cissé derive his right to rule?
(3) How, why, and by what process does the epic imply that Kumbi was abandoned?

4–5

Sundiata: the Malian epic of an empire-builder.

The Empire of Ghana was succeeded, in due course, by the even more fabulously rich and powerful Empire of Mali (c. 1230–1450 C.E.). The founder of the Empire was the redoubtable Mandinke warrior Sundiata (1230–1255 C.E.) who in the years after his reign, was transformed into a larger-than-life legend. This particular version of the Sundiata epic is that passed down to and related by the griot Djeli Mamoudou Kouyate. The first excerpt relates the background (Sundiata's lineage); the second, the exile of Sundiata and his mother; and the third, the griot's function.

Source: D. T. Niane & G.D. Pickett, trans., *Sundiata: An Epic of Old Mali* (London: Longman, 1972), pp. 2–3, 32–37, 40–41.

THE FIRST KINGS OF MALI

Listen then, sons of Mali, children of the black people, listen to my word, for I am going to tell you of Sundiata, the father of the Bright Country, of the savanna land, the ancestor of those who draw the bow, the master of a hundred vanquished kings.

I am going to talk of Sundiata, Manding Diara, Lion of Mali Sogolon Djata, son of Sogolon, Naré Maghan Djata, son of Naré Maghan, Sogo Sogo Simbon Salaba, hero of many names.

I am going to tell you of Sundiata, he whose exploits will astonish men for a long time yet. He was great among kings, he was peerless among men he was beloved of God because he was the last of the great conquerors.

Right at the beginning then, Mali was a province of the Bambara kings; those who are today called Mandingo, inhabitants of Mali, are not indigenous; they come from the East. Bilali Bounama, ancestor of the Keitas, was the faithful servant of the Prophet Muhammad (may the peace of God be upon him). Bilali Bounama had seven sons of whom the eldest, Lawalo, left the Holy City and came to settle in Mali;

Lawalo had Latal Kalabi for a son, Latal Kalabi had Damul Kalabi who then had Lahilatoul Kalabi.

Lahilatoul Kalabi was the first black prince to make the Pilgrimage to Mecca. On his return he was robbed by brigands in the desert; his men were scattered and some died of thirst, but God saved Lahilatoul Kalabi, for he was a righteous man. He called upon the Almighty and jinn appeared and recognized him as king. After seven years' absence Lahilatoul was able to return, by the grace of Allah the Almighty, to Mali where none expected to see him any more.

Lahilatoul Kalabi had two sons, the elder being called Kalabi Bomba and the younger Kalabi Dauman; the elder chose royal power and reigned, while the younger preferred fortune and wealth and became the ancestor of those who go from country to country seeking their fortune.

Kalabi Bomba had Mamadi Kani for a son. Mamadi Kani was a hunter king like the first kings of Mall. It was he who invented the hunter's whistle; he communicated with the jinn of the forest and bush. These spirits had no secrets from him and he was loved by Kondolon Ni Sané. His followers were so numerous that he formed them into an army which became formidable; he often gathered them together in the bush and taught them the art of hunting. It was he who revealed to hunters the medicinal leaves which heal wounds and cure diseases. Thanks to the strength his followers, he became king of a vast country; with them Mamadi Kani conquered all the lands which stretch from the Sankarani to the Bouré. Mamadi Kani had four sons—Kani Simbon, Kamignogo Simbon, Kabala Simbon and Simbon Tagnogokelin. They were all initiated into the art of hunting and deserved the title of Simbon. It was the lineage of Bamari Tagnogokelin which held on to the power; his son was M'Bali Nènè whose son was Bello. Bello's son was called Bello Bakon and he had a son called Maghan Kon Fatta, also called Frako Maghan Keigu, Maghan the handsome.

Maghan Kon Fatta was the father of the great Sundiata and had three wives and six children—three boys and three girls. His first wife was called Sassouma Bérété, daughter of a great divine; she was the mother of King Dankaran Touman and Prince Nana Triban. The second wife, Sogolon Kedjou, was the mother of Sundiata and the two princesses Sogolon Kolonkan and Sogolon Djamarou. The third wife was one of the Kamaras and was called Namandjé; she was the mother of Manding Bory (or Manding Bakary), who was the best friend of his half-brother, Sundiata…

The country of Ghana is a dry region where water is short. Formerly the Cissés of Ghana were the most powerful of princes. They were descended from Alexander the Great, the king of gold and silver, but ever since the Cissés had broken the ancestral taboo their power had kept on declining. At the time of Sundiata the descendants of Alexander were paying tribute to the king of Sosso. After several days of travelling the caravan arrived outside Wagadou. The merchants showed Sogolon and her children the great forest of Wagadou, where the great serpent-god used to live. The town was surrounded with enormous walls, very badly maintained. The travellers noticed that there were a lot of white traders at Wagadou and many encampments were to be seen all around the town. Tethered camels were everywhere.

Ghana was the land of the Soninke, and the people there did not speak Mandingo any more, but nevertheless there were many people who understood it, for the Soninke travel a lot. They are great traders. Their donkey caravans came heavily laden to Niani every dry season. They would set themselves up behind the town and the inhabitants would come out to barter.

The merchants made their way towards the colossal city gate. The head of the caravan spoke to the guards and one of then beckoned to Sundiata and his family to follow him, and they entered the city of the Cissés. The terraced houses did not have straw roofs in complete contrast to the towns of Mali. There were also a lot of mosques in this city, but that did not astonish Sundiata in the least, for he knew that the Cissés

were very religious; at Niani there was only one mosque. The travellers noticed that the anterooms were incorporated in the houses whereas in Mali the anteroom or 'bollon' was a separate building. As it was evening everybody was making his way to the mosque. The travellers could understand nothing of the prattle which the passers-by exchanged when they saw them on their way to the palace.

The palace of the king of Ghana was an imposing building. The walls were very high and you would have thought it was dwelling-place for jinn not for men. Sogolon and her children were received by the king's brother, who understood Mandingo. The king was at prayer, so his brother made them comfortable in an enormous room and water was brought for them to quench their thirst. After the prayer the king came back into his palace and received the strangers. His brother acted as interpreter.

'The king greets the strangers.'

'We greet the king of Ghana,' said Sogolon.

'The strangers have entered Wagadou in peace, may peace be upon them in our city.'

'So be it.'

'The king gives the strangers permission to speak.'

'We are from Mali,' began Sogolon. 'The father of my children was the king Naré Maghan, who, a few years ago sent a goodwill embassy to Ghana. My husband is dead but the council has not respected his wishes and my eldest son,' (she pointed at Sundiata) 'has been excluded from the throne. The son of my co-wife was preferred before him. I have known exile. The hate of my co-wife has hounded me out of every town and I have trudged along every road with my children. Today I have come to ask for asylum with the Cissés of Wagadou.'

There was silence for a few moments; during Sogolon's speech the king and his brother had not taken their eyes off Sundiata for an instant. Any other child of eleven would have been disconcerted by the eyes of adults, but Sundiata kept cool and calmly looked at the rich decorations of the king's reception hall—the rich carpets, the fine scimitars hanging on the wall—and the splendid garments of the courtiers.

To the great astonishment of Sogolon and her children the king also spoke in the very same Mandingo language.

'No stranger has ever found our hospitality wanting. My court is your court and my palace is yours. Make yourself at home. Consider that in coming from Niani to Wagadou you have done no more than change rooms. The friendship which unites Mali and Ghana goes back to a very distant age, as the elders and griots know. The people of Mali are our cousins.'

And, speaking to Sundiata, the king said in a familiar tone of voice, 'Approach, cousin, what is your name?'

'My name is Mari-Djata and I am also called Maghan, but most commonly people call me Sundiata. As for my brother, he is called Manding Boukary, my youngest sister is called Djamarou and the other Sogolon-Kolonkan.'

'There's one that will make a great king. He forgets nobody,'

Seeing that Sogolon was very tired, the king said, 'Brother, look after our guests. Let Sogolon and her children be royally treated and from tomorrow let the princes of Mali sit among our children.'

Sogolon recovered fairly quickly from her exertions. She was treated like a queen at the court of king Soumaba Cissé. The children were clothed in the same fashion as those of Wagadou. Sundiata and Manding Bory had long smocks splendidly embroidered. They were showered with so many attentions the Manding Bory was embarrassed by them, but Sundiata found it quite natural to be treated like this. Modesty is the portion of the average man, but superior men are ignorant of humility. Sundiata even became exacting, and the more exacting he became the more the servants trembled before him. He was held in high esteem by the king, who said to his brother one day, 'If he has a kingdom one day everything will obey him because he knows how to command.'

However, Sogolon found no more lasting peace at Wagadou than she had found at the courts of Djedeba or Tabon; she fell ill after a year.

King Sonmaba Cissé decided to send Sogolon and her people to Mema to the court of his cousin, Tounkara. Mema was the capital of a great kingdom on the Niger beyond the land of Do. The king reassured Sogolon of the welcome she would be given there. Doubtless the air which blew from the river would be able to restore Sogolon's health.

The children were sorry to leave Wagadou for they had made many friends, but their destiny lay elsewhere and they had to go away.

King Soumaba Cissé entrusted the travellers to some merchants who were going to Mema. It was a large caravan and the journey was done by camel. The children had for a long time accustomed themselves to these animals which were unknown in Mali. The king had introduced Sogolon and her children as members of his family and they were thus treated with much consideration by the merchants. Always keen to learn, Sundiata asked the caravaneers many questions. They were very well-informed people and told Sundiata a lot of things. He was told about the countries beyond Ghana; the land of the Arabs; the Hejaz, cradle of Islam and of Djata's ancestors (for Bibali Bounama, the faithful servant of the Prophet, came from Hejaz). He learnt man things about Alexander the Great, too, but it was with terror that the merchants spoke of Soumaoro, the sorcerer-king, the plunderer who would rob the merchants of everything when he was in a bad mood.

A courier, despatched earlier front Wagadou, had heralded the arrival of Sogolon at Mema; a great escort was sent to meet the travellers and a proper reception was held before Mema. Archers and spearmen formed up in a double line and the merchants showed even more respect to their travelling companions. Surprisingly enough, the king was absent. It was his sister who had organized this great reception. The whole of Mema was at the city gate and you would have thought it was the king's homecoming. Here many people could speak Mandingo and Sogolon and her children could understand the amazement of the people, who were saying to each other, 'Where do they come from? Who are they?'

The king's sister received Sogolon and her children in the palace. She spoke Maninkakan very well and talked to Sogolon as if she had known her for a long time. She lodged Sogolon in a wing of the palace. As usual, Sundiata very soon made his presence felt among the young princes of Mema and in a few days he knew every corner of the royal enclosure.

The air of Mema, the air of the river, did Sogolon's health a lot of good, but she was even more affected by the friendliness of the king's sister, who was called Massiran. Massiran disclosed to Sogolon that the king had no children and that the new companions of Sundiata were only the sons of Mema's vassal kings. The king had gone on a campaign against the mountain tribes who lived on the other side of the river. It was like this every year, because as soon as these tribes were left in peace they came down from the mountains to pillage the country.

Sundiata and Manding Bory again took up their favourite pastime, hunting, and went out with the young vassals of Mema.

At the approach of the rainy season the king's return was announced. The city of Mema gave a triumphal welcome to its king. Moussa Tounkara, richly dressed, was riding on a magnificent horse while his formidable cavalry made an impressive escort. The infantry marched in ranks carrying on their heads the booty taken from the enemy. The war drums rolled while the captives, heads lowered and hands tied behind their backs, moved forward mournfully to the accompaniment of the crowd's derisive laughter.

When the king was in his palace, Massiran, his sister, introduced Sogolon and her children and handed him the letter from the king of Ghana. Moussa Tounkara was very affable and said to Sogolon, 'My cousin Soumaba recommends you and that is enough. You are at home. Stay here as long as you wish.'

It was at the court of Mema that Sundiata and Manding Bory went on their first campaign. Moussa Tounkara was a great warrior and therefore he admired strength. When Sundiata was fifteen the king took him with him on campaign. Sundiata astonished the whole army with his strength and with his dash in the charge.

In the course of a skirmish against the mountaineers he hurled himself on the enemy with such vehemence that the king feared for his life, but Mansa Tounkara admired bravery too much to stop the son of Sogolon. He followed him closely to protect him and he saw with rapture how the youth sowed panic among the enemy. He had remarkable presence of mind, struck right and left and opened up for himself a glorious path. When the enemy had fled the old 'sofas' said, 'There's one that'll make a good king.' Moussa Tounkara took the son of Sologon in his arms and said, 'It is destiny that has sent you to Mema. I will make a great warrior out of you.'

From that day Sundiata did not leave the king any more. He eclipsed all the young princes and was the friend of the whole army. They spoke about nothing but him in the camp. Men were even more surprised by the lucidity of his mind. In the camp he had an answer to everything and the most puzzling situations resolved themselves in his presence.

Soon it was in Mema itself that people began to talk about Sundiata. Was it not Providence which had sent this boy at time when Mema had no heir? People already averred that Sundiata would extend his dominion from Mema to Mali. He went on all the campaigns. The enemy's incursions became rarer and rarer and the reputation of Sogolon's son spread beyond the river.

After three years the king appointed Sundiata Kan-Koro-Sigu his Viceroy, and in the king's absence it was he who governed. Djata had now seen eighteen winters and at that time he was tall young man with a fat neck and a powerful chest. Nobody else could bend his bow. Everyone bowed before him and he was greatly loved. Those who did not love him feared him and his voice carried authority.

The king's choice was approved of both by the army and the people; the people love all who assert themselves over them. The soothsayers of Mema revealed the extraordinary destiny of Djata. It was said that he was the successor of Alexander the Great and that he would be even greater; the soldiers already had a thousand dreams of conquest. What was impossible with such a gallant chief? Sundiata inspired confidence in the sofas by his example, for the sofa loves to see his chief share the hardship of battle.

HISTORY

We are now coming to the great moments in the life of Sundiata. The exile will end and another sun will arise. It is the sun of Sundiata. Griots know the history of kings and kingdoms and that is why they are the best counsellors of kings. Every king wants to have a singer to perpetuate his memory, for it is the griot who rescues the memories of kings from oblivion as men have short memories.

Kings have prescribed destinies just like men, and seers who probe the future know it. They have knowledge of the future, whereas we griots are depositories of the knowledge of the past. But whoever knows the history of a country can read its future.

Other peoples use writing to record the past, but this invention has killed the faculty of memory among them. They do not feel the past any more, for writing lacks the warmth of the human voice. With them everybody thinks he knows, whereas learning should be a secret. The prophets did not write and their words have been all the more vivid as a result. What paltry learning is that which is congealed in dumb books!

I, Djeli Mamoudou Kouyaté, am the result of a long tradition. For generations we have passed on the history of kings from father to son. The narrative was passed on to me without alteration and I deliver it without alteration, for I received it free from all untruth.

Questions
(1) What importance appears to be attached to hunting in Malian culture?
(2) What are set forth as young Sundiata's most significant attributes as a potential leader?
(3) What aspects of Ghana in its years of decline strike the griot as being of particular note?
(4) What, according to Kouyate's account, does the profession of griot encompass, and what is the griot's role in West African society?

4–6
The Mesoamerican mind: Tezcatlipoca, Quetzatcoatl, and music.

Two deities, Tezcatlipoca ("Smoking Mirror") and Quetzalcoatl ("Feathered Serpent"), though under varying names and guises, appear to be common to all Mesoamerican cultures, from Maya to Aztec. Tezcatlipoca is sometimes given a benign, and at other times evil, aspect; and is often equated with being in charge of the Heavens.

Quetzalcoatl, who is much more consistently depicted as being sympathetic to humans, is often equated with the Wind. On occasion, the two are antagonistic towards each other. However, in the Nahua manuscript presented here, they cooperate in order to bring to the Earth that most pleasant, sacred and healing element; music.

Source: Irene Nicholson, *Mexican and Central American Mythology* (London: Paul Hamlyn, 1967), pp. 31, 32, 35, 37.

Tezcatlipoca - god of heaven
and of the four quarters of the heavens -
came to earth and was sad.
He cried from the uttermost depths of the four
quarters:

> 'Come, O wind!
> Come, O wind!
> Come, O wind!
> Come, O wind!'

The querulous wind, scattered over earth's sad bosom,
rose higher than all things made;
and, whipping the waters of the oceans
and the manes of the trees,
arrived at the feet of the god of heaven.
There he rested his black wings
and laid aside his endless sorrow.
Then spoke Tezcatlipoca:

> 'Wind, the earth is sick from silence.
> Though we possess light and colour and fruit,
> yet we have no music.
> We must bestow music upon all creation.
> To the awakening dawn,
> to the dreaming man,
> to the waiting mother,
> to the passing water and the flying bird,
> life should be all music!
> Go then through the boundless sadness
> between the blue smoke and the spaces
> to the high House of the Sun.
> There the father Sun is surrounded
> by makers of music
> who blow their flutes sweetly
> and, with their burning choir,
> scatter light abroad.
> Go, bring back to earth a cluster - the most flowering
> - of those musicians and singers.'

Wind traversed the earth that was plunged in silence
and trod with his strength of breath pursued,
till he reached the heavenly roof of the World
where all melodies lived in a nest of light.
The Sun's musicians were clad in four colours.
White were those of the cradle songs;
red those of the epics of love and of war;
sky blue the troubadours of wandering cloud;
yellow the flute players enjoying gold
milled by the Sun from the peaks of the World.
There were no musicians the colour of darkness.

All shone translucent and happy, their gaze turned
forward.
When the Sun saw the wind approaching he told his
musician:

> 'Here comes the bothersome
> wind of earth:
> Stay your music!
> Cease your singing!
> Answer him not!
> Whoever does so
> will have to follow him
> back down there into silence.'

From the stairways of light
of the House of the Sun,
Wind with his dark voice shouted:

> 'Come, O musicians!'

None replied.
The clawing wind raised his voice and cried:

> 'Musicians, singers!
> The supreme Lord of the World is calling you...!'

Now the musicians were silent colours;
they were a circling dance held fast
in the blinding flame of the Sun.
Then the god - he of the heaven's four quarters -
waxed wroth.
From the remotest places,
whipped by his lightning lash,
flocks of cloud whose blackened wombs
were stabbed and torn by lightning
assembled to besiege the House of the Sun.
His bottomless throat let loose the thunder's roar
Everything seemed to fall flat in a circle
beneath the World's mad roof, in whose breast
the Sun like a red beast drowned.
Spurred on by fear,
the musicians and singers then ran for shelter
to the wind's lap.
Bearing them gently
lest he should harm their tender melodies,
the wind with that tumult of happiness in his arms
set out on his downward journey, generous and
contented.
Below, Earth raised its wide dark eyes to heaven
and its great face shone, and it smiled.
As the arms of the trees were uplifted,

there greeted the wind's wanderers
the awakened voice of its people,
the wings of the quetzal birds,
the face of the flowers
and the cheeks of the fruit.
When all that flutter of happiness landed on earth,
and the Sun's musicians spread to the four quarters,
then Wind ceased his complaining and sang,

caressing the valleys, the forests and seas.
Thus was music born on the bosom of earth.
Thus did all things learn to sing:
the awakening dawn,
the dreandng man,
the waiting mother,
the passing water and the flying bird.
Life was all music from that time on.

Questions

(1) Based on the words of their gods in the manuscript, what positive religious properties did the Mesoamericans attribute to music?

(2) What methods of persuasion does Wind (Quetzalcoatl) employ in order to complete his mission?

(3) What role does the Sun play in this tale?

4–7

The Mesoamerican mind: the Aztecs and holy warfare.

The last of the great Mesoamerican empires, that of the Aztecs at Tenochtitlan in Mexico, viewed the waging of war and all that accompanied it almost as part of a natural, even inexorable, cycle of existence. Insatiable Aztec gods were to be fed on sacrificial human blood of warriors slain in battle and (with others) in priestly ceremonies. This belief seemed to dictate that the Aztec empire had to be in a constant state of aggression towards its neighbors, which left the Aztecs isolated during the time of their most serious crisis—invasion by Spanish Europeans. A song which the Aztecs attributed to Tezcatlipoca seems to strike an ominous note, and the three war songs amplify and illustrate the overall cultural response to martial values.

Source: Edward Kissam & Michael Schmidt, trans., *Poems of the Aztec Peoples,* (Ypsilanti, MI: Bilingual Press, 1983), pp. 90, 104–109.

TEZCATLIPOCA'S SONG

I myself am the enemy.
I search out the servants and messengers
of my relatives
who are dressed in dark plumes,
who are plumes of rain.

I have to see them there,
not tomorrow or the next day.

I have my magic mirror with me,
smoking with stars,
and my allies

until those others, my relatives, those
dark plumes of rain in glistening sun

until they're put away.

HOMAGE TO TLACAHUEPAN

With shields, you paint nobility.

With arrows, you write battle.
Now, you dress yourself in plumes
and paint your face with chalk for the sacrifice.
Oh Tlacahuepan,
you are going to take them with you, into the realm of mystery.

Oh Tlacahuepan, you are over the princes.
You cry out, the eagle who is red answers you.
Like a dancer, who is to die,
with whistling hands,
and at the end, to the realm
of mystery.

Your song is like a mottled jaguar.
Your flower is like the spread wings of an eagle.
Oh my prince, as a dancer, who is to die,
there in the clash of shields.
How beautifully you play your drum.

You garland the nobles with flowers of the eagle,
the gathering of friends, oh dancer, who is to die,
the wine of precious flowers makes men drunk and

brave
and he will dress himself with his flowers and songs
in the realm of mystery.

Perhaps the Mexicans are singing there too.

ELEGY FOR THE TLACAHUEPANTZIN

God of rattlesnakes!
your flowers tremble—
tiger, eagle warriors roar.

The War Prince befriends
and favours us. But flowers
of flesh wither.
There, by the drums,
they are shuddering like women.

The war-dead! in the flowering water
with shields and banners raised!
Not by spears or arrows
the precious flower falls.
  The flower made of human body
will never taint the moss
of Moctezuma, will not ever
sprout again in Mexico.

Smoke-stained, your red bird of light:
you pass, prince Tlacahuepan.
Smoke-stained, the god renews him.
God, god tears your flesh away!

…

…desolate my heart,
I see a child
tremble like a feather
shattered.
I go to the garden
where princes
make each other proud with flowers.
I see a child…

NEZAHUALPILLI'S LAMENT

Drunk,
my heart is drunk:
dawn
and the zacuan bird is singing
over the shield stockade,
stockade of spears.

Tlacahuepan, neighbour, friend,
rejoice! You with your shaven head
are like none of the Cuexteca tribe
drunk with the flower waters,

by the shore of bird-river,
with your shaven head.

Rocks fracture
jewels, precious feathers,
my princes:
those who were drunk with death
in the plain of water,
on the shore—there,
the Mexicans among cactus.

The eagle screams,
warrior with tiger's face roars,
O prince Macuil Malinalli;
there in the field of smoke,
field of red…
it is right, it is right
the Mexicans make war!

…

My prince
blood-stained, death-yellow
the lord of the Cuextecas,
his skirt now black as the zapote fruit.
The glory of war clothes my friend
Tlacahuepan—in the mystery
where one perhaps lives on.

My prince
Matlaccuiatzin is drunk
with the flower of war, death-yellow
lord of the Cuextecas,
bathed in the liquid of war.
Together they go
where one perhaps lives on.

Sound the tiger's trumpet!
Eagle on the war-stone screams,
there on the carcasses of our dead lords.
The old men pass, Cuextecas
drunk with the flower of shields.
In Atlixco they dance!

Sound the turquoise drum.
Cactuses are drunk with fallen flowers;
you with the heron head-dress,
you with the painted body.
They hear him, go beside him,
birds with flower-bright beaks
accompany the strong youth
with the tiger shield. He has returned to them.

I weep
from my heart, I, Nezahualpilli.
I search for my comrades
but the old lord is gone,

that petal-green quetzal,
and gone
the young warrior.

Let the sky-blue be your dwelling!
Are Tlatohuetzin and Acapipiyol coming
to taste the water here
as I am weeping?

Nezahualpilli

I see the eagle and the tiger warrior.
Their glory saddens me who will depart
from earth, from the friendship of warriors.

Ipalnemoani,
you fly to us, bird
with a sword in your claw
and darts. Perched
in your own temple you preen
and sway among the drums.

Rain of down:
like a sacred heron you preen
and sway among the drums,

You tint the fire
and colour the throne of warriors.
My friends, you are princes
in the springtime palace.
What does Ipalnemoani require of us?

You will not remain long
in this palace. Nezahualpilli,
our friend, deserts you. War
sends up its flowers. Some grow,
some wither. They are eagles, tigers of war.

Those that wither
come back to you,
Ipalnemoani.

A march of warriors
to the region of Death:
every lord descended
but returned
in a flash
to live in the face of the sun.

Now they wander
the endless plain of the dead.

Questions

(1) How might the image of Tezcztlipoca in the song compare/contrast to the image presented in Document # 6?

(2) What passages are indicative of the "glorious" or sacred view of warfare?

(3) Do any other sentiments come out in the war songs? If so, what are they and how are they expressed?

CHAPTER 5

5–1

Sargon of Assyria records his deeds for posterity.

In their emphasis on racial exclusivity and their eager employment of terror, genocide, and forced deportations, the Assyrians had, by 700 B.C.E., forged the most militarily-intimidating empire yet seen in the Near East. Scorning loyalty and demanding only submission and heavy tribute from those they conquered, they became the most widely-hated peoples of antiquity. The chronicles of their emperors read like a monotonous catalog of warfare and atrocities, as evidenced in this selection from the Annals of Sargon II.

Source: Daniel David Luckenbill, ed., *The Ancient Records of Assyria and Babylonia* (New York: Greenwood Press, 1968), pp. 2–5, 19–21, 33–35, 63–65.

Year I. The deportation of the Israelites; a minor raid into Babylonia (ll. Iob—23)

4..........[At the beginning of my rule, in my first year of reign].............⌈Samerinai⌉ (the people of Samaria).................[of Shamash] who causes me to attain victory........[27,290 people, who lived therein] I carried away; 50 chariots for my royal equipment, I selected from [among them].....[The city I rebuilt], I made it greater than it was before; people of the lands [my hand had conquered, I settled therein. My official I placed over them as governor]. Tribute, tax, I imposed upon them as upon the Assryrians..........I mixed together, I made the price to be...........had sinned and invited me to fight.........[in the plain of Dêr(?)] I defeated him. On the Tu'munu tribe I imposed Assur's yoke...........[Merodachbaladan, king of Chaldea], who exercised the kingship over Babylon against the will of the gods........x+7 people, together with their possessions, I snatched away........[In the land] of Hatti (Syria) I settled (them).

Year 2. Against the rebels in Syria (ll. 23–31)

5. In my second year of reign, Ilu-'bi'di [of Hamath].....of the wide [land of Amurru?] he gathered together at the city of Karkar and the oath..........[the cities of Arpad, Simirra], Damascus and Samaria [revolted against me]............⌈I established⌉ and Sib'u ordered his *turtan* to go to his (Hanno's) aid, and he came forth against me, offering battle and fight. At the command of Assur, my lord, I defeated them and Sib'u ran off alone like a shepherd whose sheep have been carried off, and he died. Hanûni (Hanno) I seized with my own hand and took him to my city, Assur, in chains. The city of ⌈Rapihu⌉ I destroyed, I devastated, I burned with fire; 9,033 people, together with their many possessions, I carried off.

Year 3. Against the Mannean rebels (ll. 32–42)

6. [In my third year of reign,] Shuandahul and ⌈Durdakka⌉, strong cities, planned to fight against Iranzu, the ⌈Mannean⌉, their king and lord, who was subject to me (drew my yoke), and they put their trust in Mitatti of Zikirtu, Mitatti of Zikurtu gave them his warriors with their cavalry, and (thus) aid was provided for them. I mustered the hosts (*lit.,* masses) of Assur's armies, and went forth to capture those cities. With mighty battering rams (?) I smashed their fortified walls, and leveled them to the ground (*lit.,* reckoned them as ground). The people and their possessions I carried off. Those cities I destroyed, I devastated, I burned with fire. [The people] of the cities of Sukka, Bala, and Abitkna, conceived a wicked plan of tearing up the roots of (their) land and with Ursâ, of Urartu (Armenia), they came to terms. Because of the sin which they had committed, I tore them away from their homes (*lit.,* places) and settled them in Hatti of Amurru.

Year 4. Against Kiakki, of Shinuhtu (ll. 42–45)

7. In my fourth year of reign, Kiakki of the city of Shinuhtu forgot the oath (he took by) the great gods and decided not to pay tribute......To the great gods, my lords, I raised my hand and I overthrew Shinuhtu, his royal city, like a storm. Himself, together with his warriors, 7,350 people, his wife, his sons, his daughters, the people of his palace, together with much property, I reckoned as its booty. Shinuhtu, his royal city, I gave to Mati of Atuna and imposed upon him (the payment of) more horses, mules, gold and silver than he had paid before.

Year 5. Against Carchemish (ll. 46–52)

8. In my fifth year of reign, Pisîri of Carchemish sinned

against the oath by the great gods and sent (messages of) hostility against Assyria to Mitâ of the land of Muski. I lifted my hand to Assur, my lord, and brought him and his family out (of his city) in chains. Gold, silver, together with the property of his palace and the rebellious people of Carchemish, who were with him, with their goods, I carried off and brought (them) into Assyria. 50 chariots, 200 steeds (or, cavalry-men), 300 foot soldiers, I selected from among them and added them to my royal host. People of Assyria I settled in Carchemish and placed the yoke of Assur, my lord, upon them.

9. The people of the cities of Pâpa and Lallukna, dogs who had been brought up in my palace, plotted openly against the land of Kakmê. I tore them from their homes (places) and brought them to Damascus of Amurru.

Year 6. The beginning of the subjugation of Armenia (ll. 52–74)

10. In my sixth year of reign, Ursâ, the Armenian.....[Mitatti] of Zikirtu, the governors of the Mannean land,.....set them at enmity with Sargon (and) with Azâ, the son of their lord.......on Mount Uaush, a steep mountain, started to destroy the land of the Manneans and cast out the body of Azâ, their lord. To Assur, my lord, that the Mannean land might be avenged and that it might be restored to Assyria's rule(?), I raised my hand (in prayer) and in Mount Uaush, the mountain where they had cast out the body of Azâ, I flayed Bagdattu, and showed him to the Manneans. *Ullusunu*, his brother, I placed on the royal throne, the whole of the Mannean land I made subservient to him. [Ullusunu, the Mannean]............put his trust in Rusâ, the Armenian. Assur-li'u of the land of Karalla and Ittî of the land of Allabria he caused to revolt against me and called upon them to become vassals of Armenia. In the anger of my heart I overran (*lit.*, covered) these lands like [a swarm] of locusts and Izirtu, the royal city of the Manneans, I overwhelmed as with a net. Multitudes of them I slew. Izirtu I burned with fire and I captured the cities of Zibia and Armaid. Ullusunu, the Mannean, and all of his land gathered together as one man and seized my feet. I had mercy upon them. I forgave Ullusunu his transgression, on the royal throne [I placed him]........Ittî of [Allabria], together with his family, I snatched away, and Assur-li'u of Karalla The city of Ganu—,....[of the district of Niksama], I captured Shêpâsharri, the mayor,.....of the city of Shurgadia I seized with my own hand. Those cities I added to the province of [Parsuash]. Bêl-shar-usur, of the city of Kishesim, my hand captured and himself, together with the property of his palace, I carried off to Assyria. My official I set over his city as governor. The gods, who go before me, therein I caused to dwell and I called its name Kâr-Urta. My royal

image I set up in its midst. The lands of Bît-Sagbat, Bît-Hirmami, Bît-Umargi, the cities of Harhubarban(?), Kilambâti, Armangu, I conquered and added to his province...

36.....of the lands of Arime (*v.*, Arame), Bît-Amukkani, Bît-Dakkuri,......their heavy [tribute] I received. The former Borsippa Canal, which the kings, who lived before me, had dug,—I dug a new canal as a way for Nabû, my lord's(?), procession into Shuanna (Babylon).

37. The Hamarânu folk, who had fled before my weapons and had entered Sippar, who had kept plundering the Babylonians who went abroad (or, the caravans of the Babylonians),—I sent my officials, my governors, against them and they surrounded them completely—not one escaped, great or small—and smote them with the sword, and conquered (them).

38. In the month of *Nisânu*, the month the going forth of the lord of the gods, I took the hand(s) of the great lord, Marduk (and) Nabû, king of all of heaven and earth, and finished the march (*lit.*, road) to the temple of the New Year's Feast. Sleek bullocks and fat sheep, (barnyard) fowl (and) geese(?), together with (an) unceasing (supply) of (other) gifts, I presented (*lit.*, spread out) before them. To the gods of Sumer and Akkad I offered [pure] sacrifices,........Marduk-apal-iddina (Merodach-baladan), son of Iakinu,........I received from him,......in prayer and......of the great lord,......the cities of Sumer and Akkad,........

Year 13. Final attempt to subdue the Aramean tribes who had settled in Babylonia (ll. 317–401[?])

39. In the ⌈thirteenth⌉ year of my reign, in the month of *Airu*, I made ready my chariot (*lit.*, span) and set my camp in order in Shuanna (Babylon)......before me, the cities of......—bidaia, Ikbi-Bêl, Hi—........their (them) and the people of Ur, Uruk, Kisik and Nimid-Laguda he had carried off and brought into Dûr-Iakini, whose defenses he had strengthened. (The length) of a chain he removed (the earth) from the front of its great wall and made the moat 200 cubits wide. 1½ *GAR* (9 cubits) he made it deep and reached the nether waters. He cut a channel (leading) from the Euphrates and carried it up to its (the city's) environs. The city's meadows, where battles (are fought), he filled with water and cut the bridges (dykes). That one, with his allies (and) his warriors, pitched the royal tent in the midst of the ditches (canals) like a pelican(?), and set his camp in order. At the command of Assur, Shamash and Marduk, I caused my picked fighters to fly across his ditches like eagles. They defeated him. Himself, together with the whole of his royal host, I besieged and I slaughtered them in front of his feet like lambs. His warriors, his horses, broken to the yoke, I decimated with (my) arrows, and him I pierced through the hand with the point of my javelin. Like mice through holes, he

entered the gate of his city. The Pukudu tribesmen, his mainstay(?), the Marshanai, together with the Sutû, who.......I slaughtered before the city gate.........I bespattered his people with the venom of death. His royal tent, his golden palanquin, his royal throne, (his) golden scepter, (his) golden couch, (his) golden footstool, (his) *udini* of gold and silver, his *kurgangani* weapons (and) implements of war, I took away from him. All of his people, who dwelt in the villages about his land, who had fled before my weapons, I...........I caused to run loose (? wild) with the herds of cattle, camels, asses and sheep which..........that.....the great hosts of Assur plundered for three days and nights and carried off countless spoil. 90,580 people, 2,500 horses, 610 mules, 854 camels,—[this does not include] sheep (?), which my army carried off,—I received in the midst of my camp.......cattle and sheep, which of their own accord.....at the sides of his city I banded together and like swine they.......the palms I cut down,.....the mighty.....of his city moat........and fear for his own (safety) fell upon him and........he fled and his (abiding) place was seen no more. (*Eight lines gone.*) Dûr-Iakini, his stronghold, I burned with fire; its high defenses I destroyed, I devastated; its foundation I tore up, and made it like a mound left by the flood.

40. The people of Sippar, Nippur, Babylon, Borsippa, who were imprisoned therein through no fault of theirs,—I broke their bonds and caused them to behold the light (of day). Their fields, which since days of old, during the anarchy in the land, the Sutû had seized, I returned to them. The Sutû, desert folk, I cut down with the sword. Their (*i.e.*, the people of Sippar, etc.) borders, which had been encroached upon (*lit.*, seized), I restored to their former limits (*lit.*, place). The independence (freedom) of Ur, Erech, Eridu, Larsa, Kisik and Nimid-Laguda, I (re-)established, and brought back their captured gods to their cities. Their (the gods') revenues, which had stopped, I restored.

41. Bit-Iakin, north and south, as far as the cities of Sam'una. Bâb-dûri, Dûr-Telite, Bubê, Til-Humba, which is (are) on the border of Elam, I brought completely under my sway. The people of Kummuhu, which I had captured in Hatti, with the help of the great gods, my lords, I settled therein and made them occupy all of its waste places. On the Elamite border I had Nabû-dumuk-ilâni build a fortress, in the city of Sagbat, "to hinder the feet of the Elamite." That land I divided totally, and put it under the hand of my official, the viceroy of Babylon, and my official, the viceroy of Gambulu. And Upêri, king of Dilmun, who lives (*lit.*, whose camp is situated), like a fish, *30 bêru* ("double-hours") away in the midst of the sea of the rising sun, heard of my lordly might and brought his gifts.

42. While I was bringing about the overthrow of (the tribes) of Kaldu (and) Arimu, (on the shores) of the sea of the rising sun, I waged bitter warfare against the people of Elam. My official, the viceroy of Kue (Cilicia), whom I had set up in the land of.....of the west, and who ruled (some) people of (?) Mitâ (Midas, *v. adds,* king) of Muski, made raids(?) into his (Mitâ's) province, three times,—where the terrain was favorable, in the chariot, where it was difficult, on foot, and 1,000 warriors.....their horses he took away from them;—not a sinner escaped. Two of the fortresses which defend his province, which were situated on a steep mountain, at the side of staggering [cliffs],......he captured and smote the picked troops who fought his battle(s)....his fortresses.....he spared (*lit.,* allowed to live)....

63. The king of Meluhha (Ethiopia), who in the midst of....., an inapproachable region, a....road (path)...(dwelt), whose fathers since the far-off days of the moon-god's time (era), had not sent messengers to the kings my fathers, to bring their greetings,—(that Ethiopian king) heard from afar of the might of Assur, Nabû and Marduk and the terrifying splendor of my royalty overpowered (*lit.,* covered) him and fright overcame (*lit.,* was poured upon) him, in fetters, shackles and bonds of iron, he cast him (the fugitive Iamanî) and they brought him before me into Assyria, (after) a most difficult journey.

64. Mutallum of the land of Kummuhu, a wicked Hittite, who did not fear the name of the gods, a planner of evil, plotter of iniquity, put his trust in Argisti, king of Urartu, an ally who could not save him, and stopped the yearly payment of tribute and tax and withheld his gifts. In the anger of my heart, with my battle chariot and cavalry, who never leave the place of danger (?) at my side, I took the road against him. He saw the approach of my expedition, left his city and was seen no more. That city, together with 62 strong cities of the rest of his (land), I besieged, I captured. His wife, his sons, his daughters, the property, goods and all kinds of valuables of his palace, together with the people of his land, I tore away,—not one escaped. That district I reorganized. The people of Bît-Iakin, which my hand had seized, I settled therein; my official as governor I set over them. The yoke of my sovereignty I laid upon them. 150 chariots, 1,500 cavalry, 20,000 bowmen, 1,000 bearers of the shield (and) bearers of the lance, I selected from among them and put them under his control.

65. At that time Taltâ, king of Ellipi, a subservient slave who bore my yoke, reached the appointed limit (of life) and trod the path of death. Nibê (and) Ispabâra, sons of (different) wives, each claimed the (right of) accession to his royal throne, his wide land they totally divided, and got into a fight. Nibê, seeking vengeance, hurried a messenger to Shutur-Nahundu, the Elamite (king); he lent him aid and came to his rescue. Ispabâra, (also) seeking vengeance, and the safety of his life, besought me with prayer and fervent entreaty and begged aid of me. Seven of my officials, together with their armies, I sent to avenge him. The defeat of Nibê and the Elamite army, (which had come) to his

aid, they brought about in the city of Marubishti. Ispabâra I placed on the royal throne, I repaired the damage Ellipi (had suffered) and put it under his control.

66. Merodach-baladan, son of Iakin, king of Chaldea, seed of a murderer (*lit., murder*), prop of a wicked devil, who did not fear the name of the lord of lords, put his trust in the Bitter Sea, (with its) tossing waves, violated the oath of the great gods and withheld his gifts. Humbanigash, the Elamite, he brought to (his) aid and all of the Sutû, desert folk, he caused to revolt against me; he prepared for battle and made straight for Sumer and Akkad. Twelve years he ruled and governed Babylon, the city of the lord of the gods, against the will of the gods. At the command of Assur, father of the gods, and the great lord Marduk I made ready my span (*i.e.*, battle chariot), set my camp in order and gave the word to advance against the Chaldean, the treacherous enemy. And that Merodach-baladan heard of the approach of my expedition, he was seized with anxiety for his own (safety) and fled from Babylon to the city of Ikbi-Bêl, like a *sudinnu*-bird (a bat?), at night. The inhabitants of his cities (*lit.*, his inhabited cities) and the gods who dwelt therein he gathered together into one (body) and brought them into Dûr-Iakin, whose defenses he strengthened.

67. The (tribes of) Gambulu, Pukudu, Damunu, Ru'ua (and) Hindaru, he invited and brought into it. He raised the battle cry. (Ground) by the chain, he removed from the front of its great wall and made the moat 200 cubits wide. 1½ *GAR* (9 cubits) he made it deep and reached the nether waters. He cut a channel (leading) from the Euphrates, and carried it up to its (the city's) plain. The city's meadows, where battles (are fought), he filled with water and cut the bridges (dykes). That one, with his allies and his warriors, pitched the royal tent in the midst of the ditches (canals), like a pelican(?), and set his camp in order. I caused my fighters to fly across his ditches like eagles(?). They defeated him. The waters of his ditches they dyed with the blood of his warriors, like wool. The Sutû, his allies, who had turned aside to rescue him and had come to his aid, together with the Marshanians, I slaughtered like lambs and bespattered with the venom of death the rest of the rebellious people. And that one left his royal tent (with its) couch of gold, the golden throne, golden footstool(?), golden scepter, silver chariot, golden palanquin, and the chain about his neck, in the midst of his camp and fled alone. Like a rat(?) he crept along the side of the city wall and entered ⌈his city⌉.

68. Dûr-Iakin I besieged, I captured. Himself, together with his wife, his sons, his daughters, the gold, silver, property, goods and treasures of his palace, all that there was, and the rich spoil of his city, the rest of his rebellious people as well, who had fled from before my weapons,—I gathered them all together and count-

ed them as spoil. Dûr-Iakin, the royal city, I burned with fire; its high battlements I destroyed, I devastated; its foundation platform I tore up, like a mound (left by) a flood, I made it. The citizens of Sippar, Nippur, Babylon and Borsippa, who were imprisoned therein for no crime (*or,* detained against their will) I set free and let them see the light (of day). I restored to them their fields which the Sutû had seized long since, during the disturbances in the land. The Sutû, desert folk, I cut down with the sword; their abandoned (*lit.*, forgotten) districts (ranges, stamping-grounds) which had been given up during the anarchy in the land, I put at their disposal.

69. The freedom of Ur, Uruk, Eridu, Larsa, Kullab, Kisik (and) Nimid-Laguda I (re-)established and returned their captured gods to their shrines (places). Bît-Iakin, north and south, as far as the cities of Sam'una, Bâb-Telitum, Bubê, (and) Til-Humba which are on the Elamite border, I brought completely under my sway and settled therein people of Kummuhu, which is in the Hittite-land, whom my hand had captured with the aid of the great gods, my lords; I had them inhabit its devastated areas. On the Elamite border, at Sagbat, I had Nabû-dumuk-ilâni build a fortress to hinder any advance (*lit.*, the feet) of the Elamite. That land I divided totally and turned it over to (*lit.*, counted it into the hands of) my official, the governor of Babylon, and my official, the governor of Gambulu…

119. The sagacious king, full of kindness (words of grace), who gave his thought to the restoration of (towns) that had fallen to ruins, to bringing fields under cultivation, to the planting of orchards, who set his mind on raising crops on steep (high) slopes whereon no vegetation had flourished since the days of old; whose heart moved him to set out plants in waste areas where a plow was unknown in (all the days) of former kings, to make (these regions) ring with (the sound) of jubilation, to cause the springs of the plain to gush forth, to open ditches, to cause the waters of abundance to rise high, north and south, like the waves of the sea. The king endowed with clear understanding, sharp (*lit.*, strong) of eye, in all matters the equal of the Master (Adapa), who waxed great in wisdom and insight and grew old in understanding:—(in my time) for the wide land of Assyria, the choicest food, to repletion and revival of spirit (*lit.*, heart), as was befitting my reign, their (the gods') rains made plentiful; (there were) the choicest things to save from want and hunger and (even) the beggar was not forced, through the spoiling of the wine, (to drink) what he did not want (what was not to his liking); there was no lack (*lit.*, cessation) of grain of the heart's desire, that the oil of abundance which eases the muscles of men should not be too costly in my land, sesame was sold at the (same) price as (other) grain; that the feasts be richly provided with covers and vessels, befitting the table of god and king,

the price of every article had its limit(s) fixed. Day and night I planned (how) to build that city. I ordered a sanctuary to be built therein for Shamash, the great judge of the gods, who made me attain unto victory. The town of Magganubba, which lay at the foot of Mount Musri, a mountain (standing) above the water-courses and cultivable area of Nineveh like a pillar, whose site none among the 350 ancient princes who lived before me, who exercised dominion over Assyria and ruled the subjects of Enlil, had thought of (*lit.*, remembered), nor knew they how to make it habitable, whose canal none thought to dig,—(but I), in my all-embracing wisdom, which at the bidding of the god Ea (*lit.*, Shar-apsi, the king of the nether waters), lord of profundity, was made rich in understanding and filled with craftiness, and by the fertile planning of my brain, which thinking had been made to surpass that of the kings, my fathers, by Nin-men-anna, ("Lady of the Heavenly Disk"), mother (creatress) of the gods, planned day an night to settle that town, to raise aloft a noble shrine, a dwelling of the great gods, and palaces for my royal abode. I gave the order and I commanded that it be built.

120. In accordance with the name which the great gods have given me,—to maintain justice and right, to give guidance to those who are not strong, not to injure the weak,—the price (*lit.*, silver) of the fields of that town I paid back to their owners according to the record of the purchase documents, in silver and copper, and to avoid wrong (or, ill feeling), I gave to those who did not want to (take) silver for their fields, field for field, in locations over against (facing) the old. The "way of its (the city's) building I lifted up(?) with fervor, opposite—, to the gods Damku and Sharilâni, the judges of men, the full brothers, and that, in future days, entrance thereinto might be in joy of heart and gladness, I raised my hands in prayer, in the chamber of the "masterbuilder of the land," to Shaushka, the powerful goddess of Nineveh. The pious word of my mouth, which she made pleasing(?), was exceedingly pleasing to the great gods(?), my lords, and they commanded that the town be built and the canal dug. I trusted in their word which cannot be brought to naught, mustered my masses of (work)men and made (them) carry the basket and headpad(?). At the beginning of the month of the son of Dara-gal, the god who renders decisions, who reveals snares, Nannar of heaven and earth, the strong one among the gods, Sin, whose name,

by decree of Anu, Enlil and Ea, was called "Month of the Brick-God," (because of) the making of bricks, the building of cities and houses (undertaken therein), on the feast day of the son of Bêl, the exceedingly wise Nabû, recorder (scribe, of all things, leader of all of the gods, I had its bricks made; to the brick-god, lord of foundation (and) brickwork, and chief architect of Bêl, I offered sacrifices, I poured out libations, and raised my hand in prayer.

121. In the month of *Abu*, the month of the descent of the fire-god, destroyer of growing (cultivated) vegetation, when one lays (*lit.*, who lays) the foundation platform for city and house, I laid its foundation walls, I built its brickwork. Substantial shrines, built firm as the foundation of eternity, I constructed therein for Ea, Sin and Ningal, Adad, Shamash, Urta. Palaces of ivory, mulberry, cedar, cypress, juniper, and pistachio-wood I built at their lofty command for my royal dwelling-place. A *bît-hilanni*, a copy of a Hittite (Syrian) palace, I erected in front of their doors. Beams cedar and cypress I laid over them for roofs. 16,283 cubits, the numeral of my name, I made the circuit (*lit.*, measure) of its wall, establishing its foundation platform upon the bed rock of the high mountain. Front and back, and on both sides, I opened eight gates toward the eight winds of heaven. *Shamash-mushakshid-irnittia* ("Shamash Makes My Might Prevail"), *Adad-mukîl-hegallishu* ("Adad Is the Bringer of Its Abundance"), I called the names of the gate of Shamash and the gate of Adad which face the east; *Bêl-mukîn-ishdi-alia* ("Bê1 Establishes the Foundation of My City"), *Bêlit-mudishshat-hisbi* ("Bêlit Increases Plenty"), I designated as names for the gates of Bêl and Bêlit which face the north; *Anu-mushallim-ipshit-kâtia* ("Anu Prospers the Work of My Hands"), *Ishtar-mushammihat-nishêshu* ("Ishtar Enriches His People"), I gave as names to the gates of Anu and Ishtar which face the west; *Ea-mushtêshir-nakbishu* ("Ea Makes His Springs Flow Abundantly"), *Bêlit-ilâni-murap-pishat-talittishu* ("Bêlit-ilâni Spreads Abroad His Offspring"), I called the names of the gates of Ea and Bêlit-ilâni which face the south; *Ashur-mulabbir-palê-sharri-êpishishu-nâsir-ummânâtishu* ("Ashur Makes the Years of the King, Its Builder, Grow Old and Guards Its Troops") was (the name of) its wall, *Urta-mukîn-temen-adushshi-ana-labar-ûmê-rukûti* ("Urta Establishes Foundation Platform of the House for All Time to Come") was (the name of) its outer wall.

Questions

(1) What were the principal reasons that Sargon lists for launching attacks on his various foes?

(2) What were his different methods in dealing with those he had defeated?

(3) Are there instances of the employment of mercy in these Annals? If so, what are they?

(4) How did Sargon actually see himself? Do the Annals reveal anything resembling a constructive value system? If so, what specifically?

5–2

The other side of Imperialism: how outsiders viewed Assyria—the Book of Nahum.

When the Assyrian capital Nineveh fell to the might of an aroused coalition of Egyptians, Medes, Chaldeans, Scythians, Arameans, and others in 612 B.C.E., and the surviving Assyrians were visited in their turn with slavery and deportation, the rejoicing was universal. The Old Testament Book of Nahum the prophet (about whom nothing further is known) contains one of the Bible's most scathing denunciations and foreshadows Nineveh's impending doom.

Source: *The New English Bible, with the Apocrypha* (Oxford & Cambridge University Presses, 1970), pp. 1135–1138.

The vengeance of the LORD on his enemies

The LORD is a jealous god, a god of vengeance;
the LORD takes vengeance and is quick to anger.
In whirlwind and storm he goes on his way,
  and the clouds are the dust beneath his feet.
He rebukes the sea and dries it up
  and makes all the streams fail.
Bashan and Carmel languish,
  and on Lebanon the young shoots wither.
The mountains quake before him,
  the hills heave and swell,
and the earth, the world and all that lives in it,
  are in tumult at his presence.
Who can stand before his wrath?
  Who can resist his fury?
His anger pours out like a stream of fire,
and the rocks melt before him.
The LORD is a sure refuge
for those who look to him in time of distress;
he cares for all who seek his protection
and brings them safely through the sweeping flood;
he makes a final end of all who oppose him
and pursues his enemies into darkness.
No adversaries dare oppose him twice;
all are burnt up, like tangled briars.
Why do you make plots against the LORD?
He himself will make an end of you all.
From you has come forth a wicked counsellor,
plotting evil against the LORD.
The LORD takes vengeance on his adversaries,
against his enemies he directs his wrath;
with skin scorched black, they are consumed
like stubble that is parched and dry.

Israel and Judah rid of the invaders

These are the words of the LORD:

  Now I will break his yoke from your necks
    and snap the cords that bind you.
  Image and idol will I hew down in the house of
    your God
  This is what the LORD has ordained for you:
  never again shall your offspring be scattered;
  and I will grant you burial, fickle though you

have been
Has the punishment been so great?
Yes, but it has passed away and is gone.
I have afflicted you, but I will not afflict you again.

See on the mountains the feet of the herald
  who brings good news.
Make your pilgrimages, O Judah,
  and pay your vows.
For wicked men shall never again overrun you;
  they are totally destroyed.
The LORD will restore the pride of Jacob and
  Israel alike,
  although plundering hordes have stripped them bare
  and pillaged their vines.

Nineveh's enemies triumphant

The battering-ram is mounted against your bastions,
  the siege is closing in.
Watch the road and brace yourselves;
  put forth all your strength.
The shields of their warriors are gleaming red,
  their soldiers are all in scarlet;
  their chariots, when the line is formed,
  are like flickering fire;
squadrons of horse advance on the city in mad frenzy;
they jostle one another in the outskirts, like
  waving torches;
    the leaders display their prowess
    as they dash to and fro like lightning,
    rushing in headlong career;
they hasten to the wall, and mantelets are set
  in position.
The sluices of the rivers are opened, the palace
  topples down;
  the train of captives goes into exile,
    their slave-girls are carried off,
  moaning like doves and beating their breasts;
    and Nineveh has become like a pool of water,
  like the waters round her, which are ebbing away.
  'Stop! Stop!' they cry; but none turns back.

Spoil is taken, spoil of silver and gold;
  there is no end to the store,
    treasure beyond the costliest that man can desire.

Plundered, pillaged, stripped bare!
Courage melting and knees giving way,
writhing limbs, and faces drained of colour!
    Where now is the lions' den,
the cave where the lion cubs lurked,
where the lion and lioness and young cubs
    went unafraid,
the lion which killed to satisfy its whelps
and for its mate broke the neck of the kill,
mauling its prey to all its lair,
    filling its den with the mauled prey?

I am against you, says the LORD of Hosts,
    I will smoke out your pride,
    and a sword shall devour your cubs.
    I will leave you no more prey on the earth,
    and the sound of your feeding shall no more
        be heard.

Ah! blood-stained city, steeped in deceit,
full of pillage, never empty of prey!
    Hark to the crack of the whip,
the rattle of wheels and stamping of horses,
bounding chariots, chargers rearing,
    swords gleaming, flash of spears !
    The dead are past counting, their bodies lie in heaps,
corpses innumerable, men stumbling over corpses—
all for a wanton's monstrous wantonness,
    fair-seeming, a mistress of sorcery,
who beguiled nations and tribes
    by her wantonness and her sorceries.
I am against you, says the LORD of Hosts,
    I will uncover your breasts to your disgrace
    and expose your naked body to every nation,
        to every kingdom your shame.
    I will cast loathsome filth over you,
    I will count you obscene and treat you
        like excrement.

Then all who see you will shrink from you and say,
'Nineveh is laid waste; who will console her?'
Where shall I look for anyone to comfort you?
    Will you fare better than No-amon?—
    she that lay by the streams of the Nile,

    surrounded by water,
    whose rampart was the Nile, waters her wall;
    Cush and Egypt were her strength, and it
        was boundless,
    Put and the Libyans brought her help.
She too became an exile and went into captivity,
    her infants too were dashed to the ground at every
        street-corner,
    her nobles were shared out by lot,
    all her great men were thrown into chains.
You too shall hire yourself out, flaunting your sex;
you too shall seek refuge from the enemy.
Your fortifications are like figs when they ripen:
if they are shaken, they fall into the mouth of
    the eater.
The troops in your midst are a pack of women,
the gates of your country stand open to the enemy,
    and fire consumes their bars.
    Draw yourselves water for the siege,
        strengthen your fortifications;
down into the clay, trample the mortar,
        repair the brickwork.
    Even then the fire will consume you,
        and the sword will cut you down.
    Make yourselves many as the locusts,
        make yourselves many as the hoppers,
    a swarm which spreads out and then flies away.
    You have spies as numerous as the stars in the sky;
        your secret agents are like locusts,
        your commanders like the hoppers
    which lie dormant in the walls on a cold day;
    but when the sun rises, they scurry off,
    and no one knows where they have gone.
    Your shepherds slumber, O king of Assyria,
        your flock-masters lie down to rest;
    your troops are scattered over the hills,
        and no one rounds them up.
Your wounds cannot be assuaged, your injury
    is mortal;
all who have heard of your fate clap their hands
    in joy.
Are there any whom your ceaseless cruelty has not
    borne down?

Questions

(1) Are there specific references in the Book of Nahum that point to Assyrian policy as revealed in Sargon II's "Annals" (Document 5–1)? What are they?

(2) What parallels of warfare and military strategy and technology of the period might be found in Documents 5–1 and 5–2?

(3) What attributes are assigned to the Hebrew God in these passages?

Ramses II at the Battle of Kedesh: the Egyptian version of events.

A clash between the Egyptian and Hittite empires, the competing West Asian superpowers, was probably inevitable, but the murderous proportions of the conflict astounded everyone. For over a century (c. 1395–1285 B.C.E.) the adversaries attempted to crush one another. The battle at Kadesh in Syria proved to be a turning point. Under the audacious generalship of Pharaoh Ramses II, a potentially devastating Egyptian defeat was turned into a hard-fought standoff that left both sides exhausted and led to peace negotiations. The official account of Pharaoh Ramses, in the form of a bulletin and of a poem, naturally shows the Egyptian achievement over the Hittites ("Khatti" in the document) in the best possible light.

Source: Miriam Lichtheim, *Ancient Egyptian Literature* (Berkeley: University of California Press, 1975), v. 2, pp. 60–71.

THE BULLETIN

Year 5, third month of summer, day 9, under the majesty of Re-Harakhti: The Strong-Bull-beloved-of-Maat; the King of Upper and Lower Egypt: *Usermare-sotpenre;* the Son of Re: *Ramesse, Beloved of Amun,* given life eternally. Now his majesty was in Djahi on his second campaign of victory. A good awakening in life, prosperity, and health, in the tent of his majesty in the hill country south of Kadesh. Thereafter, in the morning, his majesty appeared like the rising of Re, clad in the panoply of his father Mont. The Lord proceeded northward and arrived in the region south of the town of Shabtuna. Then came two Shosu of the tribes of Shosu to say to his majesty: "Our brothers who are chiefs of tribes with the Foe from Khatti have sent us to his majesty to say that we will be servants of Pharaoh and will abandon the Chief of Khatti." His majesty said to them: "Where are they, your brothers who sent you to tell this matter to his majesty?" They said to his majesty: "They are where the vile Chief of Khatti is; for the Foe from Khatti is in the land of Khaleb to the north of Tunip. He was too fearful of Pharaoh to come southward when he heard that Pharaoh had come northward."

Now the two Shosu who said these words to his majesty said them falsely, for it was the Foe from Khatti who had sent them to observe where his majesty was, in order to prevent his majesty's army from making ready to fight with the Foe from Khatti. For the Foe from Khatti had come with his infantry and his chariotry, and with the chiefs of every land that was in the territory of the land of Khatti, and their infantry and their chariotry, whom he had brought with him as allies to fight against the army of his majesty, he standing equipped and ready behind Kadesh the Old, and his majesty did not know that they were there.

When the two Shosu who were in the Presence had been ⌈released⌉, his majesty proceeded northward and reached the northwest of Kadesh. The camp of his majesty's army was pitched there, and his majesty took his seat on a throne of fine gold to the north of Kadesh on the west side of the Orontes. Then came a scout who was in his majesty's retinue bringing two scouts of the Foe from Khatti. When they had been brought into the Presence, his majesty said to them: "What are you?" They said: "We belong to the Chief of Khatti. It is he who sent us to observe where his majesty is." His majesty said to them: "Where is he, the Foe from Khatti? I have heard he is in the land of Khaleb to the north of Tunip."

They said to his majesty: "Look, the vile Chief of Khatti has come together with the many countries who are with him, whom he has brought with him as allies, the land of Dardany, the land of Nahrin, that of Keshkesh, those of Masa, those of Pidasa, the land of Karkisha and Luka, the land of Carchemish, the land of Arzawa, the land of Ugarit, that of Irun, the land of Inesa, Mushanet, Kadesh, Khaleb, and the entire land of Kedy. They are equipped with their infantry and their chariotry, and with their weapons of war. They are more numerous than the sands of the shores. Look, they stand equipped and ready to fight behind Kadesh the Old."

Thereupon his majesty summoned the leaders into the Presence, to let them hear all the words which the two scouts of the Foe from Khatti who were in the Presence had spoken. Then his majesty said to them: "Observe the situation in which the governors of foreign countries and the chiefs of the lands of Pharaoh are. Every day they stood up to tell Pharaoh: 'The vile Chief of Khatti is in the land of Khaleb north of Tunip, having fled before his majesty when he heard that Pharaoh had come.' So they said daily to his majesty. But now, this very moment, I have heard from these two scouts of the Foe from Khatti that the vile Foe from Khatti has come with the many countries that are with him, men and horses as numerous as the sand. Look, they stand concealed behind Kadesh the Old, while my governors of foreign countries and my chiefs of the land of Pharaoh were unable to tell us that they had come."

Then spoke the chiefs who were in the Presence in answer to the Good [God]: "It is a great crime that the governors of foreign countries and the chiefs of Pharaoh have committed in failing to discover for themselves the Foe from Khatti wherever he was, and to report him to Pharaoh daily." Then the vizier was commanded to hasten the army of Pharaoh as it marched on the way to the south of the town of Shabtuna, so as to bring it to where his majesty was.

Now while his majesty sat speaking with the chiefs, the vile Foe from Khatti came with his infantry and his chariotry and the many countries that were with him. Crossing the ford to the south of Kadesh they charged into his majesty's army as it marched unaware. Then the infantry and chariotry of his majesty weakened before them on their way northward to where his majesty was. Thereupon the forces of the Foe from Khatti surrounded the followers of his majesty who were by his side. When his majesty caught sight of them he rose quickly, enraged at them like his father Mont. Taking up weapons and donning his armor he was like Seth in the moment of his power. He mounted 'Victory-in-Thebes,' his great horse, and started out quickly alone by himself. His majesty was mighty, his heart stout, one could not stand before him.

All his ground was ablaze with fire; he burned all the countries with his blast. His eyes were savage as he beheld them; his power flared like fire against them. He heeded not the foreign multitude; he regarded them as chaff. His majesty charged into the force of the Foe from Khatti and the many countries with him. His majesty was like Seth, great-of-strength, like Sakhmet in the moment of her rage. His majesty slew the entire force of the Foe from Khatti, together with his great chiefs and all his brothers, as well as all the chiefs of all the countries that had come with him, their infantry and their chariotry falling on their faces one upon the other. His majesty slaughtered them in their places; they sprawled before his horses; and his majesty was alone, none other with him.

My majesty caused the forces of the foes from Khatti to fall on their faces, one upon the other, as crocodiles fall, into the water of the Orontes. I was after them like a griffin; I attacked all the countries, alone. For my infantry and my chariotry had deserted me; not one of them stood looking back. As I live, as Re loves me, as my father Atum favors me, everything that my majesty has told I did it in truth, in the presence of my infantry and my chariotry.

THE POEM

Beginning of the victory of the King of Upper and Lower Egypt: *Usermare-sotpenre;* the Son of Re: *Ramesse, Beloved of Amun,* given life forever, which he won over the land of Khatti, of Nahrin, the land of Arzawa, of Pidasa, that of Dardany, the land of Masa, the land of Karkisha and Luka, Carchemish, Kedy, the land of Kadesh, the land of Ugarit, and Mushanet.

His majesty was a youthful lord,
Active and without his like;

His arms mighty, his heart stout,
His strength like Mont in his hour.
Of perfect form like Atum,
Hailed when his beauty is seen;
Victorious over all lands,
Wily in launching a fight.
Strong wall around his soldiers,
Their shield on the day of battle;
A bowman without his equal,
Who prevails over vast numbers.
Head on he charges a multitude,
His heart trusting his strength;
Stout-hearted in the hour of combat,
Like the flame when it consumes.
Firm-hearted like a bull ready for battle,
He heeds not all the lands combined;
A thousand men cannot withstand him,
A hundred thousand fail at his sight.
Lord of fear, great of fame,
In the hearts of all the lands;
Great of awe, rich in glory,
As is Seth upon his mountain;
[Casting fear] in foreigners' hearts,
Like a wild lion in a valley of goats.
Who goes forth in valor, returns in triumph,
Looking straight and free of boasting;
Firm in conduct, good in planning,
Whose first response is ever right.
Who saves his troops on battle day,
Greatly aids his charioteers;
Brings home his followers, rescues his soldiers,
With a heart that is like a mountain of copper:
The King of Upper and Lower Egypt,
    Usermare-sotpenre,
The Son of Re, *Ramesse, Beloved of Amun,*
Given life forever like Re.

Now his majesty had made ready his infantry and his chariotry, and the Sherden in his majesty's captivity whom he had brought back in the victories of his strong arm. They had been supplied with all their weapons, and battle orders had been given to them. His majesty journeyed northward, his infantry and his chariotry with him, having made a good start with the march in year 5, second month of summer, day 9. His majesty passed the fortress of Sile, being mighty like Mont in his going forth, all foreign lands trembling before him, their chiefs bringing their gifts, and all rebels coming bowed down through fear of his majesty's might. His majesty's army traveled on the narrow paths as if on the roads of Egypt.

Now when days had passed over this, his majesty was in Ramesse-meramun, the town which is in the Valley of the Pine, and his majesty proceeded north-ward. And when his majesty reached the hill country of Kadesh, his majesty went ahead like Mont, the lord of Thebes. He crossed the ford of the Orontes with the first army, "Amun-gives-victory-to-Usermare-sotpenre," and his majesty arrived at the town of Kadesh.

Now the vile Foe from Khatti had come and brought together all the foreign lands as far as the end of the sea. The entire land of Khatti had come, that of Nahrin also, that of Arzawa and Dardany, that of Keshkesh, those of Masa, those of Pidasa, that of Irun, that of Karkisha, that of Luka, Kizzuwadna, Carchemish, Ugarit, Kedy, the entire land of Nuges, Mushanet, and Kadesh. He had not spared a country from being brought, of all those distant lands, and their chiefs were there with him, each one with his infantry and chariotry, a great number without equal. They covered the mountains and valleys and were like locusts in their multitude. He had left no silver in his land. He had stripped it of all its possessions and had given them to all the foreign countries in order to bring them with him to fight.

Now the vile Foe from Khatti and the many foreign countries with him stood concealed and ready to the northeast of the town of Kadesh, while his majesty was alone by himself with his attendants, the army of Amun marching behind him, the army of Pre crossing the ford in the neighborhood south of the town of Shabtuna at a distance of 1 *iter* from where his majesty was, the army of Ptah being to the south of the town of Ironama, and the army of Seth marching on the road. And his majesty had made a first battle force from the best of his army, and it was on the shore of the land of Amor. Now the vile Chief of Khatti stood in the midst of the army that was with him and did not come out to fight for fear of his majesty, though he had caused men and horses to come in very great numbers like the sand—they were three men to a chariot and equipped with all weapons of warfare—and they had been made to stand concealed behind the town of Kadesh.

Then they came forth from the south side of Kadesh and attacked the army of Pre in its middle, as they were marching unaware and not prepared to fight. Then the infantry and chariotry of his majesty weakened before them, while his majesty was stationed to the north of the town of Kadesh, on the west bank of the Orontes. They came to tell it to his majesty, and his majesty rose like his father Mont. He seized his weapons of war; he girded his coat of mail; he was like Baal in his hour. The great horse that bore his majesty was "Victory-in-Thebes" of the great stable of *Usermare-sotpenre,* beloved of Amun. Then his majesty drove at a gallop and charged the forces of the Foe from Khatti, being alone by himself, none other with him. His majesty proceeded to look about him and found 2,500 chariots ringing him on his way out, of all the fast troops of the Foe from Khatti and the many countries with him—Arzawa, Masa, Pidasa, Keshkesh, Irun, Kizzuwadna, Khaleb, Ugarit, Kadesh and Luka, three men to a team acting together.

No officer was with me, no charioteer,
No soldier of the army, no shield-bearer;

My infantry, my chariotry yielded before them,
Not one of them stood firm to fight with them.
His majesty spoke: "What is this, father Amun?
Is it right for a father to ignore his son?
Are my deeds a matter for you to ignore?
Do I not walk and stand at your word?
I have not neglected an order you gave.
Too great is he, the great lord of Egypt,
To allow aliens to step on his path!
What are these Asiatics to you, O Amun,
The wretches ignorant of god?
Have I not made for you many great monuments,
Filled your temple with my booty,
Built for you my mansion of Millions-of-Years,
Given you all my wealth as endowment?
I brought you all lands to supply your altars,
I sacrificed to you ten thousands of cattle,
And all kinds of sweet-scented herbs.
I did not abstain from any good deed,
So as not to perform it in your court.
I built great pylons for you,
Myself I erected their flagstaffs;
I brought you obelisks from Yebu,
It was I who fetched their stones.
I conveyed to you ships from the sea,
To haul the lands' produce to you.
Shall it be said: 'The gain is small
For him who entrusts himself to your will'?
Do good to him who counts on you,
Then one will serve you with loving heart.
I call to you, my father Amun,
I am among a host of strangers;
All countries are arrayed against me,
I am alone, there's none with me!
My numerous troops have deserted me,
Not one of my chariotry looks for me;
I keep on shouting for them,
But none of them heeds my call.
I know Amun helps me more than a million troops,
More than a hundred thousand charioteers,
More than ten thousand brothers and sons
Who are united as one heart.
The labors of many people are nothing,
Amun is more helpful than they;
I came here by the command of your mouth,
O Amun, I have not transgressed your command!"

Now though I prayed in the distant land,
My voice resounded in Southern On.
I found Amun came when I called to him,
He gave me his hand and I rejoiced.
He called from behind as if near by:
"Forward, I am with you,
I, your father, my hand is with you,
I prevail over a hundred thousand men,
I am lord of victory, lover of valor!"
I found my heart stout, my breast in joy,

All I did succeeded, I was like Mont.
I shot on my right, grasped with my left,
I was before them like Seth in his moment.
I found the mass of chariots in whose midst I was
Scattering before my horses;
Not one of them found his hand to fight,
Their hearts failed in their bodies through fear of me.
Their arms all slackened, they could not shoot,
They had no heart to grasp their spears;
I made them plunge into the water as crocodiles
  plunge,
They fell on their faces one on the other.
I slaughtered among them at my will,
Not one looked behind him,
Not one turned around,
Whoever fell down did not rise.

And the wretched Chief of Khatti stood among his
  troops and chariots,
Watching his majesty fight all alone,
Without his soldiers and charioteers,
Stood turning, shrinking, afraid.
Then he caused many chiefs to come,
Each of them with his chariotry,
Equipped with their weapons of warfare:
The chief of Arzawa and he of Masa,
The chief of Irun, and he of Luka,
He of Dardany, the chief of Carchemish,
The chief of Karkisha, he of Khaleb,
The brothers of him of Khatti all together,
Their total of a thousand chariots came straight into
  the fire.
I charged toward them, being like Mont,
In a moment I gave them a taste of my hand,
I slaughtered among them, they were slain on
  the spot,
One called out to the other saying:
"No man is he who is among us,
It is Seth great-of-strength, Baal in person;
Not deeds of man are these his doings,
They are of one who is unique,
Who fights a hundred thousand without soldiers
  and chariots,
Come quick, flee before him,
To seek life and breathe air;
For he who attempts to get close to him,
His hands, all his limbs grow limp.
One cannot hold either bow or spears,
When one sees him come racing along!"
My majesty hunted them like a griffin,
I slaughtered among them unceasingly.

I raised my voice to shout to my army:
"Steady, steady your hearts, my soldiers;
Behold me victorious, me alone,
For Amun is my helper, his hand is with me.
How faint are your hearts, O my charioteers,

None among you is worthy of trust!
Is there none among you whom I helped in my land?
Did I not rise as lord when you were lowly,
And made you into chiefs by my will every day?
I have placed a son on his father's portion,
I have banished all evil from the land.
I released your servants to you,
Gave you things that were taken from you.
Whosoever made a petition,
'I will do it,' said I to him daily.
No lord has done for his soldiers
What my majesty did for your sakes.
I let you dwell in your villages
Without doing a soldier's service;
So with my chariotry also,
I released them to their towns;
Saying, 'I shall find them just as today
In the hour of joining battle.'
But behold, you have all been cowards,
Not one among you stood fast,
To lend me a hand while I fought!
As the *ka* of my father Amun endures,
I wish I were in Egypt,
Like my fathers who did not see Syrians,
And did not fight them [abroad]!
For not one among you has come,
That he might speak of his service in Egypt!
What a good deed to him who raised monuments
In Thebes, the city of Amun;
This crime of my soldiers and charioteers,
That is too great to tell!"

Behold, Amun gave me his strength,
When I had no soldiers, no chariotry;
He caused every distant land to see
My victory through my strong arm,
I being alone, no captain behind me,
No charioteer, foot soldier, officer.
The lands that beheld me will tell my name,
As far as distant lands unknown.
Whoever among them escaped from my hand,
They stood turned back to see my deeds.
When I attacked their multitudes,
Their feet were infirm and they fled;
All those who shot in my direction,
Their arrows veered as they attacked me.

Now when Menena my shield-bearer saw
That a large number of chariots surrounded me,
He became weak and faint-hearted,
Great fear invading his body.
He said to his majesty: "My good lord,
Strong ruler, great savior of Egypt in wartime,
We stand alone in the midst of battle,
Abandoned by soldiers and chariotry,
What for do you stand to protect them?
Let us get clear, save us, Usermare-sotpenre!"

His majesty said to his shield-bearer:
"Stand firm, steady your heart, my shield-bearer!
I will charge them as a falcon pounces,
I will slaughter, butcher, fling to the ground;
Why do you fear these weaklings
Whose multitudes 1 disregard?"
His majesty then rushed forward,
At a gallop he charged the midst of the foe,
For the sixth time he charged them.
I was after them like Baal in his moment of power,
I slew them without pause.

Now when my soldiers and chariotry saw
That I was like Mont, strong-armed,
That my father Amun was with me,
Making the foreign lands into chaff before me,
They started coming one by one,
To enter the camp at time of night.
They found all the foreign lands 1 had charged
Lying fallen in their blood;
All the good warriors of Khatti,
The sons and brothers of their chiefs.
For I had wrecked the plain of Kadesh,
It could not be trodden because of their mass.
Thereupon my soldiers came to praise me,
Their faces [bright] at the sight of my deeds;
My captains came to extol my strong arm,
My charioteers likewise exalted my name:
"Hail, O good warrior, firm of heart,
You have saved your soldiers, your chariotry;
You are Amun's son who acts with his arms,
You have felled Khatti by your valiant strength.
You are the perfect fighter, there's none like you,
A king who battles for his army on battle day;
You are great-hearted, first in the ranks,
You heed not all the lands combined.
You are greatly victorious before your army,
Before the whole land, it is no boast;
Protector of Egypt, curber of foreign lands,
You have broken the back of Khatti forever!"

Said his majesty to his infantry,
His captains and his chariotry:
"What about you, my captains, soldiers,
My charioteers, who shirked the fight?
Does a man not act to he acclaimed in his town,
When he returns as one brave before his lord?
A name made through combat is truly good,
A man is ever respected for valor.
Have I not done good to any of you,
That you should leave me alone in the midst
   of battle?
You are lucky to be alive at all,
You who took the air while I was alone!
Did you not know it in your hearts:
I am your rampart of iron!
What will men say when they hear of it,

That you left me alone without a comrade,
That no chief, charioteer, or soldier came,
To lend me a hand while I was fighting?
I crushed a million countries by myself
On Victory-in-Thebes, Mut-is-content, my
   great horses;
It was they whom I found supporting me,
When I alone fought many lands.
They shall henceforth be fed in my presence,
Whenever I reside in my palace;
It was they whom I found in the midst of battle,
And charioteer Menena, my shield-bearer,
And my household butlers who were at my side,
My witnesses in combat, behold, I found them!"
My majesty paused in valor and victory,
Having felled hundred thousands by my strong arm.

At dawn I marshaled the ranks for battle,
I was ready to fight like an eager bull;
I arose against them in the likeness of Mont,
Equipped with my weapons of victory.
I charged their ranks fighting as a falcon pounces,
The serpent on my brow felled my foes,
Cast her fiery breath in my enemies' faces,
I was like Re when he rises at dawn.
My rays, they burned the rebels' bodies,
They called out to one another:
"Beware, take care, don't approach him,
Sakhmet the Great is she who is with him,
She's with him on his horses, her hand is with him;
Anyone who goes to approach him,
Fire's breath comes to burn his body!"
Thereupon they stood at a distance,
Touching the ground with their hands before me.
My majesty overpowered them,
I slew them without sparing them;
They sprawled before my horses,
And lay slain in heaps in their blood.

***

Then the vile Chief of Khatti wrote and worshiped my name like that of Re, saying: "You are Seth, Baal in person; the dread of you is a fire in the land of Khatti." He sent his envoy with a letter in his hand (addressed) to the great name of my majesty, greeting the Majesty of the Palace: "Re-Harakhti, The Strong-Bull-beloved-of-Maat, the Sovereign who protects his army, mighty on account of his strong arm, rampart of his soldiers on the day of battle, King of Upper and Lower Egypt: *Usermare-sotpenre*, the Son of Re, the lion lord of strength: *Ramesse, Beloved of Amun*, given life forever":

   "Your servant speaks to let it be known that you are the Son of Re who came from his body. He has given you all the lands together. As for the land of Egypt and the land of Khatti, they are your servants, under your feet. Pre, your august father, has given them to you. Do not overwhelm us. Lo, your might is great, your strength is heavy upon the land of Khatti. Is it good that you slay your servants, your face savage toward them and without pity? Look, you spent yesterday killing a hundred thousand, and today you came back and left no heirs. Be not hard in your dealings, victorious king! Peace is better than fighting. Give us breath!"

Then my majesty relented in life and dominion, being like Mont at his moment when his attack is done. My majesty ordered brought to me all the leaders of my infantry and my chariotry, all my officers assembled together, to let them hear the matter about which he had written. My majesty let them hear these words which the vile Chief of Khatti had written to me. Then they said with one voice: "Very excellent is peace, O Sovereign our Lord! There is no blame in peace when you make it. Who could resist you on the day of your wrath?" My majesty commanded to hearken to his words, and I moved in peace southward.

His majesty returned in peace to Egypt with his infantry and his chariotry, all life, stability, and dominion being with him, and the gods and goddesses protecting his body. He had crushed all lands through fear of him; his majesty's strength had protected his army; all foreign lands gave praise to his fair face.

Arrival in peace in Egypt, in Per-Ramesse-mera-mun-great-of-victories. Resting in his palace of life and dominion like Re in his horizon, the gods of this land hailing him and saying: "Welcome, our beloved son, King *Usermare-sotpenre,* the Son of Re, *Ramesse, Beloved of Amun,* given life!" They granted him millions of jubilees forever on the throne of Re, all lowlands and all highlands lying prostrate under his feet for ever and all time.

Questions

(1) Compare the tone and the nature of the accounts in the bulletin, as opposed to those in the poem. What similarities and/or divergences can be detected?

(2) In the bulletin account, how are some of the Pharaoh's officials alleged to have failed him?

(3) In the poem, what dangerous situation did the Pharaoh find himself in, but ultimately escape from?

5–4

The Ramses-Hattusilis Treaty from both perspectives.

In the wake of the baffle of Kadesh, peace was eventually hammered out between the Egyptian Empire of Ramses II and the Hittite Empire of Hattusilis. Undoubtedly, some of the nagging issues between the powers were resolved, but as there had been no clear victor the tone is generally one of compromise and "smoothing over" of differences. The first version of the Treaty is Egyptian, the second is Hittite.

Source: James B. Pritchard, *Ancient Near Eastern Text Pertaining to the Old Testament* (Princeton: Princeton University Press, 1969), pp. 199–203.

EGYPTIAN TREATY*

Year 21, 1st month of the second season, day 21, under the majesty of the King of Upper and Lower Egypt: User-maat-Re; Son of Re: Ramses Meri-Amon, given life forever, beloved of Amon-Re; Har-akhti Ptah, South-of-His-Wall, Lord of Life of the Two Lands; Mut, the Lady of Ishru; and Khonsu Neferhotep; appearing on the Horus-Throne of the Living like his father Har-akhti forever and ever.

On this day, while his majesty was in the town of Per-Ramses Meri-Amon, doing the pleasure of his father Amon-Re; Har-akhti; Atum, Lord of the Two Lands, the Heliopolitan; Amon of Ramses Meri-Amon; Ptah of Ramses Meri-Amon; and [Seth], the Great of

*Translator: John A. Wilson

Strength, the Son of Nut, according as they give him an eternity of jubilees and an infinity of years of peace, while all lands and all foreign countries are prostrate under his soles forever—there came the Royal Envoy and Deputy…Royal Envoy…[User-maat-Re] Setep-en [Re]…[Tar]-Teshub, and the Messenger of Hatti,…-silis, carrying [the *tablet of silver which*] the Great Prince of Hatti, Hattusilis [caused] to be brought to Pharaoh—life, prosperity, health!—in order to beg [peace from *the majesty* of User-maat-Re] Setep-en-Re, the Son of Re: Ramses Meri-Amon, [given] life forever and ever, like his father Re every day.

Copy of the tablet of silver which the Great Prince of Hatti, Hattusilis, caused to be brought to Pharaoh—life, prosperity, health!—by the hand of his envoy Tar-Teshub, and his envoy Ra-mose, in order to beg peace from the majesty of [User-maat-Re], Son of Re: Ramses Meri-Amon, the bull of rulers, who has made his frontier where he wished in every land.

Preamble

The regulations which the Great Prince of Hatti, Hattusilis, the powerful, the son of Mursilis, the Great Prince of Hatti, the powerful, the son of the son of Suppi[luliumas, the Great Prince of Hatti, the] powerful, made upon a tablet of silver for User-maat-Re, the great ruler of Egypt, the powerful, the son of Men-maat-Re, the great ruler of Egypt, the powerful, the son of Men-pehti-Re, the great ruler of Egypt, the powerful; the good regulations of peace and of brotherhood, giving peace…forever.

Former Relations

Now from the beginning of the limits of eternity, as for the situation of the great ruler of Egypt with the Great Prince of Hatti, the god did not permit hostility to occur between them, through a regulation. But in the time of Muwatallis, the Great Prince of Hatti, my brother, he fought with [Ramses Meri-Amon], the great ruler of Egypt. But hereafter, from this day, behold Hattusilis, the Great Prince of Hatti, [is *under*] a regulation for making permanent the situation which the Re and Seth made for the land of Egypt with the land of Hatti, in order not to permit hostility to occur between them forever.

The Present Treaty

Behold, Hattusilis, the Great Prince of Hatti, has set himself in a regulation with User-maat-Re Setep-en-Re, the great ruler of Egypt, beginning from this day, to cause that good peace and brotherhood occur between us forever, while he is in brotherhood with me and he is at peace with me, and I am in brotherhood with him and I am at peace with him forever.

Now since Muwatallis, the Great Prince of Hatti, my brother, went in pursuit of his fate, and Hattusilis sat as Great Prince of Hatti upon the throne of his father, behold, I have come to be with Ramses Meri-Amon, the great ruler of Egypt, *for we are* [*together in*] *our* peace and our brotherhood. It is better than the peace or the brotherhood which was formerly in the land.

Behold, I, as the Great Prince of Hatti, am with [Ramses Meri-Amon], in good peace and in good brotherhood. The children of the children [of] the Great Prince of Hatti *are* in brotherhood and peace with the children of the children of [Ra]mses Meri-[Amon], the great ruler of Egypt, for they are in our situation of brotherhood and our situation [of peace. *The land of Egypt*], with the land of Hatti, [*shall be*] at peace and in brotherhood like unto us forever. Hostilities shall not occur between them forever.

Mutual Renunciation of Invasion

The great Prince of Hatti shall not trespass against the land of Egypt forever, to take anything from it. And User-maat-Re Setep-en-Re, the great ruler of Egypt, shall not trespass against the land [of Hatti, to take] from it forever.

Reaffirmation of Former Treaties

As to the traditional regulation which had been here in the time of Suppiluliumas, the Great Prince of Hatti, as well as the traditional regulation which had been in the time of Muwatallis, the Great Prince of Hatti, my father, I seize hold of it. Behold, Ramses Meri-Amon, the great ruler of Egypt, seizes hold of [*the regulation which he makes*] together with us, beginning from this day. We seize hold of it, and we act in this traditional situation.

A Defensive Alliance—for Egypt

If another enemy come against the lands of User-maat-Re, the great ruler of Egypt, and he send to the Great Prince of Hatti, saying: "Come with me as reinforcement against him, the Great Prince of Hatti shall [come to him and] the Great Prince of Hatti shall slay his enemy. However, if it is not the desire of the Great Prince of Hatti to go (himself), he shall send his infantry and his chariotry, and he shall slay his enemy. Or, if Ramses Meri-Amon, [the great ruler of Egypt], is enraged against servants belonging to him, and they commit another offence against him, and he go to slay them, the Great Prince of Hatti shall act with him [*to slay*] everyone [against whom] they shall be enraged.

Defensive Alliance—for Hatti

But [if] another enemy [come] against the Great Prince [of Hatti, User]-maat-[Re] Setep-en-Re, [the great ruler of Egypt, shall] come to him as reinforcement to slay his enemy. If it is (not) the desire of Ramses Meri-Amon, the great ruler of Egypt, to come, he shall…Hatti, [and he shall send his infantry and his] chariotry, besides returning answer to the land of Hatti. Now if the servants of the Great Prince of Hatti trespass against him, and Ramses Meri-Amon…

The Contingency of Death?

…the [land] of Hatti and the land [of Egypt]…the life. *Should it be that* I shall go [in] pursuit of my fate, *then* Ramses Meri-[Amon], the great ruler of Egypt, living forever, *shall go and come* [*to*] the [land of] Hatti,...to cause..., to make him lord for them, to make User-maat-Re Setep-en-[Re] the great ruler of Egypt, silent with his mouth forever. Now after he...the land of Hatti, and he *returns*...the Great Prince of Hatti, as well as the...

Extradition of Refugees to Egypt

[If a great man flee from the land of Egypt and come to] the Great Prince of Hatti, or a town belonging to the lands of Ramses Meri-Amon, the great ruler of Egypt, and they come to the Great Prince of Hatti, the Great Prince of Hatti shall not receive them. The Great Prince of Hatti shall cause them to be brought to User-maat-Re Setep-en-Re, the great ruler of Egypt, their lord, [because] of it. Or if a man or two men—no matter who—flee, and they come to the land of Hatti to be servants of someone else, they shall not be left in the land of Hatti; they shall be brought to Ramses Meri-Amon, the great ruler of Egypt.

Extradition of Refugees to Hatti

Or if a great man flee from the land of Hatti and [come to User]-maat-[Re] Setep-en-Re, the [great] ruler of Egypt, or a town or a district or a...belonging to the land of Hatti, and they come to Ramses Meri-Amon, the great ruler of Egypt, (then) User-maat-Re Setep-en-Re, the great ruler of Egypt, shall not receive them. Ramses Meri-Amon, the great ruler of Egypt, shall cause them to be brought to the Prince [*of Hatti*]. They shall not be left. Similarly, if a man or two men—[no] matter who—flee, and they come to the land of Egypt to be servants of other people, User-maat-Re Setep-en-Re, the great ruler of Egypt, shall not leave them. He shall cause them to be brought to the Great Prince of Hatti.

The Divine Witnesses to the Treaty

As for these words of the regulation [*which*] the Great Prince of Hatti [*made*] with Ramses [Meri-Amon], the great ruler [of Egypt], in writing upon this tablet of silver—as for these words, a thousand gods of the male gods and of the female gods of them of the land of Hatti, together with a thousand gods of the male gods and of the female gods of them of the land of Egypt, are with me as witnesses [*hearing*] these words: the Re, the lord of the sky; the Re of the town of Arinna; Seth, the lord of the sky; Seth of Hatti; Seth of the town of Arinna; Seth of the town of Zippalanda; Seth of the town of Pe(tt)iyarik; Seth of the town of Hissas(ha)pa; Seth of the town of Sarissa; Seth of the town of Aleppo; Seth of the town of Lihzina; Seth of the town...;...; Seth of the town of

Sahpin; *Antaret* of the land of Hatti; the god of Zithari(as); the god of *Karzis;* the god of Hapantaliyas; the goddess of the town of Karahna; the goddess of...; the Queen of the Sky; the gods, the lords of oaths; this goddess, the Lady of the Ground; the Lady of the Oath, Ishara; the Lady (*of the*) mountains and the rivers of the land of Hatti; the gods of the land of Kizuwadna; Amon; the Re; Seth; the male gods; the female gods; the mountains; and the rivers of the land of Egypt; the sky; the earth; the great sea; the winds; and the clouds.

Curses and Blessings for this Treaty

As for these words which are on this tablet of silver of the land of Hatti and of the land of Egypt—as for him who shall not keep them, a thousand gods of the land of Hatti, together with a thousand gods of the land of Egypt, shall destroy his house, his land, and his servants. But, as for him who shall keep these words which are on this tablet of silver, whether they are Hatti or whether they are Egyptians, and they are not *neglectful of* them, a thousand gods of the land of Hatti, together with a thousand gods of the land of Egypt, shall cause that he be well, shall cause that he live, together with his houses and his (land) and his servants.

Extradition of Egyptians from Hatti

If a man flee from the land of Egypt—or two or three—and they come to the Great Prince of Hatti, the Great Prince of Hatti shall lay hold of them, and he shall cause that they be brought back to User-maat-Re Setep-en-Re, the great ruler of Egypt. But, as for the man who shall be brought to Ramses Meri-Amon, the great ruler of Egypt, do not cause that his crime be raised against him; do not cause that his house or his wives or his children be destroyed; [do not cause that] he be [slain]; do not cause that injury be done to his eyes, to his ears, to his mouth, or to his legs; do not let any [crime be raised] against him.

Extradition of Hittites from Egypt

Similarly, if men flee from the land of Hatti—whether he be one or two or three—and they come to User-maat-Re Setep-en-Re, the great ruler of Egypt, let Ramses Meri-Amon, the [great] ruler [of Egypt], lay hold [of them and cause] that they be brought to the Great Prince of Hatti, and the Great Prince of Hatti shall not raise their crime against them, and they shall not destroy his house or his wives or his children, and they shall not slay him, and they shall not do injury to his ears, to his eyes, to his mouth, or to his legs, and they shall not raise any crime against him.

Description of the Tablet

What is in the middle of the tablet of silver. On its front side: figures consisting of an image of Seth embracing an image of the Great Prince [of Hatti], surrounded by a border with the words: "the seal of Seth, the ruler of the sky; the seal of the regulation which Hattusilis made, the Great Prince of Hatti, the powerful, the son of Mursilis, the Great Prince of Hatti, the powerful." What is within that which surrounds the figures: the seal [of Seth. What is on] its other side: figures consisting of a female image of [the] goddess of Hatti embracing a female image of the Princess of Hatti, surrounded by a border with the words: "the seal of the Re of the town of Arinna, the lord of the land; the seal of Putuhepa, the Princess of the land of Hatti, the daughter of the land of Kizuwadna, the [*priestess*] of [*the town of*] Arinna, the Lady of the Land, the servant of the goddess." What is within the surrounding (frame) of the figures: the seal of the Re of Arinna, the lord of every land.

HITTITE TREATY*

Title

Treaty of Rea-mashesha mai Amana, the great king, the king of the land of Egypt, the valiant, with Hattusilis, the great king of the Hatti land, his brother, for establishing [good] peace [and] good brotherhood [worthy of] great [king]ship between them forever.

Preamble

These are the words of Rea-mashesha mai Amana, the great king of the land of Egypt, the valiant of all lands, the son of Min-mua-rea, the great king, the king of the land of Egypt, the valiant, the grandson of Minpakhtarea, the great king, the king of the land of Egypt, the valiant, (spoken) to Hattusilis, the great king, the king of the Hatti land, the valiant, the son of Mursilis, the great king, the king of the Hatti land, the valiant, the grandson of Suppiluliumas, the great king, the king of the Hatti land, the valiant.

Relations up to the Conclusion of the Treaty

Now I have established good brotherhood (and) good peace between us forever. In order to establish good peace (and) good brotherhood in [the relationship] of the land of Egypt with the Hatti land forever (I speak) thus: Behold, as for the relationship between the land of Egypt and the Hatti land, since eternity the god does not permit the making of hostility between them because of a treaty (valid) forever. Behold, Rea-mashesha mai Amana, the great king, the king of the land of

Translator: Albrecht Goetze

Egypt, in order to bring about the relationship that the Sun-god and the Storm-god have effected for the land of Egypt with the Hatti land finds himself in a relationship valid since eternity which [does not permi]t the making of hostility between [them] until all and everlasting time.

The Present Treaty

Rea-mashesha mai Amana, the great king, the king of the land of Egypt, has entered into a treaty (written) upon a silver tablet with Hattusilis, the great king, the king of the Hatti land, [his] brother, [from] this [da]y on to establish good peace (and) good brotherhood be[tween us] forever. He is a brother [to me] and I am a brother to him and at peace with him forever. And as for us, our brotherhood and our peace is being brought about and it will be better than the brotherhood and the peace which existed formerly for the land of Egypt with the Hatti land.

Future Relations of the Two Countries

Behold Rea-mashesha mai Amana, the king of the land of Egypt, is in good peace (and) in good brotherhood with [Hattusilis], the great king, the king of the Hatti land.

Behold, the sons of Rea-mashesha mai Amana, the king of the land of Egypt, are in peace with (and) brothers of the sons of Hattusilis, the great king, the king of the Hatti land, forever. They are in the same relationship of brotherhood and peace as we.

And as for (the relationship of) the land of Egypt with the Hatti land, they are at peace and brothers like us forever.

Mutual Renunciation of Aggression

Rea-mashesha mai Amana, the great king, the king of the land of Egypt, shall not tresspass into the Hatti land to take anything therefrom in the future. And Hattusilis, the great king, the king of the Hatti land, shall not tresspass into the land of Egypt to take anything therefrom in the future.

Behold, the holy ordinance (valid) forever which the Sun-god and the Storm-god had brought about for the land of Egypt with the Hatti land (calls for) peace and brotherhood so as not to make hostility between them. Behold, Rea-mashesha mai Amana, the great king, the king of the land of Egypt, has seized hold of it in order to bring about well-being from this day on. Behold, the land of Egypt (in its relation) with the Hatti land—they are at peace and brothers forever.

Defensive Alliance

If an enemy from abroad comes against the Hatti land,

and Hattusilis, the great king, the king of the Hatti land, sends to me saying: "Come to me to help me against him," Rea-mashesha mai Amana, the great king, the king of the land of Egypt, shall send his foot soldiers (and) his charioteers and they shall slay [his enemy and] take revenge upon him for the sake of the Hatti land.

And if Hattusilis, the great king, the king of the Hatti land, is angry with servants belonging to him (and it) they have failed against him and sends to Rea-mashesha mai Amana, the great king, the king of the land of Egypt, on their account—lo! Rea-mashesha mai Amana shall send his foot soldiers (and) his charioteers and they shall destroy all those with whom he is angry.

If an enemy from abroad comes against the land of Egypt and Rea-mashesha mai Amana, the king of the land of Egypt, your brother, sends to Hattusilis, the king of the Hatti land, his brother, saying: "Come here to help me against him"—lo! Hattusilis, the king of the Hatti land, shall send his foot soldiers (and) his charioteers and shall slay my enemies.

And if Rea-mashesha ma[i Amana, the king of] the land of Egypt, is angry with servants belonging to him—(and if) they have committed sin again[st him and I send] to Hattusilis, the king of the Hatti land, my brother, on his account—lo! Hattusilis, [the king of the Hatti land,] my brother, shall send his foot soldiers (and) his charioteers and they shall destroy all those with whom he is angry.

Succession to the Throne

Behold, the son of Hattusilis, the king of the Hatti land, shall be made king of the Hatti land in place of Hattusilis, his father, after the many years of Hattusilis, the king of the Hatti land. If the noblemen the Hatti land commit sin against him—lo! [Rea-mashesha mai Amana, the king of Egypt, shall send foot soldiers] (and) charioteers to take revenge upon them [for the sake of the Hatti land. And after they have established order] in the country of the king of the Hatti land, [they shall return] to the country [of Egypt].

(Corresponding provision concerning Egypt lost in a gap.)

Extradition of Fugitives

[If a nobleman flees from the Hatti land and i]f one (such) man comes [to Rea-mashesha mai Amana, the great king, the king of the land of Egypt,] in order to enter his services—[be it a...belonging to Ha]ttusilis, the king of the Hatti land, [be it a…] or a single town—[Rea-mashesha mai Amana, the great king, the king of the land Egypt, shall seize them and] shall have them brought back to the king of the Hatti land.

(several badly broken lines)

[If a nobleman] flees [from Rea-mashesha mai Amana, the king of the land of Egypt, and if one (such) man] comes to the [Hatti] land, [Ha]ttusilis, [the great king, the king of the Hatti land, shall seize him and] shall have him brought back to R[ea-mashesha mai] Amana, the great king, the king of Egypt, his brother.

If one man flees from the [Hatti land or] two men, [or three men and come to] Rea-mashesha mai [Amana, the great king, the king of the land of Egyp]t, [Rea-mashesha] mai Amana, the great king, [the king of the land of Egypt, shall seize them and have them brought back t]o Hattusilis, his brother. [Rea-mashesha mai Amana and Hattusilis are verily] brothers; hence [let them not *exact punishment for*] their sins, [let them not] tear out [their eyes; let them not *take revenge upon*] their people […together with] their [wives and wi]th their children.

If [one man flees from Egypt] or two men or three men [and come to Hattusilis, the great king, the king of the Hatti land, Hattusilis, the great king], the king of the Hatti land, his brother, shall seize them and have them brought [back to Rea-mashesha mai Amana, the great king, the king of] the land of Egypt. [Hattusilis, the king of the Hatti land], and Rea-mashesha, the great king, the k[ing of the land of Egypt, are verily brothers; hence let them not *exact punishment for* their sins,] […] let them not tear out their eyes; [let them not *take revenge upon* their people…together with] their wives (and) with their children.

(After some fragmentary lines the text breaks off altogether. With the end of the treaty the list of the gods who were invoked as witnesses is missing.)

Questions
(1) From making a comparison of the two versions of the Treaty, what provisions seem to be accorded the greatest priority?

(2) What differences might be detected in the two versions? To what extent are they of significance?

(3) Does either side appear to have derived any definite advantages over the other? Explain.

5–5
Cyrus of Persia: a study in Imperial success.

Persia, the last of the great Near Eastern empires of the ancient world, was also the largest, most diverse in its population, and the best-organized. The empire itself was, in the main, the handiwork of one individual, Cyrus the Great (553–529 B.C.E.). Xenophon, the Greek historian-adventurer and a foe of the Persians, nonetheless stood in awe of their achievement and, in some of his works, sought to ferret out the factors behind Cyrus' success and to analyze the character of the founder-emperor.

Source: Xenophon, "The Persian Expedition," Rex Warner, ed. (Hammondsworth, England: Penguin, 1972), pp. 91–95.

THE CHARACTER OF CYRUS

Of all the Persians who lived after Cyrus the Great, he was the most like a king and the most deserving of an empire, as is admitted by everyone who is known to have been personally acquainted with him. In his early life, when he was still a child being brought up with his brother, and the other children, he was regarded the best of them all in every way. All the children of Persian nobles are brought up at the Court, and there a child can pick up many lessons in good behaviour while having no chance of seeing or hearing anything bad. The boys see and hear some people being honoured by the King and others being dismissed in disgrace, and so from their childhood they learn how to command and how to obey. Here, at the Court, Cyrus was considered, first, to be the best-behaved of his contemporaries and more willing even than his inferiors to listen to those older than himself; and then he was remarkable for his fondness for horses and being able to manage them extremely well. In the soldierly arts also of archery and javelin-throwing they judged him to be most eager to learn and most willing to practise them. When he got to the age for hunting, he was most enthusiastic about it, and only too ready to take risks in his encounters with wild animals. There was one occasion when a she-bear charged at him and he, showing no fear, got to grips with the animal and was pulled off his horse. The scar from the wounds he got then were still visible on his body, but he killed the animal in the end, and as for the first man who came to help him Cyrus made people think him very lucky indeed.

When he was sent down to the coast by his father as satrap of Lydia and Great Phrygia and Cappadocia, and had been declared Commander-in-Chief of all who are bound to muster in the plain of Castolus, the first thing he did was to make it clear that in any league or agreement or undertaking that he made he attached the utmost importance to keeping his word. The cities which were in his command trusted him and so did the men. And the enemies he had were confident that once Cyrus had signed a treaty with them nothing would happen to them contrary to the terms of the treaty. Consequently when he was at war with Tissaphernes all the cities, with the exception of the Milesians, chose to follow him rather than Tissaphernes. The Milesians

were afraid of him because he refused to give up the cause of the exiled government. Indeed, he made it clear by his actions, and said openly that, once he had become their friend, he would never give them up, not even if their numbers became fewer and their prospects worse than they were.

If anyone did him a good or an evil turn, he evidently aimed at going one better. Some people used to refer to an habitual prayer of his, that he might live long enough to be able to repay with interest both those who had helped him and those who had injured him. It was quite natural then that he was the one man in our times to whom so many people were eager to hand over their money, their cities and their own persons.

No one, however, could say that he allowed criminals and evil-doers to mock his authority. On the contrary, his punishments were exceptionally severe, and along the more frequented roads one often saw people who had been blinded or had had their feet or hands cut off. The result was that in Cyrus's provinces anyone, whether Greek or native, who doing no harm could travel without fear wherever he liked and could take with him whatever he wanted.

Of course it is well known that he treated with exceptional distinction all those who showed ability for war. In his first war, which was against the Pisidians and Mysians, he marched into their country himself and made those whom he saw willing to risk their lives governors over the territory which he conquered; and afterwards he gave them other honours and rewards, making it clear that the brave were going to be the most prosperous while the cowards only deserved to be their slaves. Consequently there was never any lack of people who were willing to risk their lives when they thought that Cyrus would get to know of it.

As for justice, he made it his supreme aim to see that those who really wanted to live in accordance with its standards became richer than those who wanted to profit by transgressing them. It followed from this that not only were his affairs in general conducted justly, but he enjoyed the services of an army that really was an army. Generals and captains who crossed the sea to take service under him as mercenaries knew that to do Cyrus good service paid better than any monthly wage. Indeed, whenever anyone carried out effectively a job which he had assigned, he never allowed his good work to go unrewarded. Consequently it was said that Cyrus got the best officers for any kind of job.

When he saw that a man was a capable administrator, acting on just principles, improving the land under his control and making it bring in profit, he never took his post away from him, but always gave him additional responsibility. The result was that his administrators did their work cheerfully and made money confidently. Cyrus was the last person whom they kept in the dark about their possessions, since he showed no envy for those who became rich openly, but, on the contrary, tried to make use of the wealth of people who attempted to conceal what they had.

Everyone agrees that he was absolutely remarkable for doing services to those whom he made friends of and knew to be true to him and considered able to help him in doing whatever job was on hand. He thought that the reason why he needed friends was to have people to help him, and he applied exactly the same principle to others, trying to be of the utmost service to his friends whenever he knew that any of them wanted anything. I suppose that he received more presents than any other single individual, and this for a variety of reasons. But more than anyone else he shared. them with his friends, always considering what each individual was like and what, to his knowledge, he needed most. When people sent him fine things to wear, either armour or beautiful clothes, they say that the remark he made about these was that he could not possibly wear all this finery on his own body, but he thought the finest thing for a man was that his friends should be well turned out. There is, no doubt, nothing surprising in the fact that he surpassed his friends in doing them great services, since he had the greater power to do so. What seems to me more admirable than this is the fact that he outdid them in ordinary consideration and in the anxiety to give pleasure. Often, when he had had a particularly good wine, he used to send jars half full of it to his friends with the message: 'Cyrus has not for a long time come

across a better wine than this; so he has sent some to you and wants you to finish it up today with those whom you love best.' Often too he used to send helpings of goose and halves of loaves and such things, telling the bearer to say when he presented them 'Cyrus enjoyed this; so he wants you to taste it too.' When there was a scarcity of fodder,—though he himself, because of the number of his servants and his own wise provision, was able to get hold of it,—he used to send round to his friends and tell them to give the fodder he sent to the horses they rode themselves, so that horses which carried his friends should not go hungry.

Whenever he went on an official journey, and was likely to be seen by great numbers of people, he used to call his friends to him and engage them in serious conversation, so that he might show what men he honoured. My own opinion therefore, based on what I have heard, is that there has never been anyone, Greek or foreigner, more generally beloved. And an additional proof of this is in the fact that, although Cyrus was a subject, no one deserted him and went over to the King,—except that Orontas tried to do so; but in his case he soon found that the man whom he thought reliable was more of a friend to Cyrus than to him. On the other hand there were many who left the King and came over to Cyrus, when war broke out between the two, and these also were people who had been particularly favoured by the King; but they came to the conclusion that if they did well under Cyrus their services would be better rewarded than they would be by the King. What happened at the time of his death is also a strong proof not only of his own courage but of his ability to pick out accurately people who were reliable, devoted and steadfast. For when he died every one of his friends and table-companions died fighting for him, except Ariaeus, who had been posted on the left wing in command of the cavalry. When Ariaeus heard that Cyrus had fallen, he and the whole army which he led took to flight.

Questions

(1) To what formative influences of Cyrus' youth does Xenophon attach the greatest importance?

(2) In what ways did Cyrus work to build and maintain the trust of others?

(3) What was the Emperor's attitude towards the acquisition of wealth?

(4) How did the circumstances of Cyrus' death bear witness to certain of his abilities?

5–6

Empires and military glory: Herodotus relates the story of Thermopylae.

Imperialism often goes hand-in-hand with a tradition of martial heroism and a glorification of wartime exploits. In rationalizing their future imperial aspirations, the Greek city-states would often hark back to the deeds of valour during the Persian Wars (490–479 B.C.E.), as in this description of the Spartan stand at the pass of Thermopylae by the historian Herodotus.

Source: Bernard Knox, ed.. *The Norton Book of Classical Literature (N.Y.: W.W. Norton, 1993), p. 288–293.*

The Persian army was now close to the pass, and the Greeks, suddenly doubting their power to resist, held a conference to consider the advisability of retreat. It was proposed by the Peloponnesians generally that the army should fall back upon the Peloponnese and hold the Isthmus; but when the Phocians and Locrians expressed their indignation at that suggestion, Leonidas gave his voice for staying where they were and sending, at the same time, an appeal for reinforcements to the various states of the confederacy, as their numbers were inadequate to cope with the Persians.

During the conference Xerxes sent a man on horseback to ascertain the strength of the Greek force and to observe what the troops were doing. He had heard before he left Thessaly that a small force was concentrated here, led by the Lacedaemonians under Leonidas of the house of Heracles. The Persian rider approached the camp and took a thorough survey of all he could see—which was not, however, the whole Greek army; for the men on the further side of the wall which, after its reconstruction, was now guarded, were out of sight. He did, nonetheless, carefully observe the troops who were stationed on the outside of the wall. At that moment these happened to be the Spartans, and some of them were stripped for exercise, while others were combing their hair. The Persian spy watched them in astonishment; nevertheless he made sure of their numbers, and of everything else he needed to know, as accurately as he could, and then rode quietly off. No one attempted to catch him, or took the least notice of him.

Back in his own camp he told Xerxes what he had seen. Xerxes was bewildered; the truth, namely that the Spartans were preparing themselves to kill and to be killed according to their strength, was beyond his comprehension, and what they were doing seemed to him merely absurd. Accordingly he sent for Demaratus, the son of Ariston, who had come with the army, and questioned him about the spy's report, in the hope of finding out what the unaccountable behaviour of the Spartans might mean. "Once before," Demaratus said, "when we began our march against Greece, you heard me speak of these men. I told you then how I saw this enterprise would turn out, and you laughed at me. I strive for nothing, my lord, more earnestly than to observe the truth in your presence; so hear me once more. These men have come to fight us for possession of the pass, and for that struggle they are preparing. It is the common practice of the Spartans to pay careful attention to their hair when they are about to risk their lives. But I assure you that if you can defeat these men and the rest of the Spartans who are still at home, there is no other people in the world who will dare to stand firm or lift a hand against you. You have now to deal with the finest kingdom in Greece, and with the bravest men."

Xerxes, unable to believe what Demaratus said, asked further how it was possible that so small a force could fight with his army. ""My lord," Demaratus replied, "treat me as a liar, if what I have foretold does not take place." But still Xerxes was unconvinced.

For four days Xerxes waited, in constant expectation that the Greeks would make good their escape; then, on the fifth, when still they had made no move and their continued presence seemed mere impudent and reckless folly, he was seized with rage and sent forward the Medes and Cissians with orders to take them alive and bring them into his presence. The Medes charged, and in the struggle which ensued many fell; but others took their places, and in spite of terrible losses refused to be beaten off. They made it plain enough to anyone, and not least to the king himself, that he had in his army many men, indeed, but few soldiers. All day the battle continued; the Medes, after their rough handling, were at length withdrawn and their place was taken by Hydarnes and his picked Persian troops—the King's Immortals—who advanced to the attack in full confidence of bringing the business to a quick and easy end. But, once engaged, they were no more successful than the Medes had been; all went as before, the two armies fighting in a confined space, the Persians using shorter spears than the Greeks and having no advantage from their numbers.

On the Spartan side it was a memorable fight; they were men who understood war pitted against an inexperienced enemy, and amongst the feints they employed was to turn their backs in a body and pretend to be retreating in confusion, whereupon the enemy would come on with a great clatter and roar, supposing the battle won; but the Spartans, just as the Persians were on them, would wheel and face them and inflict in the new struggle innumerable casualties. The Spartans had their losses too, but not many. At last the Persians, finding that their assaults upon the pass, whether by divisions or by any other way they could think of, were all useless, broke off the engagement and withdrew. Xerxes was watching the battle from where he sat; and it is said that in the course of the attacks three times, in terror for his army, he leapt to his feet.

Next day the fighting began again, but with no better success for the Persians, who renewed their onslaught in the hope that the Greeks, being so few in number, might be badly enough disabled by wounds to prevent further resistance. But the Greeks never slackened; their troops were ordered in divisions corresponding to the states from which they came, and each division took its turn in the line except the Phocian, which had been posted to guard the track over the mountains. So when the Persians found that things were no better for them than on the previous day, they once more withdrew.

How to deal with the situation Xerxes had no idea; but while he was still wondering what his next move should be, a man from Malis got himself admitted to his presence. This was Ephialtes, the son of Eurydemus, and he had come, in hope of a rich reward, to tell the king about the track which led over the hills to Thermopylae—and the information he gave was to prove the death of the Greeks who held the pass.

Later on, Ephialtes, in fear of the Spartans, fled to Thessaly, and during his exile there a price was put upon his head at an assembly of the Amphictyons at Pylae. Some time afterwards he returned to Anticyra, where he was killed by Athenades of Trachis. In point of fact, Athenades killed him not for his treachery but for another reason, which I will explain further on; but the Spartans honoured him nonetheless on that account. According to another story, which I do not at all believe, it was Onetes, the son of Phanagoras, a native of Carystus, and Corydallus of Anticyra who spoke to Xerxes and showed the Persians the way round by the mountain track; but one may judge which account is the true one, first by the fact that the Amphictyons, who must surely have known everything about it, set a price not upon Onetes and Corydallus but upon Ephialtes of Trachis, and, secondly, by the fact that there is no doubt that the accusation of treachery was the reason for Ephialtes' flight. Certainly Onetes, even though he was not a native of Malis, might have known about the track, if he had spent much time in the neighbourhood—but it was Ephialtes, and no one else, who showed the Persians the way, and I leave his name on record as the guilty one.

Xerxes found Ephialtes' offer most satisfactory. He was delighted with it, and promptly gave orders to Hydarnes to carry out the movement with the troops under his command. They left camp about the time the lamps are lit.

The track was originally discovered by the Malians of the neighbourhood; they afterwards used it to help the Thessalians, taking them over to attack Phocis at the time when the Phocians were protected from invasion by the wall which they had built across the pass. That was a long time ago, and no good ever came of it since. The track begins at the Asopus, the stream which flows through the narrow gorge, and, running along the ridge of the mountain—which, like the track itself, is called Anopaea—ends at Alpenus, the first Locrian settlement as one comes from Malis, near the rock known as Black-Buttocks' Stone and the seats of the Cercopes. Just here is the narrowest part of the pass.

This, then, was the mountain track which the Persians took, after crossing the Asopus. They marched throughout the night, with the mountains of Oeta on their right hand and those of Trachis on their left. By early dawn they were at the summit of the ridge, near the spot where the Phocians, as I mentioned before, stood on guard with a thousand men, to watch the track and protect their country. The Phocians were ready enough to undertake this service, and had, indeed, volunteered for it to Leonidas, knowing that the pass at Thermopylae was held as I have already described.

The ascent of the Persians had been concealed by the oak-woods which cover this part of the mountain range, and it was only when they reached the top that the Phocians became aware of their approach; for there was not a breath of wind, and the marching feet made a loud swishing and rustling in the fallen leaves. Leaping to their feet, the Phocians were in the act of arming themselves when the enemy was upon them. The Persians were surprised at the sight of troops preparing to resist; they had not expected any opposition—yet here was a body of men barring their way. Hydarnes asked Ephialtes who they were, for his first uncomfortable thought was that they might be Spartans; but on learning the truth he prepared to engage them. The Persian arrows flew thick and fast, and the Phocians, supposing themselves to be the main object of the attack, hurriedly withdrew to the highest point of the mountain, where they made ready to face destruction. The Persians, however, with Ephialtes and Hydarnes paid no further attention to them, but passed on along the descending track with all possible speed.

The Greeks at Thermopylae had their first warning of the death that was coming with the dawn from the seer Megistias, who read their doom in the victims of sacrifice; deserters, too, had begun to come in during the night with news of the Persian movement to take them in the rear, and, just as day was breaking, the look-out men had come running from the hills. At once a conference was held, and opinions were divided, some urging that they must on no account abandon their post, others taking the opposite view. The result was that the army split: some dispersed, the men returning to their various homes, and others made ready to stand by Leonidas.

There is another account which says that Leonidas himself dismissed a part of his force, to spare their lives, but thought it unbecoming for the Spartans under his command to desert the post which they had originally come to guard. I myself am inclined to think that he dismissed them when he realized that they had no heart for the fight and were unwilling to take their share of the danger; at the same time honour forbade that he himself should go. And indeed by remaining at his post he left a great name behind him, and Sparta did not lose her prosperity, as might otherwise have happened; for right at the outset of the war the Spartans had been told by the oracle, when they asked for advice, that either their city must be laid waste by the foreigner or one of their kings be killed. The prophecy was in hexameter verse and ran as follows:

Hear your fate, O dwellers in Sparta of the
  wide spaces;
Either your famed, great town must be sacked by
  Perseus' sons,
Or, if that be not, the whole land of Lacedaemon
Shall mourn the death of a king of the house
  of Heracles,
For not the strength of lions or of bulls shall
  hold him,
Strength against strength; for he has the power
  of Zeus,
And will not be checked till one of these two he has
  consumed.

I believe it was the thought of this oracle, combined with his wish to lay up for the Spartans a treasure of fame in which no other city should share, that made Leonidas dismiss those troops; I do not think that they deserted, or went off without orders, because of a difference of opinion. Moreover, I am strongly supported in this view by the case of Megistias, the seer from Acarnania who foretold the coming doom by his inspection of the sacrificial victims: this man—he was said to be descended from Melampus—was with the army, and quite plainly received orders from Leonidas to quit Thermopylae, to save him from sharing the army's fate. But he refused to go, sending away instead an only son of his, who was serving with the forces.

Thus it was that the confederate troops, by Leonidas' orders, abandoned their posts and left the pass, all except the Thespians and the Thebans who remained with the Spartans. The Thebans were detained by Leonidas as hostages very much against their will—unlike the loyal Thespians, who refused to desert Leonidas and his men, but stayed, and died with them. They were under the command of Demophilus the son of Diadromes.

In the morning Xerxes poured a libation to the rising sun, and then waited till about the time of the filling of the market-place, when he began to move forward. This was according to Ephialtes' instructions, for the way down from the ridge is much shorter and more direct than the long and circuitous ascent. As the Persian army advanced to the assault, the Greeks under Leonidas, knowing that the fight would be their last, pressed forward into the wider part of the pass much further than they had done before; in the previous days' fighting they had been holding the wall and making sorties from behind it into the narrow neck, but now they left the confined space and battle was joined on more open ground. Many of the invaders fell; behind them the company commanders plied their whips, driving the men remorselessly on. Many fell into the sea and were drowned, and still more were trampled to death by their friends. No one could count the number of the dead. The Greeks, who knew that the enemy were on their way round by the mountain track and that death was inevitable, fought with reckless desperation, exerting every ounce of strength that was in them against the invader. By the time most of their spears were broken, and they were killing Persians with their swords.

In the course of that fight Leonidas fell, having fought like a man indeed. Many distinguished Spartans were killed at his side—their names, like the names of all the three hundred, I have made myself acquainted with, because they deserve to be remembered. Amongst the Persian dead, too, were many men of high distinction—for instance, two brothers of Xerxes, Habrocomes and Hyperanthes, both of them sons of Darius by Artanes' daughter Phratagune.

There was a bitter struggle over the body of Leonidas; four times the Greeks drove the enemy off, and at last by their valour succeeded in dragging it away. So it went on, until the fresh troops with Ephialtes were close at hand; and then, when the Greeks knew that they had come, the character of the fighting changed. They withdrew again into the narrow neck of the pass, behind the walls, and took up a position in a single compact body—all except the Thebans—on the little hill at the entrance to the pass, where the stone lion in memory of Leonidas stands today. Here they resisted to the last, with their swords, if they had them, and, if not, with their hands and teeth, until the Persians, coming on from the front over the ruins of the wall and closing in from behind, finally overwhelmed them.

Translated by Aubrey de Sélincourt

Questions
(1) What was the cause for King Xerxes' amazement before the battle took place at Thermopylae?
(2) What role was played by Ephialtes?
(3) What did the prophecy of the oracle say about Sparta?
(4) What was behind Leonidas' decision to fight to the end?

5–7

Thucydides writes concerning the negative by-products of Imperialism.

The imperial pretentions of Athens were a major factor in the outbreak of the Peloponnesian War (431–404 B.C.E.) where Greek fought Greek, and Athens' ambitions were brought to naught. Thucydides (c. 455–c. 400 B.C.E.), himself a combatant, wrote a lucid and largely impartial account of the conflict between Athens and Sparta, and their respective allies. In his account, no detail was spared in describing the miseries brought on by a great epidemic and horrific rioting in the city of Corcyra.

Source: Thucydides, "The Peloponnesian War," Rex Warner, ed. (Hammondsworth, England; Penguin, 1956), pp. 123–127, 207–211.

IN this way the public funeral was conducted in the winter that came at the end of the first year of the war. At the beginning of the following summer the Peloponnesians and their allies, with two-thirds of their total forces as before, invaded Attica, again under the command of the Spartan King Archidamus, the son of Zeuxidamus. Taking up their positions, they set about the devastation of the country.

They had not been many days in Attica before the plague first broke out among the Athenians. Previously attacks of the plague had been reported in from many other places in the neighbourhood of Lemnos and elsewhere, but there was no record of the disease being so virulent anywhere else or causing so many deaths as it did in Athens. At the beginning the doctors were quite incapable of treating the disease because of their ignorance of the right methods. In fact mortality among the doctors was the highest of all, since they came more frequently in contact with the sick. Nor was any other human art or science of any help at all. Equally useless were prayers made in the temples, consultation of oracles, and so forth; indeed, in the end people were so overcome by their sufferings that they paid no further attention to such things.

The plague originated, so they say, in Ethiopia in upper Egypt, and spread from there into Egypt itself and Libya and much of the territory of the King of Persia. In the city of Athens it appeared suddenly, and the first cases were among the population of Piraeus, so that it was supposed by them that the Peloponnesians had poisoned the reservoirs.[*] Later, however, it appeared also in the upper city, and by this time the deaths were greatly increasing in number. As to the question of how it could first have come about or what causes can be found adequate to explain its powerful effect on nature, I must leave that to be considered by other writers, with or without medical experience. I myself shall merely describe what it was like, and set down the symptoms, knowledge of which will enable it to be recognized, if should ever break out again. I had the disease myself and saw others suffering from it.

That year, as is generally admitted, was particularly free from other kinds of illness, though those who did have any illness previously all caught the plague in

There were no wells at that time in Piraeus.

the end. In other cases, however, there seemed to be no reason for the attacks. People in perfect health suddenly began to have burning feelings in the head; their eyes became red and inflamed; inside their mouths there was bleeding from the throat and tongue, and the breath became unnatural and unpleasant. The next symptoms were sneezing and hoarseness of voice, and before long the pain settled on the chest and was accompanied by coughing. Next the stomach was affected with stomach-aches and with vomitings of every kind of bile that has been given a name by the medical profession, all this being accompanied by great pain and difficulty. In most cases there were attacks of ineffectual retching, producing violent spasms; this sometimes ended with this stage of the disease, but sometimes continued long afterwards. Externally the body was not very hot to the touch, nor was there any pallor: the skin was rather reddish and livid, breaking out into small pustules and ulcers. But inside there was a feeling of burning, so that people could not bear the touch even of the lightest linen clothing, but wanted to be completely naked, and indeed most of all would have liked to plunge into cold water. Many of the sick who were uncared for actually did so, plunging into the water-tanks in an effort to relieve a thirst which was unquenchable; for it was just the same with them whether they drink much or little. Then all the time they were afflicted with insomnia and the desperate feeling of not being able to keep still.

In the period when the disease was at its height, the body, so far from wasting away, showed surprising powers of resistance to all the agony, so that there was still some strength left on the seventh or eighth day, which was the time when, in most cases, death came from the internal fever. But if people survived this critical period, then the disease descended to the bowels, producing violent ulceration and uncontrollable diarrhoea, so that most of them died later as a result of the weakness caused by this. For the disease, first settling in the head, went on to affect every part of the body in turn, and even when people escaped its worst effects, it still left its traces on them by fastening upon the extremities of the body. It affected the genitals, the fingers, and the toes, and many of those who recovered lost the use of these members; some, too, went blind.

There were some also who, when they first began to get better, suffered from a total loss of memory, not knowing who they were themselves and being unable to recognize their friends.

Words indeed fail one when one tries to give a general picture of this disease; and as for the sufferings of individuals, they seemed almost beyond the capacity of human nature to endure. Here in particular is a point where this plague showed itself to be something quite different from ordinary diseases: though there were many dead bodies lying about unburied, the birds and animals that eat human flesh either did not come near them or, if they did taste the flesh, died of it afterwards. Evidence for this may be found in the fact that there was a complete disappearance of all birds of prey: they were not to be seen either round the bodies or anywhere else. But dogs, being domestic animals, provided the best opportunity of observing this effect of the plague.

These, then, were the general features of the disease, though I have omitted all kinds of peculiarities which occurred in various individual cases. Meanwhile, during all this time there was no serious outbreak of any of the usual kinds of illness; if any such cases did occur, they ended in the plague. Some died in neglect, some in spite of every possible care being taken of them. As for a recognized method of treatment, it would be true to say that no such thing existed: what did good in some cases did harm in others. Those with naturally strong constitutions were no better able than the weak to resist the disease, which carried away all alike, even those who were treated and dieted with the greatest care. The most terrible thing of all was the despair into which people fell when they realized that they had caught the plague; for they would immediately adopt an attitude of utter hopelessness, and, by giving in this way, would lose their powers of resistance. Terrible, too, was the sight of people dying like sheep through having caught the disease as a result of nursing others. This indeed caused more deaths than anything else. For when people were afraid to visit the sick, then they died with no one to look after them; indeed, there were many houses in which all the inhabitants perished through lack of any attention. When, on the other hand, they did visit the sick, they lost their own lives, and this was particularly true of those who made it a point of honour to act properly. Such people felt ashamed think of their own safety and went into their friends' houses at times when even the members of the household were so overwhelmed by the weight of their calamities that they had actually given up the usual practice of making laments for the dead. Yet still the ones who felt most pity for the sick and the dying were those who had had the plague themselves and had recovered from it. They knew what it was like and at the same time felt themselves to be safe, for no one caught the disease twice, or, if he did, the second attack was never fatal. Such

people were congratulated on all sides, and they themselves were elated at the time of their recovery that they fondly imagined that they could never die of any other disease in the future.

A factor which made matters much worse than they were already was the removal of people from the country into the city, and this particularly affected the incomers. There were no houses for them, and, living as they did during the hot season in badly ventilated huts, they died like flies. The bodies of the dying were heaped one on top of the other, and half-dead creatures could be seen staggering about the streets or flocking around the fountains in their desire for water. The temples in which they took up their quarters were full of the dead bodies of people who had died inside them. For the catastrophe was so overwhelming that men, not knowing what would happen next to them, became indifferent to every rule of religion or of law. All the funeral ceremonies which used to be observed were now disorganized, and they buried the dead as best they could. Many people lacking the necessary means of burial because so many deaths had already occurred in their households, adopted the most shameless methods, They would arrive first at a funeral pyre that had been made by others, put their own dead upon it and set it alight; or, finding another pyre burning, they would throw the corpse that they were carrying on top of the other one and go away.

In other respects also Athens owed to the plague the beginnings of a state of unprecedented lawlessness. Seeing how quick and abrupt were the changes of fortune which came to the rich who suddenly died and to those who had previously been penniless but now inherited their wealth, people now began openly to venture on acts of self-indulgence which before then they used to keep dark. Thus they resolved to spend their money quickly and to spend it on pleasure, since money and life alike seemed equally ephemeral. As for what is called honour, no one showed himself willing to abide by its laws, so doubtful was it whether one would survive to enjoy the name for it. It was generally agreed that what was both honourable and valuable was the pleasure of the moment and everything that might conceivably contribute to that pleasure. No fear of god or law of man had a restraining influence. As for the gods, it seemed to be same thing whether one worshipped them or not, when one saw the good and the bad dying indiscriminately. As for offences against human law, no one expected to live long enough to be brought to trial and punished: everyone felt that already a far heavier sentence had been passed on him, and was hanging over him, and that before the time for its execution arrived it was only natural to get some pleasure out of life.

This, then, was the calamity which fell upon Athens, and the times were hard indeed, with men dying inside the city and the land outside being laid waste. At this time of distress people naturally recalled old oracles, and among them was a verse which the old men claimed had been delivered in the past and which said:

> War with the Dorians comes, and a death will come
> at the same time.

There had been a controversy as to whether the word in this ancient verse was 'dearth' rather than 'death'; but in the present state of affairs the view that the word was 'death' naturally prevailed; it was a case of people adapting their memories to suit their sufferings. Certainly I think that if there is ever another war with the Dorians after this one, and if a dearth results from it, then in all probability people will quote the other version.

Then also the oracle that was given to the Spartans was remembered by those who knew of it: that when they inquired from the god whether they should go to war, they received the reply that, if they fought with all their might, victory would be theirs and that the god himself would be on their side. What was actually happening seemed to fit in well with the words of this oracle; certainly the plague broke out directly after the Peloponnesian invasion, and never affected the Peloponnese at all, or not seriously; its full force was felt at Athens, and, after Athens, in the most densely populated of the other towns.

***

The Corcyraeans were now in a state of the utmost confusion, alarmed both at what was happening inside their city and at the approach of the enemy fleet. They immediately got ready sixty ships and sent them straight out against the enemy, as soon as they were manned, neglecting the advice of the Athenians, which was to let them sail out first and then come out in support of them later with all their ships together. As the Corcyraean ships approached the enemy in this disorganized way, two of them immediately deserted, in other ships the crews were fighting among themselves, and no sort of order was kept in anything. The Peloponnesians observed the confusion in which they were, set aside twenty of their ships to meet the Corcyraeans, and put all the rest of their fleet against the twelve Athenian ships, among which were the *Salaminia* and the *Paralus*.

The Corcyraeans, in their part of the battle, were soon in difficulties, since they were making their attacks inefficiently and in small detachments. The Athenians, afraid of the numbers of the enemy and of the risk of encirclement, did not commit themselves to a general engagement and did not even charge the fleet opposed to them in the centre. Instead they fell upon its wing, where they sank one ship. After this the Peloponnesians formed their ships up in a circle and the Athenians rowed round them, trying to create confusion among them. Seeing this, and fearing a repetition of what had happened at Naupactus, the other Peloponnesians, who had been dealing with the Corcyraeans, came up in support, and then the whole Peloponnesian fleet together bore down on the Athenians, who now began to back water and to retire in front of them. They carried out the manoeuvre in their own good time, wishing to give the Corcyraean ships the fullest opportunity to escape first by keeping the enemy facing them in battle formation. So the fighting went, and it continued until sunset.

The Corcyraeans now feared that the enemy would follow up the victory by sailing against the city, or rescuing the men from the island, or by taking some other bold step. So they brought the men back again from the island to the temple of Hera, and put the defences of the city in order. The Peloponnesians, however, in spite of their victory on the sea, did not risk sailing against the town, but sailed back to their original station on the mainland, taking with them the thirteen Corcyraean ships which they had captured. Nor were they any the more disposed to sail against the city on the next day, although the Corcyraeans were thoroughly disorganized and in a state of panic, and although Brasidas is said to have urged Alcidas to do so. Brasidas, however, was overruled, and the Peloponnesians merely made a landing on the headland of Leukimme and laid waste the country.

Meanwhile the democratic party in Corcyra were still terrified at the prospect of an attack by the enemy fleet. They entered into negotiations with the suppliants and with others of their party with a view to saving the city, and they persuaded some of them to go on board the ships. Thus they succeeded in manning thirty ships to meet the expected attack.

The Peloponnesians, however, having spent the time up till midday in laying waste the land, sailed away again, and about nightfall were informed by fire signals that a fleet of sixty Athenian ships was approaching from the direction of Leucas. This fleet, which was under the command of Eurymedon, the son of Thucles, had been sent out by the Athenians when they heard that the revolution had broken out and that Alcidas's fleet was about to sail for Corcyra. Thus the Peloponnesians set off by night, at once and in a hurry, for home, sailing close in to the shore. They hauled their ships across the isthmus of Leucas, so as to avoid being seen rounding the point, and so they got away.

When the Corcyraeans realized that the Athenian fleet was approaching and that their enemies had gone, they brought the Messenians, who had previously been outside the walls, into the city and ordered the fleet which they had manned to sail round into the Hyllaic harbour. While it was doing so, they seized upon all their enemies whom they could find and put them to death. They then dealt with those whom they had persuaded to go on board the ships, killing them as they landed. Next they went to the temple of Hera and persuaded about fifty of the suppliants there to submit to a trial. They then condemned every one of them to death. Seeing what was happening, most of the other suppliants, who had refused to be tried, killed each other there in the temple; some hanged themselves on the trees, and others found various other means of committing suicide. During the seven days that Eurymedon stayed there with his sixty ships, the Corcyraeans continued to massacre those of their own citizens whom they considered to be their enemies. Their victims were accused of conspiring to overthrow the democracy, but in fact men were often killed on grounds of personal hatred or else by their debtors because of the money that they owed. There was death in every shape and form. And, as usually happens in such situations, people went to every extreme and beyond it. There were fathers who killed their sons; men were dragged from the temples or butchered on the very altars; some were actually walled up in the temple of Dionysus and died there.

So savage was the progress of this revolution, and it seemed all the more so became it was one of the first which had broken out. Later, of course, practically the whole of the Hellenic world was convulsed, with rival parties in every state—democratic leaders trying to bring in the Athenians, and oligarchs trying to bring in the Spartans. In peacetime there would have been no excuse and no desire for calling them but in time of war, when each party could always count upon an alliance which would do harm to its opponents and at the same time strengthen its own position, it became a natural thing for anyone who wanted a change of government to call in help from outside. In the various cities these revolutions were the cause of many calamities—as happens and always will happen while human nature is what it is, though there may be different degrees of savagery, and, as different circumstances arise, the general rules will admit of some variety. In times of peace and prosperity cities and individuals alike follow higher standards, because they are not forced into a situation where they have to do what they do not want to do. But war is a stern teacher; in depriving them of the power of easily satisfying their daily wants, it brings most people's minds down to the level of their actual circumstances.

So revolutions broke out in city after city, and in places where the revolutions occurred late the knowledge of what had happened previously in other places caused still new extravagances of revolutionary zeal, expressed by an elaboration in the methods of seizing power and by unheard-of atrocities in revenge. To fit in with the change of events, words, too, had to change their usual meanings. What used to be described as a thoughtless act of aggression was now regarded as the courage one would expect to find in a party member; to

think of the future and wait was merely another way of saying one was a coward; any idea of moderation was just an attempt to disguise one's unmanly character; ability to understand a question from all sides meant that one was totally unfitted for action. Fanatical enthusiasm was the mark of a real man, and to plot against an enemy behind his back was perfectly legitimate self-defence. Anyone who held violent opinions could always be trusted, and anyone who objected to them became a suspect. To plot successfully was a sign of intelligence, but it was still cleverer to see that a plot was hatching. If one attempted to provide against having to do either, one was disrupting the unity of the party and acting out of fear of the opposition. In short, it was equally praiseworthy to get one's blow in first against someone who was going to do wrong, and to denounce someone who had no intention of doing any wrong at all. Family relations were a weaker tie than party membership, since party members were more ready to go to any extreme for any reason whatever. These parties were not formed to enjoy the benefits of the established laws, but to acquire power by overthrowing the existing regime; and the members of these parties felt confidence in each other not because of any fellowship in a religious communion, but because they were partners in crime. If an opponent made reasonable speech, the party in power, so far from giving it a generous reception, took every precaution to see that it had no practical effect.

Revenge was more important than self-preservation. And if pacts of mutual security were made, they were entered into by the two parties only in order to meet some temporary difficulty, and remained in force only so long as there was no other weapon available. When the chance came, the one who first seized it boldly, catching his enemy off his guard, enjoyed a revenge that was all the sweeter from having been taken, not openly, but because of a breach of faith. It was safer that way, it was considered, and at the same time a victory won by treachery gave one a title for superior intelligence. And indeed most people are more ready to call villainy cleverness than simple-mindedness honesty. They are proud of the first quality and ashamed of the second.

Love of power, operating through greed and through personal ambition, was the cause of all these evils. To this must be added the violent fanaticism which came into play once the struggle had broken out. Leaders of parties in the cities had programmes which appeared admirable—on one side political equality for the masses, on the other the safe and sound government of the aristocracy—but in professing to serve the public interest they were seeking to win the prizes for themselves. In their struggles for ascendancy nothing was barred; terrible indeed were the actions to which they committed themselves, and in taking revenge they went farther still. Here they were deterred neither by the claims of justice nor by the interests of the state; their one standard was the pleasure of their own party at that particular moment, and so, either by means of condemning their enemies on an illegal vote or by violently usurping power over them, they were always ready to satisfy the hatreds of the hour. Thus neither side had any use for conscientious motives; more interest was shown in those who could produce attractive arguments to justify some disgraceful action. As for the citizens who held moderate views, they were destroyed by both the extreme parties, either for not taking part in the struggle or in envy at the possibility that they might survive.

As the result of these revolutions, there was a general deterioration of character throughout the Greek world. The simple way of looking at things, which is so much the mark of a noble nature, was regarded as a ridiculous quality and soon ceased to exist. Society had become divided into two ideologically hostile camps, and each side viewed the other with suspicion. As for ending this state of affairs, no guarantee could be given that would be trusted, no oath sworn that people would fear to break; everyone had come to the conclusion that it was hopeless to expect a permanent settlement and so, instead of being able to feel confident in others, they devoted their energies to providing against being injured themselves. As a rule those who were least remarkable for intelligence showed the greater powers of survival. Such people recognized their own deficiencies and the superior intelligence of their opponents; fearing that they might lose a debate or find themselves out-manoeuvred in intrigue by their quick-witted enemies, they boldly launched straight into action; while their opponents, over-confident in the belief that they would see what was happening in advance, and not thinking it necessary to seize by force what they could secure by policy, were the more easily destroyed because they were off their guard.

Certainly it was in Corcyra that there occurred the first examples of the breakdown of law and order. There was the revenge taken in their hour of triumph by those who had in the past been arrogantly oppressed instead of wisely governed; there were the wicked resolutions taken by those who, particularly under the pressure of misfortune, wished to escape from their usual poverty and coveted the property of their neighbours; there were the savage and pitiless actions into which men were carried not so much for the sake of gain as because they were swept away into an internecine struggle by their ungovernable passions. Then, with the ordinary conventions of civilized life thrown into confusion, human nature, always ready to offend even where laws exist, showed itself proudly in its true colours, as something incapable of controlling passion, insubordinate to the idea of justice, the enemy to anything superior to itself; for, if it had not been for the pernicious power of envy, men would not so have exalted vengeance above innocence and profit above justice. Indeed, it is true that in these acts of revenge on others men take it upon themselves to begin the process of repealing those general laws of humanity which are there to give a hope of salvation to all who are in distress, instead of leaving those laws in existence, remembering that there may come a time when they, too, will be in danger and will need their protection.

Questions

(1) Where does Thucydides surmise the epidemic originated, and what group experienced the highest mortality rate?

(2) What happened to those who were in the Temple of Hera at Corcyra?

(3) What murderous motives does Thucydides believe to have touched off the revolution?

(4) Describe and characterize the breakdown/deterioration that occurred, according to Thucydides, in the wake of the Corcyrean revolution.

5–8

The first Philippic: a great orator warns of Macedonian imperialism.

Philip II, King of Macedonia was at first not taken seriously by his Greek adversaries, who considered him uncouth and uncultured and labeled him "Philip the Barbarian." However, the Athenian Demosthenes, arguably the most persuasive speaker of his day, was well aware of the danger, and the growth of Macedonian power confirmed these fears. In a series of impassioned speeches known as the "Philippics," Demosthenes tried to rally his countrymen, as it later proved without avail, to meet the challenge.

Source: J. R. Ellis & R. D. Milne, eds., The Spectre of Philip: Demosthenes' first Phillipic (Sydney, Australia: Sydney University Press, 1970), pp. 16–19; 30–33.

Men of Athens, if some new topic were being proposed for discussion, I would have held back until most of the regular speakers had disclosed their views, and then, if I were satisfied with anything they said, I would have held my peace, and if I were not satisfied, I would have tried to put forward my own point of view. But, since it so happens that the present debate is concerned with matters that these regular speakers have discussed many times, I think that I may reasonably be excused for standing up to speak first of all; for had these men given the requisite advice in the past there would be no need for your deliberations now.

Firstly then, men of Athens, you must not be despondent at the present state of affairs even though they seem to be in a pretty bad way. For the aspect of the situation in the past that is worst is, in fact, the aspect that holds out most hope for the future. And what is this? It is the fact that your affairs are in an evil plight *because* you do none of the things that duty imposes on you; whereas if you were doing all you ought and they were still in such a state, there would be no hope of their improving. Again, it must be borne in mind, both by those hearing the story from others and by those having first-hand knowledge as they recall the occasion, how strong and powerful the Spartans were only a short time ago, yet how nobly and befittingly you did nothing unworthy of the city, but undertook, in defence of the cause of justice, the war against them. And why do I say this? So that you may look and see that when you are on your guard there is nothing that can alarm you, but when you let things slide nothing is the way you would wish it to be. Take as an example to prove this the might of Sparta at that time and the wanton violence of Philip at the present; the former you overcame because you gave your attention to affairs of state, while the latter is throwing us into confusion because we have no concern for the things that matter.

And if anyone thinks that Philip is a tough opponent, as he considers the size of Philip's available resources and the fact that our city has lost all her territories, then he thinks rightly, though he should consider this: that there was a time when we had Pydna, Potidaea and Methone, with all the surrounding area, well disposed towards us, and that many of the tribes that are now with him were then free and autonomous and preferred to be on good terms with us rather than him. If Philip at that time had formed the opinion that waging war on Athens was a hard and difficult task, since the city possessed so many fortresses in his own territory and he himself was without allies, he would never have done any of the things he has now achieved, nor would he have won such great power. But, men of Athens, Philip saw full well that all these places are the prizes of war, ready for the taking, and that the possessions of those who are absent naturally belong to those on the spot, the possessions of the neglectful to those who will endure toil and danger. This is his attitude and because of it he has sub-

dued and possesses all the places in question. Some he now holds by right of conquest, others he has brought into alliance and friendship; for all men are prepared to ally themselves and give attention to those whom they see are ready and willing to do what should be done. Men of Athens, if you are ready to put yourselves in such a frame of mind as this now—for, to date, you have not been—and if each one of you puts aside all his shilly-shallying and shows himself ready to act where he ought to act and where he could be of use to the city (that is, the man with money must pay the property-tax and the man of military age must go on active service); if, I say, to sum up plainly and briefly, you will agree to become your own masters and will cease, each one of you, from expecting to do nothing yourself and your neighbour to do everything on your behalf, then you will redeem what is your own, you will recover what you have let slip through your own carelessness and you will take your revenge upon Philip.

For you must not regard his present position as being invested with an eternal immutability, as though he were a god; he is hated, feared and envied, even by some of the people who now appear to be particularly well disposed towards him. And you must recognize that all the desires and emotions that other men have are present also in the people ranged on Philip's side, although they are all now repressed and have no outlet, thanks to your indolence and indifference-of which I urge you to rid yourselves immediately. Look at the situation, men of Athens, and see what a peak of insolence the fellow has reached. He gives you no choice between action and living at peace, but threatens, utters arrogant statements—so it is said—and cannot be satisfied by his conquests, but is always seeking fresh acquisitions and trying to hedge us in on all sides, while we procrastinate and sit idly by. Men of Athens, when will you do your duty? What must happen before you will do it? 'When' comes the reply, 'the need arises.' But how ought we to regard what is happening now? For my part, I think that for free men a sense of shame over the conduct of their affairs is the most compelling necessity of all. Or, tell me, are you content with going around asking one another: 'Is there any news?' Could there be any hotter news than a Macedonian beating Athenians in war and administering the affairs of the Greeks? 'Is Philip dead?' 'No, but he's ill!' What difference does it make to you? If he dies you will soon make yourselves another Philip, if this is the way you give your attention to your affairs. For Philip has not become great so much by his own strength as by our neglect. And a further point: if anything happens to Philip, if our good fortune—which has always looked after us better than we look after ourselves—should bring this about, I would have you know that if you were close at hand you could take advantage of the general confusion and handle the situation as you wish. But as you now stand, you could not take over Amphipolis even if the opportunity was offered to you, for you are far from ready for it, both in your state of preparations and in your whole outlook....

It seems to me, men of Athens, that some god, ashamed on the city's behalf at what is being done, has inspired Philip with this meddlesome activity of his. For if Philip, holding the places he has already subdued and seized, were willing to keep quiet and do no more, I think that some of you would be quite satisfied with a situation whereby we would stand convicted, as a people, of shameful conduct, of cowardice, of all that is most disgraceful. But as it is, by always making new attempts and always striving for more, he might perhaps stir you to action, if you have not completely given up the struggle. For my part, I am amazed that none of you either takes it to heart or is filled with indignation when he sees that although the war was begun with the object of punishing Philip its end is already concerned with avoiding harm at Philip's hands. And yet it is quite obvious that he will not halt his progress unless he is compelled. Shall we wait for this? Do you think that all is well if you dispatch empty triremes and send off the mere expectations that are being raised by so-and-so? Shall we not embark in our ships? Shall we not set out ourselves with at least part of our own citizen-forces now, even if we have not done so before? Shall we not sail against Philip's territory? But where, somebody asks me, shall we anchor off his coast? The war itself, men of Athens, will discover the weak point in his dispositions, if we make the attempt. But if we sit idly at home listening to the politicians abusing and blaming each other then certainly nothing will ever be done that should be done. For in my opinion, wheresoever any part of our city-even if not the whole-is dispatched in company with the forces there fights along with it the good will of Heaven and of Fortune. But whenever you send out a commander, an empty decree and expressions of hope from the speaker's platform none of the things are done that should be; instead, our enemies laugh at us while our allies stand in mortal fear of such expeditions. For it is not possible, no, quite impossible that one single man could ever achieve for you all that you want achieved. He can, however, make promises, say 'yes' and accuse this man and that man; and the result of this is the ruin of our interests. For when the commander leads miserable, unpaid mercenaries, and when there are men here who glibly give you false information on his activities, when, on the basis of the stories you hear, you pass any decrees that come into your heads, then what must we expect?

How, then, will this situation be ended? It will cease when you, men of Athens, appoint the same men as sol-diers and as witnesses what the generals do, and as judges, when they have returned home, of the generals' auditing; in this way you will not only hear about your own affairs but will also be present and see them. As things are, our affairs have reached such a shameful state that each of the commanders is put on trial for his life twice or thrice in your courts, but none of them dares engage in a struggle for life with your enemies even once; they prefer to die the death of a kidnapper or a highwayman rather than the death appropriate to a soldier. For a criminal should die as the result of a court's sentence, a general fighting the enemy. Some of us go about saying that Philip is planning with Sparta the destruction of Thebes and the dissolution of the demo-cratic states, others that he has sent envoys to the Persian king, and still others that he is fortifying cities in Illyria—each one of us goes around inventing his own story.

For my part, men of Athens, I definitely think that Philip is intoxicated with the magnitude of his achievements and has many similar aspirations revolving in his mind; for he sees that there is nobody to stop him and he is buoyed up with his successes. I do not think; however, that he has chosen to act in such a way that the most foolish of our citizens know what he intends to do-for the rumour-mongers are the most foolish of our citizens.

But if we give these tales short shrift and recognize that the fellow is an enemy, that he is depriving us of our possessions, that he has been wantonly outraging and insulting us for a long time, that all we ever expected anyone to do on our behalf has turned out to our detriment, that the future is in our own hands, that if we are not willing to fight Philip there we may perhaps be forced to fight him here—if, I say, we recognize these things then we shall have made the necessary decision and have done with useless talk. For you must not inquire what the future will be; you must fully recognize that it will be bad if you do not give it your attention and are not willing to act appropriately.

I have never chosen on other occasions to speak with a view to pleasing you unless I was fully convinced it would be of benefit, and I have now given you my opinion freely and straightforwardly, with no reservations. I could wish that, just as I know it is beneficial for you to hear the best advice, so I knew that it would also be beneficial to the men who gave it; then I should be much happier. As it is, although it is not clear what will befall me as a result of this advice, I offer it nevertheless, convinced that it is to your benefit if you heed it. May that prevail which is going to be to the advantage of all!

Questions

(1) For what does Demosthenes most criticize his fellow Athenians?

(2) What arguments does Demosthenes produce in support of his contention that Philip poses a serious threat?

(3) What solutions and course of action does Demosthenes propose?

CHAPTER 6

6–1
A hero under fire: Livy relates the trials and tribulations of Scipio Africanus.

Livy (59–17 B.C.E.) wrote the lengthiest account of the formative years of Roman civilization, the "History of Rome." Writing to please the tastes and biases of Caesar Augustus' court, Livy certainly wrote in a great deal of mythology and propaganda concerning the earliest centuries. In his account of later events, however, there is much that rings true, as in his description of the political problems faced by General Scipio Africanus, who had bested the formidable Carthaginian Hannibal at the Battle of Zama (202 B.C.E), and thus secured the Roman triumph over arch-rival Carthage in the Second Punic War.

Source: P. G. Walsh, ed., *Livy* (Warminster, England: Aris and Phillips, 1993), pp. 105–111.

On that day the accusations would have prevailed over the defence if the senators had not drawn out the dispute until a late hour. When the senate was dismissed, the general belief was that it seemed to have been on the point of refusing a triumph. But the following day relatives and friends of Gnaeus Manlius brought all their resources to bear, and in addition the authority of older members was decisive, for they argued that it was unprecedented for a commander who had vanquished the enemies of the state, completed his sphere of duty, and brought back his army, to enter the city without chariot and laurel-wreath as a private citizen deprived of glory. This impression of indignity prevailed over ill-will, and the senators in large numbers voted a triumph.

The entire mention and recollection of this dispute were subsequently overshadowed by the rise of a greater controversy, involving a greater and more celebrated man. Valerius Antias states that the two Quinti Petilii indicted Publius Scipio Africanus; individuals reacted to this according to their temperaments. Some attacked not the plebeian tribunes but the entire state for envisaging the possibility of allowing this. Their argument was that the two greatest cities of the world had been seen to show ingratitude to their leading men at virtually the same time, but that Rome's ingratitude was the greater, for when Carthage exiled Hannibal both city and leader had been conquered, whereas Rome was driving out Africanus when both were victorious. Others claimed that no one citizen should be so outstanding that he could not be subjected to interrogation under the laws; nothing was so important for the impartial application of liberty as that all most powerful men should be liable to defend themselves against indictment. Could any individual be safely entrusted with anything, let alone the direction of the state, if he were not to be accountable? Constraints applied to anyone who could not brook the equality of the law were by no means unjust. These were the issues under discussion until the day of the impeachment came. No-one

before that date, even including Scipio himself as consul or censor, was attended on his way to the forum by a greater crowd of people of every rank than was the defendant on that day. When he was ordered to plead his case, he made no mention of the charges. He embarked upon a speech about his own achievements which was so splendid that it was wholly clear that no man had ever been the subject of a better or more truthful panegyric; for he recounted those achievements with the same spirit and genius with which he had performed them, and because they were uttered in the context of his trial and not for vainglory, he did not alienate the ears of his audience.

The plebeian tribunes first resurrected ancient charges of degenerate life in the winter-quarters at Syracuse, and the disturbances associated with Pleminius at Locri, to lend credence to their immediate accusations. Then they charged the defendant with peculation on the basis of suspicions rather than proofs. They stated that his son, previously captured, had been restored without a ransom, and that Scipio had been courted by Antiochus in all other matters, as though the issue of peace and war with Rome rested in the hands of him alone. He had acted not as legate but as dictator towards the consul in his province; his only purpose in going there was so that Greece, Asia, and all the kings and nations facing eastward should recognise the reality of what Spain, Gaul, Sicily and Africa had long been persuaded: namely, that one man was the source and stay of the Roman empire, that the state which was mistress of the world lay hidden under Scipio's shadow, that his nod represented senatorial decrees and the people's commands. They hounded this man, who was untouched by ill-repute, with the spite which was their strength. The speeches were prolonged until nightfall, when the date for resumption of the trial was announced.

When that day came, the tribunes took their seats at dawn on the platform. The defendant was summoned, and he made his way to the Rostra, attended by a large retinue of friends and dependants, through the midst of the gathering. Once silence had been imposed, Scipio spoke: "On this day, plebeian tribunes and you, citizens, I joined battle with Hannibal and the Carthaginians, and fought well and successfully. Since therefore today it is right to renounce disputes and reproaches, I shall at once make my way from here to the Capitol to hail Jupiter greatest and best, Juno, Minerva and the other deities who preside over the Capitol and citadel; and I shall thank them for having granted me, both today and often on other occasions, the intention and capacity to perform public service with distinction. I invite those of you, citizens, who find it convenient, to accompany me and to pray to the gods that you may have leaders like me, with this proviso: if from when I was seventeen up to my old age you have always bestowed your distinctions earlier than my years warranted, and if my achievements have preceded the distinctions you awarded."

He mounted from the Rostra to the Capitol, and at the same moment the entire assembly moved off and followed Scipio, so that finally the clerks and messengers forsook the tribunes, and no-one was left in their company except their slave-retinue and the herald whose job from the platform was to summon the defendant. Scipio, accompanied by the Roman people, toured all the gods' temples not only on the Capitol but throughout the entire city. This day became almost more famous through the citizens' affection and appreciation of his true greatness than the day on which he rode into the city in triumph over king Syphax and the Carthaginians.

This was the last day of glory to shine on Publius Scipio. Since he foresaw following it the onset of odium and struggles with the tribunes, when a quite lengthy adjournment of the trial was announced he retired to his estate at Liternum, for he had made up his mind not to attend to plead his case. His spirit and disposition were too lofty, and he was too accustomed to a loftier fortune, to reconcile himself to undergo a trial, and to abase himself to the humiliation of joining the ranks of defendants. When the day of the resumption came and his name began to be called in his absence, Lucius Scipio entered the excuse of illness for his non-appearance. The tribunes who had indicted him refused to accept this explanation. They maintained that the reason for his non-arrival to plead his case was the same arrogance with which he had previously quitted the trial, the plebeian tribunes, and the assembly; accompanied by those whom he had deprived of the right and freedom of passing judgment on him, he had dragged them along like captives to celebrate a triumph over the Roman people, and on that day he had organized a secession from the plebeian tribunes to the Capitol. "So now you have your reward for that rash gesture. You yourselves have been abandoned by the man who led

and induced you to abandon us. Our native spirit has so declined day by day that we do not dare to dispatch men to drag this private citizen from his farmhouse to plead his case, though seventeen years ago, when he commanded an army and a fleet, we steeled ourselves to send plebeian tribunes and an aedile to Sicily to arrest him and bring him back to Rome." Lucius Scipio formally appealed to the plebeian tribunes, who decreed that if the plea of illness was being cited as excuse, their ruling was that this be accepted, and that their colleagues should adjourn the trial to a later date.

One of the plebeian tribunes at that time was Tiberius Sempronius Gracchus; personal enmity existed between him and Publius Scipio. He forbade his name to be appended to his colleagues' decree, and all were anticipating a more hostile proposal. But his resolution was that since Lucius Scipio had pleaded illness as excuse for his brother, he considered this sufficient; he would not allow Publius Scipio to be indicted before he returned to Rome, and even then, if he appealed to him, he would support him in a refusal to plead his case. Publius Scipio, by the general assent of gods and men, had attained such high distinction by his achievements and the honours conferred by the Roman people, that for him to stand indicted beneath the Rostra, and to listen to the reproaches of young men, was more dishonourable for the Roman people than for himself.

To his proposal he appended this expression of anger: "Is Scipio, the man who reduced Africa, to be set beneath your feet, tribunes? Was it for this that he scattered and routed four most illustrious Carthaginian generals and four armies in Spain? Was it for this that he captured Syphax, overthrew Hannibal, made Carthage pay tribute to us, and expelled Antiochus behind the ridges of Taurus (for Lucius Scipio admitted his brother to partnership in that glorious exploit), that he should bow the knee to the two Petilii, and that you should seek the palm of victory over Publius Africanus? Will eminent men never through their own merits, or through the honours bestowed by you, attain a stronghold affording them safety and virtual veneration, in which their old age can find rest—if not with respect, at any rate with immunity from attack?"

This resolution and the speech appended to it affected not only the other listeners but also the accusers themselves, and they said that they would weigh carefully their rights and duties. Then, following the adjournment of the people's council, a meeting of the senate began, in which profuse thanks were offered by the whole order, and especially by those of consular rank and the older senators, to Tiberius Gracchus, because he had put the public interest before private disagreements; and the Petilii were assailed with reproaches for having sought prominence by bringing odium on another, and plunder by triumphing over Africanus. Thereafter no more was heard of Africanus; he spent his life at Liternum without hankering after

Rome. They say that as he was dying, he gave instructions that he be buried in that same country area, and that his tombstone should be erected there so that his funeral should not be held in his ungrateful native city. He was a man worthy of remembrance, but for his skills in war rather than in peace. The earlier years of his life were more noteworthy than the later, because wars were waged continually in his young days, whereas with the onset of old age his achievements too lost their bloom, and his talents were offered no scope.

His second consulship was as nothing compared with the first, even if you added the censorship as well; similarly his tenure of office as legate in Asia, for it was ineffective through ill-health and disfigured by his son's misfortune, and following his return, by the need either to stand trial or to absent himself from both the trial and his native region. Yet he and no other gained the outstanding glory of bringing to a close the Punic war, and no war which the Romans waged was greater or more hazardous.

Questions

(1) How does the treatment handed out to Scipio compare to that meted out to Hannibal by Carthage, according to the arguments advanced by certain Romans?

(2) What decision did Scipio enter into regarding attending his trial, and why?

(3) In the final analysis, how does Livy rate the career of Scipio?

6–2
"The War with Catiline": Sallust's insights into the Roman Republic's decline.

Gaius Sallustius Crispus, known as Sallust (86–35? B.C.E.) was a plebeian-born historian-public official who witnessed the death throes of Republican Rome and contributed to its demise as an ardent supporter of Julius Caesar. In his account of Catiline's 63 B.C.E. plot to seize control of the state, Sallust lucidly analyses the decay of the old republican spirit and republican institutions that sent Rome down the path of autocracy. While bemoaning the general corruption, Sallust may have been guilty of it himself: he was once expelled from the Senate for alleged immorality and accused of using his position as governor of Africa Nova to commit extortion and embezzlement, but was never brought to trial because of Caesar's intervention.

Source: J. C. Rolfe, trans., *Sallust* (Cambridge, MA: Harvard University Press, 1965), pp.17–23.

...But the Roman people never had that advantage, since their ablest men were always most engaged with affairs; their minds were never employed apart from their bodies; the best citizen preferred action to words, and thought that his own brave deeds should be lauded by others rather than that theirs should be recounted by him.

IX. Accordingly, good morals were cultivated at home and in the field; there was the greatest harmony and little or no avarice; justice and probity prevailed among them, thanks not so much to laws as to nature. Quarrels, discord, and strife were reserved for their enemies; citizen vied with citizen only for the prize of merit. They were lavish in their offerings to the gods, frugal in the home, loyal to their friends. By practising these two qualities, boldness in warfare and justice when peace came, they watched over themselves and their country. In proof of these statements I present this convincing evidence: firstly, in time of war punishment was more often inflicted for attacking the enemy contrary to orders, or for withdrawing too tardily when recalled from the field, than for venturing to abandon

the standards or to give ground under stress; and secondly, in time of peace they ruled by kindness rather than fear, and when wronged preferred forgiveness to vengeance.

X. But when our country had grown great through toil and the practice of justice, when great kings had been vanquished in war, savage tribes and mighty peoples subdued by force of arms, when Carthage, the rival of Rome's away, had perished root and branch, and all seas and lands were open, then Fortune began to grow cruel and to bring confusion into all our affairs. Those who had found it easy to bear hardship and dangers, anxiety and adversity, found leisure and wealth, desirable under other circumstances, a burden and a curse. Hence the lust for money first, then for power, grew upon them; these were, I may say, the root of all evils. For avarice destroyed honour, integrity, and all other noble qualities; taught in their place insolence, cruelty, to neglect the gods, to set a price on everything. Ambition drove many men to become false; to have one thought locked in the breast, another ready on the tongue; to value friendships and enmities not on their merits but by the standard of self-interest, and to show a good front rather than a good heart. At first these vices grew slowly, from time to time they were punished; finally, when the disease had spread like a deadly plague, the state was changed and a government second to none in equity and excellence became cruel and intolerable.

XI. But at first men's souls were actuated less by avarice than by ambition—a fault, it is true, but not so far removed from virtue; for the noble and the base alike long for glory, honour, and power, but the former mount by the true path, whereas the latter, being destitute of noble qualities, rely upon craft and deception. Avarice implies a desire for money, which no wise man covets; steeped as it were with noxious poisons, it renders the most manly body and soul effeminate; it is ever unbounded and insatiable, nor can either plenty or want make it less. But after Lucius Sulla, having gained control of the state by arms, brought everything to a bad end from a good beginning, all men began to rob and pillage. One coveted a house, another lands; the victors showed neither moderation nor restraint, but shamefully and cruelly wronged their fellow citizens. Besides all this, Lucius Sulla, in order to secure the loyalty of the army which he led into Asia, had allowed it a luxury and license foreign to the manners of our forefathers; and in the intervals of leisure those charming and voluptuous lands had easily demoralized the warlike spirit of his soldiers. There it was that an army of the Roman people first learned to indulge in women and drink; to admire statues, paintings, and chased vases, to steal them from private houses and public places, to pillage shrines, and to desecrate everything, both sacred and profane. These soldiers, therefore, after they had won the victory, left nothing to the vanquished. In truth, prosperity tries the souls even of the wise; how then should men of depraved character like these make a moderate use of victory?

XII. As soon as riches came to be held in honour,when glory, dominion, and power followed in their train, virtue began to lose its lustre, poverty to be considered a disgrace, blamelessness to be termed malevolence. Therefore as the result of riches, luxury and greed, united with insolence, took possession of our young manhood. They pillaged, squandered; set little value on their own, coveted the goods of others; they disregarded modesty, chastity, everything human and divine; in short, they were utterly thoughtless and reckless.

It is worth your while, when you look upon houses and villas reared to the size of cities, to pay a visit to the temples of the gods built by our forefathers, most reverent of men. But they adorned the shrines of the gods with piety, their own homes with glory, while from the vanquished they took naught save the power of doing harm. The men of to-day, on the contrary, basest of creatures, with supreme wickedness are robbing our allies of all that those heroes in the hour of victory had left them; they act as though the one and only way to rule were to wrong.

XIII. Why, pray, should I speak of things which are incredible except to those who have seen them, that a host of private men have levelled mountains and built upon the seas? To such men their riches seem to me to have been but a plaything; for while they might have enjoyed them honourably, they made haste to squander them shamefully. Nay more, the passion which arose for lewdness, gluttony, and the other attendants of luxury was equally strong; men played the woman, women offered their chastity for sale; to gratify their palates they scoured land and sea; they slept before they needed sleep; they did not await the coming of hunger or thirst, of cold or of weariness, but all these things their self-indulgence anticipated. Such were the vices that incited the young men to crime, as soon as they had run through their property. Their minds, habituated to evil practices, could not easily refrain from self-indulgence, and so they abandoned themselves the more recklessly to every means of gain as well as of extravagance.

Questions

(1) In Sallust's estimation, which two qualities practiced by the early Romans were most instrumental in maintaining domestic peace and moral strength?
(2) When, and through what factors, does Sallust see a change as having taken place?
(3) According to Sallust's assessment, how did the later Romans compare/contrast with those of an earlier era?

6–3

Suetonius: a critical writer has, for once, very few negative comments about an Emperor.

Gaius Suetonius Tranquillus (72?–122? C.E.) was an aristocratic lawyer whose life spanned the Roman

Empire's most prosperous years. His semi-anecdotal "The Lives of the Twelve Caesars," which contained biographical material on the first eleven Roman emperors and Julius Caesar, is often uncompromising in its criticism. The chapter on Emperor Titus (79–81 C.E.) is exceptional in that the ruler is depicted as a role model, both in the exercise of his administrative duties and in his personal life, in contrast to the degenerate conduct of Nero, Tiberius, Caligula, and Domitian.

Source: Suetonius, "The Lives of the Twelve Caesars," John Gavorse, ed. (NY: Modern Library, 1959), pp. 337–343.

THE DEIFIED TITUS

TITUS, of the same surname as his father, was the delight and darling of the human race; such surpassing ability had be, by nature, art, or good fortune, to win the affections of all men, and that, too, which is no easy task, while he was Emperor. For as a private citizen and even during his father's rule, he did not escape hatred, much less public criticism.

He was born on the third day before the Kalends of January, in the year memorable for the death of Caligula in a mean house near the Septizonium and in a very small dark room besides; for it still remains and is shown to the curious. He was brought up at court in company with Britannicus and taught the same subjects by the same masters. At that time, so they say, a physiognomist was brought in by Narcissus, the freedman of Claudius, to examine Britannicus and declared most positively that he would never become Emperor, but that Titus, who was standing near by at the time, would surely rule. The boys were so intimate too, that it is believed that when Britannicus drained the fatal draught, Titus, who was reclining at his side, also tasted of the potion and for a long time suffered from an obstinate disorder. Titus did not forget all this, but later set up a golden statue of his friend in the palace, and dedicated another equestrian statue of ivory, which is to this day carried in the procession in the Circus, and attended it on its first appearance.

Even in boyhood his bodily and mental gifts were conspicuous and they became more and more so as he advanced in years. He had a handsome person, in which there was no less dignity than grace, and was uncommonly strong, although he was not tall of stature and had a rather protruding belly. His memory was extraordinary and he had an aptitude for almost all the arts, both of war and of peace, Skillful in arms and horsemanship, he made speeches and wrote verses in Latin and Greek with ease and readiness, and even offhand. He was besides not unacquainted with music, but sang and played the harp agreeably and skillfully. I have heard from many sources that he used also to write shorthand with great speed and would amuse himself by playful contests with his secretaries; also that he could imitate any handwriting that he had ever seen and often declared that he might have been the prince of forgers.

He served as military Tribune both in Germany and in Britain, winning a high reputation for energy and no less for integrity, as is evident from the great number of his statues and busts in both those provinces and from the inscriptions they bear.

After his military service he pleaded in the Forum, rather for glory than as a profession, and at the same time took to wife Arrecina Tertulla, whose father, though only a Roman Knight, had once been Prefect of the praetorian cohorts. On her death he replaced her by Marcia Furnilla, a lady of very distinguished family, but divorced her after he had acknowledged a daughter which she bore him.

Then, after holding the office of Quaestor, as commander of a legion he subjugated the two strong cities of Tarichaeae and Gamala in Judaea, having his horse killed under him in one battle and mounting another, whose rider had fallen fighting by his side.

Presently he was sent to congratulate Galba on becoming ruler of the state, and attracted attention wherever he went through the belief that he had been sent for to be adopted. But observing that everything was once more in a state of turmoil, he turned back, and visiting the oracle of the Paphian Venus, to consult it about his voyage, he was also encouraged to hope for imperial power. Soon realizing his hope and left behind to complete the conquest of Judaea, in the final attack on Jerusalem he slew twelve of the defenders with as many arrows. He took the city on his daughter's birthday, so delighting the soldiers and winning their devotion that they hailed him as Imperator and detained him from time to time when he would leave the province, urging him with prayers and even with threats either to stay or to take them all with him. This aroused the suspicion that he had tried to revolt from his father and make himself King of the East. He strengthened this suspicion on his way to Alexandria by wearing a diadem at the consecration of the bull Apis in Memphis, an act quite in accord with the usual ceremonial of that ancient religion, but unfavorably interpreted by some. Because of this he hastened to Italy, and putting in at Regium and then at Puteoli in a transport ship, he went with all speed from there to Rome, where, as if to show that the reports about him were groundless, he surprised his father with the greeting, "I am here, father; I am here."

From that time on he never ceased to act as the Emperor's partner and even as his protector. He took part in his father's triumph and was Censor with him. He was also his colleague in the tribunicial power and in seven consulships. He took upon himself the discharge of almost all duties, personally dictated letters and wrote edicts in his father's name, and even read his speeches in the Senate in lieu of a Quaestor. He also assumed the command of the praetorian guard, which before that time had never been held except by a Roman Knight, and in this office conducted himself in a somewhat arrogant and tyrannical fashion. For whenever he himself regarded any one with suspicion, he would secretly send some of the guard to the various theaters and camps, to demand their punishment, as if by consent of all who were present. He would then put them out of the way without delay. Among these was Aulus Caecina, an ex-consul, whom he invited to dinner and then ordered to be stabbed almost before he left the dining-room. But in this case he was led by a pressing danger, having got possession of an autograph copy of an harangue which Caecina had prepared to deliver to the soldiers. Although by such conduct he provided for his safety in the future, he incurred such odium at the time that hardly any one ever came to the throne with so evil a reputation or so much against desires of all.

Besides cruelty, he was also suspected of riotous living since he protracted his revels until the middle of the night with the most prodigal of his friends; likewise of unchastity because of his troops of catamites and eunuchs, and his notorious passion for Queen Berenice, to whom it was even said that he promised marriage. He was suspected of greed as well, for it was well known that in cases which came before his father he put a price on his influence and accepted bribes. In short, people not only thought, but openly declared, that he would be a second Nero. But this reputation turned out to his advantage and gave place to the highest praise, when no fault was discovered in him, but on the contrary the highest virtues.

His banquets were pleasant rather than extravagant. He chose as his friends men whom succeeding Emperors also retained as indispensable alike to themselves and to the State, and of whose services they made special use. Berenice he sent from Rome at once, against her will and against his own. Some of his most beloved paramours, although they were such skillful dancers that they later became stage favorites, he only ceased to cherish any longer, but even to witness their public performances.

He took away nothing from any citizen. He respected others' property, if any one ever did. In fact, he would not accept even proper and customary presents. And yet he was second to none of his predecessors in munificence. At the dedication of the amphitheater, and of the baths which were hastily built near it he gave a most magnificent and costly gladiatorial show. He presented a sham sea-fight too in the old Naumachia, and in the same place a combat of gladiators, exhibiting in one day five thousand wild beasts of every kind.

He was most kindly by nature, and whereas in accordance with a custom established by Tiberius, all the Caesars who followed him refused to regard favors granted by previous Emperors as valid, unless they had themselves conferred the same ones on the same individuals, Titus was the first to ratify them all in a single edict, without allowing himself to be asked. Moreover, in the case of other requests made of him, it was his fixed rule not to let any one go away without hope. Even when his household officials warned him that he was promising more than he could perform, he said that it was not right for any one to go away sorrowful from an interview with his Emperor. On another occasion, remembering at dinner that he had done nothing for anybody all that day, he gave utterance to that memorable and praiseworthy remark: "Friends, I have lost a day."

The whole body of the people in particular he treated with such indulgence on all occasions, that once at a gladiatorial show he declared that he would give it, "not after his own inclinations, but those of the spectators"; and what is more, he kept his word. For he refused nothing which any one asked, and even urged them to ask for what they wished. Furthermore, he openly displayed his partiality for Thracian gladiators and bantered the people about it by words and gestures, always, however, preserving his dignity, as well as observing justice. Not to omit any act of condescension, he sometimes bathed in the baths which he had built, in company with the common people.

There were some dreadful disasters during his reign, such as the eruption of Mount Vesuvius in Campania, a fire at Rome which continued three days and as many nights, and a plague the like of which had hardly ever been known before. In these many great calamities he showed not merely the concern of an Emperor, but even a father's surpassing love, now offering consolation in edicts, and now lending aid so far as his means allowed. He chose commissioners by lot from among the ex-consuls for the relief of Campania, and the property of those who lost their lives by Vesuvius and had no heirs left alive he applied to the rebuilding of the buried cities. During the fire in Rome he made no remark except "I am ruined," and he set aside all the ornaments of his villas for the public buildings and temples, and put several men of the equestrian order in charge of the work, that everything might be done with the greater dispatch. For curing the plague and diminishing the force of the epidemic there was no aid, human or divine, which he did not employ, searching for every kind of sacrifice and all kinds of medicines.

Among the evils of the times were the informers and their instigators, who had enjoyed a long standing license. After these had been soundly beaten in the Forum with scourges and cudgels, and finally led in procession across the arena of the amphitheater, he had some of them put up and sold, and others deported to the wildest of the islands. Further to discourage for all time any who might think of venturing on similar practices, among other precautions he made it unlawful for any one to be tried under several laws for the same offense, or for any inquiry to be made as to the legal status of any deceased person after a stated number of years.

Having declared that he would accept the office of Pontifex Maximus for the purpose of keeping his hands unstained, he was true to his promise. For, after that he neither caused nor connived at the death of any man, although he sometimes had no lack of reasons for taking vengeance; but he swore that he would rather be killed than kill. When two men of patrician family were found guilty of aspiring to the throne, he satisfied himself with warning them to abandon their attempt, saying that imperial power was the gift of fate, and promising that if there was anything else they desired, he himself would bestow it. Then he sent his couriers with all speed to the mother of one of them, for she was some distance off, to relieve her anxiety by reporting that her son was safe. And he not only invited the men themselves to dinner among his friends, but on the following day at a gladiatorial show he purposely placed them near him, and when the swords of the contestants were offered him, handed them over for their inspection. It is even said that he inquired into the horoscope of each of them, and declared that danger threatened them both, but at some future time and from another, as turned out to be the case.

Although his brother, never ceased plotting against him, but almost openly stirred up the armies to revolt and meditated flight to them, he had not the heart to put him to death or banish him from the court, or even to hold him in less honor than before. On the contrary, as he had done from the very first day of his rule, he continued to declare that he was his partner and successor, and sometimes he privately begged him with tears and prayers to be willing at least to return his affection.

In the meantime he was cut off by death, to the loss of mankind rather than to his own. After finishing the public games, at the close of which he wept bitterly in the presence of the people, he went to the Sabine territory, somewhat cast down because a victim had escaped as he was sacrificing and because it had thundered from a clear sky. Then at the very first stopping place he was seized with a fever, and as he was being carried on from there in a litter, it is said that he pushed back the curtains, looked up to heaven, and lamented bitterly that his life was being taken from him contrary to his deserts. For he said that there was no act of his life of which he had cause to repent, save one only. What this was he did not himself disclose at the time, nor could any one easily divine? Some think that he recalled the intimacy which he had with his brother's wife. But Domitia swore most solemnly that this did not exist, although she would not have denied it if it had been in the least true, but on the contrary would have boasted of it, as she was most ready to do of all her scandalous actions.

He died in the same farmhouse as his father, on the Ides of September, two years two months and twenty days after succeeding Vespasian, in the forty-second year of his age. When his death was made known, the whole populace mourned as they would for a loss in their own families, the Senate hastened to the House before it was summoned by proclamation, and with the doors still shut, and then with them open, rendered such thanks to him and heaped such praise on him after death as they had never done even when he was alive and present.

Questions

(1) In what ways did Titus acquire a sinister reputation before he came to the throne? How does Suetonius assert that this reputation actually worked to his advantage?

(2) In what ways did Titus deal with the disasters of the Vesuvius eruption and the fire at Rome?

(3) How did Titus deal with two patricians who had conspired against him and in what manner was this unusual?

(4) What was Titus' relationship with his brother, and how did he react to certain of his brother's actions?

6–4

Pliny the Younger on the Vesuvius eruption and the Christian "controversy."

Gaius Plinius Secondus, or "Pliny the Younger" (62–113 C.E.), has always stood in the shadow of his illustrious uncle and adoptive father, Pliny the Elder, but grew up to be a competent official in his own right. His letters "Epistulae" provide a significant insight into major events and problems in the early Roman Empire. The first of these describes, for the historian Tacitus, the Mount Vesuvius explosion of 79 C.E., and the second is an exchange with the Emperor Trajan over how Pliny, in his capacity as governor of Bithynia, might best deal with members of the illegal sect of Christianity.

Source: Betty Radice, trans., *The Letters of the Younger Pliny* (Baltimore: Penguin, 1963), pp. 166–168, 293–295.

TO CORNELIUS TACITUS

Thank you for asking me to send you a description of my uncle's death so that you can leave an accurate account of it for posterity; I know that immortal fame awaits him if his death is recorded by you. It is true that he perished in a catastrophe which destroyed the loveliest regions of the earth, a fate shared by whole cities and their people, and one so memorable that it is likely to make his name live for ever: and he himself wrote a number of books of lasting value: but you write for all time and can still do much to perpetuate his memory. The fortunate man, in my opinion, is he to whom the gods have granted the power either to do something which is worth recording or to write what is worth reading, and most fortunate of all is the man who can do both. Such a man was my uncle, as his own books and yours will prove. So you set me a task I would choose for myself, and I am more than willing to start on it.

My uncle was stationed at Misenum in active command of the fleet. On 24 August, in the early afternoon, my mother drew attention to a cloud of unusual size and appearance. He had been out in the sun, had taken a cold bath, and lunched while lying down, and was then working at his books. He called for his shoes and climbed up to a place which would give him the best view of the phenomenon. It was not clear at that distance from which mountain the cloud was rising (it was afterwards known to be Vesuvius); its general appearance can best be expressed as being like an umbrella pine, for it rose to a great height on a sort of trunk and then split off into branches, I imagine because it was thrust upwards by the first blast and then left unsupported as the pressure subsided, or else it was borne down by its own weight so that it spread out and gradually dispersed. In places it looked white, elsewhere blotched and dirty, according to the amount of soil and ashes it carried with it. My uncle's scholarly acumen saw at once that it was important enough for a closer inspection, and he ordered a boat to be made ready, telling me I could come with him if I wished. I replied that I preferred to go on with my studies, and as it happened he had himself given me some writing to do.

As he was leaving the house he was handed a message from Rectina, wife of Tascus whose house was at the foot of the mountain, so that escape was impossible except by boat. She was terrified by the danger threatening her and implored him to rescue her from her fate. He changed his plans, and what he had begun in a spirit of inquiry he completed as a hero. He gave orders for the warships to be launched and went on board himself with the intention of bringing help to many more people besides Rectina, for this lovely stretch of coast was thickly populated. He hurried to the place where everyone else was hastily leaving, steering his course straight for the danger zone. He was entirely fearless, describing each new movement and phase of the portent to be noted down exactly as he observed them. Ashes were already falling, hotter and thicker as the ships drew near, followed by bits of pumice and blackened stones, charred and cracked by the flames: then suddenly they were in shallow water, and the shore was blocked by debris from the mountain. For a moment my uncle wondered whether to turn back, but when the helmsman advised this he refused, telling him that Fortune stood by the courageous and that they must make for Pomponianus at Stabiae. He was cut off there by the breadth of the bay (for the shore gradually curves round a basin filled by the sea) so that he was not as yet in danger, though it was clear that this would come nearer as it spread. Pomponianus had therefore already put his belongings on board ship, intending to escape if the contrary wind fell. This wind was of course full in my uncle's favour, and he was able to bring his ship in. He embraced his terrified friend, cheered and encouraged him, and thinking he could calm his fears by showing his own composure, gave orders that he was to be carried to the bathroom. After his bath he lay down and dined; he was quite cheerful, or at any rate he pretended he was, which was no less courageous.

Meanwhile on Mount Vesuvius broad sheets of fire and leaping flames blazed at several points, their bright glare emphasized by the darkness of night. My uncle tried to allay the fears of his companion by repeatedly declaring that these were nothing but bonfires left by the peasants in their terror, or else empty homes on fire in the districts they had abandoned. Then he went to rest and certainly slept, for as he was a stout man his breathing was rather loud and heavy and could be heard by people coming and going outside his door. By this time the courtyard giving access to his room was full of ashes mixed with pumice-stones, so that its level had risen, and if he had stayed in the room any longer he would never have got out. He was wakened, came out and joined Pomponianus and the rest of the household who had sat up all night. They debated whether to stay indoors or take their chance in the open, for the buildings were now shaking with violent shocks, and seemed to be swaying to and fro as if they were torn from their foundations. Outside on the other hand, there was the danger of falling pumice-stones, even though these were light and porous; however, after comparing the risks they chose the latter. In my uncle's case one reason outweighed the other, but for the others it was a choice of fears. As a protection against falling objects they put pillows on their heads tied down with cloths.

Elsewhere there was daylight by this time, but they were still in darkness, blacker and denser than any ordinary night, which they relieved by lighting torches and various kinds of lamp. My uncle decided to go down to the shore and investigate on the spot the possibility of any escape by sea, but he found the waves still wild and dangerous. A sheet was spread on the ground for him to lie down, and he repeatedly asked for cold water to drink. Then the flames and smell of sulphur which gave warning of the approaching fire drove the others to take flight and roused him to stand up. He stood leaning on two slaves and then suddenly collapsed, I imagine because the dense fumes choked his breathing by blocking his windpipe which was constitutionally weak and narrow and often inflamed. When daylight returned on the 26th—two days after the last day he had seen—his body was found intact and uninjured, still fully clothed and looking more like sleep than death.

Meanwhile my mother and I were at Misenum, but this is not of any historic interest, and you only wanted to hear about my uncle's death. I will say no more, except to add that I have described in detail every incident which I either witnessed myself or heard about immediately after the event, when reports were most likely to be accurate. It is for you to select what best suits your purpose, for there is a great difference between a letter to a friend and history written well for all to read.

PLINY TO THE EMPEROR TRAJAN

It is my custom to refer all my difficulties to you, Sir, for no one is better able to resolve my doubts and to inform my ignorance.

I have never been present at an examination of Christians. Consequently, I do not know the nature of the extent of the punishments usually meted out to them, nor the grounds for starting an investigation and how far it should be pressed. Nor am I at all sure whether any distinction should be made between them on the grounds of age, or if young people and adults should be treated alike; whether a pardon ought to be granted to anyone retracting his beliefs, or if he has once professed Christianity, he shall gain nothing by renouncing it; and whether it is the mere name of Christian which is punishable, even if innocent of crime, or rather crimes associated with the name.

For the moment this is the line I have taken with all persons brought before me on the charge of being Christians. I have asked them in person if they are Christians, and if they admit it, I repeat the question a second and a third time, with a warning of punishment awaiting them. If they persist, I order them to be led away for execution; for, whatever the nature of their admission, I am convinced that their stubbornness and unshakeable obstinacy ought not to go unpunished. There have been others similarly fanatical who are Roman citizens. I have entered them on the list of persons to be sent to Rome for trial.

Now that I have begun to deal with this problem, as so often happens, the charges are becoming more widespread and increasing in variety. An anonymous pamphlet has been circulated which contains the names of a number of accused persons. Amongst these I con-

sidered that I should dismiss any who denied that they were or had been Christians when they had repeated after me a formula of invocation to the gods and had made offerings of wine and incense to your statue (which I had ordered to be brought into court for this purpose along with the images of the gods), and furthermore had reviled the name of Christ: none of which things, I understand, any genuine Christian can be induced to do.

Others, whose names were given to me by an informer, first admitted the charge and then denied it; they said that they had ceased to be Christiana two or more years previously, and some of them even twenty years ago. They all did reverence to your statue and the images of the gods in the same way as the others, and reviled the name of Christ. They also declared that the sum total of their guilt or error mounted to no more than this: they had met regularly before dawn on a fixed day to chant verses alternately amongst themselves in honour of Christ as if to a god, and also to bind themselves by oath, not for any criminal purpose, but to abstain from theft, robbery, and adultery, to commit no breach of trust and not to deny a deposit when called upon to restore it. After this ceremony it had been their custom to disperse and reassemble later to take food of an ordinary, harmless kind; but they had in fact given up this practice since my edict, issued on your instructions, which banned all political societies. This made me decide it was all the more necessary to extract the truth by torture from two slave-women, whom they call deaconesses. I found nothing but a degenerate sort of cult carried to extravagant lengths.

I have therefore postponed any further examination and hastened to consult you. The question seems to me to be worthy of your consideration, especially in view of the number of persons endangered; for a great many individuals of every age and class, both men and women, are being brought to trial, and this is likely to continue. It is not only the towns, but villages and rural districts too which are infected through contact with this wretched cult. I think though that it is still possible for it to be checked and directed to better ends, for there is no doubt that people have begun to throng the temples which had been almost entirely deserted for a long time; the sacred rites which had been allowed to lapse are being performed again, and flesh of sacrificial victims is on sale everywhere, though up till recently scarcely anyone could be found to buy it. It is easy to infer from this that a great many people could be reformed if they were given an opportunity to repent.

TRAJAN TO PLINY

You have followed the right course of procedure, my dear Pliny, in your examination of the cases of persons charged with being Christians, for it is impossible to lay down a general rule to a fixed formula. These people must not be hunted out; if they are brought before you and the charge against them is proved, they must be punished, but in the case of anyone who denies that he is a Christian, and makes it clear that he is not by offering prayers to our gods, he is to be pardoned as a result of his repentance however suspect his past conduct may be. But pamphlets circulated anonymously must play no part in any accusation. They create the worst sort of precedent and are quite out of keeping with the spirit of our age.

Questions

(1) What traits exhibited by Pliny's uncle during the crisis of the Vesuvius eruption are held up as being the most admirable, and why?

(2) From certain comments made by Pliny in his letter to Tacitus, what does he envision as being the historian's task?

(3) What dilemma was Pliny faced with regarding people accused of practicing Christianity, and what administrative procedures did he follow?

(4) To what extent and in what manner does the Emperor both praise and criticize Pliny in his letter of reply?

6–5

A Roman expresses grudging admiration for some of his country's barbarian adversaries.

The historian Cornelius Tacitus (55?–116? C.E.) often acted as a travelling administrator for outlying regions of the Roman Empire at a time when it was attaining its greatest expansion. He culminated his career as proconsul of Asia Minor under Emperor Trajan. In his work "On the Origin, Geography, Institutions and Tribes of the Germans" ("Germania"), Tacitus ruefully compares the virtues and vigor of the semi-civilized Germanic peoples to what he viewed as an effete and deteriorating Roman society.

Source: H. Mattingly & S.A. Handford, trans., *Tacitus: The Agricola & The Germania* (Harmondsworth, England: Penguin, 1970), pp. 106–123.

They choose their kings for their noble birth, their commanders for their valour. The power even of the kings is not absolute or arbitrary. The commanders rely on example rather than on the authority of their rank—on the admiration they win by showing conspicuous energy and courage and by pressing forward in front of their own troops. Capital punishment, imprisonment, even flogging, are allowed to none but the priests, and are not inflicted merely as punishments or on the commanders' orders, but as it were in obedience to the god whom the Germans believe to be present on the field of battle. They actually carry with them into the fight certain figures and emblems taken from their sacred groves. A specially powerful incitement to valour is that the squadrons and divisions are not made up at random by the mustering of chance-comers, but are each composed of men of one family or clan. Close by them, too, are their nearest and dearest, so that they can hear the shrieks of their womenfolk and the wailing of their children. These are the witnesses whom each man reverences most highly, whose praise he most desires. It is to their mothers and wives that they go to have their wounds treated, and the women are not afraid to count

and compare the gashes. They also carry supplies of food to the combatants and encourage them.

It stands on record that armies already wavering and on the point of collapse have been rallied by the women, pleading heroically with their men, thrusting forward their bared bosoms, and making them realize the imminent prospect of enslavement—a fate which the Germans fear more desperately for their women than for themselves. Indeed, you can secure a surer hold on these nations if you compel them to include among a consignment of hostages some girls of noble family. More than this, they believe that there resides in women an element of holiness and a gift of prophecy; and so they do not scorn to ask their advice, or lightly disregard their replies. In the reign of the emperor Vespasian we saw Veleda long honoured by many Germans as a divinity; and even earlier they showed a similar reverence for Aurinia and a number of others—a reverence untainted by servile flattery or any pretence of turning women into goddesses.

Above all other gods they worship Mercury, and count it no sin, on certain feast-days, to include human victims in the sacrifices offered to him. Hercules and

Mars they appease by offerings of animals, in accordance with ordinary civilized custom. Some of the Suebi sacrifice also to Isis. I do not know the origin or explanation of this foreign cult; but the goddess's emblem, being made in the form of a light warship, itself proves that her worship came in from abroad. The Germans do not think it in keeping with the divine majesty to confine gods within walls or to portray them in the likeness of any human countenance. Their holy places are woods and groves, and they apply the names of deities to that hidden presence which is seen only by the eye of reverence.

For omens and the casting of lots they have the highest regard. Their procedure in casting lots is always the same. They cut off a branch of a nut-bearing tree and slice it into strips; these they mark with different signs and throw them completely at random onto a white cloth. Then the priest of the state, if the consultation is a public one, or the father of the family if it is private, often a prayer to the gods, and looking up at the sky picks up three strips, one at a time, and reads their meaning from the signs previously scored on them. If the lots forbid an enterprise, there is no deliberation that day on the matter in question; if they allow it, confirmation by the taking of auspices is required. Although the familiar method of seeking information from the cries and the flight of birds is known to the Germans, they have also a special method of their own—to try to obtain omens and warnings from horses. These horses are kept at the public expense in the sacred woods and groves that I have mentioned; they are pure white and undefiled by any toil in the service of man. The priest and the king, or the chief of the state, yoke them to a sacred chariot and walk beside them, taking note of their neighs and snorts. No kind of omen inspires greater trust, not only among the common people, but even among the nobles and priests; who think that they themselves are but servants of the gods, whereas the horses are privy to the gods' counsels. There is yet another kind of omen-taking used to forecast the issue of serious wars. They contrive somehow to secure a captive from the nation with which they are at war and match him against a champion of their own, each being armed with his national weapons. The victory of one or the other is thought forecast the issue of the war.

On matters of minor importance only the chiefs debate; on major affairs, the whole community. But even where the commons have the decision, the subject is considered in advance by the chiefs. Except in case of accident or emergency, they assemble on certain particular days, either shortly after the new moon or shortly before the full moon. These, they hold, are the most auspicious times for embarking on any enterprise. They do not reckon time by days, as we do, but by nights. All their engagements and appointments are made on this system. Night is regarded as ushering in the day. It is a drawback of their independent spirit that they do not take a summons as a command: instead of coming to a meeting all together, they waste two or three days by their unpunctuality. When the assembled crowd thinks fit, they take their seats fully armed. Silence is then commanded by the priests, who on such occasions have power to enforce obedience. Then such hearing is given to the king or state-chief as his age, rank, military distinction, or eloquence can secure—more because his advice carries weight than because he has the power to command. If a proposal displeases them, the people shout their dissent; if they approve, they clash their spears. To express approbation with their weapons is their most complimentary way of showing agreement.

The Assembly is competent also to bear criminal charges, especially those involving the risk of capital punishment. The mode of execution varies according to the offence. Traitors and deserters are hanged on trees; cowards, shirkers, and sodomites are pressed down under a wicker hurdle into the slimy mud of a bog. This distinction in the punishments is based on the idea that offenders against the state should be made a public example of, whereas deeds of shame should be buried out of men's sight. Less serious offences, too, have penalties proportioned to them. The man who is found guilty has to pay a fine of so many horses or cattle, part of which goes to the king of the state, part to the victim of the wrongful act or to his relatives. These same assemblies elect, among other officials, the magistrates who administer justice in the districts and villages. Each magistrate is assisted by a hundred assessors chosen from the people to advise him and to add weight to his decisions.

They transact no business, public or private, without being armed. But it is a rule that no one shall carry arms until the state authorities are satisfied that he will be competent to use them. Then, in the presence of the Assembly, either one of the chiefs or the young man's father or some other relative presents him with a shield and a spear. These, among the Germans, are the equivalent of the man's toga with us—the first distinction publicly conferred upon a youth, who now ceases to rank merely as a member of a household and becomes a citizen. Particularly noble birth, or great services rendered by their fathers, can obtain the rank of 'chief' for boys still in their teens. They are attached to others of more mature strength who have been approved some years before and none of them blushes to be seen in a chief's retinue of followers. There are grades of rank even in these retinues, determined at the discretion of the chief whom they follow; and there is great rivalry, both among the followers to obtain the highest place in their leader's estimation and among the chiefs for the honour of having the biggest and most valiant retinue. Both prestige and power depend on being continually attended by a large train of picked young warriors, which is a distinction in peace and a protection in war.

And it is not only in a chief's own nation that the superior number and quality of his retainers brings him glory and renown. Neighbouring states honour them also, courting them with embassies and complimenting them with presents. Very often the mere reputation of such men will virtually decide the issue of a war.

On the field of battle it is a disgrace to a chief to be surpassed in courage by his followers, and to the followers not to equal the courage of their chief. And to leave a battle alive after their chief has fallen means lifelong infamy and shame. To defend and protect him, and to let him get the credit for their own acts of heroism, are the most solemn obligations of their allegiance. The chiefs fight for victory, the followers for their chief. Many noble youths, if the land of their birth is stagnating in a long period of peace and inactivity, deliberately seek out other tribes which have some war in hand. For the Germans have no taste for peace; renown is more easily won among perils, and a large body of retainers cannot be kept together except by means of violence and war. They are always making demands on the generosity of their chief, asking for a coveted war-horse or a spear stained with the blood of a defeated enemy. Their meals, for which plentiful if homely fare is provided, count in lieu of pay. The wherewithal for this openhandedness comes from war and plunder. A German is not so easily prevailed upon to plough the land and wait patiently for harvest as to challenge a foe an earn wounds for his reward. He thinks it tame and spiritless to accumulate slowly by the sweat of his brow what can be got quickly by the loss of a little blood.

When not engaged in warfare they spend a certain amount of time in hunting, but much more in idleness, thinking of nothing else but sleeping and eating. For the boldest and most warlike men have no regular employment, the care of house, home, and fields being left to the women, old men, and weaklings of the family. In thus dawdling away their time they show a strange inconsistency—at one and the same time loving indolence and hating peace.

It is a national custom for gifts of cattle or agricultural produce to be made to the chiefs, individual citizens making voluntary contributions for this purpose. These are accepted as tokens of honour, but serve also to supply their wants. They take particular pleasure in gifts received from neighbouring states, such as are sent not only by individuals but by communities as well—choice horses, splendid arms, metal discs, and collars. And we have now taught them to accept presents of money also.

It is a well-known fact that the peoples of Germany never live in cities and will not even have their houses adjoin one another. They dwell apart, dotted about here and there, wherever a spring, plain, or grove takes their fancy. Their villages are not laid out in the Roman style, with buildings adjacent and connected. Every man leaves an open space round his house, perhaps as a precaution against the risk of fire, perhaps because they are inexpert builders. They do not even make use of stones or walltiles, for all purposes they employ rough-hewn timber, ugly and unattractive-looking. Some parts, however, they carefully smear over with a clay of such purity and brilliance that it looks like painting or coloured design. They also have the habit of hollowing out underground caves, which they cover with masses of manure and use both as refuges from the winter and as storehouses for produce. Such shelters temper the keenness of the frosts; and if an invader comes, he ravages the open country; while these hidden excavations are either not known to exist, or else escape detection simply because they cannot be found without a search.

The universal dress in Germany is a cloak fastened with a brooch or, failing that, a thorn. They pass whole days by the fireside wearing no garment but this. It is a mark of great wealth to wear undergarments, which are not loose like those of the Sarmatians and Parthians, but fit tightly and follow the contour of every limb. They also wear the skins of wild animals—the tribes near the river frontiers without any regard to appearance, the more distant tribes with some refinement of taste, since in their part of the country there is no finery to be bought. These latter people select animals with care, and after stripping off the hides decorate them with patches of the skin of creatures that live in the unknown seas of the outer ocean. The dress of the women differs from that of the men in two respects only: women often wear outer garments linen ornamented with a purple pattern; and as the upper part of these is sleeveless, the whole of their arms, and indeed the parts of their breasts nearest the shoulder are exposed.

Their marriage code, however, is strict, and no feature of their morality deserves higher praise. They are almost unique among barbarians in being content with one wife apiece—all of them, that is, except a very few who take more than one wife not to satisfy their desires but because their exalted rank brings them many pressing offers of matrimonial alliances. The dowry is brought by husband to wife, not by wife to husband. Parents and kinsmen attend and approve the gifts—not gifts chosen to please a woman's fancy or gaily deck a young bride, but oxen, a horse with its bridle, or a shield, spear, and sword. In consideration of such gifts a man gets his wife, and she in her turn brings a present of arms to her husband. The interchange of gifts typifies for them the most sacred bond of union, sanctified by mystic rites under the favour of the presiding deities of wedlock. The woman must not think that she is excluded from aspirations to manly virtues or exempt from the hazards of warfare. That is why she is reminded, in the very ceremonies which bless her marriage at its outset, that she enters her husband's home to be the partner of his toils and perils, that both in peace and in war she is to share his sufferings and adventures. That is the meaning of the team of oxen, the horse ready for its rider, and the gift of arms. On these terms she must live her life and bear her children. She is receiving something that she must hand over intact and undepreciated to her children, something for her sons' wives to receive in their turn and pass on to her grandchildren.

By such means is the virtue of their women protected, and they live uncorrupted by the temptations of public shows or the excitements of banquets. Clandestine love—letters are unknown to men and women alike. Adultery is extremely rare, considering the size of the population. A guilty wife is summarily punished by her husband. He cuts off her hair, strips her naked, and in the presence of kinsmen turns her out of his house and flogs her all through the village. They have in fact no mercy on a wife who prostitutes her chastity. Neither beauty, youth, nor wealth can find her another husband. No one in Germany finds vice amusing, or calls it 'up-to-date' to seduce and be seduced. Even better is the practice of those states in which only virgins may marry, so that a woman who has once been a bride has finished with all such hopes and aspirations. She takes one husband, just as she has one body and one life. Her thoughts must not stray beyond him or her desires survive him. And even that husband she must love not for himself, but as an embodiment of the married state. To restrict the number of children, or to kill any of those born after the heir, is considered wicked. Good morality is more effective in Germany than good laws are elsewhere.

In every home the children go naked and dirty, and develop that strength of limb and tall stature which excite our admiration. Every mother feeds her child at the breast and does not depute the task to maids or nurses. The young master is not distinguished from the slave by any pampering in his upbringing. They live together among the same flocks and on the same earthen floor, until maturity sets apart the free and the spirit of valour claims them as her own. The young men are slow to mate, and thus they reach manhood with vigour unimpaired. The girls, too, are not hurried into marriage. As old and full-grown as the men, they match their mates in age and strength, and the children inherit the robustness of their parents. The sons of sisters are as highly honoured by their uncles as by their own fathers. Some tribes even consider the former the closer and more sacred of the two, and in demanding hostages prefer nephews to sons, thinking that this gives them a firmer grip on men's hearts and a wider hold on the family. However, a man's heirs and successors are his own children, and there is no such thing as a will. When there is no issue, the first in order of succession are brothers, and then uncles, first on the father's, then on the mother's side. The more relatives and connections by marriage a man has, the greater authority he commands in old age. There is nothing to be gained by childlessness in Germany.

Heirs are under an obligation to take up both the feuds and the friendships of a father or kinsman. But feuds do not continue for ever unreconciled. Even homicide can be atoned for by a fixed number of cattle or sheep, the compensation being received by the whole family. This is to the advantage of the community: for private feuds are particularly dangerous where there is such complete liberty.

No nation indulges more freely in feasting and entertaining than the German. It is accounted a sin to turn any man away from your door. The host welcomes his guest with the best meal that his means allow. When he has finished entertaining him, the host undertakes a fresh role: he accompanies the guest to the nearest house where further hospitality can be had. It makes no difference that they come uninvited; they are welcomed just as warmly. No distinction is ever made between acquaintance and stranger as far as the right to hospitality is concerned. As the guest takes his leave, it is customary to let him have anything he asks for; and the host, with as little hesitation, will ask for a gift in return. They take delight in presents, but they expect no repayment for giving them and feel no obligation in receiving them.

As soon as they wake, which is often well after sunrise, they wash, generally with warm water—as one might expect in a country where winter lasts so long. After washing they eat a meal, each man having a separate seat and table. Then they go out to attend to any business they have in hand, or, as often as not, to partake in a feast—always with their weapons about them. Drinking-bouts lasting all day and all night are not considered in any way disgraceful. The quarrels that inevitably arise over the cups are seldom settled merely by hard words, but more often by killing and wounding. Nevertheless, they often make a feast an occasion for discussing such affairs as the ending of feuds, the arrangement of marriage alliances, the adoption of chiefs, and even questions of peace or war. At no other time, they think, is the heart so open to sincere feelings or so quick to warm to noble sentiments. The Germans are not cunning or sophisticated enough to refrain from blurting out their inmost thoughts in the freedom of festive surroundings, so that every man's soul is laid completely bare. On the following day the subject is reconsidered, and thus due account is taken of both occasions. They debate when they are incapable of pretence but reserve their decision for a time when they cannot well make a mistake.

Their drink is a liquor made from barley or other grain which is fermented to produce a certain resemblance to wine. Those who dwell nearest the Rhine or the Danube also buy wine. Their food is plain—wild fruit, fresh game, and curdled milk. They satisfy their hunger without any elaborate cuisine or appetizers. But they do not show the same self-control in slaking their thirst. If you indulge their intemperance by plying them with as much drink as they desire, they will be as easily conquered by this besetting weakness as by force of arms.

They have only one kind of public show, which is performed without variation at every festive gathering. Naked youths, trained to the sport, dance about among swords and spears levelled at them. Practice begets skill, and skill grace; but they are not professionals and do not receive payment. Their most daring flings have their only reward in the pleasure they give the spectators. They play at dice—surprisingly enough—when they are sober, making a serious business of it; and they are so reckless in their anxiety to win, however often they lose, that when everything else is gone they will stake their personal liberty on a last decisive throw. A loser willingly discharges his debt by becoming a slave: even though he may be the younger and stronger man, he allows himself to be bound and sold by the winner. Such is their stubborn persistence in a vicious practice—though they call it 'honour'. Slaves of this description are disposed of by way of trade, since even their owners want to escape the shame of such a victory.

Slaves in general do not have particular duties about the house and estate allotted to them, as our slaves do. Each has control of a holding and home of his own. The master demands from him a stated quantity of grain, live-stock, or cloth, as he would from a tenant. To this extent the slave is under an obligation of service; but all other duties, including household work, are carried out by the housewife and her children. To flog a slave, or to punish him by imprisonment and hard labour, is very unusual; yet to kill one outright is quite common. But they do this, not as a strict enforcement of discipline, but in a fit of passion, as they might kill an enemy—except that they do not have to pay for it. Freedmen rank little higher than slaves: they seldom have any influence in a household, never in the state, except among the tribes that are ruled by kings. There they rise above free men and even above noblemen. Elsewhere, the inferior status of freedmen is a proof of genuine liberty.

The employment of capital in order to increase it by usury is unknown in Germany; and ignorance is here a surer defence than any prohibition. Lands proportioned to their own number are appropriated in turn for tillage by the whole body of tillers. They then divide them among themselves according to rank; the division is made easy by the wide tracts of cultivable ground available. These ploughlands are changed yearly, and still there is enough and to spare. The fact is that although their land is fertile and extensive, they fail to take full advantage of it because they do not work sufficiently hard. They do not plant orchards, fence off meadows, or irrigate gardens; the only demand they make upon the soil is to produce a corn-crop. Hence even the year itself is not divided by them into as many seasons as it is with us: winter, spring and summer are the seasons they understand and have names for; the name of autumn is as completely unknown to them as· are the blessings that it can bring.

There is no ostentation about their funerals. The only special observance is that the bodies of famous men are burned with particular kinds of wood. When they have heaped up the pyre they do not throw garments or spices on it; only the dead man's arms, and sometimes his horse too, are cast into the flames. The tomb is a raised mound of turf. They disdain to show honour by laboriously rearing high monuments of stone, which they think would only lie heavy on the dead....

Questions

(1) What value did German society seem to place on women? What might be surmised about gender relationships in Germanic society?

(2) On what particular virtues of the Germanic societies does Tacitus seem to lay the greatest stress?

(3) What seems to be noteworthy regarding the Germanic attitude towards their slaves?

(4) What are the governmental and/or judicial functions of the kings? the priests? the Assembly?

6–6
Petronius: Insights into Roman private life and upper-middle-class values.

Gaius Petronius Arbiter (died c. 66 C.E.) served as governor of Bithynia Province and later as master-of-ceremonies at Emperor Nero's decadent court; and is widely-held to have been the author of the "Satyrica," a humorous narrative depicting the seamy side of Neronian Rome. In his description of a banquet held by the wealthy but ludicrous Trimalchio, Petronius lampoons the habits and attitudes of the nouveau riche.

Source: R. Bracht Branham & Daniel Kinney. trans., *Petronius: Satyrica* (Berkeley: University of California Press, 1996), pp. 23–31, 46–49.

The third day had already arrived, and that meant the prospect of a free meal. But we were so tattered and bruised we felt more like running away than resting. While we morosely pondered how to avoid the coming storm, one of Agamemnon's slaves interrupted us: 'What's wrong? Don't you know who your host is today? It's Trimalchio, a most elegant man…He has a waterclock in his dining room and a trumpeter on call to announce the time, so that he knows at any moment how much of life he's already lost.'

We promptly forgot all our troubles, dressed up, and asked Giton, who so willingly played the servant's role, to accompany us to the baths…

While we wandered the grounds in our evening clothes—or rather joked around and mingled with groups of guests playing games—we suddenly encountered a bald old man in a blood-red tunic playing ball with some long-haired boys. It was not so much the boys who caught our attention—although they were well worth it—as the paterfamilias himself. He stood there in his slippers playing intently with a leek-green ball. If the ball hit the ground, he didn't chase it, but had a slave with a bag full of balls give the players a new one. We noticed some other novelties: there were two eunuchs stationed at different points in a circle; one was holding a silver chamber pot, the other was counting the balls—not those batted back and forth by the players, but only those that fell on the ground!

While we wondered at the extravagance of all this, Menelaus ran up and said, '*This* is the guy who's throwing the party! What you see is only the prelude to dinner.' As Menelaus spoke, Trimalchio snapped his fingers as a signal to the eunuch to hold out the chamber pot for him as he continued to play. After emptying his bladder, he called for water for his hands, sprinkled it lightly on his fingers and then wiped them dry on the head of a young slave…

There wasn't time to take it all in, so we entered the baths, and the minute we began to sweat moved on to the cold pool. Trimalchio was already drenched in perfume and being towelled down, not with linen, but with Greek comforters of the softest wool. Right in front of him three masseurs were guzzling a fine Falernian wine. When they proceeded to spill most of it in a scuffle, he blithely observed that this was 'a libation in his honor'.

He was then wrapped in a scarlet cloak and placed upon a litter. Four runners bristling with decorations pranced before him along with a little wagon on which his darling was riding—a boy past his prime, puffy eyed, and even uglier than his master. As Trimalchio was being carried out, a musician holding a tiny flute ran up to his side and—just as if he were whispering a secret in his ear—played for him the whole way!

Utterly astonished, we made our way to the door with Agamemnon. By the entrance we saw a notice posted:

ANY SLAVE WHO LEAVES THE PREMISES WITHOUT PERMISSION OF THE MASTER WILL RECEIVE ONE HUNTED LASHES

Just inside stood a doorman dressed entirely in green except for a cherry-red belt around his waist. He was shucking peas into a silver dish. Over the doorsill hung a golden cage from which a motley-colored magpie called salutations to the guests.

While I stared in stupefaction at all this, I almost fell over backwards and broke a leg. For just to the left of the entrance (not far from the porter's lodge), was the most enormous dog tethered by a chain—painted on the wall under some large block letters that said:

BEWARE OF DOG

My companions laughed at my fright, but I pulled myself together to look at the rest of the wall. It depicted a slave market complete with price tags. Trimalchio himself was in the picture; his hair is long and in his hand he grips the wand of Mercury. Minerva leads the way as our hero enters Rome. A painstaking artist had carefully portrayed the whole course of his career, complete with captions: how he first learned to keep the books and then was put in charge of the cash. In the last scene of the fresco Mercury lifts him by the chin up to a lofty dais. Fortuna is at his side carrying her burgeoning cornucopia, as the three Fates spin the golden threads.

I also noticed a team of runners in the nearby colonnade exercising with their trainer. In the corner stood an imposing cabinet: inside I saw a little shrine containing the household gods sculpted in silver, a marble statuette of Venus, and a none-too-small golden casket, which, they said, preserved the master's first beard…

I started to ask the steward what they had painted in the atrium. 'The *Iliad* and the *Odyssey*', he said, 'and the gladiator show put on by Laenas.' It was too much to contemplate…

We had already reached dining room. In the entryway a bookkeeper was poring over the accounts. But what caught my eye were the rods and axes fixed on the doorposts. They were mounted on top of what looked like the bronze prow of a ship that bore the inscription:

PRESENTED TO C. POMPEIUS TRIMALCHIO
PRIEST OF THE COLLEGE OF AUGUSTUS
BY CINNAMUS THE STEWARD

Beneath this inscription was a double lamp suspended from the ceiling and two wooden tablets, one on each doorpost. I seem to remember that one of them read:

OUR GAIUS IS DINING OUT
ON THE 30TH AND 31ST OF DECEMBER

On the other were painted the phases of the moon and images of the seven planets, and lucky and unlucky days were marked with studs of different colors.

When we had had enough of these diversions and were ready to enter the dining room, a slave—evidently assigned this job—shouted, 'Right foot first!' We were momentarily taken aback, for fear one of us should commit some faux pas as he entered the room. But just as we moved our right feet forward in unison, a slave stripped for flogging threw himself at our feet and begged us to save him! He was only guilty of a minor offense, it seemed: the bookkeeper's clothes had been stolen from him at the baths. They were only worth a pittance. We drew back our right feet and begged a pardon from the bookkeeper as he sat there counting gold pieces in the hallway. He looked up like royalty and said, 'It is not the financial loss that irks me, but the sheer negligence of this worthless slave! He lost *my* dress clothes, a birthday present from a client, dyed of course in the finest Tyrian purple. Admittedly they had been washed once. Well what can I say? You can have him!'

Grateful for the bookkeeper's munificence, we now entered dining room. Then the slave we had just saved ran up and, before we knew what had hit us, smothered us in kisses and thanked us effusively for our kindness. 'Listen,' he whispered, 'you'll see in a minute who it is you've befriended: the master's wine, courtesy of your waiter!'

At last we took our places. Some Alexandrian slave-boys poured melted snow over our hands, while others tended our feet, meticulously paring our hangnails. Not even this distasteful task was done in silence: they kept singing as they worked. I wanted to find out whether the entire household sang, so I ordered a drink. A most attentive slave promptly responded in a grating soprano. In fact, every request was answered in song. You would have thought you were in a pantomime, not a formal dining room. Nonetheless, they served great antipasto. Everyone was now in their place except for Trimalchio, who, following the current fashion, had reserved the most prominent seat for himself.

On the hors d'oeuvres tray stood a donkey of Corinthian bronze bearing saddlebags stuffed with olives, white in one side, black in the other. Two platters flanked the animal; their weight in silver and Trimalchio's name were engraved along their edges. Little bridges welded to the plate supported dormice sprinkled with honey and poppyseeds. There were even sausages sizzling on a silver gridiron, which arched over some Syrian plums and pomegranate seeds.

We were in the midst of these delicacies when Trimalchio was carried in to a fanfare of trumpets and placed amid a veritable fortress of cushions—a sight that elicited some indiscreet laughter from the guests. For his shaven head poked out of a scarlet shawl, and round his muffled neck he had tucked a napkin bearing a stripe of senatorial purple and a fringe of tassels that dangled here and there. On the smallest finger of his left hand he wore a huge gilded ring. On the very last joint of the next finger he wore a smaller ring that appeared to be pure gold, but actually was studded with little iron stars. But his display of wealth didn't stop there; he exposed his right biceps, which was adorned with a golden armlet and a bangle of ivory fastened by a bright metal clasp.

After picking his teeth with a silver toothpick, he began: 'Friends, I really wasn't in the mood to come to dinner yet; but rather than keep you waiting, I have denied myself every pleasure. At least allow me to finish my game.'

A slave followed with a board of terebinth and a pair of crystal dice. Then I noticed the most extravagant touch yet: instead of the usual white and black counting-stones, he had substituted coins of gold and silver. While he chattered away over his game and we tasted the hors d'oeuvres, a tray was served with a basket on it. There sat a wooden hen with her wings spread out in a circle, just as they do when they're hatching eggs. Two slaves immediately came up and, as the music blared on, began to search through the straw. Peahens' eggs were found and promptly distributed to the guests.

Trimalchio looked over at this scene and said, 'Friends, I had peahens' eggs placed under the chicken. But to tell the truth, I'm afraid they may have already been fertilized! Let's try them and see if they can still be sucked.'

We picked up our spoons —weighing no less than half a pound each—and poked at the eggs, which were encased in fine pastry. I was about to throw mine away, because it already seemed to have a chick inside it. Then I overheard a more experienced guest remark, 'I'll bet there's something good in here!' So I pushed my finger through the shell and found the fattest little fig-pecker marinated in peppered egg yolk.

Since his game was now interrupted, Trimalchio had ordered all the same dishes for himself and announced in a loud voice that whoever wanted a second glass of aperitif could have one. Then, suddenly, a musical cue was given and all at once our hors d'oeuvres were whisked away by a chorus of singing slaves. Amid all the commotion one of the dishes was accidentally dropped and a slave retrieved it from the floor. Trimalchio noticed this, had the servant's ears boxed, and ordered him to throw the dish back on the floor. A house slave appeared and began to sweep up the silverware along with the rest of the mess. Then two long-haired Ethiopians came in holding little wineskins—like those used to dampen the sand at the amphitheatre—and they poured wine over our hands. No one even offered water.

When complimented on his elegant service, Trimalchio replied, 'Mars loves a level playing field. So I've had each guest assigned his own table. And that way the bustle of these smelly slaves won't bother us so.'

Carefully sealed wine bottles were promptly served; attached to their necks were labels:

FALERNIAN WINE
BOTTLED IN THE CONSULSHIP OF OPIMIUS
ONE HUNDRED YEARS OLD

While we were studying the labels, Trimalchio clapped his hands together and cried, 'How sad! Even a bottle of wine outlives a mere man. So, let's wet our whistles, friends. Wine is life—and *this* wine's real Opimian! I didn't serve anything this good yesterday, and the guests were much classier.'

We were drinking the wine and thoroughly relishing all the luxuries of the feast when a slave brought in a silver skeleton so loosely jointed that its limbs swivelled in every direction. He promptly threw it down on the table several times. Each time its floppy limbs fell in a different pattern. Trimalchio responded in verse:

'Alas! Poor us! We all add up to squat;
once Hades gets his hooks in, that's the lot;
so live while it's your turn,' 'cause then it's not.'

Our applause was followed by a dish that was disappointingly small, but so odd it had everyone staring at it. On a round serving tray the twelve signs of the zodiac were arranged in a circle. Over each sign the specialty chef had placed the kind of food that fit its character: over Aries the ram, a ramifying pea; on Taurus the bull, a slice of rump roast; over Gemini the twins, testicles and kidneys; on the Crab, crown of flowers; over the Lion, a virile African fig; on Virgo, the womb of a barren sow; over Libra, a set of scales with a cheesetart on one side, balanced by a pancake on the other; on Scorpio, [the scorpion fish]; on Sagittarius, a seahorse; on Capricorn, a lobster; on Aquarius, a goose; on Pisces, a pair of snapper. In the middle of all this was a piece of turf, torn out roots and all, with a honeycomb sitting on it. An Egyptian slave boy was bringing bread around in a silver chafing dish…while the master himself belted out a tune from the mime, *The North African Quack,* in a hideous voice.

We were looking gloomily at this vile fare when Trimalchio piped up, 'Please let's eat! This is just the preamble to our dinner!'

As he spoke, four male dancers bounced up in time to the music and snatched the lid off the next dish. Inside we saw some fowl and sows' udders and a hare adorned with wings to look like Pegasus. At the corners of the dish we noticed four little statues of Marsyas the satyr; from their wineskins a pepper sauce poured over fish that looked as if they were swimming in a little canal. We all joined in the applause started by the slaves, and, grinning broadly, proceeded to attack the choicest items.

…As he was talking, a slave dropped a drinking cup. Trimalchio glared at him and said, 'Quickly, off with your head, since you're good-for-nothing.' Instantly, the boy's face fell and he begged Trimalchio's pardon. 'Why do you ask me, as if I were your problem? I suggest you beg yourself not to be a good-for-nothing.' Finally, we prevailed on him to pardon the boy. As soon as he was off the hook, he danced about the table…

'Water for the outside, wine for the insides,' shouted Trimalchio, and we laughed approvingly at his jest, especially Agamemnon, who certainly knew how to get invited back to dinner. Feeling appreciated, Trimalchio drank happily and, when he was virtually drunk, said, 'Won't any of you ask my Fortunata to dance? Believe me, no one does the bump and grind better!'

He then held his hands up in front of his forehead and impersonated the actor Syrus, while the whole household chanted, 'Do it! Do it!' He would have taken the floor, if Fortunata hadn't whispered something in his ear. I imagine she told him that such clownery didn't become him. But nothing was so unpredictable: one moment he would cower before Fortunata, and the next, revert to his natural self.

The impulse to dance was checked by a clerk who read aloud as if from a government document:

'July 26th: on the estate at Cumae, which belongs to Trimalchio, there were born thirty male slaves, forty females; 500,000 pecks of wheat were transferred from the threshing floor to the barn; 500 oxen were broken in.

'On the same day, the slave Mithridates was crucified for speaking disrespectfully of the guardian spirit of our Gaius.'

'On the same day, 10,000,000 in coin that could not be invested was returned to the strong-box.

'On the same day, there was a fire in the gardens at Pompeii that started in the house of Nasta the caretaker.

'What's that? When did I buy gardens in Pompeii?' asked Trimalchio.

'Last year,' said the clerk. 'So they are not yet on the books.'

Trimalchio was incensed: 'I forbid any property

bought for me to be entered on the books unless I know of it within six months!'

Even the police reports were being read and the wills of some game-keepers, in which Trimalchio was disinherited in a codicil. The names of some caretakers followed and a divorce was announced—of a night watchman from a freedwoman: she had been caught *in flagrante* with a bath attendant. A porter had been exiled to Baiae; a steward was being prosecuted; and a law suit between some valets had been decided.

But finally, the acrobats arrived: some big lug stood there with a ladder and had a boy jump from rung to rung and dance a jig at the top. Then he made the boy jump through burning hoops, and pick up a large wine bottle with his teeth! All this impressed Trimalchio alone, who kept saying, 'the arts are unappreciated.' But the two things he most enjoyed watching in all the world were acrobats and trumpeters; the other shows he thought were 'lightweight'. 'I even bought a troupe of professional actors,' he said, 'but I had them do Atellan farces and told my chorister to sing in Latin.'

Just as he was speaking, the acrobat...slipped and fell smack into our Trimalchio. The guests cried out as did the slaves, not on account of this pathetic creature whose neck they would happily have seen broken, but because it would spoil the dinner to end with a lament

over a perfect stranger. Trimalchio himself groaned aloud and bent over his arm as if he'd been wounded. Doctors ran up, and leading the way was Fortunata with her hair down and a goblet in hand crying out what a poor, unhappy creature she was. The boy who had fallen was already crawling around our feet begging for mercy. What was worse, as far as I was concerned, was that these pleadings might be the set-up for some kind of joke: I still remembered the cook who'd forgotten to gut the pig. So I was looking all over the dining room to see what kind of jack-in-the-box was about to spring out at us, especially after a slave was beaten for dressing Trimalchio's bruised arm in white instead of purple wool! My suspicion wasn't misplaced: instead of punishing the acrobat, Trimalchio gave him his freedom! That way no one could say that a man of his stature had been wounded by a lowly slave.

We applauded his clemency and chatted about the mutability of fortune. 'We mustn't let this event pass without a trace,' said Trimalchio; he immediately called for writing paper and, with scarcely a moment's thought, composed these verses:

'Things always spin the way no one expects;
Fortune on High all our affairs directs;
more good wine, boy, to counter these effects!'

Questions

(1) From the overall tone of the narrative and from individual examples, what observation might be made, or implications drawn, about the status and conditions of slaves in Rome?
(2) Are there correlations between Petronius' story and some of the points made by Sallust in Document 6–2? In what ways might the account of Trimalchio's banquet parallel or dispel Sallust's assessments?
(3) From Petronius' account, what can possibly be discerned about Roman middle-class values and priorities during the reign of Nero?

6–7

Julian Imperator: the ultimate pagan.

Julian, Emperor of Rome (reigned 361–363 B.C.E.), was a throwback to the Augustan period. Having been baptized and raised a Christian, he reverted to the ancestral paganism of the Civic cult, and was thus labelled by future (Christian) historians with the uncomplimentary term: "the Apostate," Julian was running against the spirit of his age and his attempted pagan revival collapsed upon his death. During his brief reign—as his letters demonstrate—he endeavored to straddle both worlds with a policy of toleration. The following excerpts from his letters address: the ironic punishment of Arian Christians; the lingering of paganist sentiment and forms, even in Christian settings; admiration for Christian charity; and adminitions for restraint while dealing with Christians ("Galileans").

Source: Finley Hooper & Matthew Schwartz, ed., *Roman Letters: History from a Personal Point of View* (Detroit: Wayne State University Press, 1991), pp. 133, 136, 139, 140, 142.

I have behaved to all the Galilaeans [Christians] with such kindness and benevolence that none of them has

suffered violence anywhere or been dragged into a temple or threatened into anything else of the sort against his own will. But the followers of the Arian church, in the insolence bred by their wealth, have attacked the followers of Valentine [founder of an obscure sect of Gnostics] and have committed in Edessa such rash acts as could never occur in a well-ordered city. Therefore, since by their most admirable law they are bidden to sell all they have and give to the poor that so they may attain more easily to the kingdom of the skies, in order to aid those persons in that effort, I have ordered that all their funds, namely, that belong to the church of the people of Edessa, are to be taken over that they may be given to the soldiers, and that its property be confiscated to my private purse. This is in order that poverty may teach them to behave properly and that they may not be deprived of that heavenly kingdom for which they still hope.

***

I stayed [in Beroea, modern Aleppo in northwest Syria] for a day and saw the Acropolis and sacrificed to Zeus in imperial fashion a white bull. Also I conversed briefly with the senate about the worship of the gods. But though they all applauded my arguments very few were converted by them, and these few were men who even before I spoke seemed to me to hold sound views. But they were cautious and would not strip off and lay aside their modest reserve, as though afraid of too frank speech. For it is the prevailing habit of mankind, O ye gods, to blush for their noble qualities, manliness of soul and piety, and to plume themselves, as it were, on what is most depraved, sacrilege and weakness of mind and body.

***

I should never have favoured Pegasius unhesitatingly if I had not had clear proofs even in former days, when he had the title of the Bishop of the Galileans [Christians], he was wise enough to revere and honour the gods.…after rising at early dawn I came from Troas to Ilois about the middle of the morning. Pegasius came to meet me, as I wished to explore the city—this was my excuse for visiting the temples—and he was my guide and showed me all the sights. So now let me tell you what he did and said, and from it one may guess that he was not lacking in right sentiments towards the gods.

Hector has a hero's shrine there and his bronze statue stands in a tiny little temple. Opposite this they have set up a figure of the great Achilles in the unroofed court.…Now I found that the altars were still alight a I might almost say still blazing, and that the statue of Hector had been anointed till it shone. So I looked at Pegasius and said: "What does this mean? Do the people of Ilios offer sacrifices?" This was to test him cautiously, to find out his own views. He replied: "Is it not natural that they should worship a brave man

who was their own citizen, just as we worship the martyrs?" Now the analogy was far from sound; but his point of view and intentions were those of a man of culture, if you consider the times in which we then lived. Observe what followed. "Let us go," said he, "to the shrine of Athene of Ilios." Thereupon with the greatest eagerness he led me there and opened the temple, and as though he were producing evidence he showed me all the statues in perfect preservation, nor did he behave at all as those impious men do usually, I mean when they make the sign on their impious foreheads, nor did he hiss to himself as they do. For these two things are the quintessence of their theology, to hiss at demons and make the sign of the cross on their foreheads.…This same Pegasius went with me to the temple of Achilles as well and showed me the tomb in good repair; yet I had been informed that this also had been pulled to pieces by him. But he approached it with great reverence; I saw this with my own eyes.

***

Why…do we not observe that it is their benevolence to strangers, their care for the graves of the dead and the pretended holiness of their lives that have done most to increase atheism [Julian often refers to Christianity this way]? I believe that we ought really and truly to practice every one of these virtues. And it is not enough for you alone to practice them, but so must all the priests in Galatia, without exception…In the second place, admonish them that no priest may enter a theatre or drink in a tavern or control any craft or trade that is base and not respectable. Honour those who obey you, but those who disobey, expel from office. In every city establish frequent hostels in order that strangers may profit by our benevolence; I do not mean for our own people only, but for others also who are in need of money.…For it is disgraceful that, when no Jew ever has to beg and the impious Galilaeans [Christians] support not only their own poor but ours as well, all men see that our people lack aid from us.

***

I thought that the leaders of the Galilaeans would be more grateful to me than to my predecessor in the administration of the Empire. For in his reign it happened to the majority of them to be sent into exile, prosecuted, and cast into prison, and moreover, many whole communities of those who are called "heretics" were actually butchered, as at Samosata and Cyzicus, in Paphlagonia, Bithynia, and Galatia, among many other tribes also villages were sacked and completely devastated; whereas, during my reign, the contrary has happened. For those who had been exiled have had their exile remitted, and those whose property was confiscated have, by a law of mine received permission to recover all their possessions. Yet they have reached such a pitch of raving madness and folly that they are exasperated because they are not allowed to behave like tyrants or to persist in the conduct in which they at one time indulged against one another, and afterwards carried on towards us who revered the gods....but do you, the populace, live in agreement with one another, and let no man be quarrelsome or act unjustly. Neither let those of you who have strayed from the truth outrage those who worship the gods duly and justly, according to the beliefs that have been handed down to us from time immemorial; nor let those of you who worship the gods outrage or plunder the houses of those who have strayed rather from ignorance than of set purpose. It is by reason that we ought to persuade and instruct men,

not by blows, or insults, or bodily violence. Wherefore, again and often I admonish those who are zealous for true religion not to injure the communities of the Galilaeans or attack or insult them....

***

I affirm by the gods that I do not wish the Galilaeans to be either put to death or unjustly beaten, or to suffer any other injury; but nevertheless I do assert absolutely that the god-fearing must be preferred to them. For through the folly of the Galilaeans almost everything has been overturned, whereas through the grace of the gods are we all preserved. Wherefore we ought to honour the gods and the god-fearing, both men and cities.

Questions

(1) How does Julian administer an ironic/humorous penalty upon the Arians?

(2) What do the letters referring to the Emperor's stay in Beroea and his meeting with Bishop Pegasius reveal about the state of pagan worship?

(3) What significant Christian virtue does Julian grudgingly concede, and how does he describe his administrative policy towards the Christian church?

(4) How does Julian's attitude contrast with that of Pliny and Trajan in Document 6–4? What inferences can be drawn?

6–8

Sidonius Appolinaris: Rome's decay, and a glimpse of the new order.

Sidonius Appolinaris (430?–485? C.E.) descended from an aristocratic family that had, by the time of his birth, completely converted to Christianity. Sidonius would witness the final agonizing years of the western Roman Empire, ending his days as Bishop of Clermont in Southern France. Like many people of his rank and position, Sidonius had to come to terms with the half-civilized Germanic invaders (in his case, the Visigoths). He writes admiringly of the Visigothic king, Theodoric II (first letter); and of wedding of the Frankish prince Sigismer (second letter). All the same, his third letter reflects a pervasive concern over the power of the Germans, and their potential for destruction.

Source: Finley, Hooper & Matthew Schwartz, ed., *Roman Letters: History from a Personal Point of View* (Detriot: Wayne State University, 1991), pp. 272–277.

1

You have often begged a description of Theodoric the Gothic king, whose gentle breeding fame commends to every nation; you want him in his quantity and quality, in his person, and the manner of his existence. I gladly accede, as far as the limits of my page allow, and highly approve so fine and ingenuous a curiosity.

Well, he is a man worth knowing, even by those who cannot enjoy his close acquaintance, so happily have Providence and Nature joined to endow him with the perfect gifts of fortune; his way of life is such that not even the envy which lies in wait for a king can rob

him of his proper praise. And first as to his person. He is well set up, in height above the average man, but below the giant. His head is round, with curled hair retreating somewhat from brow to crown. His nervous neck is free from disfiguring knots. The eyebrows are bushy and arched; when the lids droop, the lashes reach almost half-way down the cheeks. The upper ears are buried under overlying locks, after the fashion of his race. The nose is finely aquiline; the lips are thin and not enlarged by undue distention of the mouth. Every day the hair springing from his nostrils is cut back; that on the face springs thick from the hollow of the temples, but the razor has not yet come upon his cheek, and his barber is assiduous in eradicating the rich growth on the lower part of the face. Chin, throat, and neck art full, but not fat, and all of fair complexion; seen close, their colour is fresh as that of youth; they often flush, but from modesty, and not from anger. His shoulders are smooth, the upper- and forearms strong and hard; hands broad, breast prominent; waist receding. The spine dividing the broad expanse of back does not project, and you can see the spring of the ribs; the sides swell with salient muscle, the well-girt flanks are full of vigour. His thighs are like hard horn; the knee-joints firm and masculine; the knees themselves the comeliest and least wrinkled in the world. A full ankle supports the leg, and the foot is small to bear such mighty limbs.

Now for the routine of his public life. Before day-break he goes with a very small suite to attend the service of his priests. He prays with assiduity, but, if I may speak in confidence, one may suspect more of habit than conviction in this piety. Administrative duties of the kingdom take up the rest of the morning. Armed nobles stand about the royal seat; the mass of guards in their garb of skins are admitted that they may be within call but kept at the threshold for quiet's sake; only a murmur of them comes in from their post at the doors, between the curtain and the outer barrier. And now the foreign envoys are introduced. The king hears them out, and says little; if a thing needs more discussion he puts it off, but accelerates matters ripe for dispatch. The second hour arrives; he rises from the throne to inspect his treasure-chamber or stable. If the chase is the order of the day, he joins it, but never carries his bow at his side, considering this derogatory to royal state. When a bird or beast is marked for him, or happens to cross his path, he puts his hand behind his back and takes the bow from a page with the string all hanging loose; for as he deems it a boy's trick to bear it in a quiver, so he holds it effeminate to receive the weapon ready strung. When it is given him, he sometimes holds it in both hands and bends the extremities towards each other; at others he sets it, knot-end downward, against his lifted heel, and runs his finger up the slack and wavering string. After that, he takes his arrows, adjusts, and lets fly. He will ask you beforehand what you would like him to transfix; you choose, and he hits. If there is a miss through either's error, your vision will mostly be at fault, and not the archer's skill.

On ordinary days, his table resembles that of a private person. The board does not groan beneath a mass of dull and unpolished silver set on by panting servitors; the weight lies rather in the conversation than in the plate; there is either sensible talk or none. The hangings and draperies used on these occasions are sometimes of purple silk, sometimes only of linen; art, not costliness, commends the fare, as spotlessness rather than bulk the silver. Toasts are few, and you will oftener see a thirsty guest impatient, than a full one refusing cup or bowl. In short, you will find elegance of Greece, good cheer of Gaul, Italian nimbleness, the state of public banquets with the attentive service of a private table, and everywhere the discipline of a king's house. What need for me to describe the pomp of his feast days? No man is so unknown as not to know of them. But to my theme again. The siesta after dinner is always slight and sometimes intermitted. When inclined for the board-game, he is quick to gather up the dice, examines them with care, shakes the box with expert hand, throws rapidly, humorously apostrophizes them, and patiently waits the issue. Silent at a good throw, he makes merry over a bad, annoyed by neither fortune, and always the philosopher. He is too proud to ask or to refuse a revenge; he disdains to avail himself of one if offered; and if it is opposed will quietly go on playing. You effect recovery of your man without obstruction on his side; he recovers his without collusion upon yours. You see the strategist when he moves the pieces; his one thought is victory. Yet at play he puts off a little of his kingly rigour, inciting all to good fellowship and the freedom of the game: I think he is afraid of being feared. Vexation in the man whom he beats delights him; he will never believe that his opponents have not let him win unless their annoyance proves him really victor. You would be surprised how often the pleasure born of these little happenings may favour the march of great affairs....I myself am gladly beaten by him when I have a favor to ask, since the loss of my game may mean the gaining of my cause. About the ninth hour, the burden of government begins again. Back come the importunates, back the ushers to remove them; on all sides buzz the voices of petitioners, a sound which lasts till evening, and does not diminish till interrrupted by the royal repast; even then they disperse to attend their various patrons among the courtiers, and are astir till bedtime. Sometimes, though this is rare, supper is enlivened by sallies of mimes, but no guest is ever exposed to the wound of a biting tongue. Withal there is no noise of hydraulic organ, or choir with its conductor intoning a set piece; you will hear no players of lyre of flute, no master of the music, no girls with cithara or tabor; the king cares for no strains but those which no less charm the mind with virtue than the ear with melody. When he rises to withdraw, the treasury watch begins its vigil; armed sentries stand on guard during the first hours of slumber. But I am wandering from my subject. I never promised a whole chapter on the kingdom, but a few words about the king. I must stay my pen; you asked for nothing more than one or two facts about the person and the tastes of Theodoric; and my own aim was to write a letter, not a history.

2

You take such pleasure in the sight of arms and those

who wear them, that I can imagine your delight if you could have seen the young prince Sigismer on his way to the palace of his father-in-law in the guise of a bridegroom or suitor in all the pomp and bravery of the tribal fashion. His own steed with its caparisons, other steeds laden with flashing gems, paced before and after; but the conspicuous interest in the procession centred in the prince himself as with a charming modesty he went afoot amid his bodyguard and footmen, in flame-red mantle, with much glint of ruddy gold, and gleam of snowy silken tunic, his fair hair, red cheeks and white skin according with the three hues of his equipment. But the chiefs and allies who bore him company were dread of aspect, even thus on peace intent. Their feet were laced in boots of bristly hide reaching to the heels; ankles and legs were exposed. They wore high tight tunics of varied colour hardly descending to their bare knees, the sleeves covering only the upper arm. Green mantles they had with crimson borders; baldrics supported swords hung from their shoulders, and pressed on sides covered with cloaks of skin secured by brooches. No small part of their adornment consisted of their arms; in their hands they grasped barbed spears and missile axes; their left sides were guarded by shields, which flashed with tawny golden bosses and snowy silver borders, betraying at once their wealth and their good taste. Though the business in hand was wedlock, Mars was no whit less prominent in all his pomp than Venus. Why need I say more? Only your presence was wanting to the full enjoyment of so fine a spectacle. For when I saw you had missed the things you love to see, I longed to have you with me in all the impatience of your longing soul.

3

Rumour has it that the Goths have occupied Roman soil; our unhappy Auvergne is always their gateway on every such incursion. It is our fate to furnish fuel to the fire of a peculiar hatred, for, by Christ's aid, we are the sole obstacle to the fulfilment of their ambition to extend their frontier to the Rhone, and so hold all the country between that river, the Atlantic, and the Loire. Their menacing power has long pressed us hard; it has already swallowed up whole tracts of territory round us, and threatens to swallow more. We mean to resist with spirit, though we know our peril and the risks which we incur. But our trust is not in our poor walls impaired by fire, or in our rotting palisades, or in our ramparts worn by the breasts of the sentries, as they lean on them in continual watch. Our only present help we find in those Rogations which you introduced; and this is the reason why the people of Clermont refuse to recede, though terror surge about them on every side. By inauguration and institution of these prayers we are already new initiates; and if so far we have effected less than you have, our hearts are affected equally with yours. For it is not

unknown to us by what portents and alarms the city entrusted to you by God was laid desolate at the time when first you ordained this form of prayer. Now it was earthquake, shattering the outer palace walls with frequent shocks; now fire, piling mounds of glowing ash upon proud houses fallen in ruin; now, amazing spectacle! wild deer grown ominously tame, making their lairs in the very forum. You saw the city being emptied of its inhabitants, rich and poor taking to flight. But you resorted in our latter day to the example shown of old in Nineveh, that you at least might not discredit the divine warning by the spectacle of your despair. And, indeed, you of all men have been least justified in distrusting the providence of God, after the proof of it vouchsafed to your own virtues. Once, in a sudden conflagration, your faith burned stronger than the flames. In full sight of the trembling crowd you stood forth all alone to stay them, and lo! the fire leapt back before you, a sinuous beaten fugitive. It was miracle, a formidable thing, unseen before and unexampled; the element which naturally shrinks from nothing, retired in awe at your approach. You therefore first enjoined a fast upon a few members of our sacred order, denouncing gross offences, announcing punishment, promising relief. You made it clear that if the penalty of sin was nigh, so also was the pardon; you proclaimed that by frequent prayer the menace of coming desolation might be removed. You taught that it was by water of tears rather than water of rivers that the obstinate and raging fire could best be extinguished, and by firm faith the threatening shock of earthquake stayed. The multitude of the lowly forthwith followed your counsel, and this influenced persons of higher rank, who had not scrupled to abandon the town, and now were not ashamed to return to it. By this devotion God was appeased, who sees into all hearts; your fervent prayers were counted to you for salvation; they became an example for your fellow citizens, and a defence about you all, for after those days there were neither portents to alarm, nor visitations to bring disaster.

We of Clermont know that all these ills befell your people of Vienne before the Rogations, and have not befallen them since; and therefore it is that we are eager to follow the lead of so holy a guide, beseeching your Beatitude from your own pious lips to give us the advocacy of those prayers now known to us by the examples which you have transmitted. Since the Confessor Ambrose discovered the remains of Gervasius and Protasius, it has been granted to you alone in the West to translate the relics of two martyrs—all the holy body of Ferteolus, and the head of our martyr Julian, which once the executioner's gory hand brought to the raging persecutor from the place of testimony. It is only fair, then, in compensation for the loss of this hallowed relic, that some part of your patronage should come to us from Vienne, since a part of our patronal saint has migrated thither. Deign to hold us in remembrance, my Lord Bishop.

Questions

(1) What is the overall impression given by Sidonius in his decription of Theodoric II—admiration or fear? What specific evidence might support either viewpoint?

(2) On what does Sidonius seem to focus in his description of Sigismer's wedding festivities?

(3) For what reasons does Sidonius fear for the future of his native region of Auvergne? What does he single out as his peoples' main hope for survival?

(4) What do the letters reveal about the character, policy, and priorities of Sidonius himself?

CHAPTER 7

7–1

Kung Fu-tzu: "The Master" and his persistent legacy.

It would not be possible to understand Chinese civilization prior to 1949 without considering the lasting influence of the scholar/official/philosopher Kung Fu-tzu (551–478 B.C.E.), more popularly known by the Westernized form of his name: Confucius. His ethical and educational standards and stress on the universal harmony of interrelationships have attained, for many, a religious status. Certainly, his teachings have had the most pervasive and dominant impact on the Chinese mind and conscience through the centuries. During his lifetime he is alleged to have compiled the most significant of the Xia, Shang, and Zhou documents into the "Classics" of China. Confucius did not write much of his own and accounts of his life ("Li-chi" documents) and sayings ("Analects," selections) were only put together by his disciples after his death.

Source: William Theodore de Bary, et al., eds., *Sources of Chinese Tradition* (N.Y.: Columbia University Press,1960), p. 24–25, 28–31, 191–192. Quoted in Mircea Eliade, *From Medicine Men to Muhammad* (N.Y.: Harper & Row, 1974), pp. 146–149.

LI-CHI', 9

Once Confucious was taking part in the winter sacrifice. After the ceremony was over, he went for a stroll along the top of the city gate and sighed mournfully. He sighed for the state of Lu.

His disciple Yet Yen [Tzu lu], who was by his side, asked: 'Why should the gentleman sigh?'

Confucius replied: 'The practice of the Great Way, the illustrious men of the Three Dynasties—these I shall never know in person. And yet they inspire my ambition! When the Great Way was practised, the world was shared by all alike. The worthy and the able were promoted to office and men practised good faith and lived in affection. Therefore they did not regard as parents only their own parents, or as sons only their own sons. The aged found a fitting close to their lives, the robust their proper employment; the young were provided with an upbringing and the widow and widower, the orphaned and the sick, with proper care. Men had their tasks and women their hearths. They hated to see goods lying about in waste, yet they did not hoard them for themselves; they disliked the thought that their energies were not fully used, yet they used them not for private ends. Therefore all evil plotting was prevented and thieves and rebels did not arise, so people could leave their outer gates unbolted. This was the age of Grand Unity.

'Now the Great Way has become hid and the world is the possession of private families. Each regards as parents only his own parents, as sons only his sons; goods and labour are employed for selfish ends. Hereditary offices and titles are granted by ritual law while walls and moats must provide security. Ritual and righteousness are used to regulate the relationship between ruler and subject, to insure affection between father and son, peace between brothers, and harmony between husband and wife, to set up social institutions, organize the farms and villages, honour the brave and wise, and bring merit to the individual. Therefore intrigue and plotting come about and men take up arms. Emperor Yu, kings T'ang, Wen, Wu, and Ch'eng and the Duke of Chou achieved eminence for this reason: that all six rulers were constantly attentive to ritual, made manifest their righteousness and acted in complete faith. They exposed error, made humanity their law and humility their practice, showing the people wherein they should constantly abide. If there were any who did not abide by these principles, they were dismissed from their positions and regarded by the multitude as dangerous. This is the period of Lesser Prosperity.'

'ANALECTS,' SELECTIONS

Confucius said: 'At fifteen, I set my heart on learning. At thirty, I was firmly established. At forty, I had no more doubts. At fifty, I knew the will of Heaven. At sixty, I was ready to listen to it. At seventy I could follow my heart's desire without transgressing what was right.'

When Confucius was in Ch'i, he heard the Shao music and for three months he forgot the taste of meat, saying: 'I never thought music could be so beautiful.'

Confucius said: 'When walking in a party of three, I always have teachers, I can select the good qualities of the one for imitation, and the bad ones of the other and correct them in myself.'

Confucius said: 'I am a transmitter and not a creator. I believe in and have a passion for the ancients. I venture to compare myself with our old P'eng (China's Methuselah).'

Confucius said: 'Sometimes I have gone a whole day without food and a whole night without sleep, giving myself to thought. It was no use. It is better to learn.'

There were four things that Confucius was determined to eradicate: a biased mind, arbitrary judgments, obstinacy, and egotism.

Confucius said: 'Those who know the truth are not up to those who love it; those who love the truth are not up to those who delight in it.'

Confucius said: 'Having heard the Way (Tao) in the morning, one may die content in the evening.'

Humanity (*jen*)

Fan Ch'ih asked about humanity. Confucius said: 'Love men.'

Tzu Chang asked Confucius about humanity. Confucius said: 'To be able to practise five virtues anywhere in the world constitutes humanity.' Tzu Chang begged to know what these were. Confucius said: 'Courtesy, magnaminity, good faith, diligence, and kindness. He who is courteous is not humiliated, he who is magnanimous wins the multitude, he who is of good faith is trusted by the people, he who is diligent attains his objective, and he who is kind can get service from the people.'

Confucius said: 'Without humanity a man cannot long endure adversity, nor can he long enjoy prosperity.

The humane rest in humanity; the wise find it beneficial.'

Confucius said: 'Only the humane man can love men and can hate men.'

Filial Piety

Tzu Yu asked about filial piety. Confucius said: 'Nowadays a filial son is just a man who keeps his parents in food. But even dogs or horses are given food. If there is no feeling of reverence, wherein lies the difference?'

Tzu Hsia asked about filial piety. Confucius said: 'The manner is the really difficult thing. When anything has to be done the young people undertake it; when there is wine and food the elders are served—is this all there is to filial piety?'

Religious Sentiment

Tzu Lu asked about the worship of ghosts and spirits. Confucius said: 'We don't know yet how to serve men, how can we know about serving the spirits?' 'What about death,' was the next question. Confucius said: 'We don't know yet about life, how can we know about death?'

Fan Ch'ih asked about wisdom. Confucius said: 'Devote yourself to the proper demands of the people, respect the ghosts and spirits but keep them at a distance—this may be called wisdom.' (VI, 20.)

Questions

(1) In "Li-chi," what did Confucius regard as being responsible for China's moral deterioration?

(2) At what age did Confucius believe that he had attained an ideal state of knowledge?

(3) What are Confucius' ideas regarding the hereafter?

7–2

Government by centralization and mistrust: the Legalist credo of Han Fei-tzu.

Legalism arose out of the breakdown in order that prevailed during the later Zhou period. As defined by its founder Han Fei-tzu (d. 233 B.CE.) and implemented by the first Qin Emperor Shi Huang Ti (221–210 B.C.E.), Legalism settled for nothing short of the vesting of total political authority in the hands of a single individual and utter regulation of all aspects of human society by the government. It worked on the premise that human nature tended towards anarchy and that people, in Alexander Hamilton's words, were "a great beast." Han Fei-tzu, a prince of the Han kingdom, was never able to personally implement his ideas; he was forced to commit suicide after losing a political power-struggle.

Source: Burton Watson, trans., *Han Fei Tzu, Basic Writings* (N.Y.: Columbia University Press, 1964), pp. 16–17, 35–42, passim. Quoted in Marc Anthony Meyer, *Landmarks of World Civilization*, Vol.1 (Guilford, CT: Dushkin, 1994), pp. 193–197.

The Way [Tao] is the beginning of all beings and the measure of right and wrong. Therefore the enlightened ruler holds fast to the beginning in order to understand the wellspring of all beings, and minds the measure in order to know the source of good and bad. He waits, empty and still, letting **names** define themselves and affairs reach their own settlement. Being empty, he can comprehend the true aspect of fullness; being still, he can correct the mover.

Those whose duty it is to speak will come forward to name themselves; those whose duty it is to act will produce results. When names and results match, the ruler need do nothing more and the true aspect of all things will be revealed.

Hence it is said: The ruler must not reveal his desires; for if he reveals his desires his ministers will put on the mask that pleases him. He must not reveal his will; for if he does so his ministers will show a different face. So it is said: Discard likes and dislikes and the ministers will show their true form; discard wisdom and wile and the ministers will watch their step. Hence, though the ruler is wise, he hatches no schemes from his wisdom, but causes all men to know their place. Though he has worth, he does not display it in his deeds, but observes the motives of his ministers. Though he is brave, he does not flaunt his bravery in shows of indignation, but allows his subordinates to display their valor to the full. Thus, though he discards wisdom, his rule is enlightened; though he discards worth, he achieves merit; and though he discards bravery, his state grows powerful. When the ministers stick to their posts, the hundred officials have their regular duties, and the ruler employs each according to his particular ability, this is known as the state of manifold constancy.

Hence it is said: "So still he seems to dwell nowhere at all; so empty no one can seek him out." The enlightened ruler reposes in nonaction above, and below his ministers tremble with fear....

If you do not guard the door, if you do not make fast the gate, then tigers will lurk there....

The ruler of men stands in danger of being blocked in five ways. When the ministers shut out their ruler, this is one kind of block. When they get control of the wealth and resources of the state, this is a second kind of block. When they are free to issue orders as they please, this is a third kind. When they are able to do righteous deeds in their own name, this is a fourth kind. When they are able to build up their own cliques, this is a fifth kind. If ministers shut out the ruler, then he loses the effectiveness of his position. If they control wealth and resources, he loses the means of dispensing bounty to others. If they issue orders as they please, he loses the means of command. If they are able to carry out righteous deeds in their own name, he loses his claim to enlightenment. And if they can build up cliques of their own, he loses his supporters. All these are rights that should be exercised by the ruler alone; they should never pass into the hands of his ministers....

The enlightened ruler in bestowing rewards is as benign as the seasonable rain; the dew of his bounty profits all men. But in doling out punishment he is as terrible as the thunder; even the holy sages cannot assuage him. The enlightened ruler is never over-liberal in his rewards, never over-lenient in his punishments. If his rewards are too liberal, then ministers who have won merit in the past will grow lax in their duties; and if his punishments are too lenient, then evil ministers will find it easy to do wrong. Thus if a man has truly won merit, no matter how humble and far removed he may be, he must be rewarded; and if he has truly committed error, no matter how close and dear to the ruler he may be, he must be punished. If those who are humble and far removed can be sure of reward, and those close and dear to the ruler can be sure of punishment, then the former will not stint in their efforts and the latter will not grow proud.

***

Both Heaven [Nature] and man have their fixed destinies. Fragrant aromas and delicate flavors, rich wine and fat meat delight the palate but sicken the body. Fair lineaments and pearly teeth warm the heart but waste the spirit. Therefore renounce riot and excess, for only then can you keep your health unharmed.

Don't let your power be seen; be blank and actionless. Government reaches to the four quarters, but its source is in the center. The sage holds to the source and the four quarters come to serve him. In emptiness he awaits them, and they spontaneously do what is needed. When all within the four seas have been put in their proper places, he sits in darkness to observe the light. When those to the left and right have taken their places, he opens the gate to face the world. He changes nothing, alters nothing, but acts with the two handles of reward and punishment, acts and never ceases: this is what is called walking the path of principle....

The Way is vast and great and without form; its Power is clear and order and extends everywhere. Since it extends to all living beings, they use it proportionately; but, though all things flourish through it, it does not rest among things. The Way pervades all affairs here below. Therefore examine and obey the decrees of Heaven and live and die at the right time; compare names, differentiate events, comprehend their unity, and identify yourself with the Way's true nature....

The way to listen to the words of the ministers is to take the statements that come from them and compare them with the powers that have been invested in them. Therefore you must examine names carefully in order to establish ranks, clarify duties in order to distinguish worth. This is the way to listen to the words of others: be silent as though in a drunken stupor. Say to yourself: Lips! teeth! do not be the first to move; lips! teeth! be thicker, be clumsier than ever! Let others say their piece—I will gain knowledge thereby.

Though right and wrong swarm about him, the

ruler does not argue with them. Be empty, still, inactive, for this is the true nature of the Way. Study, compare, and see what matches, for this will reveal how much has been accomplished. Compare with concrete results; check against empty assertions. Where the root and base of the affair are unshaken, there will be no error in movement or stillness. Whether you move or remain still, transform all through inaction. If you show delight, your affairs will multiply; if you show hatred, resentment will be born. Therefore discard both delight and hatred and with an empty mind become the abode of the Way.

The ruler does not try to work side by side with his people, and they accordingly respect the dignity of his position. He does not try to tell others what to do, but leaves them to do things by themselves. Tightly he bars his inner door, and from his room looks out into the courtyard; he has provided the rules and yardsticks, so that all things know their place. Those who merit reward are rewarded; those who deserve punishment are punished. Reward and punishment follow the deed; each man brings them upon himself. Therefore, whether the result is pleasant or hateful, who dares to question it? When compass and rule have marked out one corner of truth, the other three corners will become evident them-selves. If the ruler is not godlike in his isolation, his subordinates will find ways to move him. If his management of affairs is not impartial, they will guess at his inclinations. Be like Heaven, be like earth, and all coils will be untangled. Be like Heaven, be like earth; then who will be close to you, who will be distant? He who can model himself on Heaven and earth may be called a sage....

In ferreting out evil within the palace and controlling it outside, you yourself must hold fast to your standards and measurements. Whittle away from those who have too much, enhance those who have too little, but let the taking and the giving be according to measure. Never allow men to form cliques or join together to deceive their superiors. Let your whittling be as gradual as the slimming moon, your enhancing like a slow-spreading heat. Simplify the laws and be cautious in the use of penalties but, where punishments are called for, make certain they are carried out. Never loosen your bow, or you will find two cocks in a single roost, squawking in fierce rivalry. When wildcat and wolf break into the fold, the sheep are not likely to increase. When one house has two venerables, its affairs will never prosper. When husband and wife both give orders, the children are at a loss to know which one to obey....

Questions

(1) Is it fair to characterize Han's portrait of the effective ruler as being "unprincipled" or "immoral"? Explain.

(2) What, according to Han, must never slip from a ruler's control if he wishes to govern properly?

(3) What value does Han place on a ruler's use of silence, and why?

7–3

Mencius: the counterattack on Legalism.

So deep was the hatred engendered by the Legalist policies of Emperor Shi Huang Ti that those who had taken an opposing point of view by championing the idea of humane and moral political leadership were regarded as sages. The individual who exemplified this attitude was the philosopher Mencius (372–289 B.C.E.). A follower of Confucianism, Mencius went further than The Master in emphasizing a government's ethical mission to those it governed. His book, the "Meng-tze," is considered one of the "Four Books" of Confucianism.

Source: S.E. Frost, Jr., ed., *The Sacred Writings of the World's Great Religions* (N.Y.: McGraw-Hill, 1972), pp. 113–117.

Mencius went to visit King Hui of Liang. The King said to him: You are an old man, yet you have not shrunk from a journey of a thousand *li* in order to come hither. Doubtless you have something in your mind which will profit my kingdom?

Mencius replied: Why must your Majesty use that word "profit"? My business is with benevolence and righteousness and nothing else. If the King says, How shall I profit my kingdom? the great officers will say, How shall we profit our families? and the petty officers and common people will say, How shall we profit our-selves? And while upper and lower are thus engaged in a fierce struggle for profits, the State will be brought into peril. If the ruler of ten thousand chariots is slain, it will be by a family of a thousand; if the ruler of a thousand chariots is slain, it will be by a family of a hundred. A thousand out of ten thousand or a hundred out of one thousand, is no small proportion of the whole. But if righteousness be considered of less importance than profit, people will never be satisfied without grasping more than they possess. As benevolence is incompatible with neglect of one's parents, so righteousness never puts the interests of one's sovereign last. Let me, then, hear your Majesty speak only of benevolence and righteousness. There is no need to use the word "profit" at all.

Kung-sun Ch'ou asked, saying: If, Sir, you were appointed Chancellor of the Ch'i State, you would be able to put your principles into practice; and it would not be at all surprising if you thereby succeeded in obtaining the hegemony, or the royal dignity itself, for your prince. In such circumstances, would you feel agitated in mind?—No, replied Mencius; by the age of forty I had achieved imperturbability of mind. In that case, you are far superior to Meng Pen.—It is not hard to acquire. The philosopher Kao achieved the same result before I did. Is there any special method of acquiring it?—Oh, yes. Pei-kung Yu trained himself in physical courage so as not to flinch from a blow or to relax the steadiness of his gaze. He would resent the slightest push from anybody as fiercely as a thrashing in the market-place; he would not stomach an insult either from a coarsely clad man of the people or from a lord of ten thousand chariots. When it came to stabbing, prince and pauper were all the same to him. He stood in no awe of the feudal princes, and if an abusive word was addressed to him, he would be sure to retort.

Meng Shih-she had another method of fostering his courage. He used to say: "I care not whether I win or lose. One who weighs up the enemy before he advances, and plans for victory before he joins battle, is in reality afraid of the army he is fighting. How can I make certain of victory? "All I can do is to have no fear." Meng Shih-she was like Tseng Tzu and Pei-kung Yu was like Tzu Hsia. Which of the two was the more courageous I do not know, but Meng Shih-she held to the essential point. Tseng Tzu once said to his disciple Tzu Hsiang: "Do you admire courage? On the subject of courage in its highest form I once heard our Master say: If on self-examination I find that I am not in the right, shall I not be afraid even of the humblest yokel? But if I find that I am in the right, I will face the enemy in his thousands and tens of thousands." After all, Meng Shih-she's hold on his spirit was not so good as Tseng Tzu's hold on the essential point.

Mencius said: He is a tyrant who uses force while making a show of benevolence. To be a tyrant one must have a large kingdom at one's command. He is a true king who practises benevolence in a virtuous spirit. To be a true king, one need not wait for a large kingdom. T'ang ruled over seventy square li, and King Wen over

a hundred. When men are subdued by force, it is not their hearts that are won but their strength that gives out. When men are won by goodness, their hearts are glad within them and their submission is sincere. Thus were the seventy disciples of Confucius won by their Master. This is what is meant in the *Book of Songs* where it says: "From east and west, from north and south, came no thought but of surrender."

Mencius said: Benevolence brings honour, without it comes disgrace. To hate disgrace and yet to be content to live without benevolence, is like hating damp and yet living in a hollow. If a ruler hates disgrace, his best way is to prize virtue and do honour to the scholar. With worthy men in high places and able men in office, his country may enjoy a season of peace and quiet; and if he uses this opportunity to clarify law and government, even a great kingdom will be wary of him. It is said in the *Book of Songs*:

> "Ere that the rain-clouds gathered,
> I took the bark of the mulberry tree
> And wove it into window and door.
> Now, ye people below,
> Which of you will dare to affront me?"

Confucius said of the maker of this ode that he knew the principles of statecraft; for who will dare to affront a ruler that can order his kingdom well? But, now that the State is enjoying a season of quiet, to use the opportunity for junketing and idle amusement is nothing less than seeking out misfortune. Happiness and misfortune are indeed always of man's own seeking. That is the lesson conveyed in the *Book of Songs*:

> "Ever adjust thyself to the will of Heaven,
> And great happiness will be thine;"

and in the T'ai Chia: "Heaven-sent calamities you may stand up against, but you cannot survive those brought on by yourself."

Mencius said: All men have a certain sympathy towards their fellows. The great monarchs of old had this human sympathy, and it resulted in their government being sympathetic. Having this feeling of sympathy for his fellows, he who acts upon it in governing the Empire will find that his rule can be conducted as it were in the palm of his hand. What I mean by this feeling of sympathy which all men possess is this: If anyone were to see a child falling into a well, he would have a feeling of horror and pity, not because he happened to be an intimate friend of the child's parents, nor because he sought the approbation of his neighbours and friends, nor yet because he feared to be thought inhumane. Looking at the matter in the light of this example, we may say that no man is devoid of a feeling of compassion, nor of a feeling of shame, nor of a feeling of consideration for others, nor of a feeling of plain right and wrong. The feeling of compassion is the origin of benevolence; the feeling of shame is the origin of righteousnes; the feeling of consideration for others is the origin of good manners; the feeling of right and wrong is the origin of wisdom. The presence of these four elements in man is as natural to him as the possession of his four limbs. Having these four elements within him, the man who says he is powerless to act as he should is doing a grave injury to himself. And the man who says the same of his prince is likewise doing him a grave injury. Let a man but know how to expand and develop these four elements existing in the soul and his progress becomes as irresistible as a newly kindled fire or a spring that has just burst from the ground. If they can be fully developed, these virtues are strong enough to safeguard all within the Four Seas; if allowed to remain undeveloped, they will not suffice for the service due to one's parents.

Mencius said: If you love others but are not loved in return examine your own feeling of benevolence. If you try to govern others and do not succeed, turn inwards and examine your wisdom. If you treat others with courtesy but evoke no response, examine your inward feeling of respect. Whenever our actions fail to produce the effect desired, we should look for the cause in ourselves. For when a man is inwardly correct, the world will not be slow in paying him homage.

A man must insult himself before others will. A family must begin to destroy itself before others do so. State must smite itself before it is smitten from without.

With one who does violence to his own nature words are of no avail. For one who throws himself away, nothing can be done. To discard decency and right feeling in one's speech is what I mean by doing violence to one's nature. To profess inability to abide in benevolence and follow the road of righteousness is what I mean by throwing oneself away. Benevolence is man's peaceful abode and righteousness his true road. Alas for those who desert the peaceful abode, and dwell not therein! Alas for those who abandon the true road and follow it not!

The path of duty lies close at hand, yet we seek for it afar. Our business lies in what is simple, yet we seek for it in what is difficult. If every man would love his parents and treat his elders as they should be treated, the Empire would be at peace.

What trouble is he not laying up for himself who discourses on other people's faults!

The great man makes no effort to be sincere in his speech nor resolute in his acts: he simply does as his conscience prompts him.

The great man is one who has never lost the heart of a child.

Not the support of one's parents when alive but rather the performance of their obsequies after death, is to be accounted the greatest of filial piety.

The disciple Hsü said: Confucius used to apostrophize water in terms of praise. What did he find to admire in it?—Mencius replied: A spring of water flows in a copious stream, never ceasing day and night filling all cavities and, continuing its course, finding its way at last into the ocean. Such is the behaviour of water that flows from a spring, and this is what he admired. But where there is no spring, though channels and ditches are filled after rainfall in the seventh and eighth months, yet the water may soon be expected to dry up again. Thus the princely man is ashamed to enjoy a reputation which exceeds his real deserts.

The princely man is distinguished from others by the feelings laid up in his heart, and these are the feelings of benevolence and propriety. The benevolent man loves his fellows; the man of propriety respects his fellows. He who loves his fellows is loved by them in return; he who respects his fellows is respected by them in return. The nobler type of man, when treated by anybody in a rude and churlish manner, will turn his eyes inward and say: "I must have been lacking in benevolence; I must have shown a want of propriety; or how could this have happened?" Having examined himself thus, he may find that he has really been inspired by benevolence and propriety. If the other man is none the less rude and churlish, he will again subject himself to a searching examination, saying: "I cannot have been true to myself." But if he finds that he has been true to himself, and the rudeness of the other still persists he will say to himself: "This must be an unreasonable sort of fellow after all. If he behaves thus, there is little to choose between him and a bird or beast. And why should I be unduly concerned about a bird or beast?"

Thus it is that the nobler type of man, while constantly solicitous, never suffers grief of any duration. Solicitude, indeed, he feels; for he will argue thus: "Shun was a man; I too am a man. But Shun was an example to the Empire, worthy of being handed down to posterity, whereas I have not yet risen above the level of an ordinary villager." This, then, causes him solicitude, which is nothing more than anxiety to become like Shun himself. But anything that would cause him real grief simply does not exist. He never acts without a feeling of benevolence, never moves without a sense of propriety. Even if some transient cause for grief were to come his way, he would not regard it as such.

The philosopher Kao said: Man's nature is like a current of water: deflected in an easterly direction, it will flow to the east; deflected in an westerly direction, it will flow to the west. And just as water has no predilection either for east or for west, so man's nature is not predisposed either to good or to evil.—Mencius replied: It is true that water has no predilection for east or west, but will it flow equally well up or down? Human nature is disposed towards goodness just as water flows downwards. There is no water but flows down, and no men but show this tendency to good. Now, if water is splashed up, it can be made to go over your head; by forcing it along, it can be made to go uphill. But how can that be termed its natural bent? It is some external force that causes it to do so. And likewise, if men are made to do what is not good, nature is being distorted in a similar way.

Mencius said: I am fond of fish, and I am also fond of bear's paws. If I cannot have both, I will give up the fish and take the bear's paws. Similarly, I hold life dear, and also hold righteousness dear, If I cannot have both, I will give up my life and keep my righteousness. Although I hold life dear, there are things which I hold dearer than life, therefore I will not keep it at the expense of what is right. Although I hate death, there are things which I

hate more than death, therefore there are certain dangers from which I will not flee. If there was nothing that men desired more than life, would they not use any possible means of preserving it? And if there was nothing men hated more than death, would they not do anything to escape from danger? Yet there are means of preserving one's life which men will not use, ways of avoiding danger which men will not adopt. Thus it appears that men desire some things more than life, and some things more than death. And it is not only the virtuous man who has such feelings; all men have them. What distinguishes the virtuous man is that he can keep those feelings from being stifled within him.

The disciple Kung-tu asked, saying: Human nature is common to us all. How is it, then, that some are great men and some are small men?—Mencius replied: Those that follow their higher nature are great men; those that follow their lower nature are small men.—Kung-tu said: Seeing that all alike are men, how is it that some follow their higher nature and some their lower nature?—Mencius replied: The function of the eye and the ear is not thought, but is determined by material objects; for when objects impinge on the senses these cannot but follow wherever they lead. Thought is the function of the mind: by thinking, it achieves; by not thinking, it fails to achieve. These faculties are implanted in us by Nature. If we take our stand from the first on the higher part of our being, the lower part will not be able to rob us of it. It is simply this that constitutes the great man.

Questions

(1) Why is Mencius so opposed to the term "profit" as it relates to government?

(2) What is Mencius' understanding of what should distinguish a prince from others?

(3) Contrast "Meng-tze" to Document 7–2; what precise differences of approach can you discern?

7–4

Sima Qian: the historian's historian writes about the builder of the Great Wall.

Sima Qian, or Ssu -ma Ch'ien (145–86 B.C.E.), was China's first scientific historian. As the official court historian for the Han Dynasty, he developed a definitive history of China by pioneering methods of reconstructing the past through primary sources, finishing—towards the end of his life the "Records of the Grand Historian." So devoted (some might say obsessed) was he to the historian's craft that, when given the choice between death and castration for transgressing the will of the Emperor, he opted for castration on the sole basis of at least being able to complete his book. Here he relates the life of Meng Tian, designer of the Great Wall.

Source: Raymond Dawson, trans., *Sima Qian: Historical Records* (Oxford & N.Y.: Oxford University Press,1994), pp. 55–61.

As for Meng Tian, his forebears were men of Qi. Tian's paternal grandfather, Meng Ao, came from Qi to serve

King Zhaoxiang of Qin, and attained the office of senior minister. In the first year of King Zhuangxiang of Qin, Meng Ao became general of Qin, made an assault on Hann and took Chenggao and Xingyang, and established the Sanchuan province. In the second year Meng Ao attacked Zhao and took thirty-seven cities. In the third year of the First Emperor, Meng Ao attacked Han and took thirteen cities. In the fifth year Meng Ao attacked Wei, took twenty cities, and established Dong province. In the seventh year of the First Emperor, Meng Ao died. Ao's son was called Wu and Wu's son was called Tian. Tian at one time kept legal records and was in charge of the relevant literature. In the twenty-third year of the First Emperor, Meng Wu became an assistant general of Qin and, together with Wang Jian, made an attack on Chu and inflicted a major defeat upon it and killed Xiang Yan. In the twenty-fourth year Meng Wu attacked Chu and took the King of Chu prisoner. Meng Tian's younger brother was Meng Yi.

In the twenty-sixth year of the First Emperor, Meng Tian was able to become a general of Qin on account of the long-term service given by his family. He attacked Qi and inflicted a major defeat upon it, and was appointed Prefect of the Capital. When Qin had unified all under Heaven, Meng Tian was consequently given command of a host of 300,000 to go north and drive out the Rong and Di barbarians and take over the territory to the south of the Yellow River. He built the Great Wall, taking advantage of the lie of the land and making use of the passes. It started from Lintao and went as far as Liaodong, extending more than 10,000 *li*. Crossing the Yellow River, it followed the Yang Mountains and wriggled northwards. His army was exposed to the elements in the field for more than ten years when they were stationed in Shang province, and at this time Meng Tian filled the Xiongnu with terror.

The First Emperor held the Meng family in the highest esteem. Having confidence in them and so entrusting them with responsibility, he regarded them as men of quality. He allowed Meng Yi to be on terms of close intimacy, and he reached the position of senior minister. When he went out, he took him with him in his carriage, and within the palace he was constantly in the imperial presence. Tian was given responsibility for matters outside the capital, but Yi was constantly made to take part in internal planning. They were reputed to be loyal and trustworthy, so that none even of the generals or leading ministers dared to take issue with them in these matters.

Zhao Gao was a distant connection of the various Zhaos. He had several brothers, and all of them were born in the hidden part of the palace. His mother had been condemned to death, and her descendants were to be of low station for generations to come. When the King of Qin heard that Zhao Gao was forceful and well acquainted with the law, he promoted him and made him Director of Palace Coach-houses. Thereupon Gao privately served Prince Huhai and gave him instruction in judicial decisions. When Zhao Gao committed a major crime, the King of Qin ordered Meng Yi to try him at law. Yi did not dare to show partiality, so he condemned Gao to death and removed him from the register of officials, but because of Gao's estimable performance in the conduct of affairs, the Emperor pardoned him and restored his office and rank.

The First Emperor intended to travel throughout the Empire and go via Jiuyuan directly to Ganquan, so he made Meng Tian open up a road from Jiuyuan straight to Ganquan, hollowing out mountains and filling in valleys for 1,800 *li*. The road had not yet been completed when the First Emperor in the winter of the thirty-seventh year went forth on his journey and travelled to Kuaiji. Going along the sea coast, he went north to Langye. When he fell ill on the way, he made Meng Yi return to offer prayers to the mountains and streams. He had not yet got back when the First Emperor passed away on reaching Shaqiu. It was kept a secret, and none of the officials knew. At this time Chief Minister Li Si, Prince Huhai, and Director of Palace Coach-houses Zhao Gao were in constant attendance. Gao had regularly obtained favours from Huhai and wanted him to be set on the throne. He was also resentful that when Meng Yi had tried him at law he had not been in favour of letting him off. Consequently he felt like doing him harm, and so he secretly plotted together with Chief Minister Li Si and Prince Huhai to establish Huhai as crown prince. When the Crown Prince had been established, messengers were sent to bestow death on Prince Fusu and Meng Tian because of their alleged crimes. Even after Fusu was dead, Meng Tian felt suspicious and requested confirmation of it. The messengers handed Meng Tian over to the law officers and replaced him.

The messengers returned and made their report, and when Huhai heard that Fusu was dead he intended to free Meng Tian. But Zhao Gao, fearing that the Meng family would again be treated with honour and be employed on affairs, felt resentful about this.

So when Meng Yi got back, Zhao Gao, making his plans on the pretext of loyalty towards Huhai, intended on this account to wipe out the Meng family. 'Your servant hears that the previous Emperor had long intended to promote a man of quality and set up a crown prince,' he therefore said, 'but Meng Yi had remonstrated and said that this would be improper. But if he was aware that you were a man of quality and yet insisted that you should not be set up, this would be acting disloyally and deluding one's sovereign. In your servant's foolish opinion, the best thing would be to put him to death.' Paying heed, Huhai had Meng Yi put in bonds at Dai. (Previously he had taken Meng Tian prisoner at Yangzhou.) When the announcement of mourning reached Xianyang and the funeral had taken place, the Crown Prince was set up as Second Generation Emperor and Zhao Gao, being admitted to terms of close intimacy; slandered the Meng family day and night, seeking out their crimes and mistakes so as to recommend their impeachment.

Ziying came forward to remonstrate, saying: 'I hear that in ancient times King Qian of Zhao killed his good minister Li Mu and employed Yan Ju, and King Xi of Yan secretly employed the strategems of Jing Ke and ignored the pact with Qin, and King Jian of Qi killed loyal ministers from ancient families which had given long-standing service and made use of the counsels of Hou Sheng. Each of these three rulers lost their states through changing ancient ways so that disaster befell them. Now the Meng family are important officials and counsellors of Qin and yet our sovereign intends to get rid of them all in a single morning, but your servant humbly considers this to be improper. Your servant hears that it is impossible for one who plans frivolously to govern a state and it is impossible for one who exercises wisdom on his own to preserve his ruler. If you put to death loyal servants and set up people who have nothing to do with integrity, then within the palace this will cause all your servants to lose confidence in each other, and in the field it will cause the purposes of your fighting men to lose their cohesion. Your servant humbly considers this to be improper.'

Huhai did not take any notice, but dispatched the imperial scribe Qu Gong to ride relay and go to Dai and instruct Meng Yi as follows: 'You, minister, made things difficult when our previous sovereign wanted to set up a crown prince. Now the Chief Minister considers that you are disloyal, and that your whole clan is implicated in the crime. But in the kindness of Our heart We bestow death upon you, minister, which is surely extremely gracious. It is for you to give this your consideration!'

'If it is thought that your servant was incapable of grasping the wishes of our previous sovereign,' replied Meng Yi, 'then when he was young he was in his service and obediently received his patronage until he passed away, so it may be said that he knew what he wanted. Or if it is thought that your servant was unaware of the abilities of the Crown Prince, then he went all over the Empire with the Crown Prince in sole attendance, and left all the other princes far behind, so your servant had no doubts. Our previous sovereign's proposal to employ him as crown prince had been building up over several years, so what words would your servant have dared to utter in remonstrance, and what plan would he dare to have devised! It is not that I dare to produce showy verbiage for the purpose of avoiding death and implicate the reputation of our previous sovereign by creating an embarrassment, but I would like you, sir, to devote your thoughts to this, and make sure that the circumstances which cause your servant to be put to death are true. Moreover, perfect obedience is what the Way honours, and killing as a punishment is what the Way puts an end to. In former times Duke Mu of Qin died having killed three good men, and charged

Baili Xi with a crime although it was not his. Therefore he was given the title of "False." King Zhaoxiang killed Bai Qi, Lord Wan. King Ping of Chu killed Wu She. Fucha King of Wu killed Wu Zixu. These four rulers all made major mistakes and so all under Heaven regarded them as wrong and thought such rulers were unenlightened, and as such they were recorded by the feudal lords. Therefore it is said that "Those who govern in accordance with the Way do not kill the guiltless and punishment is not inflicted on the innocent." It is up to you, my lord, to take notice!' But the messengers were aware of what Huhai wanted, so they took no notice of Meng Yin's words, and killed him forthwith.

Second Generation also dispatched messengers to go to Yangzhou, with the following instructions for Meng Tian: 'Your errors, my lord, have become numerous, and your younger brother Yi bears a great burden of guilt, so the law has caught up with you.' 'From my grandfather right down to his sons and grandsons,' said Meng Tian, 'their achievements and trustworthiness have been built up in Qin over three generations. Now your servant has been in command of more than 300,000 soldiers, and although he personally is a prisoner, his influence is sufficient to instigate a revolt. But as one who safeguards righteousness although he is aware he is bound to die, he does not dare to disgrace the teachings of his forbears, and in this way does not forget his former sovereign. In former times when King Cheng of Zhou was first set on the throne and had not yet left his swaddling clothes, Dan Duke of Zhou carried the King on his back to go to court, and ultimately restored order in all under Heaven. When King Cheng had an illness and was in extreme danger, Duke Dan personally cut his finger-nails and sank the parings in the Yellow River. "The King does not yet possess understanding and it is I who handle affairs," he said. "If there is a crime-engendered disaster, I accept the unfortunate consequences of it." Accordingly he made an account and stored it away in the repository of records, and he may be said to have behaved with good faith. When the time came when the King was able to govern the country, there was a malicious official who said: "Dan Duke of Zhou has long intended to make a rebellion, and if the King is not prepared, there is bound to be a major crisis." The King was consequently furious and Dan Duke of Zhou ran away and fled to Chu. When King Cheng looked at the repository of records, he got hold of the account of the sinking, and so he said, with tears streaming down his face: "Who said that Dan Duke of Zhou intended to make a rebellion?" He killed the one who had said this and restored Dan Duke of Zhou. Thus the *Book Zhou* says: "One must put them in threes and fives." Now for generations my family has avoided duplicity, so if our affairs are finally in such straits, this is bound to be due to the methods of a wicked minister rebelliously stirring up trouble. That King Cheng made a mistake, but when he restored the situation, he ultimately flourished; but Jie killed Guan Longfeng and Zhou killed Prince Bi Gan, and they did not repent, and when they died their country was destroyed. Your servant therefore says that errors can be remedied and remonstrance can be understood. To examine into threes and fives is the method of supreme sages. All in all, your servant's words have not been for the purpose of seeking to escape from blame. He is about to die because he is making a remonstrance, and he wishes Your Majesty would think about following the Way for the sake of the myriad people.' 'Your servants have received an imperial decree to carry out the law on you, general,' said the messengers, 'and they do not dare to report your words to the Supreme One.' Meng Tian sighed deeply. 'For what am I being blamed by Heaven,' he cried, 'that I should die although I have avoided error?' After a good long while he solemnly said: 'There is a crime for which I certainly ought to die. I built a wall stretching more than 10,000 *li* from Lintao as far as Liaodong, and so in the course of this I surely could not avoid cutting through the earth's arteries. This then is my crime.' And so he swallowed poison and killed himself.

The Grand Historiographer says: 'I have been to the northern border and returned via the direct road. On my journey I observed the ramparts of the Great Wall which Meng Tian built for Qin. He hollowed out the mountains and filled in the valleys and opened up a direct road. To be sure, he showed little concern for the efforts of the people. Qin had only just destroyed the feudal states and the hearts of the people of all under Heaven had not yet been restored to order, and the wounded had not yet been healed; but Tian, although he had become a famous general, did not use this occasion to remonstrate strongly and remedy the distresses of the people, minister to the old and enable the orphans to survive, and strive to cultivate harmony among the masses. Instead he embarked on great enterprises to pander to imperial ambition, so was it not therefore reasonable that both he and his brother should suffer the death penalty? Why in that case should cutting the arteries of the earth be made a crime?'

Questions

(1) Into what professions were Meng Tian's ancestors and relatives appointed?
(2) Under what circumstances did Meng Tian build the Wall and how long was he engaged in this task?
(3) For what crime—after Meng's own words—did he commit suicide?
(4) What is Sima's assessment of Meng Tian's life and character?

7–5
Shi Huang Ti of Qin: a study in absolutism.

Seldom has any one individual tried so intensively to personify, dominate, and mold a nation as Shi Huang Ti, ruler of the state of Qin who succeeded in unifying China under his iron hand from 221–210 B.C.E., and styled himself "First Emperor." This harsh dictatorial figure went so far as to attempt to destroy all records referring to anything that occurred prior to his reign, exclaiming "History begins with me!" Years later, Sima Qian left us this portrait of a man of power.

Source: Raymond Dawson, trans., *Sima Qian: Historical Records* (Oxford & N.Y.: Oxford University Press, 1994), pp. 68–70, 80–81.

He then proceeded to the east of Bohai, passed through Huang and Chui, did a complete tour of Mount Cheng, ascended Zhifu, and set up a stone tablet there extolling the virtue of Qin and then left.

He then went south and ascended Langye and, since he greatly enjoyed it, he stayed for three months. Then he moved 30,000 households of the black-headed people to the foot of Langye terrace, giving them tax and labour exemption for twelve years. When he built Langye terrace, he set up a stone inscription extolling the virtue of Qin, to make clear that he had achieved his ambition. It said:

In his twenty-eighth year, the August Emperor makes a beginning.

Laws and standards are corrected and adjusted, as a means of recording the myriad things.

Thus he clarifies human affairs, and brings concord to father and son.

With sagacity, wisdom, humaneness, and righteousness, he has made manifest all principles.

In the east he has pacified the eastern lands, and thus he has inspected officers and men.

When this task had been magnificently accomplished, he then turned towards the sea.

Through the achievements of the August Emperor, the basic tasks are diligently worked on.

Farming is put first and non-essentials are abolished, and it is the black-headed people who are made wealthy.

All people under Heaven, have heart and mind in unison.

Implements are given a uniform measure, and the characters used in writing are standardized.

Wherever the sun and moon shine, wherever boats and carts carry goods.

Everyone completes his destiny, and nobody does not get what he wants.

He makes things move in accord with the seasons, such is the August Emperor.

To rectify diverse customs, he has traversed land and water.

Feeling sorrow for the black-headed people, he relaxes not morning or evening.

Removing doubt he fixes the laws, so that all understand what they are forbidden to do.

The regional earls have their separate duties, and all government is regulated and made easy.

What is put into practice is bound to be right, and everything goes according to plan.

The intelligence of the August Emperor, oversees and inspects all four quarters.

High and low, noble and base, do not step out of their rank.

Evil and depravity are not allowed, and all strive to be upright and good.

Putting all their effort into both the trivial and the important, nobody dares to be indolent and careless.

Both far and near and both in developed and in obscure places, they concentrate their efforts on

being majestic and sturdy.

Upright, correct, sincere, and loyal, they show constancy in their work.

The virtue of our August Emperor, preserves and settles the far extremes.

Punishes disorder and banishes harm, promotes advantage and attracts prosperity.

The practice of economy accords with the seasons, and all creation abounds.

The black-headed people are at peace, and do not employ armour and weapons.

Relations care for each other, and there are absolutely no bandits or robbers.

Joyful recipients of the teachings, they completely understand the framework of the law.

The area within the six directions, is the August Emperor's land.

To the west it crosses the shifting sands, and in the south takes in the whole of the north-facing households.

In the east there is the eastern sea, and to the north it extends beyond Daxia.

Wherever human footsteps reach, there are none who are not his subjects.

His achievements surpass those of the Five Emperors, and his beneficence even extends to cattle and horses.

No one does not receive the benefit of his virtue, and everyone is at peace in his dwelling-place.

***

…he flew into a great rage and said: 'Previously I collected together the writings of all under Heaven and got rid of all which were useless. I called together all the scholars and magicians, an extremely large gathering, intending to promote an era of great peace by this means, and the magicians I intended to pick out to go in search of strange elixirs. Now I hear that Han Zhong has left and not made a report, and the expenses of Xu Shi and his colleagues may be reckoned in millions, but they have totally failed to obtain elixirs, and it is only the charges of corruption they make against each other which I hear of daily. I was extremely generous in the honours and gifts I bestowed on Master Lu and the others, but now they even slander me so as to emphasize the fact that I am not virtuous. I have had people investigate all the scholars who are in Xianyang, and some have been fabricating weird rumours in order to confuse the black-headed people.'

Thereupon he made the Imperial Secretary investigate all the scholars, who were reported to have informed on each other; but in fact, although they tried to exonerate themselves, more than 460 who had infringed the prohibitions were all buried alive at Xianyang, and the whole Empire was made to know about this to serve as a warning for the future. And increasingly people were banished to the frontiers. Fusu, the eldest son of the First Emperor, remonstrated and said: 'All under Heaven has only just been restored to order and the black-headed people in the distant regions have not yet been brought together, and all the scholars sing the praises of Master Kong and adopt him as a model, but now the Supreme One restrains them all by emphasizing the law, and your servant is afraid that all under Heaven will not be at peace. It is up to the Supreme One to investigate this.' The First Emperor was angry, and he made Fusu go north and act as inspector of Meng Tian in the Shang province.

In the thirty-sixth year Mars was stationed in the mansion of the Heart. There was a meteor which fell in the Dong province, and when it reached the earth it turned into a stone, and someone among the black-headed people inscribed the stone concerned with the words: 'When the First Emperor dies, the land will be divided up.' When the First Emperor heard this, he sent the Imperial Secretary to investigate and, when nobody confessed, all those who lived near the stone were taken and condemned to death, and as a consequence the stone concerned was destroyed by burning.

The First Emperor was not happy, and he made the scholars of broad learning compose poems about immortals and true beings and also on wherever in the Empire he went on his travels, and musicians were instructed to sing and play them....

Questions

(1) Judging from his own words and standards, what did the Emperor set as China's most pressing priorities?

(2) What was the reason behind, and what were the results of, the Emperor's investigation of scholars?

(3) What light does this episode, and that of the meteor, shed on the Emperor's character and personality?

7–6

Prince Shotoku's Seventeen Article Constitution.

During the reign of the Japanese Empress Suiko, the true power behind the throne and chief administrator was her nephew, Prince Shotoku (574–622 B.C.E.). Japan was just recovering from a bitter and sometimes bloody power struggle between court traditionalists and nobles like Shotoku, who desired to reform the government along the lines of Chinese administrative methods morally buttressed with Buddhist precepts. The main purpose was, of course, to centralize and bureaucratize authority along Chinese Confucian lines, but the idea of a moral responsibility was stated explicitly.

Source: Ryusaku Tsunoda, ed., *Sources of the Japanese Tradition*, Vol.1 (N.Y.: Columbia University Press, 1964), pp. 49–51.

12th year [604], Summer, 4th month, 3rd day. The Prince Imperial in person prepared for the first time laws. There were seventeen clauses, as follows:

I. Harmony is to be valued and an avoidance of wanton opposition to be honored. All men are influenced by partisanship, and there are few who are intelligent. Hence there are some who disobey their lords and fathers, or who maintain feuds with the neighboring villages. But when those above are harmonious and those below are friendly, and there is concord in the discussion of business, right views of things spontaneously gain acceptance. Then what is there which cannot be accomplished?

II. Sincerely reverence the three treasures. The three treasures, viz. Buddha, the Law, and the Monastic orders, are the final refuge of the four generated beings, and are the supreme objects of faith in all countries. Few men are utterly bad. They may be taught to follow it. But if they do not betake them to the three treasures, wherewithal shall their crookedness be made straight?

III. When you receive the imperial commands,

fail not scrupulously to obey them. The lord is Heaven, the vassal is Earth. Heaven overspreads, and Earth upbears. When this is so, the four seasons follow their due course, and the powers of Nature obtain their efficacy. If the Earth attempted to overspread, Heaven would simply fall in ruin. Therefore is it that when the lord speaks, the vassal listens; when the superior acts, the inferior yields compliance. Consequently when you receive the imperial commands, fail not to carry them out scrupulously. Let there be a want of care in this matter, and ruin is the natural consequence.

IV. The ministers and functionaries should make decorous behavior their leading principle, for the leading principle of the government of the people consists in decorous behavior. If the superiors do not behave with decorum, the inferiors are disorderly: if inferiors are wanting in proper behavior, there must necessarily be offenses. Therefore it is that when lord and vassal behave with decorum, the distinctions of rank are not confused: when the people behave with decorum, the government of the commonwealth proceeds of itself.

V. Ceasing from gluttony and abandoning covetous desires, deal impartially with the suits which are submitted to you. Of complaints brought by the people there are a thousand in one day. If in one day there are so many, how many will there be in a series of years? If the man who is to decide suits at law makes gain his ordinary motive, and hears cases with a view to receiving bribes, then will the suits of the rich man be like a stone flung into water, while the plaints of the poor will resemble water cast upon a stone. Under these circumstances the poor man will not know whither to betake himself. Here too there is a deficiency in the duty of the minister.

VI. Chastise that which is evil and encourage that which is good. This was the excellent rule of antiquity. Conceal not, therefore, the good qualities of others, and fail not to correct that which is wrong when you see it. Flatterers and deceivers are a sharp weapon for the overthrow of the State, and a pointed sword for the destruction of the people. Sycophants are also fond, when they meet, of dilating to their superiors on the errors of their inferiors; to their inferiors, they censure the faults of their superiors. Men of this kind are all wanting in fidelity to their lord, and in benevolence towards the people. From such an origin great civil disturbances arise.

VII. Let every man have his own charge, and let not the spheres of duty be confused. When wise men are entrusted with office, the sound of praise arises. If unprincipled men hold office, disasters and tumults are multiplied. In this world, few are born with knowledge: wisdom is the product of earnest meditation. In all things, whether great or small, find the right man, and they will surely be well managed: on all occasions, be they urgent or the reverse, meet but with a wise man, and they will of themselves be amenable. In this way

will the State be lasting and the Temples of the Earth and of Grain will be free from danger. Therefore did the wise sovereigns of antiquity seek the man to fill the office, and not the office for the sake of the man.

VIII. Let the ministers and functionaries attend the court early in the morning, and retire late. The business of the State does not admit of remissness, and the whole day is hardly enough for its accomplishment. If, therefore, the attendance at court is late, emergencies cannot be met: if officials retire soon, the work cannot be completed.

IX. Good faith is the foundation of right. In everything let there be good faith, for in it there surely consists the good and the bad, success and failure. If the lord and the vassal observe good faith one with another, what is there which cannot be accomplished? If the lord and the vassal do not observe good faith towards one another, everything without exception ends in failure.

X. Let us cease from wrath, and refrain from angry looks. Nor let us be resentful when others differ from us. For all men have hearts, and each heart has its own leanings. Their right is our wrong, and our right is their wrong. We are not unquestionably sages, nor are they unquestionably fools. Both of us are simply ordinary men. How can any one lay down a rule by which to distinguish right from wrong? For we are all, one with another, wise and foolish, like a ring which has no end. Therefore, although others give way to anger, let us on the contrary dread our own faults, and though we alone may be in the right, let us follow the multitude and act like them.

XI. Give clear appreciation to merit and demerit, and deal out to each its sure reward or punishment. In these days, reward does not attend upon merit, nor punishment upon crime. Ye high functionaries who have charge of public affairs, let it be your task to make clear rewards and punishments.

XII. Let not the provincial authorities or the Kuni no Miyakko levy exaction on the people. In a country there are not two lords; the people have not two masters. The sovereign is the master of the people of the whole country. The officials to whom he gives charge are all his vassals. How can they, as well as the Government, presume to levy taxes on the people?

XIII. Let all persons entrusted with office attend equally to their functions. Owing to their illness or to their being sent on missions, their work may sometimes be neglected. But whenever they become able to attend to business, let them be as accommodating as if they had had cognizance of it from before, and not hinder public affairs on the score of their not having had to do with them.

XIV. Ye ministers and functionaries! Be not envious. For if we envy others, they in turn will envy us. The evils of envy know no limit. If others excel us in intelligence, it gives us no pleasure; if they surpass us in ability, we are envious. Therefore it is not until after a lapse of five hundred years that we at last meet with a wise man, and even in a thousand years we hardly obtain one sage. But if we do not find wise men and sages, wherewithal shall the country be governed?

XV. To turn away from that which is private, and to set our faces towards that which is public—this is the path of a minister. Now if a man is influenced by private motives, he will assuredly feel resentments, and if he is influenced by resentful feelings, he will assuredly fail to act harmoniously with others. If he fails to act harmoniously with others, he will assuredly sacrifice the public interests to his private feelings. When resentment arises, it interferes with order, and is subversive of law. Therefore in the first clause it was said, that superiors and inferiors should agree together. The purport is the same as this.

XVI. Let the people be employed [in forced labor] at seasonable times. This is an ancient and excellent rule. Let them be employed, therefore, in the winter months, when they are at leisure. But from Spring to Autumn, when they are engaged in agriculture or with the mulberry trees, the people should not be so employed. For if they do not attend to agriculture, what will they have to eat? if they do not attend to the mulberry trees, what will they do for clothing?

XVII. Decisions on important matters should not be made by one person alone. They should be discussed with many. But small matters are of less consequence. It is unnecessary to consult a number of people. It is only in the case of the discussion of weighty affairs, when there is a suspicion that they may miscarry, that one should arrange matters in concert with others, so as to arrive at the right conclusion.

Questions

(1) Which element of the "Seventeen Articles is the more dominant, the political or the ethical? Why?

(2) What particular areas of deficiency of the old system does Shotoku imply are in need of reform?

(3) Are there passages that seem to express sympathy for, and a wish to alleviate the burden of, ordinary people? Explain.

7–7
"Kagero Nikki": a noblewoman's lot in ancient Japan.

Japanese women, even those of aristocratic rank like the anonymous authoress of the autobiography "Kagero Nikki" (c. 934–995 C.E), were not immune from the pain and humiliation of marital infidelity. Though her husband ("the Prince") was an influential man who provided his wife with all the material comforts of the time, this hardly seems to have made up for the consequences of his extramarital dalliances.

Source: Donald Keene, ed., *Anthology of Japanese Literature* (N.Y.: Grove Press, 1960), pp. 97–105.

The years of my youth have passed, and I can see little in them that suggests greatness. It is, I suppose, natural that I should have fallen into such mediocrity. I am less handsome than most, and my character is hardly remarkable. But as the days and nights have gone by in monotonous succession, I have had occasion to read most of the old romances, and I have found them masses of the rankest fabrication. Perhaps, I think to myself, the events of my own life, if I were to put them down in a journal, might attract attention, and indeed those who have been misled by the romancers might find in it a description of what the life of a well-placed lady is really like. But I must begin at the beginning, and I see that my memories of those first years have blurred. I shall not be surprised then if one finds traces of fiction here too....

It had become clear that I was to have a child. I passed a most unpleasant spring and summer, and toward the end of the eighth moon gave birth to a boy. The Prince showed every sign of affection.

But the following month I received a shock. Toying with my writing box one morning just after he had left, I came upon a note obviously intended for another woman. My chagrin was infinite, and I felt that I must at least send something to let him know I had seen the thing. "Might this be a bill of divorcement," I wrote, "this note that I see for another?"

As the weeks went by my anxiety increased. Toward the end of the tenth moon he stayed away three nights running, and when he finally appeared he explained nonchalantly that he had hoped by ignoring me for a few days to find out what my feelings really were. But he could not stay the night: he had an appointment, he said, which could not very well be broken. I was of course suspicious, and I had him trailed. I found that he spent the night in a house off a certain narrow side street. It was so, then, I thought. My worst suspicions were confirmed.

Two or three days later I was awakened toward dawn by a pounding on the gate. It was he, I knew, but I could not bring myself to let him in, and presently he went off, no doubt to the alley that interested him so....

His visits became still more infrequent. I began to feel listless and absent-minded as I had never been before, and I fell into the habit of forgetting things I had left lying around the house. "Perhaps he has given me up completely," I would say to myself; "and has he left behind nothing to remember him by?" And then, after an interval of about ten days, I got a letter asking me to send him an arrow he had left attached to the bed pillar. He had indeed left that behind—I remembered now.

I returned it with a verse: "I am aroused by this call for an arrow, even as I wonder what is to bring memories."

My house was directly on his way to and from the palace, and in the night or early in the morning I would hear him pass. He would cough to attract my attention. I wanted not to hear, but, tense and unable to sleep, I would listen through the long nights for his approach. If only I could live where I would not be subjected to this, I thought over and over. I would hear my women talking among themselves of his current indifference— "He used to be so fond of her," they would say—and my wretchedness would increase as the dawn came on....

Summer came, and a child was born to his paramour. Loading the lady into his carriage and raising a commotion that could be heard through the whole city, he came hurrying past my gate—in the worst of taste, I thought. And why, my women loudly asked one another, had he so pointedly passed our gate when he had all the streets in the city to choose from? I myself was quite speechless, and thought only that I should like to die on the spot. I knew that I would be capable of nothing as drastic as suicide, but I resolved not to see him again.

Three or four days later I had a most astonishing letter: "I have not been able to see you because we have been having rather a bad time of it here. Yesterday the child was born, however, and everything seems to have gone off well. I know that you will not want to see me until the defilement has worn off."

I dismissed the messenger without a reply. The child, I heard, was a boy, and that of course made things worse.

He came calling three or four days later, quite as though nothing unusual had happened. I did my best to make him uncomfortable, and shortly he left....

It began to appear that the lady in the alley had fallen from favor since the birth of her child. I had prayed, at the height of my unhappiness, that she would live to know what I was then suffering, and it seemed that my prayers were being answered. She was alone, and now her child was dead, the child that had been the cause of that unseemly racket. The lady was of frightfully bad birth—the unrecognized child of a rather odd prince, it was said. For a moment she was able to use a noble gentleman who was unaware of her short-comings, and now she was abandoned. The pain must be even sharper than mine had been. I was satisfied....

It had become painful even to get his rare letters, little flashes into the past, and I was sure, moreover, that there would be more insults like the recent one as long as he could pass my gate. I determined therefore to go away, as I had planned earlier, to that temple in the western mountains, and to do so before he emerged from his penance.

The mountain road was crowded with associations. We had traveled it together a number of times, and then there had been that time, just at this season, when he had played truant from court and we had spent several days together in this same temple. I had only three attendants with me this time.

I hurried up to the main hall. It was warm, and I left the door open and looked out. The hall was situated on an eminence in a sort of mountain basin. It was heavily wooded and the view was most effective, although it was already growing dark and there was no moon. The priests made preparations for the early watch, and I began my prayers, still with the door open.

Just as the conch shells blew ten there was a clamor at the main gate. I knew that the Prince had arrived. I quickly lowered the blinds, and, looking out, saw two or three torches among the trees.

"I have come to take your mother back," he said to the boy, who went down to meet him. "I have suffered a defilement, though, and cannot get out. Where shall we have them pick her up?"

The boy told me what he had said, and I was quite at a loss to know how to handle such madness. "What can you be thinking of," I sent back, "to come off on such a weird expedition? Really, I intend to stay here only the night. And it would not be wise for you to defile the temple. Please go back immediately—It must be getting late."

Those were the first of a great number of messages the boy had to deliver that night, up and down a flight of stairs that must have been more than a hundred yards long. My attendants, sentimental things, found him most pathetic.

Finally the boy came up in tears: "He says it is all my fault—that I am a poor one not to make a better case for him. He is really in a rage." But I was firm—I could not possibly go down yet, I said.

"All right, all right," the Prince stormed. "I can't stay here all night. There is no help for it—hitch the oxen."

I was greatly relieved. But the boy said that he would like to go back to the city with his father, and that he would probably not come again. He went off weeping. I was quite desolate: how could he, whom of all in the world I had come most to rely on, leave me like this? But I said nothing, and presently, after everyone had left, he came back alone.

He was choked with tears. "He says I am to stay until I am sent for."

I felt extremely sorry for the boy, but I tried to distract him by ridiculing his weakness. Surely he did not think his father would abandon him, too, I said.…

I spent the days in the usual observances and the nights praying before the main Buddha. Since the place was surrounded by hills and there seemed no danger of my being seen, I kept the blinds up; but once, so great still was my lack of self-possession, I hastily started to lower them when an unseasonal thrush burst into song in a dead tree nearby.

Then the expected defilement approached, and I knew I should have to leave. But in the city a rumor had spread that I had become a nun, and I felt sure I could not be comfortable there. I decided therefore to withdraw to a house some distance below the temple. My aunt visited me there, but she found it a strange and unsettling place.

Five or six days after my removal came the night of the full moon. The scene was a lovely one. The moon flooded through the trees, while over in the shadow of the mountain great swarms of fireflies wheeled about. An uninhibited cuckoo made me think ironically of how once, long ago and back in the city, I had waited with some annoyance for a cuckoo that refused to repeat his call. And then suddenly, so near at hand that it seemed almost to be knocking on the door, came the drumming of a moor hen. All in all it was a spot that stirred in one the deepest emotions.

There was no word from the Prince. But I had come here by my own choice, and I was content.

In the evenings came the booming of the great sunset bells and the hum of the cicadas, and the choruses of small bells from the temples in the hills around us, chiming in one after another as though afraid to be left out, and the chanting of Sutras from the shrine on the hill in front of us.

Five days or so later the defilement passed and I returned to the temple.…

Then, after a time, I got several letters from the city. They all said the same thing: it appeared that the Prince was starting out to see me again, and that if I did not go back with him this time public opinion would label my behavior completely outrageous; that this was surely the last time he would come after me, and that if, after he had thus done everything possible to move me, I should come weakly back to the city by myself, I would be publicly laughed at.

My father had just that day come back from the provinces, and he hurried up to see me. "I had thought it would not be unwise for you to go away for a little while by yourself," he said, "but now that I see how the boy has wasted away I think it would be best for you to return. I can take you back today or tomorrow, whichever would be better. I shall come for you whenever you say."

It was clear that he was ordering me home. I felt quite drained of strength.

"Well, tomorrow then," he said, and started for the city.

My mind jumped about like the fisherman's bob in the poem—what could I do? And then came the usual shouting, and I knew the Prince had arrived. This time there was no hesitation. He marched straight in. I pulled up a screen to hide behind, but it was no use.

"Terrible," he exclaimed, as he watched me burning incense and fingering my beads, the Sutras spread out in front of me. "Worse even than I had expected. You really do seem to have run to an extreme. I thought you might be ready to leave by this time, but I now suspect that it would be a sin and a crime to take you back." And, turning to my son, "How about it? Do you feel like staying on?"

"I don't like the idea at all," the boy answered, his eyes on the floor, "but what can we do?"

"Well, I leave it to you. If you think she should go back, have the carriage brought up."

And almost before he had finished speaking, the boy began dashing about, picking things up, poking them into bags, loading the carts, tearing the curtains down and rolling them into bundles. I was taken quite by surprise, and could only watch helplessly. The Prince was most pleased with himself. Now and then he would exchange an amused wink with the boy.

"Well, we have everything cleaned up," he finally said. "There is not much for you to do but come with us. Tell your Buddha politely that you are leaving—that is the thing to do, I hear." He seemed to think it all a great joke.

I was too numb to answer, but somehow I managed to keep the tears back, and still I held out. The carriage was brought up at about four, and at dark, when I Still showed no sign of getting in, the Prince turned to my son in great annoyance.

"All right, all right, I am going back," he exclaimed. "I leave everything to you."

The boy, almost in tears, took my hand and pleaded with me to get in, and finally, since nothing else seemed possible, I allowed myself to be taken away, quite in a daze. Outside the main gate we divided up for the trip back, and the Prince got in with me. He was in a fine humor, but I was unable to appreciate his witty remarks. My sister was riding with us, however—she felt it would be all right since it was already dark—and now and then she took up the conversation.

We reached the city at about ten in the evening. My people had of course known of his trip and my probable return, and had cleaned the place thoroughly and left the gates open for us. Barely conscious, I lay down behind a curtain. Immediately one of my women came bustling up. "I thought of gathering seeds from the pinks," she said, "but the plants died. And then one of your bamboos fell over, but I had it put back up again." I thought it would be better to discuss these problems some other time, and did not answer....

The New Year lists were published on the twenty-fifth, and the Prince, I heard, was made a senior councilor. I knew that his promotion probably would keep him from me more than ever, and when people came around to congratulate me it was as if they were joking. My son, however, appeared more delighted than he could say.

The following day the Prince sent a note: "Does this happy event mean nothing to you? Is that why you have sent no congratulations?" And toward the end of the month, "Has something happened to you? We have been very busy here, but it is not kind of you to ignore me." And thus my silence had the effect of making him the petitioner, a position that had to then been exclusively mine. "It is sad that your duties keep you so busy," I answered. I was sure that he had no intention of visiting me.

The days went by, and it became clear that I was right. But I had finally learned not to let his silence bother me. I slept very well at night.

Then one evening after I had gone to bed I was startled by a most unusual pounding outside. Someone opened the gate. I waited rather nervously, and presently the Prince was at the end door demanding to be let in. My people, all in night dress, scurried about for shelter. I was no better dressed than they, but I crawled to the door and let him in.

"You so seldom come any more even to pass the time of day," I said, "that the door seems to have gotten a little stiff."

"It is because you are always locking me out that I do not come," he retorted pleasantly. And how would one answer that?...

My house was meanwhile going to ruin. My father suggested that it would be best to let it out, since my retinue was a small one, and move into his place on the Nakagawa. I had spoken to the Prince many times of the possibility that I might move, but now that the time approached I felt I should let him know I was finally leaving. I sent to tell him that I wanted to talk to him, but he replied coldly that he was in retreat. "If that is how he feels," I said to myself. l went ahead with the move.

The new place fronted on the river, near the mountains. I found it rather satisfying to think that I was there by my own choice.

The Prince apparently did not hear for two or three days that l had moved. Then, on the twenty-fifth or twenty-sixth, I had a letter complaining that I had not informed him.

"I did think of telling you," I answered, "but this is such a poor place that I assumed you would not want to visit it. I had hoped to see you once more where we used to meet."

I spoke as though I considered our separation final, and he seemed to agree. "You are perhaps right. It might not be easy for me to visit you there." And I heard no more for some weeks.

The ninth moon came. Looking out early one morning after the shutters were raised, I saw that a mist had come in over the garden from the river, so that only the summits of the mountains to the east were visible. Somehow it seemed to shut me in from the world, alone....

The New Year came, and on the fifteenth the boy's men lit ceremonial fires to chase out the devils. They made rather a party of it, well on into the night. "Quiet down a bit," someone shouted, and I went to the edge of the room for a look. The moon was bright, and the mountains to the east shone dim and icy through the mist. Leaning quietly against a Pillar, I thought about myself and my loneliness, how I should like to go off to a mountain temple somewhere if only I could, and how I had not seen him for five months, not since the end of the summer. I could not keep back my tears. "I would join my song with the song thrush," I whispered to myself, "but the thrush has forgotten the New Year."

Translated by Edward Seidensticker

Questions

(1) How does the wife discover her husband's infidelity, and what were the results of his affair?

(2) What was their son's position during the time of their estrangement, and what role did he ultimately play?

(3) What general and specific insights does the "Kagero Nikki" provide about gender status and convention amongst the Japanese nobility?

CHAPTER 8

8–1
"Artha-sastra": a wily courtier's handbook on political survival.

The identity of the author of the "Artha-sastra" is not known with any certainty, but tradition has long designated Kautilya, a chief minister at the court of Emperor Chandragupta I Maurya (c. 322–298 B.C.E.). Whoever the author might have been, "Artha-satra" is certainly the work of a cunning political operative who was well versed on the dynamics of power and the methods by which a monarch might maintain that power while sufficiently meeting the expectations of his subjects.

Source: Kautilya, *Artha-sastra,* 2nd ed., trans. R. Shamasastry (Mysore, India: Wesleyan Mission Press, 1923) passim. Quoted in Marc Anthony Meyer, *Landmarks of World Civilization,* vol. 1 (Guilford, CT: Dushkin, 1994), pp. 161–165.

…When in the court, he shall never cause his petitioners to wait at the door, for when a king makes himself inaccessible to his people and entrusts his work to his immediate officers, he may be sure to engender confusion in business, and to cause thereby public disaffection, and himself a prey to his enemies.

…Of a king, the religious vow is his readiness to action; satisfactory discharge of duties is his performance of sacrifice; equal attention to all is the offer of fees and ablution towards consecration.

In the happiness of his subjects lies his happiness; in their welfare his welfare; whatever pleases himself he shall not consider as good, but whatever pleases his subjects he shall consider as good.

Hence the king shall ever be active and discharge his duties; the root of wealth is activity, and of evil its reverse.

In the absence of activity acquisitions present and to come will perish; by activity be can achieve both his desired ends and abundance of wealth.

BOOK THREE: CONCERNING LAW

1....In virtue of his power to uphold the observance of the respective duties of the four castes and of the **four divisions of religious life,** and in virtue of his power to guard against the violation of the dharmas, the king is the fountain of justice.

Sacred law, evidence, history, and edicts of kings are the four legs of Law. Of these four in order, the later is superior to the one previously named.

Dharma is eternal truth holding its sway over the world; evidence is in witnesses; history is to be found in the tradition of the people; and the order of kings is what is called *sasana.*

As the duty of a king consists in protecting his subjects with justice, its observance leads him to heaven. He who does not protect his people or upsets the social order wields his royal sceptre in vain.

It is power and power alone which, only when exercised by the king with impartiality and in proportion to guilt, either over his son or his enemy, maintains both this world and the next.

The king who administers justice in accordance with sacred law, evidence, history, and edicts of kings, which is the fourth, will be able to conquer the whole world bounded by the four quarters.

Whenever there is disagreement between history and sacred law or between evidence and sacred law, then the matter shall be settled in accordance with sacred law.

But whenever sacred law is in conflict with rational law, then reason shall be held authoritative; for there the original text on which the sacred law has been based is not available.…

BOOK SIX: THE SOURCE OF SOVEREIGN STATES

1. The king, the minister, the country, the fort, the treasury, the army, and the friend are the elements of sovereignty.

Of these, the best qualities of the king are:

Born of a high family, godly, possessed of valor, seeing through the medium of aged persons, virtuous, truthful, not of a contradictory nature, grateful, having large aims, highly enthusiastic, not addicted to procrastination, powerful to control his neighboring kings, of resolute mind, having an assembly of ministers of no mean quality, and possessed of a taste for discipline—these are the qualities of an inviting nature.

Inquiry, hearing, perception, retention in memory, reflection, deliberation, inference and steadfast adherence to conclusions are the qualities of the intellect.

Valor, determination of purpose, quickness, and probity are the aspects of enthusiasm.

Possessed of a sharp intellect, strong memory, and keen mind, energetic, powerful, trained in all kinds of arts, free from vice, capable of paying in the same coin by way of awarding punishments or rewards, possessed of dignity, capable of taking remedial measures against dangers, possessed of foresight, ready to avail himself of opportunities when afforded in respect of place, time, and manly efforts, clever enough to discern the causes necessitating the cessation of treaty or war with an enemy, or to lie in wait keeping treaties, obligations and pledges, or to avail himself of his enemy's weak points, making jokes with no loss of dignity or secrecy, never brow-beating and casting haughty and stern looks, free from passion, anger, greed, obstinacy, fickleness, haste and back-biting habits, talking to others with a smiling face, and observing customs as taught by aged persons—such is the nature of self-possession....

Possessed of capital cities both in the center and the extremities of the kingdom, productive of subsistence not only to its own people, but also to outsiders on occasions of calamities, repulsive to enemies, powerful enough to put down neighboring kings, free from miry, rocky, uneven, and desert tracts, as well as from conspirators, tigers, wild beasts, and large tracts of wilderness, beautiful to look at, containing fertile lands, mines, timber and elephant forests, and pasture grounds, artistic, containing hidden passages, full of cattle, not depending upon rain for water, possessed of land and waterways, rich in various kinds of commercial articles, capable of bearing the burden of a vast army and heavy taxation, inhabited by agriculturists of good and active character, full of intelligent masters and servants, and with a population noted for its loyalty and good character—these are the characteristics of a good country.

A wise king can make even the poor and miserable elements of his sovereignty happy and prosperous; but a wicked king will surely destroy the most prosperous and loyal elements of his kingdom.

Hence a king of unrighteous character and of vicious habits will, though he is an emperor, fall prey either to the fury of his own subjects or to that of his enemies.

But a wise king, trained in politics, will, though he possesses a small territory, conquer the whole earth with the help of the best-fitted elements of his sovereignty, and will never be defeated.

2. Acquisition and security of property are dependent upon peace and industry.

Effort to achieve the results of works undertaken is industry.

Absence of disturbance to the enjoyment of the results achieved from works is peace.

The application of the six-fold royal policy is the source of peace and industry.

Deterioration, stagnation, and progress are the three aspects of position.

Those causes of human design which affect position are policy and impolicy; fortune and misfortune are providential causes. Causes, both human and providential, govern the world and its affairs.

What is unforeseen is providential; here, the attainment of that desired and which seemed almost lost is termed fortune.

What is anticipated is human; and the attainment of a desired end as anticipated is due to policy.

What produces unfavorable results is impolicy. This can be foreseen; but misfortune due to providence cannot be known.

The king who, being possessed of good character and best-fitted elements of sovereignty, is the fountain of policy, is termed the conqueror.

The king who is situated anywhere immediately on the circumference of the conqueror's territory is termed the enemy.

The king who is likewise situated close to the enemy, but separated from the conqueror only by the enemy, is termed the friend of the conqueror.

A neighboring foe of considerable power is styled an enemy; and when he is involved in calamities or has taken himself to evil ways, he becomes assailable; and when he has little or no help, he becomes destructible; otherwise, when he is provided with some help, he deserves to be harassed or reduced. Such are the aspects of an enemy....

Strength is of three kinds: power of deliberation is intellectual strength; the possession of a prosperous treasury and a strong army is the strength of sovereignty; and that which is to be secured by perseverance is the end of martial power.

The possession of power and happiness in a greater degree makes a king superior to another; in a less degree, inferior; and in an equal degree, equal. Hence a king shall always endeavor to augment his own power and elevate his happiness.

BOOK SEVEN: THE END OF THE SIX-FOLD POLICY

1....The Circle of States is the source of the six-fold policy.

[Kautilya] says that peace, war, observance of neutrality, marching, alliance, and making peace with one and waging war with another are the six forms of state policy.

But Vatavyadhi holds that there are only two forms of policy, peace and war, inasmuch as the six forms result from these two primary forms of policy.

While Kautilya holds that, as their respective conditions differ, the forms of policy are six.

Of these, agreement with pledges is peace; offensive operation is war; indifference is neutrality; making preparations is marching; seeking the protection of another is alliance; and making peace with one and waging war with another, is termed a double policy. These are the six forms.

Whoever is inferior to another shall make peace with him; whoever is superior in power shall wage war; whoever thinks, "No enemy can hurt me, nor am I strong enough to destroy my enemy," shall observe neutrality; whoever is possessed of necessary means shall march against his enemy; whoever is devoid of necessary strength to defend himself shall seek the protection of another; whoever thinks that help is necessary to work out an end shall make peace with one and wage war with another. Such is the aspect of the six forms of policy.

Of these, a wise king shall observe that form of policy which, in his opinion, enables him to build forts, to construct buildings and commercial roads, to open new plantations and villages, to exploit mines and timber and elephant forests, and at the same time to harass similar works of his enemy.

Whoever thinks himself to be growing in power more rapidly both in quality and quantity than his enemy, and the reverse of his enemy, may neglect his enemy's progress for the time.

If any two kings, hostile to each other, find the time of achieving the results of their respective works to be equal, they shall make peace with each other.

No king shall keep that form of policy, which causes him the loss of profit from his own works, but which entails no such loss on the enemy; for it is deterioration.

Whoever thinks that in the course of time his loss will be less than his acquisition as contrasted with that of his enemy, may neglect his temporary deterioration.

If any two kings, hostile to each other, and deteriorating, expect to acquire equal amount of wealth in equal time, they shall make peace with each other.

That position in which neither progress nor retrogression is seen is stagnation.

[Kautilya] says that if any two kings, who are hostile to each other, and are in a stationary condition, expect to acquire equal amount of wealth and power in equal time, they shall make peace with each other.

"Of course," says Kautilya, "there is no other alternative."

Questions
(1) What are the four "legs" of the law, and to which does the author assign the greatest importance?
(2) What traits must a monarch exhibit in order to achieve "self-possession"?
(3) How fair is it to characterize the "Artha-sastra" (as some historians have) as dismissive of ethical content?
(4) What is set forward as the ultimate goal of a ruler's foreign policy?

8–2
Fa-Hsien: a Chinese perspective on Gupta India.

A comparative paucity of records is one of the main handicaps confronting anyone who studies Gupta India; written documentation is not extensive. Of the intermittent glimpses we have, one of the most intriguing is the account of the Chinese Buddhist monk Fa-Hsien, who undertook a pilgrimmage to sacred sites connected with the Buddha, and made some passing observations about India itself.

Source: Samuel Beal, trans., *Travels of Fa-Hsien and Sung Yun, Buddhist Pilgrims from China to India* (N.Y.: Augustus M. Kelly, 1967), pp. xxxvi–xxxix.

XIV. After remaining here during two months of winter Fa-hian and two companions went south across the Little Snowy Mountains. The Snowy Mountains, both in summer and winter, are covered (*heaped*) with snow. On the north side of the mountains, in the shade, excessive cold came on suddenly, and all the men were struck mute with dread; Hwui-king alone was unable to proceed onwards. The white froth came from his mouth as he addressed Fa-hian and said, "I too have no power of life left; but whilst there is opportunity, do you press on, lest you all perish." Thus he died. Fa-hian, caressing him, exclaimed in piteous voice, "Our purpose was not to produce fortune!" Submitting, he again exerted himself, and pressing forward, they so

crossed the range; on the south side they reached the Lo-i country. In this vicinity there are 3,000 priests, belonging both to the Great and Little Vehicle. Here they kept the rainy season. The season past, descending south and journeying for ten days, they reached the Po-na country, where there are also some 3,000 priests or more, all belonging to the Little Vehicle. From this journeying eastward for three days, they again crossed the Sin-tu river. Both sides of it are now level.

XV. The other side of the river there is a country named Pi-t'u. The law of Buddha is very flourishing; they belong both to the Great and Little Vehicle. When they saw pilgrims from China arrive, they were much affected and spoke thus, "How is it that men from the frontiers are able to know the religion of family-renunciation and come from far to seek the law of Buddha?" They liberally provided necessary entertainment according to the rules of religion.

XVI. Going south-east from this somewhat less than 80 *yôjanas*, we passed very many temples one after another, with some myriad of priests in them. Having passed these places, we arrived at a certain country. This country is called Mo-tu-lo. Once more we followed the Pu-na river. On the sides of the river, both right and left, are twenty *sangdârâmas,* with perhaps 3,000 priests. The law of Buddha is progressing and flourishing. Beyond the deserts are the countries of Western India. The kings of these countries are all firm believers in the law of Buddha. They remove their caps of state when they make offerings to the priests. The members of the royal household and the chief ministers personally direct the food-giving; when the distribution of food is over, they spread a carpet on the ground opposite the chief seat (the president's seat) and sit down before it. They dare not sit on couches in the presence of the priests. The rules relating to the alms-giving of kings have been handed down from the time of Buddha till now. Southward from this is the so-called middle-country (Mâklhyadesa). The climate of this country is warm and equable, without frost or snow. The people are very well off, without polltax or official restrictions. Only those who till the royal lands return a portion of profit of the land. If any desire to go, they go; if they like to stop, they stop. The kings govern without corporal punishment; criminals are fined, according to circumstances, lightly or heavily. Even in eases of repeated rebellion they only cut off the right hand. The king's personal attendants, who guard him on the right and left, have fixed salaries. Throughout the country the people kill no living thing nor drink wine, nor do they eat garlic or onions, with the exception of Chandâlas only. The Chandâlas are named "evil men" and dwell apart from others; if they enter a town or market, they sound a piece of wood in order to separate themselves; then men, knowing who they are, avoid coming in contact with them. In this country they do not keep swine nor fowls, and do not deal in cattle; they have no shambles or wine-shops in their market-places. In selling they use cowrie shells. The Chandâlas only hunt and sell flesh. Down from the time of Buddha's *Nirvâna,* the kings of these countries, the chief men and householders, have raised *vihâras* for the priests, and provided for their support by bestowing on them fields, houses, and gardens, with men and oxen. Engraved title-deeds were prepared and handed down from one reign to another; no one has ventured to withdraw them, so that till now there has been no interruption. All the resident priests having chambers (*in these vihâras*) have their beds, mats, food, drink, and clothes provided without stint; in all places this is the case. The priests ever engage themselves in doing meritorious works for the purpose of religious advancement (*karma*—building up their religious character), or in reciting the scriptures, or in meditation. When a strange priest arrives, the senior priests go out to meet him, carrying for him his clothes and alms-bowl. They offer him water for washing his feet and oil for rubbing them; they provide untimely (*vikâla*) food. Having rested awhile, they again ask him as to his seniority in the priesthood, and according to this they give him a chamber and sleeping materials, arranging everything according to the *dharma.* In places where priests reside they make towers in honour of Sâriputra, of Mudgalaputra, of Ânanda, also in honour of the *Abhidharma, Vinaya,* and *Sûtra.* During a month after the season of rest the most pious families urge a collection for an offering to the priests; they prepare an untimely meal for them, and the priests in a great assembly preach the law. The preaching over, they offer to Sâriputra's tower all kinds of scents and flowers; through the night they burn lamps provided by different persons. Sâriputra originally was a Brâhman; on a certain occasion he went to Buddha and requested ordination. The great Mudgala and the great Kâsyapa did likewise. The Bhikshunîs principally honour the tower of Ânanda, because it was Ânanda who requested the lord of the world to let women take orders; Srâmanêras mostly offer to Râhula; the masters of the *Abhidharma* offer to the *Abhidharma;* the masters of the *Vinaya* offer to the *Vinaya.* Every year there is one offering, each according to his own day. Men attached to the Mahâyâna offer to *Prajña-pâramitâ,* Mañjusrî, and Avalôkitêsvara. When the priests have received their yearly dues, then the chief men and householders and Brâhmans bring every kind of robe and other things needed by the priests to offer them; the priests also make offerings one to another. Down from the time of Buddha's death the titles of conduct for the holy priesthood have been (thus) handed down without interruption.

After crossing the Indus, the distance to the Southern Sea of South India is from four to five myriads of li; the land is level throughout, without great mountains or valleys, but still there are rivers.

Questions
(1) What is Fa-Hsien's impression of the state of Buddhism in India at this time?
(2) What most impressed Fa-Hsien about the conditions under which people lived and the administration of justice?
(3) What characteristics does Fa-Hsien observe as related to Chandalas?

8–3
"Periplus of the Erythrean Sea": a European navigator's view of the Indian subcontinent.

The "Periplus of the Erythrean Sea" (Indian Ocean) is a nautical merchants handbook written, it is believed, by a Greek living in Egypt during the early days of the Roman Empire. The date of composition is thought to have fallen between 50–95 C.E. The "Periplus" indicates a thriving commercial interchange between ports on the west coast of India and the Roman Mediterranean, via northeastern Africa and southern Arabia. The selected excerpt opens with a description of India's western coast.

Source: Lionel Casson, trans., *The Periplus Erythraei* (Princeton, N.J.: Princeton University Press, 1989), pp. 79, 81, 83, 85, 89, 91, 93.

45. All over India there are large numbers of rivers with extreme ebb-and-flood tides that at the time of the new moon and the full moon last for up to three days, diminishing during the intervals. They are much more extreme in the area around Barygaza than elsewhere. Here suddenly the sea floor becomes visible, and certain parts along the coast, which a short while ago had ships sailing over them, at times become dry land, and the rivers, because of the inrush at flood tide of a whole concentrated mass of seawater, are driven headlong upstream against the natural direction of their flow for a good many stades.

46. Thus the navigating of ships in and out is dangerous for those who are inexperienced and are entering this port of trade for the first time. For, once the thrust of the flood tide is under way, restraining anchors do not stay in place. Consequently, the ships, carried along by its force and driven sideways by the swiftness of the current, run aground on the shoals and break up, while smaller craft even capsize. Even in the channels some craft, if not propped up, will tilt over on their sides during the ebb and, when the flood suddenly returns, get swamped by the first wave of the flow. So much power is generated at the inrush of the sea even during the dark of the moon, particularly if the food arrives at night, that when the tide is just beginning to come in and the sea is still at rest, there is carried from it to people at the mouth something like the rumble of an army heard from afar, and after a short while the sea itself races over the shoals with a hiss.

47. Inland behind Barygaza there are numerous peoples: the Aratroi, Arachusioi, Gandaraioi, and the peoples of Proklais, in whose area Bukephalos Alexandreia is located. And beyond these is a very warlike people, the Bactrians, under a king....Alexander, setting out from these parts, penetrated as far as the Ganges but did not get to Limyrikê and the south of India. Because of this, there are to be found on the market in Barygaza even today old drachmas engraved with the inscriptions, in Greek letters, of Apollodotus and Menander, rulers who came after Alexander.

48. There is in this region [sc. of Barygaza] towards the east a city called Ozênê the former seat of the royal court, from which everything that contributes to the region's prosperity, including what contributes to

trade with us, is brought down to Barygaza: onyx; agate (?); Indian garments of cotton; garments of *molochinon;* and a considerable amount of cloth of ordinary quality. Through this region there is also brought down from the upper areas the nard that comes by way of Proklais (the Kattyburinê, Patropapigê, and Kabalitê), the nard that comes through the adjacent part of Skythia, and costus and bdellium.

49. In this port of trade there is a market for: wine, principally Italian but also Laodicean and Arabian; copper, tin, and lead; coral and peridot (?); all kinds of clothing with no adornment or of printed fabric; multicolored girdles, eighteen inches wide; storax; yellow sweet clover (?); raw glass; realgar; sulphide of antimony; Roman money, gold and silver, which commands an exchange at some profit against the local currency; unguent, inexpensive and in limited quantity. For the king there was imported in those times precious silverware, slave musicians, beautiful girls for concubinage, fine wine, expensive clothing with no adornment, and choice unguent. This area exports: nard; costus; bdellium; ivory; onyx; agate (?); *lykion;* cotton cloth of all kinds; Chinese [sc. silk] cloth; *molochinon* cloth; [sc. silk] yarn; long pepper; and items brought here from the [sc. nearby] ports of trade. For those sailing to this port from Egypt, the right time to set out is around the month of July, that is Epeiph.

50. Immediately beyond Barygaza the coast runs from north to south. Thus the region is called Dachinabadês, for the word for south in their language is *dachanos.* The hinterland that lies beyond towards the east contains many barren areas, great mountains, and wild animals of all kinds—leopards, tigers, elephants, enormous serpents, hyenas, and a great many kinds of monkeys, as well as a great many populous nations up to the Ganges.

51. Of the trading centers in the region of Dachinabadês, two are the most outstanding: Paithana, twenty days' travel to the south from Barygaza; and, from Paithana, about ten days to the east, another very large city, Tagara. From these there is brought to Barygaza, by conveyance in wagons over very great roadless stretches, from Paithana large quantities of onyx, and from Tagara large quantities of cloth of ordinary quality, all kinds of cotton garments, garments of

molochinon, and certain other merchandise from the coastal parts that finds a market locally there. The voyage as far as Limyrikê is 7,000 steadies in all, but most vessels continue on to the strand.

52. The local ports [sc. of Dachinabadês], lying in a row, are Akabaru, Suppara, and the city of Kalliena; the last, in the time of the elder Saraganos, was a port of trade where everything went according to law. [Sc. It is so no longer] for, after Sandanês occupied it, there has been much hindrance [sc. to trade]. For the Greek ships that by chance come into these places are brought under guard to Barygaza.

53. Beyond Kalliena other local ports of trade are: Sêmylla, Mandagora, Palaipatmai, Melizeigara, Byzantion, Toparon, Tyrannosboas. Then come the Sêsekreienai Islands as they are called, the Isle of the Aigidioi, the Isle of the Kaineitoi near what is called the Peninsula, around which places there are pirates, and next White Island. Then come Naura and Tyndis, the first ports of trade of Limyrikê and, after these, Muziris and Nelkynda, which are now the active ones.

54. Tyndis, a well-known village on the coast, is in the kingdom of Kêprobotos. Muziris, in the same kingdom, owes its prosperity to the shipping from Ariakê that comes there as well as to Greek shipping. It lies on a river 500 stades distant from Tyndis by river and sea, and from [? the river mouth] to it is 20 stades. Nelkynda is just about 500 stades from Muziris, likewise by river and sea, but it is in another kingdom, Pandiôn's. It too lies on a river, about 120 stades from the sea.

55. Another settlement lies at the very mouth of the river, Bakarê, to which vessels drop downriver from Nelkynda for the outbound voyage; they anchor in the open roads to take on their cargoes because the river has sandbanks and channels that are shoal. The kings themselves of both ports of trade dwell in the interior. Vessels coming from the open sea in the vicinity of these places get an indication that they are approaching land from the snakes that emerge to meet them; these are also black in color but shorter and with dragon-shaped head and blood-red eyes.

56. Ships in these ports of trade carry full loads because of the volume and quantity of pepper and malabathron. They offer a market for: mainly a great amount of money; peridot (?); clothing with no adornment, in limited quantity; multicolored textiles; sulphide of antimony; coral; raw glass; copper, tin, lead; wine, in limited quantity, as much as goes to Barygaza; realgar; orpiment; grain in sufficient amount for those involved with shipping, because the [sc. local] merchants do not use it. They export pepper, grown for the most part in only one place connected with these ports of trade, that called Kottanarikê. They also export: good supplies of fine-quality pearls; ivory; Chinese [i.e., silk] cloth; Gangetic nard; malabathron, brought here from the interior; all kinds of transparent cut

gems; diamonds; sapphires; tortoise shell, both the kind from Chrysê Island and the kind caught around the islands lying off Limyrikê itself. For those sailing here from Egypt, the right time to set out is around the month of July, that is, Epeiph....

63. After this, heading east with the ocean on the right and sailing outside past the remaining parts to the left, you reach the Gangês region and in its vicinity the furthest part of the mainland towards the east, Chrysê. There is a river near it that is itself called the Ganges, the greatest of all the rivers in India, which has a rise and fall like the Nile. On it is a port of trade with the same name as the river, Gangês, through which are shipped out malabathron, Gangetic nard, pearls, and cotton garments of the very finest quality, the so-called Gangeric. It is said that there are also gold mines in the area, and that there is a gold coin, the *kaltis,* as it is called. Near this river is an island in the ocean, the furthest extremity towards the east of the inhabited world, lying under the rising sun itself, called Chrysê. It supplies the finest tortoise shell of all the places on the Erythraean Sea.

64. Beyond this region, by now at the northernmost point, where the sea ends somewhere on the outer fringe, there is a very great inland city called Thina from which silk floss, yarn, and cloth are shipped by land via Bactria to Barygaza and via the Ganges River back to Limyrikê. It is not easy to get to this Thina; for rarely do people come from it, and only a few. The area lies right under Ursa Minor and, it is said, is contiguous with the parts of the Pontus and the Caspian Sea where these parts turn off, near where Lake Maeotis, which lies parallel, along with [sc. the Caspian] empties into the ocean.

65. Every year there turns up at the border of Thina a certain tribe, short in body and very flat-faced...called Sêsatai....They come with their wives and children bearing great packs resembling mats of green leaves and then remain at some spot on the border between them and those on the Thina side, and they hold a festival for several days, spreading out their mats under them, and then take off for their own homes in the interior. The [? locals], counting on this, then turn up in the area, collect what the Sêsatai had spread out, extract the fibers from the reeds, which are called *petroi,* and lightly doubling over the leaves and rolling them into ball-like shapes, they string them on the fibers from the reeds. There are three grades: what is called big-ball malabathron from the bigger leaves; medium-ball from the lesser leaves; and small-ball from the smaller. Thus three grades of malabathron are produced, and then they are transported into India by the people who make them.

66. What lies beyond this area, because of extremes of storm, bitter cold, and difficult terrain and also because of some divine power of the gods, has not been explored.

Questions
(1) What evidence is presented in the "Periplus" for Greek influence in India?
(2) What appears to have been the most important Indian products exported from the west-coast ports?
(3) What European or African products did Indian merchants seem to be most interested in purchasing?
(4) What is "Gangetic," and who were "Sesatai"?

8–4
"King Milinda": the Greek world's incursion into India.

The "King Milinda" of the revered Buddhist scripture "The Questions of King Milinda" was based on the historical Greek King Menender of Bactria (c. 160–135 B.C.E.), whose realm was one of the successor-states to the empire of Alexander the Great. Buddhist tradition asserts that Menander converted to Buddhism after exchanging thought and insights with the monk Negasena.

Source:T.W. Rhys Davids, trans., *The Questions of King Milinda* (Delhi, India: Motiles Banarsidass, 1965, first published by Oxford University Press, 1894), pp. 1–10.

THE SECULAR NARRATIVE

1. King Milinda, at Sâgala the famous town of yore,
To Nâgasena, the world famous sage, repaired.
(So the deep Ganges to the deeper ocean flows.)
To him, the eloquent, the bearer of the torch
Of Truth, dispeller of the darkness of men's minds,
Subtle and knotty questions did he put, many,
Turning on many points. Then were solutions given
Profound in meaning, gaining access to the heart,
Sweet to the ear, and passing wonderful and strange.
For Nâgasena's talk plunged to the hidden depths
Of Vinaya and of Abhidhamma (Law and Thought)
Unravelling all the meshes of the Suttas' net,
Glittering the while with metaphors and reasoning
  high.
Come then! Apply your minds, and let your hearts
  rejoice,
And hearken to these subtle questionings, all grounds
Of doubt well fitted to resolve.

2. Thus hath it, been handed down by tradition—
There is in the country of the Yonakasa a great centre of trade, a city that is called Sâgala, situate in a delightful country well watered and hilly, abounding in parks and gardens and groves and lakes and tanks a paradise of rivers and mountains and woods. Wise architects have laid it out, and its people know of no oppression, since all their enemies and adversaries have been put down. Brave is its defence, with many and various strong towers and ramparts, with superb gates and entrance archways; and with the royal citadel in its midst, white walled and deeply moated. Well laid out are its streets, squares, cross roads, and market places. Well displayed are the innumerable sorts of costly merchandise with which its shops are filled. It is richly adorned with hundreds of alms-halls of various kinds; and splendid with hundreds of thousands of magnificent mansions, which rise aloft like the mountain peaks of the Himalayas. Its streets are filled with elephants, horses, carriages, and foot-passengers, frequented by groups of handsome men and beautiful women, and crowded by men of all sorts and conditions, Brahmans, nobles, artificers, and servants. They resound with cries of welcome to the teachers of every creed, and the city is the resort of the leading men of each of the differing sects. Shops are there for the sale of Benares muslin, of Koṭumbara stuffs, and of other cloths of various kinds; and sweet odours are exhaled from the bazaars, where all sorts of flowers and perfumes are tastefully set out. Jewels are there in plenty, such as men's hearts desire, and guilds of traders in all sorts of finery display their goods in the bazaars that face all quarters of the sky. So full is the city of money, and of gold and silver ware, of copper and stone ware, that it is a very mine of dazzling treasures. And there is laid up there much store of property and corn and things of value in warehouses—foods and drinks of every sort, syrups and sweetmeats of every kind. In wealth it rivals Uttara-kuru, and in glory it is as Âḷakamandâ, the city of the gods.

3. Having said thus much we must now relate the previous birth history of these two persons (Milinda and Nâgasena) and the various sorts of puzzles. This we shall do under six heads:—

1. Their previous history (Pubba-yoga).
2. The Milinda problems.
3. Questions as to distinguishing characteristics.
4. Puzzles arising out of contradictory statements.
5. Puzzles arising out of ambiguity.
6. Discussions turning on metaphor.

And of these the Milinda problems are in divisions—questions as to distinctive characteristics; and questions aiming at the dispelling of doubt; and the puzzles arising out of contradictory statements are in two divisions—the long chapter, and the problems in the life of the recluse.

THEIR PREVIOUS HISTORY (PUBBA-YOGA).

4. By Pubba-yoga is meant their past Karma (their doings in this or previous lives). Long ago, they say, when Kassapa the Buddha was promulgating the faith, there dwelt in one community near the Ganges a great company of members of the Order. There the brethren, true to established rules and duties, rose early in the morning, and taking the long-handled brooms, would sweep out the courtyard and collect the rubbish into a heap, meditating the while on the virtues of the Buddha.

5. One day a brother told a novice to remove the heap of dust. But he, as if he heard not, went about his business; and on being called a second time, and a third, still went his way as if he had not heard. Then the brother, angry with so intractable a novice, dealt him a blow with the broom stick. This time, not daring to refuse, he set about the task crying; and as he did so he muttered to himself this first aspiration: 'May I, by reason of this meritorious act of throwing out the rubbish, in each successive condition in which I may be born up to the time when I attain Nirvâna, be powerful and glorious as the midday sun!'

6. When he had finished his work he went to the river side to bathe, and on beholding the mighty billows of the Ganges seething and surging, he uttered this second aspiration: 'May I, in each successive condition in which I may be born till I attain Nirvâna, possess the power of saying the right thing, and saying it instantly, under any circumstance that may arise, carrying all before me like this mighty surge!'

7. Now that brother, after he had put the broom away in the broom closet, had likewise wandered down to the river side to bathe, and as he walked he happened to overhear what the novice had said. Then thinking: 'If this fellow, on the ground of such an act of merit, which after all was instigated by me, can harbour hopes like this, what may not I attain to?' he too made his wish, and it was thus: 'In each successive condition in which I may be born till I attain Nirvâna, may I too be ready in saying the right thing at once, and more especially may I have the power of unravelling and of solving each problem and each puzzling question this young man may put—carrying all before me like this mighty surge!'

8. Then for the whole period between one Buddha and the next these two people wandered from existence to existence among gods and men. And our Buddha saw them too, and just as he did to the son of Moggall and to Tissa the Elder, so to them also did he foretell their future fate, saying: 'Five hundred years after I have passed away with these two reappear, and the subtle Law and Doctrine taught by me will they two explain, unravelling and disentangling its difficulties by questions put and metaphors adduced.'

9. Of the two the novice became the king of the city of Sâgala in India, Milinda by name, learned eloquent, wise, and able; and a faithful observer, and that at the right time, of all the various acts of devotion and ceremony enjoined by his own sacred hymns concerning things past, present, and to come. Many were the arts and sciences he knew—holy tradition and secular law; the Sânkhya, Yoga, Nyâya, and Vaiseshika systems of philosophy; arithmetic; music; medicine; the four Vedas, the Purânas, and the Itihâsas; astronomy, magic, causation, and spells; the art of war; poetry; conveyancing—in a word, the whole nineteen.

As a disputant he was hard to equal, harder still to overcome; acknowledged superior of all the founders of the schools of thought. And as in wisdom so in strength of body, swiftness, and valour there was none equal to Milinda in all India. He was rich too, mighty in wealth and prosperity, and the number of his armed hosts knew no end.

10. Now one day Milinda the king proceeded forth out of the city to pass in review the innumerable host of his mighty army in its fourfold array (of elephants, cavalry, bowmen, and soldiers on foot). And when the numbering of the forces was over, the king, who was fond of wordy disputation, and eager for discussion with casuists, sophists, and gentry of that sort, looked at the sun (to ascertain the time), and then said to his ministers: 'The day is yet young. What would be the use of getting back to town so early? Is there no learned person, whether wandering teacher or Brahman, the head of some school or order, or the master of some band of pupils (even though he profess faith in the Arahat, the Supreme Buddha), who would be able to talk with me, and resolve my doubts?'

11. Thereupon the five hundred Yonakas said to Milinda the king: 'There are the six Masters, O king!— Pûrana Kassapa, Makkhali of the cowshed, the Nigantha of the Nâta clan, Sañgaya the son of the Belattha woman, *Agita* of the garment of hair, and Pakudha Kakkâyana. These are well known as famous founders of schools, followed by bands of disciples and hearers, and highly honoured by the people. Go, great king! put to them your problems, and have your doubts resolved.

12. So king Milinda, attended by the five hundred Yonakas, mounted the royal car with its splendid equipage, and went out to the dwelling-place of Pûrana Kassapa, exchanged with him the compliments of friendly greeting, and took his seat courteously apart. And thus sitting he said to him: 'Who is it, venerable Kassapa, who rules the world?'

'The Earth, great king, rules the world!'

'But, venerable Kassapa, if it be the Earth that rules the world, how comes it that some men go to the Avîki hell, thus getting outside the sphere of the Earth?'

When he had thus spoken, neither could Pûrana Kassapa swallow the puzzle, nor could he bring it up;

crestfallen, driven to silence, and moody, there he sat.

13. Then Milinda the king said to Makkhali of the cowshed: 'Are there, venerable Gosâla, good and evil acts? Is there such a thing as fruit, ultimate result, of good and evil acts?'

'There are no such acts, O king; and no such fruit, or ultimate result. Those who here in the world are nobles, they, O king, when they go to the other world, will become nobles once more. And those who are Brahmans, or of the middle class, or workpeople, or outcasts here, will in the next world become the same. What then is the use of good or evil acts?'

'If, venerable Gosâla, it be as you say then, by parity of reasoning, those who, here in this world

have a hand cut off, must in the next world become persons with a hand cut off, and in like manner those who have had a foot cut off or an ear or their nose!'

And at this saying Makkhali was silenced.

14. Then thought Milinda the king within himself: 'All India is an empty thing, it is verily like chaff! There is no one, either recluse or Brahman capable of discussing things with me, and dispelling my doubts.' And he said to his ministers: 'Beautiful is the night and pleasant! Who is the recluse or Brahman we can visit to-night to question him who will be able to converse with us and dispel our doubts?' And at that saying the counsellors remained silent, and stood there gazing upon the face of the king.

Questions

(1) What can be gleaned from the description of Sagala that sheds light on the city's economic/commercial life?

(2) What references might tend to bear out Milinda's Greek education and upbringing, and what traits does Milinda demonstrate that might confirm this?

(3) In what manner does the author tie in Buddhist spiritual ideas to the story?

8–5
Asoka: how a life was turned around.

Emperor Asoka (c. 274–232 B.C.E.) was the grandson of the Maurya Dynasty's founder, Chandragupta I and, in his early days, acted in the conventional manner of potentates, always seeking to enlarge his personal power and expand his domains through conquest. The sight of the horrendous slaughter and devastation caused by the Battle of Kalinga, however, brought about a spiritual crisis and a change of heart; thereafter Asoka never waged war and tried to atone for his past actions by governing his subjects in as moral and benevolent a manner as possible. A convert to Buddhism, Asoka has been, on up to this day, considered the role model for successive Indian rulers (kings, prime ministers, etc.). His decrees, sometimes inscribed on stone pillars and rocks, set forth his philosophy of government.

Source: N.A. Nikam & Richard McKeon, trans., *The Edicts of Asoka* (Chicago: University of Chicago Press, 1959), pp. 27–30, 51–52. Quoted in Mircea Eliade, *From Medicine Men to Muhammad* (N.Y.: Harper & Row, 1974), pp. 142–145.

('ROCK EDICT' XIII)

The Kalinga country was conquered by King Priyadarshī, Beloved of the Gods, in the eighth year of his reign. One hundred and fifty thousand persons were carried away captive, one hundred thousand were slain, and many times that number died.

Immediately after the Kalingas had been conquered, King Priyadarshī became intensely devoted to the study of Dharma, to the love of Dharma, and to the inculcation of Dharma.

The Beloved of the Gods, conqueror of the Kalingas, is moved to remorse now. For he has felt profound sorrow and regret because the conquest of a people previously unconquered involves slaughter, death, and deportation.

But there is a more important reason for the King's

remorse. The Brāhmanas and Shramanas [the priestly and ascetic orders] as well as the followers of other religions and the householders—who all practised obedience to superiors, parents, and teachers, and proper courtesy and firm devotion to friends, acquaintances, companions, relatives, slaves, and servants—all suffer from the injury, slaughter and deportation inflicted on their loved ones. Even those who escaped calamity themselves are deeply afflicted by the misfortunes suffered by those friends, acquaintances, companions, and relatives for whom they feel an undiminished affection. Thus all men share in the misfortune, and this weighs on King Priyadarshī's mind.

[Moreover, there is no country except that of the Yōnas (that the Greeks) where Brahmin and Buddhist ascetics do not exist] there is no place where men are not attached to one faith or another.

Therefore, even if the number of people who were killed died or who were carried away in the Kalinga war had been only one one-hundredth or one one-thousandth of what it actually was, this would still have weighed on the King's mind.

King Priyadarshī now thinks that even a person who wrongs him must be forgiven for wrongs that can be forgiven.

King Priyadarshī seeks to induce even the forest peoples who have come under his dominion [that is, primitive peoples in the sections of the conquered territory] to adopt this way of life and this ideal. He reminds them, however, that he exercises the power to punish, despite his repentance, in order to induce them to desist from their crimes and escape execution.

For King Priyadarshī desires security, self-control, impartiality, and cheerfulness for all living creatures.

King Priyadarshī considers moral conquest [that is, conquest by Dharma, *Dharma vijaya*] the most important conquest. He has achieved this moral conquest repeatedly both here and among the peoples living beyond the borders of his kingdom, even as far away as six hundred *yojanas* [about three thousand miles], where the Yōna [Greek] king Antiyoka rules, and even beyond Antiyoka in the realm of the four kings named Turamaya, Antikini, Maka, and Alikasudara and to the south among the Cholas and Pandyas [in the southern tip of the Indian peninsula] as far as Ceylon.

Here in the King's dominion also, among the Yōnas [inhabitants a northwest frontier province, probably Greeks] and the Kambōjas [neighbours of the Yōnas], among the Nābhakas and Nābhapanktis [who probably lived along the Himalayan frontier], among the Bhojas and Paitryanikas, among the Andhras and Paulindas [all peoples of the Indian peninsula], everywhere people heed his instructions in Dharma.

Even in countries which King Priyadarshī's envoys have not reached, people have heard about Dharma and about his Majesty's ordinances and instructions in Dharma, and they themselves conform to Dharma and will continue to do so.

Wherever conquest is achieved by Dharma, it produces satisfaction. Satisfaction is firmly established by conquest by Dharma [since it generates no opposition of conquered and conqueror]. Even satisfaction, however, is of little importance. King Priyadarshī attaches value ultimately to consequences of action in the other world.

This edict on Dharma has been inscribed so that my sons and great-grandsons who may come after me should not think new conquests worth achieving. If they do conquer, let them take pleasure in moderation and mild punishments. Let them consider moral conquest the only true conquest.

That is good, here and hereafter. Let their plea-sure be pleasure in [Dharma-rati]. For this alone is good, here and hereafter.

('ROCK EDICT' XII)

King Priyadarshī honours men of all faith, members of religious orders and laymen alike, with gifts and various marks of esteem. Yet he does not value either gifts or honours as much as growth in the qualities essential to religion in men of all faiths.

This growth may take many forms, but its root is in guarding one's speech to avoid extolling one's own faith and disparaging the faith of others improperly or, when the occasion is appropriate, immoderately.

The faiths of others all deserve to be honoured for one reason or another. By honouring them, one exalts one's own faith and at the same time performs a service to the faith of others. By acting otherwise, one injures one's own faith and also does disservice to that of others. For if a man extols his own faith and disparages another because of devotion to his own and because he wants to glorify it, he seriously injures his own faith.

Therefore concord alone is commendable, for through concord men may learn and respect the conception of Dharma accepted by others.

King Priyadarshī desires men of all faiths to know each other's doctrines and to acquire sound doctrines. Those who are attached to their particular faiths should be told that King Priyadarshī does not value gifts or honours as much as growth in the qualities essential to religion in men of all faiths.

Many officials are assigned to tasks bearing on this purpose—the officers in charge of spreading Dharma, the superintendents of women the royal households, the inspectors of cattle and pasture lands, and other officials.

The objective of these measures is the promotion of each man's particular faith and the glorification of Dharma.

('KALINGA EDICT' II)

King Priyadarshī says:

I command that the following instructions be communicated to my official at Samāpā:

Whenever something right comes to my attention, I want it put into practice and I want effective means devised to achieve it. My principal means to do this is to transmit my instructions to you.

All men are my children. Just as I seek the welfare and happiness of my own children in this world and the next, I seek the same things for all men.

Unconquered peoples along the borders of my dominions may wonder what my disposition is towards them. My only wish with respect to them is that they should not fear me, but trust me; that they should expect only happiness from me, not misery; that they should understand further that I will forgive them for offences which can be forgiven; that they should be induced by my example to practise Dharma; and that they should attain happiness in this world and the next.

I transmit these instructions to you in order to discharge my debt [to them] by instructing you and making known to you my will and my unshakable resolution and commitment. You must perform your duties in this way and establish their confidence in the King, assuring them that he is like a father to them, that he loves them as he loves himself, and that they are like his own children.

Having instructed you and informed you of my will and my unshakable resolution and commitment, I will appoint officials to carry out this programme in all the provinces. You are able to inspire the border peoples with confidence in me and to advance their welfare and happiness in this world and the next. By doing so, you will also attain heaven and help me discharge my debts to the people.

This edict has been inscribed here so that my officials will work at all times to inspire the peoples of neighbouring countries with confidence in me and to induce them to practise Dharma.

Questions

(1) What reasons does Asoka (Priyadarshi) give for his repentence? How does he propose to deal with the forest peoples?
(2) Taking an overview based on reading all the edicts presented here, precisely what does Asoka's concept of Dharma seem to entail?
(3) What rationale does Asoka give for his policy of religious tolerance? What benefits does he see in following such a course?

8–6
The "Shakuntala": the privileges, obligations and limits of the royal Kshatriya caste.

Practically nothing is known of the Indian dramatist Kalidasa. Even the dates of his life are unknown, and have been postulated to have occurred as early as the 5th century B.C.E. and as late as the year 56 B.C.E. Kalidasa's surviving plays and poems, however, provide a valuable degree of insight concerning the lifestyle and values of, and the importance of proper decorum to, the Kshatriya (or "Puru") caste, to which the monarchs, aristocrats and warriors belong; and the pervasive significance of living up to the dharma (standards of duty and rules of conduct) of one's own caste. The plot of the play "Shakuntala," revolves around the King, Dushyanta, who has been bewitched to the point that he no longer remembers his marriage to Shakuntala, but who is eventually reconciled to his wife once his memory is restored.

Source: P. Lal, trans., *Great Sanskrit Plays* (Norfolk, CT: New Directions Books, 1964), pp. 13–15, 48–53, 72–74.

ACT I

Enter KING DUSHYANTA'S *chariot. The* KING *is armed with a bow and arrow.*

CHARIOTEER. You are like Siva on a deer hunt:
Bow and arrow in search of the antelope.

KING. This clever beast leads us a wild-goose chase.
Look, charioteer,
There, open-mouthed and foaming: grass falls from his mouth half chewed,
He fears the arrow and pulls in his neck,
He leaps like a breath of air, gracefully,
Turning his neck toward the chariot.
But now I'm afraid I'm losing him, though I saw him clearly a minute back.

CHARIOTEER. He gave us the slip on that bumpy ground. I had to rein in tight then. But he won't get far.

KING. Faster!

CHARIOTEER. This is the fastest I can, your Majesty.
He loosens the reins.
Look at them go! Taut, intolerant, and emulous,
Ears straight and steady, careless of the kicked-up dust.

KING. They excel even the gods.
This speed is a miracle, it plays tricks with my eyes—
Small objects put on size, the crooked becomes straight.
I seem to be nowhere and everywhere.
There he is! Slow down, charioteer.

The KING aims an arrow. Shouting voices are heard off-stage.

VOICES. The sacred stag! The sacred stag! Who would kill the sacred stag?

CHARIOTEER, *looking and listening.* I see holy men everywhere, Your Majesty. Exactly where you were going to shoot.

KING, *quickly.* Stop the horses.

The chariot stops. A SAGE enters, followed by a number of disciples.

SAGE, *lifting his right hand.* This is a sacred place, sir and this stag is a sacred beast. Hunting sacred beasts is sinful.
This stag is not a scrap of paper, for boys to set fire to.
The very thought is sinful: a tender animal matched against your lightning-like arrows.
Put the arrow back in your quiver, sir.
It is meant to guard the distressed, not harm the innocent.

KING. I am sorry.

SAGE. Nobly done, sir. You prove yourself a Puru. My blessings on you: may your son be like you.

KING. I am honored.

SAGE. We were out to gather sticks for the sacrificial fire. The ashrama of our guru Kanva is over on the other side, sir, on the left bank of the Malini. If it isn't interfering with your plans, may we ask you to join us for a while? We'd be happy to perform the sacred rites in your presence.

KING. Is Sage Kanva there?

SAGE. Not at the moment. He's away on a pilgrimage to ward off the evil eye from his daughter. But Shakuntala is receiving his guests, and she will be pleased if you accept her hospitality.

KING. Then I'll come. She will speak of me to her father when he returns.

SAGE. We will see you there.

The SAGE and his disciples leave.

KING. The horses, charioteer! We shall go to the ashrama.

CHARIOTEER. Yes, Your Majesty. *He clucks to the horses.*

KING. No one briefed me, but I think I can make out where I am.
This is the edge of the Forest of Penance. It's simple really.
Here are grains near the tree roots, dropped from the beaks of wild parrots.
Fruit lies rotting, with no one to pick it.
The deer gaze nonchalantly at our strange chariot.
And the paths to the pond are wet: the sages have been bathing.

CHARIOTEER. That is true.

KING. We mustn't spoil their peace, you know. Stop the chariot here. I'll walk the rest of the distance.

CHARIOTEER. Your Majesty.

KING, *getting down.* Nor should we expect fanfare. Here, hold these. *He hands his bow, quiver, and golden ornaments to the CHARIOTEER.* See that the horses are washed and fed by the time I get back.

***

The hermits SARNGARAVA and SARADVATA, enter, bringing GAUTAMI and SHAKUNTALA with them. The CHAMBERLAIN and a PRIEST attached to the royal household follow. GAUTAMI places SHAKUNTULA in front of her. At first the group stands at some distance from the KING.

SARNGARAVA. This king is a fine man, Saradvata, and very gifted. The meanest of his subjects are well behaved. But I feel like a fish out of water with so many people around.

SARADVATA. All hermits do in a city. I'm not very happy here myself. I've a trick though: I look on the people as the pure look on the impure, the waking on the sleeping, the free on the enslaved.

SHAKUNTULA. I have a feeling it's not going to turn out right, Mother Gautami.

GAUTAMI. There's nothing to worry about, Shakuntala.

PRIEST. The king is ready to receive you, O hermits. He will hear you standing.

SARNGARAVA. You honor us, sire. We are grateful to you, but your courtesy doesn't surprise us. Trees bend with fruits, the clouds with rain, and wealth brings humility to a good man.

GUARD. You look happy, hermits. I hope your news is pleasant.

The KING *looks at* SHAKUNTALA *and speaks in an aside to the* FEMALE GUARD.

KING. Who is that veiled lady? She stands out like a glistening bud among brown leaves.

GUARD, *aside.* I couldn't say, sire. But she is very lovely.

KING, *aside.* Hold your tongue. She may be married.

SHAKUNTALA, *aside.* I must keep calm. I know he loves me.

PRIEST, *advancing toward the* KING. They carry a message from their father, sire.

KING. I am ready.

SARNGARAVA, *raising his right hand.* We bless you, O king.

KING. Thank you.

SARNGARAVA. May you receive all you wish for.

KING. Are the ashrama rites undisturbed?

SARNGARAVA. They are, sire. You have helped us greatly.
When the sun shines, we don't fear darkness.

KING. Thank you. And how is Father Kashyapa? Doing well?

SARNGARAVA. Perfectly well, sire. He is never out of sorts. He inquires after you. He sends a message.

KING. What can I do for him?

SARNGARAVA. "You fell in love with my daughter and married her," he says. "I approve of it, for you are known to be a man of honor, and she is devoted to you. When two excellent persons are brought together, there can be no blame. Take her now, for she is with child."

GAUTAMI. I can add nothing to the message, sire. You are aware of the exceptional circumstances of the case. She kept her love to herself; you didn't tell us either. It's difficult for a third person to interfere with a private arrangement.

SHAKUNTALA, *aside.* What can he possibly say to that?

KING. I don't understand.

SHAKUNTALA, *aside.* There is anger in his voice.

SARNGARAVA. We don't either. You know the custom, sire. We cannot keep her in the ashrama. We know she is pure, but what will people say? A wife must stay with her husband.

KING. Are you implying that I'm married to her?

SHAKUNTALA, *aside.* I was afraid of this.

SARNGARAVA. You may have made a mistake, but duty comes first to a king.

KING. You're presumptuous.

SARNGARAVA. I do not like the tone of your voice, sire. You speak like one drunk with power.

KING. You insult me.

GAUTAMI, *to* SHAKUNTALA. Come here, child—take off the veil. That may jog your husband's memory.

SHAKUNTALA, *removes her veil.* The KING *looks at her fixedly.*

KING, *aside.* I can't remember a thing. Until I do I can neither take nor leave her, for she is very beautiful.

The KING *continues to stare at* SHAKUNTALA *without speaking.*

SARNGARAVA. Why are you silent, sire?

KING. I am sorry, but I remember nothing, certainly not the marriage you speak of. You must excuse me if I refuse to think of myself as a adulterer.

SHAKUNTALA, *aside.* I am lost. He can't even remember what happened.

SARNGARAVA. Of course not, sire. You are no adulterer; it's Father Kashyapa who's to blame for giving his daughter in honor to the robber who stole her.

SARADVATA. Stop it, Sarngarava. We have said what we could….Shakuntala, it is your turn now.

SHAKUNTULA, *aside,* What can I possibly say that will change his mind? *She speaks aloud, hesitantly.* My husband…*She falters and speaks to herself.* But he says he never married me. *Again she summons her courage.* It is not right, O Puru, to reject so soon the girl you loved in the ashrama…

KING, *covering his ears.* This is impossible! Why must you drag my ancestral name into it?

SHAKUNTALA. If you think I am someone else's wife, this gift may remind you that I'm not.

KING. Gift?

SHAKUNTALA, *touching her finger.* Oh, no! Oh, no! The ring…it's gone! *Terrified, she looks at GAUTAMI.*

GAUTAMI. It must have slipped from your finger while you were bathing in the Ganges.

KING, *smiling.* A fertile imagination—women are famous for it.

SHAKUNTALA. Fate has intervened. But I can tell you some of the things we did. Then you will remember.

KING. From rings to incidents!

SHAKUNTALA. You remember the day you brought a lotus leaf filled with water…

KING. Go on.

SHAKUNTALA. And you offered it to Dhirgapangha, my adopted fawn, but he wouldn't drink it, for you were strange to the place; and when I gave him the water, he drank it immediately; and you said, "He trusts you, you both belong to the forest"?

KING. Very pretty. That's the way painted girls trap a man.

GAUTAMI, You're unfair, sire. You know she belongs to an ashrama and knows nothing of deceit.

KING. I am not so sure, Mother. I find even the innocent cunning. The cuckoo. for instance—she has her eggs hatched by others.

SHAKUNTALA, *in anger.* Must you judge everyone by your own small selfish heart? You are like a well that grass has grown over. Who will respect only a mask of virtue?

KING, *aside.* Her anger seems genuine. Her eyes are red, and these are hard quick words. She looks straight into my eyes: her lip quivers and her eyebrows curve like bows. *Aloud.* Dushyanta's acts are all public. Such a thing is unheard of among my subjects.

SHAKUNTALA. So I am unchaste! You tricked me—you, a Puru!—honey-mouthed and poison-hearted! *She covers her face and weeps.*

SARNGARAVA. This is the inevitable result of rashness. Those who marry in secret should know each other well before doing so.

KING. Why do you accuse me of these crimes? Have you no evidence beyond her word?

SARNGARAVA, *scornfully.* Remarkable! The words of a clean girl are suspect and the words of a man who practices professional deceit sacred!

KING. Sarcasm won't help. My mind's made up.

SARADVATA. Let us go, Sarngarava, We have done what Father Kashyapa asked us to do. *To the* KING. She is your wife, sire. Take her or leave her…Lead the way, Gautami.

They start to leave.

SHAKUNTALA. And leave me behind? Rejected by him, and now by you? *She follows.*

GAUTAMI, *stopping.* Let us take Shakuntala with us, Sarngarava. It's not her fault he won't accept her.

SARNGARAVA, *turning in sudden anger.* Never! Stay where you are! SHAKUNTALA *shrinks back.* If what he says is true, Father Kashyapa won't have you back. If your heart's pure, you might as well stay here.

KING. She can stay if she likes. As far as I'm concerned, she is another man's wife—I'm not going to molest her.

SARADVATA. If she is your wife, why don't you accept her? If she isn't, why do you let her stay?
KING. It's very simple. I may be forgetful, or she may be lying. If I am forgetful, should I not let her stay and wait till my memory comes back? If she is lying, time will tell.

***

SHAKUNTALA, *enters, her hair tied in a hermit's knot.*

KING. There she is, the pure-minded one,
Wearing saffron, her face thin with penance,
Forced to separate from a heartless husband.

SHAKUNTALA. A stranger being so familiar with my son…

BOY, *running to her.* Mother, he calls me his son.

KING. I have been cruel to you, my dearest. It does not matter. You recognize me.

SHAKUNTALA, *aside.* Be still, my heart.
My fate pities me, having done its worst.
This is my husband.

KING. My dearest, my beautiful wife,
My eyes see clearly once more.
The fates have been kind.

SHAKUNTALA. My husband. *She sobs.*

KING. Having seen you, I am happy.
Having seen your face, and your pale-red lips.

BOY. Who is he, Mother?

SHAKUNTALA. My son, a star is dancing.
She weeps.

KING. Forget the sad past of separation, my
    beautiful wife.
Delusion filled my mind.
To a blind man a garland is a snake.

He falls at her feet.

SHAKUNTALA. No, my husband, no.

The KING *rises.*

Did you remember me?

KING. Let the sorrow pass: there is time enough.
O my dearest, let me dry your eyes.
He does so.

SHAKUNTALA, *noticing the royal signet.* This is the ring.

KING. This is the ring that brought me to my senses.

MATALI, *entering.* So he has found his joy—at last!

KING. I do not think Indra knows of this.

MATALI. There is very little he does not know. Come with me. Maricha the perfect grants you an audience.

KING. Shakuntala, take the child's hand.

MARICHA, *entering.* My son, live long. And do not let self-pity overpower you. Durvasas was responsible for the curse that brought you to your error. I learned this in deep meditation.

KING. Now I know why I feel so free.

MARICHA. And this is your son.

KING. And heir, O perfect one.

MARICHA. And so—this is the end, Go to the capital with your wife and son. Indra will send you and your subjects blessings and prosperity…
See that you do the necessary acts of worship.
And all will be well…
What more can I do for you?

KING. There is no greater favor, O perfect one.
Yet perhaps there is…
May the lord of the earth seek the good of my
    subjects.
May the wise be honored.
And may I be released from further lives.

CURTAIN
***

Questions

(1) What does the opening scene indicate about the responsibilities of and restrictions on the power of the Puru caste, as personified by King Dushyanta?

(2) What further insights, along the lines of those in question 1, can be surmised from the exchange between the King and Sarngarava?

(3) In general terms, what does Kalidasa's play state or imply about gender relationships amongst members of the Indian Puru caste?

CHAPTER 9

9–1

"Upanishads": a mirror into the underpinnings of the ancient Hindu faith.

The "Upanishads" form a "second group" of Hindu scripture. They date from a later period than the "Vedas" and the "Puranas" (it is believed that they were compiled between 800–600 B.C.E). They certainly contain a greater degree of theological complexity than the earlier works. The "Upanishads" is not a single book united by a common thread, but a collection of different volumes, each of which is an entity unto itself, presenting a distinct philosophical slant on the most pressing spiritual questions of the Hindu faith. Central to the "Upanishads" is the attempt to reconcile the demands of the material world with the Infinite (referred to as "Brahman" and "The Self") that goes beyond physical existence.

Source: S.E. Frost, Jr., *The Sacred Writings of the World's Great Religions.* (N.Y.: McGraw-Hill, 1972), pp. 20–22, 27–30.

SECOND ADHYAYA

First Brahmana

1. There was formerly the proud Gargya Balaki, a man of great reading. He said to Ajatasatru of Kasi, "Shall I tell you Brahman?" Ajatasatru said. "We give a thousand (cows) for that speech (of yours), for verily all people run away, saying, Janaka (the king of Mithila) is our father (patron)."

2. Gargya said: "The person that is in the sun, that I adore as Brahman." Ajatasatru said to him: "No, no! Do not speak to me on this. I adore him verily as the supreme, the head of all beings, the king. Whoso adores him thus, becomes supreme, the head all beings, a king."

3. Gargya said: "The person that is in the moon (and in the mind) that I adore as Brahman." Ajatasatru said to him: "No, no! Do not speak to me on this. I adore him verily as the great, clad in white raiment, as Soma, the king. Whoso adores him thus, Soma is poured out and poured forth for him day by day, and his food does not fail."

4. Gargya said: "The person that is in the lightning (and in the heart), that I adore as Brahman." Ajatasatru said to him: "No, no! Do not speak to me on this. I adore him verily as the luminous. Whoso adores him thus, becomes luminous, and his offspring becomes luminous."

5. Gargya said: "The person that is in the ether (and in the ether of heart), that I adore as Brahman." Ajatasatru said to him: "No, no! Do not speak to me on this. I adore him as what is full, and quiescent. Whoso adores him thus, becomes filled with offspring and cattle, and his offspring does not cease from this world."

6. Gargya said: "The person that is in the wind (and in the breath), that I adore as Brahman." Ajatasatru said to him: "No, no! Do not speak to me on this. I adore him as Indra Vaikuntha, as the unconquer-able arm (of the Maruts). Whoso adores him thus, becomes victorious, unconquerable, conquering his enemies."

7. Gargya said: "The person that is in the fire (and in the heart), that l adore as Brahman." Ajatasatru said to him: "No, no! Do not speak to me on this. I adore him as powerful. Whoso adores him thus, becomes powerful, and his offspring becomes powerful."

8. Gargya said: "The person that is in the water (in seed, and in the heart), that I adore as Brahman." Ajatasatru said to him: "No, no! Do not speak to me on this. I adore him as likeness. Whoso adores him thus, to him comes what is likely (or proper), not what is improper; what is born from him is like unto him."

9. Gargya said: "The person that is in the mirror, that I adore as Brahman." Ajatasatru said to him: "No, no! Do not speak to me on this. I adore him verily as the brilliant. Whoso adores him thus, he becomes brilliant, his offspring becomes brilliant, and with whomsoever he comes together, he outshines them."

10. Cargya said: "The sound that follows a man while be moves, that I adore as Brahman." Ajatasatru said to him: "No, no! Do not speak to me on this. I adore him verily as life. Whoso adores him thus, he reaches his full age in this world, breath does not leave him before the time."

11. Gargya said: "The person that is in space, that I adore as Brahman." Ajatasatru said to him: "No, no! Do not speak to me on this. I adore him verily as the second who never leaves us. Whoso adores him thus, becomes possessed of a second, his party is not cut off from him."

12. Gargya said: "The person that consists of the shadow, that I adore as Brahman." Ajatasatru said to him: "No, no! Do not speak to me on this. I adore him verily as death. Whoso adores him thus, he reaches his whole age in this world, death does not approach him before the time."

13. Gargya said: "The person that is in the body,

that I adore as Brahman." Ajatasatru said to him: No, no! Do not speak to me on this. I adore him verily as embodied. Whoso adores him thus, becomes embodied, and his offspring becomes embodied."

Then Gargya became silent.

14. Ajatasatru said: "Thus far only?" "Thus far only," he replied. Ajatasatru said: "This does not suffice to know it (the true Brahman)." Gargya replied: "Then let me come to you, as a pupil."

15. Ajatasatru said: "Verily, it is unnatural that a Brahmana should come to a Kshatriya, hoping that he should tell him the Brahman. However, I shall make you know him clearly"; thus saying, he took him by the hand and rose.

And the two together came to a person who was asleep. He called him by these names, "Thou, great one, clad in white raiment, Soma, king." He did not rise. Then rubbing him with his hand, he woke him, and he arose.

16. Ajatasatru said: "When this man was thus asleep, where was then the person (purusha), the intelligent? and from whence did he thus come back?" Gargya did not know this.

17. Ajatasatru said: "When this man was thus asleep, then the intelligent person (purusha), having through the intelligence of the senses (pranas) absorbed within himself all intelligence, lies in the ether, which is in the heart. When he takes in these different kinds of intelligence, then it is said that the man sleeps (svapiti). Then the breath is kept in, speech is kept in, the ear is kept in, the eye is kept in, the mind is kept in.

18. "But when he moves about sleep in (and dream), then these are his worlds. He is, as it were, a great king; he is, as it were, a great Brahmana; he rises, as it were, and he falls. And as a great king might keep in his own subjects, and move about, according to his pleasure, within his own domain, thus does that person (who is endowed with intelliegence) keep in the various senses (pranas) and move about, according to his pleasure, within his own body (while dreaming).

19. "Next, when he is in profound sleep, and knows nothing, there are the seventy-two thousand arteries called Hita, which from the heart spread through the body. Through them he moves forth and rests in the surrounding body. And as a young man, or a great king, or a great Brahmana, having reached the summit of happiness, might rest, so does he then rest.

20. "As the spider comes out with its thread, or as small sparks come all forth from fire, thus do all senses, all worlds, all Devas, all beings come forth from that Self. The Upanishad (the true name and doctrine) of that Self is 'the True of the True.' Verily the senses are the True, and he is the True of the True."

FOURTH ADHYAYA

Fourth Brahmana

1. Yajnavalkya continued: "Now when that Self, having sunk into weakness, sinks, as it were, into unconsciousness, then gather those senses (pranas) around him, and he, taking with him those elements of light, descends into the heart. When that person in the eye turns away, then he ceases to know any forms.

2. "'He has become one' they say, 'he does not see.' 'He has become one,' they say, 'he does not smell.' 'He has become one,' they say, 'he does not taste.' 'He has become one,' they say, 'he does not speak.' 'He has become one,' they say, 'he does not hear.' 'He has become one' they say, 'he does not think.' 'He has become one,' they say, 'he does not touch.' 'He has become one' they say, 'he does not know.' The point of his heart becomes lighted up, and by that light the Self departs, either through the eye, or through the skull, or through other places of the body. And when he thus departs, life (the chief prana) departs after him, and when life thus departs, all the other vital spirits (pranas) depart after it. He is conscious, and being conscious he follows and departs.

"Then both his knowledge and his work take hold of him, and his acquaintance with former things.

3. "And as a caterpillar, after having reached the end of a blade of grass, and after having made another approach (to another blade), draws itself together towards it, thus does this Self, after having thrown off this body and dispelled all ignorance, and after making another approach (to another body), draw himself together towards it.

4. "And as a goldsmith, taking a piece of gold, turns it into another, newer and more beautiful shape, so does this Self, after having thrown off this body and dispelled all ignorance, make unto himself another, newer and more beautiful shape, whether it be like the fathers, or like the Gandharvas, of like the Devas, or like Prajapati, or like Brahman, or like other beings.

5. "That Self is indeed Brahman, consisting of knowledge, mind, life, sight, hearing, earth, water, wind, ether, light and no light, desire and no desire, anger and no anger, right or wrong, and all things. Now as a man is like this or like that, according as he acts and according as he behaves, so will he be—a man of good acts will become good, a man of bad acts, bad. He becomes pure by pure deeds, bad by bad deeds.

"And here they say that a person consists of desires. And as is his desire, so is his will; and as is his will, so is his deed; and whatever deed he does, that he will reap.

6. "And here there is this verse: 'To whatever object a man's own mind is attached, to that he goes

strenuously together with his deed; and having obtained the end (the last results) of whatever deed he does here on earth, he returns again from that world (which is the temporary reward of his deed) to this world of action.'

"So much for the man who desires. But as to the man who does not desire, who, not desiring, freed from desires, is satisfied in his desires, or desires the Self only, his vital spirits do not depart elsewhere—being Brahman, he goes to Brahman."

7. "On this there is this verse: When all desires which once entered his heart are undone, then does the mortal become immortal, then he obtains Brahman."

"And as the slough of a snake lies on an ant-hill, dead and cast away, thus lies this body; but that disembodied immortal spirit (prana, life) is Brahman only, is only light."

Janaka Vaideha said: "Sir, I give you a thousand."

8. "On this there are these verses:

"'The small, old path stretching far away has been found by me. On it sages who know Brahman move on to the Svargaloka (heaven), and thence higher on, as entirely free.

9. "'On that path they say that there is white, or blue, or yellow, or green, or red; that path was found by Brahman, and on it goes whoever knows Brahman, and who has done good, and obtained splendour.

10. "'All who worship what is not knowledge (avidya) enter into blind darkness: those who delight in knowledge, enter, as it were, into greater darkness.

11. "'There are indeed those unblessed worlds, covered with blind darkness. Men who are ignorant and not enlightened go after death to those worlds.

12. "'If a man understands the Self, saying, "I am He," what could be wish or desire that he should pine after the body?

13. "'Whoever has found and understood the Self that has entered into this patched-together hiding-place, he indeed is the creator, for he is the maker of everything, his is the world, and he is the world itself.

14. "'While we are here, we may know this; if not, I am ignorant, and there is great destruction. Those who know it become immortal, but others suffer pain indeed.

15. "'If a man clearly beholds this Self as God, and as the lord of all that is and will be, then he is no more afraid.

16. "'He behind whom the year revolves with the days, him the gods worship as the light of lights, as immortal time.

17. "'He in whom the five beings and the ether rest, him alone I believe to be the Self—I who know, believe him to be Brahman; I who am immortal, believe him to be immortal.

18. "'They who know the life of life, the eye of the eye, the ear of the ear, the mind of the mind, they have comprehended the ancient, primeval Brahman.

19. "'By the mind alone it is to be perceived, there is in it no diversity. He who perceives therein any diversity, goes from death to death.

20. "'This eternal being that can never be proved, is to be in perceived in one way only; it is spotless, beyond the ether, the unborn Self, great and eternal.

21. "'Let a wise Brahmana, after he has discovered him, practise wisdom. Let him not seek after many words, for that is mere weariness of the tongue.'

22. "And he is that great unborn Self, who consists of knowledge, is surrounded by the Pranas, the ether within the heart. In it there reposes the ruler of all, the lord of all, the king of all. He does not become greater by good works, nor smaller by evil works. He is the lord of all, the king of all things, the protector of all things. He is a bank and a boundary, so that these worlds may not be confounded. Brahmanas seek to know him by the study of the Veda by sacrifice, by gifts, by penance, by fasting, and he who knows him becomes a Muni. Wishing for that world (for Brahman) only, mendicants leave their homes.

"Knowing this, the people of old did not wish for offspring. What shall we do with offspring, they said, who have this Self' and this world of (Brahman). And they, having risen above the desire for sons, wealth, and new worlds, wander about as mendicants. For desire for sons is desire for wealth, and desire for wealth is desire for worlds. Both these are indeed desires only. He, the Self, is to be described by No, no! He is incomprehensible, for he cannot be comprehended; he is imperishable, for he cannot perish; he is unattached, for he does not attach himself; unfettered, he does not suffer, he does not fail. Him (who knows), these two do not overcome, whether he says that for some reason he has done evil, or for some reason he has done good—he overcomes both, and neither what he has done, nor what he has omitted to do, burns (affects) him.

23. "This has been told by a verse (Rich): 'This eternal greatness of the Brahmana does not grow larger by work, nor does it grow smaller. Let man try to find (know) its trace, for not having found (known) it, he is not sullied by any evil deed.'

"He therefore that knows it, after having become quiet, subdued, satisfied, patient, and collected, sees self in Self, sees all as Self. Evil does not overcome him, he overcomes all evil. Evil does not burn him, he burns all evil. Free from evil, free from spots, free from doubt, he becomes a (true) Brahmana; this is the Brahma-world, O king"—thus spoke Vajnavalkya.

Janaka Vaideha said: "Sir: I give you the Videhas, and also myself, to be together your slaves."

24. This indeed is the great, the unborn Self, the strong, the giver of wealth. He who knows this obtains wealth.

25. This great, unborn Self, undecaying, undying, immortal, fearless, is indeed Brahman. Fearless is Brahman, and he who knows this becomes verily the fearless Brahman.

Questions

(1) Compare/contrast the two conceptualizations of Brahman found in the Second Adhyaya to that in the Fourth Adhyaya; are there differences and, if so, what are they?

(2) How is the dream state explained, or employed, to illustrate a truth in each Adhyaya?

(3) How are the ideals of samsura (reincarnation) and dharma (duties and ethical standards connected to one's caste) dovetailed into the Fourth Adhyaya?

9–2

The "Apastamba": traditional Hindu law.

Much of what is now incorporated into Hinduism developed, bit by bit, over the centuries as custom became engrained into tradition. No set doctrine or codes of conduct sprouted in any one place at any one time. Only much later was there felt to be a need to codify what had become accepted practice. The "Apastamba" was thus an attempt by members of the Brahmin caste to set down a legal basis for the existing system that placed them in a position of privilege.

Source: Georg Buhler, trans., *Apastamba: The Sacred Law of the Aryans* (Delhi, India: Motilas Banarsidass, 1965), pp. 1–8, 10–11, 16–17, 54–55, 161–166. First published by Clarendon Press, 1879.

PRASNA 1, PATALA 1, KHANDA 1

1. Now, therefore, we will declare the acts productive of merit which form part of the customs of daily life, as they have been settled by the agreement (of those who know the law).

2. The authority (for these duties) is the agreement of those who know the law, (and the authorities for the latter are) the Vedas alone.

3. (There are) four castes—Brâhmanas, Kshatriyas, Vaisyas, and Sûdras.

4. Amongst these, each preceding (caste) is superior by birth to the one following.

5. (For all these), excepting Sûdras and those who have committed bad actions, (are ordained) the initiation, the study of the Veda, and the kindling of the sacred fire; and (their) works are productive of rewards (in this world and the next).

6. To serve the other (three) castes (is ordained) for the Sûdra.

7. The higher the caste (which he serves) the greater is the merit.

8. The initiation is the consecration in accordance with the texts of the Veda, of a male who is desirous of (and can make use of) sacred knowledge.

9. A Brâhmana declares that the Gâyatrî is learnt for the sake of all the (three) Vedas.

10. (Coming) out of darkness, forsooth, he enters darkness, whom a man unlearned in the Vedas, initiates, and (so does he) who, without being learned in the Vedas, (performs the rite of initiation.) That has been declared in a Brâhmana.

11. As performer of this rite of initiation he shall seek to obtain a man in whose family sacred learning is hereditary, who himself possesses it, and who is devout (in following the law)

12. And under him the sacred science must be studied until the end, provided (the teacher) does not fall off from the ordinances of the law.

13. He from whom (the pupil) gathers (âkinoti) (the knowledge of) his religious duties (dharmân) (is called) the Âkârya (teacher).

14. Him he should never offend.

15. For he causes him (the pupil) to be born (a second time) by (imparting to him) sacred learning.

16. This (second) birth is the best.

17. The father and the mother produce the body only.

18. Let him initiate a Brâhmana in spring, Kshatriya in summer, a Vaisya in autumn, a Brâmana in the eighth year after his conception, a Kshatriya in the eleventh year after his conception, (and) a Vaisya in the twelfth after his conception.

19. Now (follows the enumeration of the years to be chosen) for the fulfilment of some (particular) wish.

20. (Let him initiate) a person desirous of excellence in sacred learning in his seventh year, a person desirous of long life in his eighth year, a person desirous of manly vigour in his ninth year, a person desirous of food in his tenth year, a person desirous of strength in his eleventh year, a person desirous of cattle in his twelfth year.

21. There is no dereliction (of duty, if the initiation takes place), in the case of a Brâhmana before the completion of the sixteenth year, in the case of Kshatriya before the completion of the twenty-second year, in the case of a Vaisya before the completion of the twenty-fourth year.

22. (Let him be initiated at such an age) that he may be able to perform the duties, which we shall declare below.

23. If the proper time for the initiation has passed, he shall observe for the space of two months the duties of a student, as observed by those who are studying the three Vedas.

24. After that he may be initiated.

25. After that he shall bathe (daily) for one year.

26. After that he may be instructed.

27. He, whose father and grandfather have not been initiated, (and his two ancestors) are called 'slayers of the Brahman.'

28. Intercourse, eating, and intermarriage with them should be avoided.

29. If they wish it (they may perform the following) expiation;

30. In the same manner as for the first neglect (of the initiation), (a penance of) two months (was) prescribed, so (they shall do penance for) one year.

31. Afterwards they may be initiated, and then they must bathe (daily),

PRASNA I, PATALA 1, KHANDA 2.

I. For as many years as there are uninitiated persons, reckoning (one year) for each ancestor (and the person to be initiated himself),

2. (They should bathe daily under the recitation) of the seven Pâvamânîs, beginning with 'If near or far' of the Yagushpavitra, ('May the waters, the mothers purify us,' &c.) of the Sâmapavitra, ('With what help assists,' &c.), and of the Ângirasapavitra ('A swan, dwelling in purity'),

3. Or also under the recitation of the Vyâh*ritis* (om, bhû*h*, bhuva*h*, suva*h*).

4. After that (such a person) may be taught (the Veda).

5. But those whose great-grandfather's (grandfather's and father's) initiation is not remembered, are called 'burial-grounds.'

6. Intercourse, dining, and intermarriage with them should be avoided. For them, if they like, the (following) penance (is prescribed). (Such a man) shall keep for twelve years the rules prescribed for a student who is studying the three Vedas. Afterwards he may be initiated. Then he shall bathe under the recitation of the Pâvamânîs and of the other (texts mentioned above, I, I, 2, 2).

7. Then he may be instructed in the duties of a householder.

8. He shall not be taught (the whole Veda), but only the sacred formulas required for the domestic ceremonies.

9. When he has finished this (study of the G*ri*hyamantras), he may be initiated (after having performed the penance prescribed) for the first neglect (I, I, I, 23).

10. Afterwards (everything is performed) as in the case of a regular initiation.

11. He who has been initiated shall dwell as a religious student in the house of his teacher,

12. For forty-eight years (if he learns all the four Vedas),

13. (Or) a quarter less (i. e. for thirty-six years),

14. (Or) less by half (i.e. for twenty-four years),

15. (Or) three quarters less (i.e. for eighteen years),

16. Twelve years (should be) the shortest time (for his residence with his teacher).

17. A student who studies the sacred science shall not dwell with anybody else (than his teacher).

18. Now (follow) the rules for the studentship.

19. He shall obey his teacher, except (when ordered to commit) crimes which cause loss of caste.

20. He shall do what is serviceable to his teacher, he shall not contradict him.

21. He shall always occupy a couch or seat lower (than that of his teacher).

22. He shall not eat food offered (at a funeral oblation or at a sacrifice),

23. Nor pungent condiments, salt, honey, or meat.

24. He shall not sleep in the day-time.

25. He shall not use perfumes.

26. He shall preserve chastity.

27. He shall not embellish himself (by using ointments and the like).

28. He shall not wash his body (with hot water for pleasure).

29. But, if it is soiled by unclean things, he shall clean it (with earth or water), in a place where he is not seen by a Guru.

30. Let him not sport in the water whilst bathing; let him swim (motionless) like a stick.

31. He shall wear all his hair tied in one knot.

32. Or let him tie the lock on the crown of the head in a knot, and shave the rest of the hair....

PRASNA I, PATALA 1, KHANDA 3

...

11. Let him not look at dancing.

12. Let him not go to assemblies (for gambling, &c.), nor to crowds (assembled at festivals).

13. Let him not be addicted to gossiping.

14. Let him be discreet.

15. Let him not do anything for his own pleasure in places which his teacher frequents.

16. Let him talk with women so much (only) as his purpose requires.

17. (Let him be) forgiving.

18. Let him restrain his organs from seeking illicit objects.

19. Let him be untiring in fulfilling his duties;

20. Modest;

21. Possessed of self-command;

22. Energetic;

23. Free from anger;

24. (And) free from envy.

25. Bringing all he obtains to his teacher, he shall go begging with a vessel in the morning and in the evening, (and he may) beg (from everybody) except low-caste people unfit for association (with Âryas) and Abhisastas.

PRASNA I, PATALA 1, KHANDA 4

...

13. In the evening and in the morning he shall fetch water in a vessel (for the use of his teacher).

14. Daily he shall fetch fuel from the forest, and place it on the floor (in his teacher's house).

15. He shall not go to fetch firewood after sunset.

16. After having kindled the fire, and having swept the ground around (the altar), he shall place the sacred fuel on the fire every morning and evening, according to the prescription (of the Grihya-sûtra).

17. Some say that the fire is only to be worshipped in the evening.

18. He shall sweep the place around the fire after it has been made to burn (by the addition of fuel) with his hand, and not (with the bundle of Kusa grass called) Samûhanî.

19. But, before (adding the fuel, he is free to use the Samûhanî) at his pleasure.

20. He shall not perform non-religious acts with the residue of the water employed for the fire-worship, nor sip it.

21. He shall not sip water which has been stirred with the hand, nor such as has been received in one hand only.

22. And he shall avoid sleep (whilst his teacher is awake).

23. Then (after having risen) he shall assist his teacher daily by acts tending to the acquisition of spiritual merit and of wealth....

PRASNA I, PATALA 5, KHANDA 15.

I. When he shows his respect to Gurus or aged persons or guests, when he offers a burnt-oblation (or other sacrifice), when he murmurs prayers at dinner, when sipping water and during the (daily) recitation of the Veda, his garment (or his sacrificial thread) shall pass over his left shoulder and under his right arm.

2. By sipping (pure) water, that has been collected on the ground, he becomes pure.

3. Or he, whom a pure person causes to sip water, (becomes also pure.)

4. He shall not sip rain-drops.

5. (He shall not sip water) from a (natural) cleft in the ground.

6. He shall not sip water heated (at the fire) except for a particular reason (as sickness).

7. He who raises his empty hands (in order to scare) birds, (becomes impure and) shall wash (his hands).

8. If he can (find water to sip) he shall not remain impure (even) for a muhûrta.

9. Nor (shall he remain) naked (for a mûhutra if he can help it).

10. Purification (by sipping water) shall not take place whilst he is (standing) in the water.

11. Also, when he has crossed a river, he shall purify himself by sipping water.

12. He shall not place fuel on the fire, without having sprinkled it (with water)....

PRASNA II, PATALA 10, KHANDA 26.

1. A (king) who, without detriment to his servants, gives land and money to Brâhmanas according to their deserts gains endless worlds....

4. He shall appoint men of the first three castes, who are pure and truthful, over villages and towns for the protection of the people.

5. Their servants shall possess the same qualities.

6. They must protect a town from thieves in every direction to the distance of one yogana.

7. (They must protect the country to the distance of) one krosa from each village.

8. They must be made to repay what is stolen within these (boundaries).

9. The (king) shall make them collect the lawful taxes (sulka).

10. A learned Brâhmana is free from taxes,

11. And the women of all castes,

12. And male children before the marks (of puberty appear),

13. And those who live (with a teacher) in order to study,

14. And ascetics, who are intent on fulfilling the sacred law,

15. And a Sûdra who lives by washing the feet,

16. Also blind, dumb, deaf, and diseased persons (as long as their infirmities last),

17. And those to whom the acquisition of property is forbidden (as Sannyâsins).

18. A young man who, decked with ornaments, enters unintentionally (a place where) a married woman or (marriageable) damsel (sits), must be reprimanded.

19. But if he does it intentionally with a bad purpose, he must be fined.

20. If he has actually committed adultery, the organ shall be cut off together with the testicles.

21. But (if he has bad intercourse) with a (marriageable) girl, his property shall he confiscated and he shall be banished.

22. Afterwards the king must support (such women and damsels),

23. And protect them from defilement.

24. If they agree to undergo the (prescribed penance, he shall make them over to their (lawful) guardians.

PRASNA II, PATALA 10, KHANDA 27.

1. If (adulteresses) have performed (the prescribed penance), they are to be treated as before (their fault). For the connexion (of husband and wife) takes place through the law.

2. (A husband) shall not make over his (wife), who occupies the position of a 'gentilis,' to others (than to his 'gentiles'), in order to cause children to be begot for himself.

3. For they declare, that a bride is given to the family (of her husband, and not to the husband alone).

4. That is (at present) forbidden on account of the weakness of (men's) senses.

5. The hand (of a gentilis is considered in law to be) that of a stranger, as well as (that of any other person except the husband).

6. If the (marriage vow) is transgressed, both (husband and wife) certainly go to hell.

7. The reward (in the next world) resulting from observing the restrictions of the law is preferable offspring obtained in this manner (by means of Niyoga)

8. A man of one of the first three castes (who commits adultery) with a woman of the Sûdra caste shall be banished.

9. A Sûdra (who commits adultery) with a woman of one of the first three castes shall suffer capital punishment.

10. And he shall emaciate a woman who has committed adultery with a (Sûdra, by making her undergo penances and fasts, in case she had no child).

11. They declare, that (a Brâhmana) who has once committed adultery with a married woman of equal class, shall perform one-fourth of the penance prescribed for an outcast.

12. In like manner for every repetition (of crime), one-fourth of the penance (must be added).

13. (If the offence be committed) for the fourth time, the whole (penance of twelve years must be performed).

14. The tongue of a Sûdra who speaks evil of a virtuous person, belonging to one of the first three castes, shall be cut out.

15. A Sûdra who assumes a position equal (to that of a member of one of the first three castes), in conversation, on the road, on a couch, in sitting (and on similar occasions), shall be flogged.

16. In case (a Sûdra) commits homicide or theft, appropriates land (or commits similar heinous crimes), his property shall be confiscated and he himself shall suffer capital punishment.

17. But if these (offences be committed) by a Brâhmana, he shall be made blind (by tying a cloth over his eyes).

18. He shall keep in secret confinement him who violates the rules (of his caste or order), or any other sinner, until (he promises) amendment.

19. If he does not amend, he shall be banished.

20. A spiritual teacher, an officiating priest, a Snâtaka, and a prince shall be able to protect (a criminal from punishment by their intercession), except in case of a capital offence.

Questions

(1) What ritual/spiritual significance does Hindu law attach to water?

(2) What would entitle an individual to tax-exempt status?

(3) How does the students' training regimen compare/contrast to that of a Sumerian scribe (see Document 2–7)?

(4) To what degree of rigor is the law to be applied to Sudras? To Brahmins?

9–3
Mahavira: the "Great Hero" of the Jain religion.

As Hinduism became more legalistic and written codes like "Apastamba" reinforced the tendency towards tranforming the faith into a vehicle for perpetuating a rigid social system, there were inevitable reactions against it. One of the earliest and most effective of these was Jainism, founded by Vardhamana Mahavira (c. 540–468 B.C.E), a holy man who is reputed to have wandered for 12 years, observing isolation from human society until he attained spiritual enlightenment. Jain precepts stress nonviolence, vegetarianism, austerity, fasting, and self-denial.

Source: Hermann Jacobi, *Sacred Books of the East* (Oxford:1884, pp. 85–87. Quoted in Mircea Eliade *From Medicine Men to Muhammad* (N.Y: Harper & Row,1974), pp. 43–45.

I. 3. For a year and a month he did not leave off his robe. Since that time the Venerable One, giving up his robe, was a naked, world-relinquishing, houseless (sage).

4. Then he meditated (walking) with his eye fixed on a square space before him of the length of a man. Many people assembled, shocked at the sight; they struck him and cried.

5. Knowing (and renouncing) the female sex in mixed gathering places, he meditated, finding his way himself: I do not lead a worldly life.

6. Giving up the company of all householders whomsoever, he meditated. Asked, he gave no answer; he went and did not transgress the right path.

7. For some it is not easy (to do what he did), not to answer those who salute; he was beaten with sticks, and struck by sinful people....

10. For more than a couple of years he led a religious life without using cold water; he realized singleness, guarded his body, had got intuition, and was calm.

11. Thoroughly knowing the earth-bodies and water-bodies and fire-bodies and wind-bodies, the lichens, seeds, and sprouts,

12. He comprehended that they are, if narrowly inspected, imbued with life, and avoided to injure them; he, the Great Hero.

13. The immovable (beings) are changed to movable ones, and the movable beings to immovable ones; beings which are born in all states become individually sinners by their actions.

14. The Venerable One understands thus: he who is under the conditions (of existenece), that fool suffers pain. Thoroughly knowing (karman), the Venerable One avoids sin.

15. The sage, perceiving the double (karman), proclaims the incomparable activity, he, knowing one; knowing the current of worldliness, the current of sinfulness, and the impulse.

16. Practising the sinless abstinence from killing, he did no acts, neither himself nor with the assistance of others; he to whom woman were known as the causes of all sinful acts, he saw (the true sate of the world)....

III. 7. Ceasing to use the stick (i.e. cruelty) against living beings, abandoning the care of the body, the houseless (Mahāvīa), the Venerable One, endures the thorns of the villages (i.e. the abusive language of the peasants), (being) perfectly enlightened.

8. As an elephant at the head of the battle, so was Mahāvīa victorious. Sometimes he did not reach a village there in Ladha.

9. When he who is free from desires approached the village, the inhabitants met him on the outside, and attacked him, saying, 'Get away from here.'

10. He was struck with a stick, the fist. a lance, hit with a fruit, a clod, a potsherd. Beating him again and again, many cried.

11. When he once (sat) without moving his body, they cut his flesh, tore his hair under pains, or covered him with dust.

12. Throwing him up, they let him fall, or disturbed him in his religious postures; abandoning the care of his body. the Venerable One humbled himself and bore pain, free from desire.

13. As a hero at the head of the battle is surrounded on all sides, so was there Mahāvīa. Bearing all hardships, the Venerable One, undisturbed, proceeded (on the road to Nirvāna)....

IV. 1. The Venerable One was able to abstain from indulgence of the flesh, though never attacked by diseases. Whether wounded or not wounded, he desired not medical treatment.

2. Purgatives and emetics, anointing of the body and bathing, shampooing and cleaning of the teeth do not behove him, after he learned (that the body is something unclean).

3. Being averse from the impressions of the senses, the Brāhmana wandered about, speaking but little. Sometimes in the cold season the Venerable One was meditating in the shade.

4. In summer he exposes himself to the heat, he sits squatting in the sun; he lives on rough (food); rice, pounded jujube, and beans.

5. Using these three, the Venerable One sustained himself eight months. Sometimes the Venerable One did not drink for half a month or even for a month.

6. Or he did not drink for more than two months, or even six months, day and night, without desire (for drink). Sometimes he ate stale food.

7. Sometimes he ate only the sixth meal, or the eighth, the tenth, the twelfth; without desires, persevering in meditation.

8. Having wisdom, Mahavira committed no sin himself, nor did he induce other to do so, nor did he consent to the sins of others.

Questions

(1) In what ways might Mahāvīa's behavior have provoked such violent responses in others?

(2) What did Mahāvīa's diet consist of while he sought enlightenment?

(3) What often occurred when Mahāvīa approached a village?

(4) What admirable traits does the writer see in Mahāvīa?

9-4

Gautama: a pampered prince faces his moment of truth.

Gautama the Buddha (563–483 B.C.E) would far surpass Mahāvīa, just as his creed of Buddhism would become a far more dominant force than Jainism. Originally known as Siddhartha Gautama, the young man went from being the spoiled and insulated son of a north-Indian raja to an impoverished seeker of eternal Truth after becoming aware of death, poverty, and disease. Out of this spiritual crisis, Gautama would ultimately find what he sought, becoming the Buddha (or "Enlightened One"). The story was later set down by his disciples in the "Digha-nikaya," a Buddhist holy book.

Source: Clarence H. Hamilton, *Buddhism* (N.Y.: 1952), pp. 6–11, quoting translation by E.H. Brewster, *Life of Gotama the Buddha*, pp. 15–19. Quoted in Mircea Eliade, *From Medicine Men to Muhammed* (N.Y.: Harper & Row, 1974), pp. 51–55.

Now the young lord Gotama, when many days had passed by, bade his charioteer make ready the state carriages, saying: 'Get ready the carriages, good charioteer, and let us go through the park to inspect the pleasaunce.' 'Yes, my lord,' replied the charioteer, and harnessed the state carriages and sent word to Gotama: 'The carriages are ready, my lord; do now what you deem fit.' Then Gotama mounted a state carriage and drove out in state into the park.

Now the young lord saw, as he was driving to the park, an aged man as bent as a roof gable, decrepit, leaning on a staff, tottering as he walked, afflicted and long past his prime. And seeing him Gotama said: 'That man, good charioteer, what has he done, that his hair is not like that of other men, nor his body?'

'He is what is called an aged man, my lord.'

'But why is he called aged?'

'He is called aged, my lord, because he has not much longer to live.'

'But then, good charioteer, am I too subject to old age, one who has got past old age?'

'You, my lord, and we too, we all are of a kind to grow old; we have not got past old age.'

'Why then, good charioteer, enough of the park for today. Drive me back hence to my rooms.'

'Yea, my lord,' answered the charioteer, and drove him back. And he, going to his rooms, sat brooding sorrowful and depressed, thinking, 'Shame then verily be upon this thing called birth, since to one born old age shows itself like that!'

Thereupon the rāja sent for the charioteer and asked him: 'Well, good charioteer, did the boy take pleasure in the park? Was he pleased with it?'

'No, my lord, he was not.'

'What then did he see on his drive?'

(And the charioteer told the rāja all.)

Then the rāja thought thus: We must not have Gotama declining to rule. We must not have him going forth from the house into the homeless state. We must not let what the brāhman soothsayers spoke of come true.

So, that these things might not come to pass, he let the youth be still more surrounded by sensuous pleasures. And thus Gotama continued to live amidst the pleasures of sense.

Now after many days had passed by, the young lord again bade his charioteer make ready and drove forth as once before....

And Gotama saw, as he was driving to the park, a sick man, suffering and very ill, fallen and weltering in his own water, by some being lifted up, by others being dressed. Seeing this, Gotama asked: 'That man, good charioteer, what has he done that his eyes are not like others' eyes, nor his voice like the voice of other men?'

'He is what is called ill, my lord.'

'But what is meant by ill?'

'It means, my lord, that he will hardly recover from his illness.'

'But I am too, then, good charioteer, subject to fall ill; have not got out of reach of illness?'

'You, my lord, and we too, we are all subject to fall ill; we have not got beyond the reach of illness.'

'Why then, good charioteer, enough of the park for today. Drive me back hence to my rooms. 'Yea, my lord,' answered the charioteer, and drove him back. And he, going to his rooms, sat brooding sorrowful and depressed, thinking: Shame then verily be upon this thing called birth, since to one born decay shows itself like that, disease shows itself like that.

Thereupon the rāja sent for the charioteer and asked him: 'Well, good charioteer, did the young lord take pleasure in the park and was he pleased with it?'

'No, my lord, he was not.'

'What did he see then on his drive?'

(And the charioteer told the rāja all.)

Then the rāja thought thus: We must not have Gotama declining to rule; we must not have him going forth from the house to the homeless state; we must not let what the brāhman soothsayers spoke of come true.

So, that these things might not come to pass, he let the young man be still more abundantly surrounded by sensuous pleasures. And thus Gotama continued to live amidst the pleasures of sense.

Now once again, after many days...the young lord Gotama...drove forth.

And he saw, as he was driving to the park, a great concourse of people clad in garments of different colours constructing a funeral pyre. And seeing this he asked his charioteer: 'Why now are all those people come together in garments of different colours, and making that pile?'

'It is because someone, my lord, has ended his days.'

'Then drive the carriage close to him who has ended his days.'

'Yea, my lord,' answered the charioteer, and did so. And Gotama saw the corpse of him who had ended his days and asked: 'What, good charioteer, is ending one's days?'

'It means, my lord, that neither mother, nor father, nor other kinsfolk will now see him, nor will he see them.'

'But am I too then subject to death, have I not got beyond reach of death? Will neither the rāja, nor the ranee, nor any other of my kin see me more, or shall I again see them?'

'You, my lord, and we too, we are all subject to death; we have not passed beyond the reach of death. Neither the rāja, nor the ranee, nor any other of your kin will see you any more, nor will you see them.'

'Why then, good charioteer, enough of the park for today. Drive me back hence to my rooms.'

'Yea, my lord,' replied the charioteer, and drove him back.

And he, going to his rooms, sat brooding sorrowful and depressed, thinking: Shame verily be upon this thing called birth, since to one born the decay of life, since disease, since death shows itself like that!

Thereupon the rāja questioned the charioteer as before and as before let Gotama be still more surrounded by sensuous enjoyment. And thus he continued to live amidst the pleasures of sense.

Now once again, after many days...the lord Gotama...drove forth.

And he saw, as he was driving to the park, a shaven-headed man, a recluse, wearing the yellow robe. And seeing him he asked the charioteer, 'That man, good charioteer, what has he done that his head is unlike other men's heads and his clothes too are unlike those of others?'

'That is what they call a recluse, because, my lord, he is one who has gone forth.'

'What is that, "to have gone forth"?'

'To have gone forth, my lord, means being thorough in the religious life, thorough in the peaceful life, thorough in good action, thorough in meritorious conduct, thorough in harmlessness, thorough in kindness to all creatures.'

'Excellent indeed, friend charioteer, is what they call a recluse, since so thorough in his conduct in all those respects, wherefore drive me up to that forthgone man.'

'Yea, my lord,' replied the charioteer and drove up to the recluse. Then Gotama addressed him, saying, 'You master, what have you done that your head is not as other men's heads, nor your clothes as those of other men?'

'I, my lord, am one whose has gone forth.'

'What, master, does that mean?'

'It means, my lord, being thorough in the religious life, thorough in the peaceful life, thorough in good actions, thorough in meritorious conduct, thorough in harmlessness, thorough in kindness to all creatures.'

'Excellently indeed, master, are you said to have gone forth since thorough is your conduct in all those respects.' Then the lord Gotama bade his charioteer, saying: 'Come then, good charioteer, do you take the carriage and drive it back hence to my rooms. But I will even here cut off my hair, and don the yellow robe, and go forth from the house into the homeless state.'

'Yea, my lord,' replied the charioteer, and drove back. But the prince Gotama, there and then cutting off his hair and donning the yellow robe, went forth from the house into the homeless state.

Now at Kapilavatthu, the rāja's seat, a great number of persons, some eighty-four thousand souls, heard of what prince Gotama had done and thought: Surely this is no ordinary religious rule, this is no common going forth, in that prince Gotama himself has had his head shaved and has donned the yellow robe and has gone forth from the house into the homeless state. If prince Gotama has done this, why then should not we also? And they all had their heads shaved and donned the yellow robes, and in imitation of the Bodhisat they went forth from the house into the homeless state. So the Bodhisat went up on his rounds through the villages, towns and cities accompanied by that multitude.

Now there arose in the mind of Gotama the Bodhisat, when he was meditating in seclusion, this thought: That indeed is not suitable for me that I should live beset. 'Twere better were I to dwell alone, far from the crowd.

So after a time he dwelt alone, away from the crowd. Those eighty-four thousand recluses went one way, and the Bodhisat went another way.

Now there arose in the mind of Gotama the Bodhisat, when he had gone to his place and was meditating in seclusion, this thought: Verily, this world has fallen upon trouble—one is born, and grows old, and dies, and falls from one state, and springs up in another. And from the suffering, moreover, no one knows of any way of escape, even from decay and death. O, when shall a way of escape from this suffering be made known—from decay and from death?'

Questions
(1) How and against what does Siddhartha react after returning from his excursions in the park?

(2) What is "going forth" in this context?

(3) On what quest does Gautama embark; what does he reveal as being his ultimate purpose?

9–5

"Dhamammapada": oral tradition becomes part of the Buddhist canon.

The "Way of Virtue" or "Dhammapada" was a compilation of previously unwritten material which had been handed down from the time of the Buddha and which was asserted to have been transcribed from the words of the Buddha himself. After some deliberation, the "Dhammapada" was pronounced authentic by a religious council convened by Emperor Asoka Maurya (c. 240 BC.E).

Source: S.E. Frost, Jr., ed., *The Sacred Writing of the World's Great Religions* (N.Y.:McGraw-Hill, 1972), pp. 145–151.

1. Mind it is which gives to things their quality, their foundation, and their being: whoso speaks or acts with impure mind, him sorrow dogs, as the wheel follows the steps of the draught-ox.

2. Mind it is which gives to things their quality, their foundation, and their being: whoso speaks or acts with purified mind, him happiness accompanies as his faithful shadow.

3. "He has abused me, beaten me, worsted me, robbed me"; those who dwell upon such thoughts never lose their hate.

4. "He has abused me, beaten me, worsted me, robbed me"; those who dwell not upon such thoughts are freed of hate.

5. Never does hatred cease by hating; by not hating does it cease: this is the ancient law.

10. He who has doffed his impurities, calm and clothed upon with temperance and truth, he wears the pure robe worthily.

11. Those who mistake the shadow for the substance, and the substance for the shadow, never attain the reality, following wandering fires [lit. followers of a false pursuit].

12. But if a than knows the substance and the shadow as they are, he attains the reality, following the true trail.

18. Here and hereafter the good man rejoices; rejoices as he thinks "I have done well": yea rather rejoices when he goes to a heaven.

19. If a man is a great preacher of the sacred text, but slothful and no doer of it, he is a hireling shepherd, who has no part in the flock.

20. If a man preaches but a little of the text and practises the teaching, putting away lust and hatred and infatuation; if he is truly wise and detached and seeks nothing here or hereafter, his lot is with the holy ones.

21. Zeal is the way to Nirvana. Sloth is the day of death. The zealous die not: the slothful are as it were dead.

22. The wise who know the power of zeal delight in it, rejoicing in the lot of the noble.

23. These wise ones by meditation and reflection, by constant effort reach Nirvana, highest freedom.

24. Great grows the glory of him who is zealous in meditation, whose actions are pure and deliberate, whose life is calm and righteous and full of vigour.

25. By strenuous effort, by self-control, by tem-perance, let the wise man make for himself an island which the flood cannot overwhelm.

26. Fools in their folly give themselves to sloth: the wise man guards his vigour as his greatest posses-sion.

27. Give not yourselves over to sloth, and to dal-liance with delights: he who meditates with earnestness attains great joy.

28. When the wise one puts off sloth for zeal, ascending the high tower of wisdom he gazes sorrow-less upon the sorrowing crowd below! Wise himself, he looks upon the fools as one upon a mountain-peak gaz-ing upon the dwellers in the valley.

29. Zealous amidst the slothful, vigilant among the sleepers, go the prudent, as a racehorse outstrips a hack.

35. Good it is to tame the mind, so difficult to control, fickle, and capricious. Blessed is the tamed mind.

36. Let the wise man guard his mind, incompre-hensible, subtle and capricious though it is. Blessed is the guarded mind.

42. Badly does an enemy treat his enemy, a foe-man his foe: worse is the havoc wrought by a misdi-rected mind.

43. Not mother and father, not kith and kin can so benefit a man as a mind attentive to the right.

50. Be not concerned with other men's evil words or deeds or neglect of good: look rather to thine own sins and negligence [lit. "sins of commission and omis-sion": things done and undone].

51. As some bright flower—fair to look at, but lacking fragrance—so are fair words which bear no fruit in action.

52. As some bright flower, fragrant as it is fair, so are fair words whose fruit is seen in action.

53. As if from a pile of flowers one were to weave many a garland, so let mortals string together much merit.

54. No scent of flower is borne against the wind, though it were sandal, or incense or jasmine: but the fragrance of the holy is borne against the wind: the righteous pervade all space (with their fragrance).

55. More excellent than the scent of sandal and incense, of lily and jasmine, is the fragrance of good deeds.

56. A slight thing is this scent of incense and of

sandal-wood, but the scent of the holy pervades the highest heaven.

61. If on a journey thou canst not find thy peer or one better than thyself, make the journey stoutly alone: there is no company with a fool.

62. "I have sons and wealth," thinks the fool with anxious care; he is not even master of himself, much less of sons and wealth.

63. The fool who knows his folly is so far wise: but the fool who reckons himself wise is called a fool indeed.

64. Though for a lifetime the fool keeps company with the wise, yet does he not learn righteousness, as spoon gets no taste of soup.

65. If but for a moment the thoughtful keep company with the wise, straightway he learns righteousess, as tongue tastes soup.

66. Fools and dolts go their way,

their own worst enemies: working evil which bears bitter fruit.

67. That is no good deed which brings remorse, whose reward one receives with tears and lamentation.

68. But that is the good deed which brings no remorse, whose reward the doer takes with joy and gladness.

69. Honey-sweet to the fool is his sin—until it ripens: then he comes to grief.

76. Look upon him who shows you your faults as a revealer of treasure: seek his company who checks and chides you, the sage who is wise in reproof: it fares well and not ill with him who seeks such company.

77. Let a man admonish, and advise, and keep others from strife! So will he be dear to the righteous, and hated by the unrighteous.

103. If one were to conquer a thousand thousand in the battle—he who conquers self is the greatest warrior.

104, 105. Self-conquest is better than other victories: neither god nor demi-god, neither Mara nor Brahma, can undo the victory of such a one, who is self-controlled and always calm.

106. If month by month throughout a hundred years one were to offer sacrifices costing thousands, and if for a moment another were to reverence the self-controlled—this is the be better worship.

107. If one for a hundred years tended the sacred fire in the glade, and another for a moment reverenced the self-controlled, this is the better worship.

108. Whatsoever sacrifice or offering a man makes for a full year in hope of benefits, all is not worth a quarter of that better offering—reverence to the upright.

109. In him who is trained in contant courtesy and reverence to the old, four qualities increase: length of days, beauty, gladness, and strengh.

117. If one offends, let him not repeat his offence; let him not set his heart upon it. Sad is the piling up of sin.

118. If one does well, let him repeat his well-doing: let him set his heart upon it. Glad is the storing up of good.

119. The bad man sees good days until his wrong-doing ripens; then he beholds evil days.

120. Even a good man may see evil days till his well-doing comes to fruition; then he beholds good days.

121. Think not lightly of evil "It will not come nigh me." Drop by drop the pitcher is filled: slowly but surely the fool is saturated with evil.

122. Think not lightly of good "It will not come nigh me." Drop by drop the pitcher is filled: Slowly but surely the good are filled with merit.

129. All fear the rod, all quake at death. Judge then by thyself, and forbear from slaughter, or from causing to slay.

130. To all is life dear. Judge then by thyself, and forbear to slay or to cause slaughter.

131. Whoso himself desires joy, yet hurts them who love joy, shall not obtain it hereafter.

132. Whoso himself desires joy and hurts not them who love it, shall hereafter attain to joy.

133. Speak not harshly to any one: else will men turn upon *you*. Sad are the words of strife: retribution will follow them.

142. If even a fop fosters the serene mind, calm and controlled, pious and pure, and does no hurt to any living thing, he is the Brahmin, he is the Samana, he is the Bhikkhu.

143. Is there in all the world a man so modest that he provokes no blame, as a noble steed never deserves the whip? As a noble steed stung by the whip, be ye spirited and swift.

144. By faith, by righteousness, manliness, by meditation, by just judgment, by theory and practice, by mindfulness, leave aside sorrow—no slight burden.

145. Engineers control the water fletchers fashion their shafts, carpenters shape the wood: it is themselves that the pious fashion and control.

157. If a man love himself, let him diligently watch himself: the wise will keep vigil for one of the three watches of the night.

158. Keep first thyself aright: then mayest thou advise others. So is the wise man unblameable.

159. If one so shapes his own life as he directs others, himself controlled, he will duly control others: self, they say, is hard to tame.

160. A man is his own helper: who else is there to help? By self-control man is a rare help to himself.

161. The ill that is begun and has its growth and its being in self, bruises the foolish one, as the diamond pierces its own matrix.

162. As the creeper overpowers the tree, so he whose sin is great, works for himself the havoc his enemy would wish for him.

163. Ill is easy to do; it is easy to do harm: hard indeed it is to do helpful and good deeds.

164. Whoso fondly repudiates the teaching of the noble and virtuous Arahats, following false doctrine, is like the bamboo which bears fruit to its own destruction.

165. Thou art brought low by the evil thou hast done thyself: by the evil thou hast left undone art thou purified. Purity and impurity are things of man's inmost self; no man can purify another.

166. Even for great benefit to another let no man imperil his own benefit. When he has realised what is for his own good, let him pursue that earnestly.

173. He who covers his idle deeds with goodness lights up the world as the moon freed of clouds.

174. Blinded are the men of this world; few there are who have eyes see: few are the birds which escape the fowler's net; few are they who go to heaven.

175. Through the sky fly the swans: Rishis too pass through the air. The wise leave the world altogether, deserting Mara and his hosts.

176. There is no wrong he would not do who breaks one precept, speaking lies and mocking at the life to come.

177. Misers go not to the realm of gods: therefore he is a fool who does not delight in liberality. The wise delighting in liberality come thereby with gladness to the other world.

178. Good is kingship of the earth; good is birth in heaven; good is universal empire; better still is the fruit of conversion.

183. "Eschew all evil: cherish good: cleanse your inmost thoughts"—this is the teaching of Buddhas.

184. "Patience and fortitude is the supreme asceticism: Nirvana is above all," say the Buddhas. He is no recluse who harms others: nor is he who causes grief an ascetic (samana).

194. A blessing is the arising of Buddhas, a blessing is the true preaching. Blessed is the unity of the Sangha, blessed is the devotion of those who dwell in unity.

195, 196. Immeasurable is the merit of him who does reverence to those to whom reverence is due, Buddha and his disciples, men who have left behind them the trammels of evil, and crossed beyond the stream of sorrow and wailing, calmed and free of all fear.

197. O Joy! We live in bliss: amongst men of hate, hating none. Let us indeed dwell among them without hatred.

198. O Joy! In bliss we dwell; healthy amidst the ailing. Let us indeed dwell amongst them in perfect health.

199. Yea in very bliss we dwell; free from care amidst the careworn. Let us indeed dwell amongst them without care.

200. In bliss we dwell possessing nothing: let us dwell feeding upon joy like the shining ones in their splendour.

201. The victor breeds enmity; the conquered sleeps in sorrow. Regardless of either victory or defeat the calm man dwells in peace.

202. There is no fire like lust; no luck so bad as hate. There is no sorrow like existence: no bliss greater than Nirvana (rest).

203. Hunger is the greatest ill: existence is the greatest sorrow. Sure knowledge of this is Nirvana, highest bliss.

204. Health is the greatest boon; content is the greatest wealth; a loyal friend is the truest kinsman; Nirvana is the Supreme Bliss.

205. Having tasted the joy of solitude and of serenity, a man is freed from sorrow and from sin, and tastes the nectar of piety.

206. Good is the vision of the Noble; good is their company. He may be always happy who escapes the sight of fools.

207. He who consorts with fools knows lasting grief. Grievous is the company of fools, as that of enemies; glad is the company of the wise, as that of kinsfolk.

208. Therefore do thou consort with the wise, the sage, the learned, the noble ones who shun not the yoke of duty: follow in the wake of such a one, the wise and prudent, as the moon follows the path of the stars.

222. Whoso controls his rising anger as a running chariot, him I call the charioteer: the others only hold the reins.

223. By calmness let a man overcome wrath; let him overcome evil by good; the miser let him subdue by liberality, and the liar by truth.

224. Speak the truth, be not angry, give of thy poverty to the suppliant: by these three virtues a man attains to the company of the gods.

231. Guard against evil deeds: control the body. Eschew evil deeds and do good.

232. Guard against evil words; control the tongue. Eschew evil words and speak good ones.

233. Guard against evil thoughts; control the mind. Eschew evil thoughts and think good ones.

234. The wise, controlled in act, in word, in thought, are well controlled indeed.

235. Thou art withered as a sere leaf: Death's messengers await thee. Thou standest at the gate of death and hast made no provision for the journey.

236. Make to thyself a refuge; come, strive, and be prudent: when thy impurities are purged, thou shalt come into the heavenly abode of the Noble.

237. Thy life is ended; thou art come into the Presence of Death: there is no resting-place by the way and thou hast no provision for the journey.

238. Make for thyself a refuge; come, strive and play the sage! Burn off thy taints, and thou shalt know birth and old age no more.

239. As a smith purifies silver in the fire, so bit by bit continually the sage burns away his impurities.

245. Hard it is for the modest, the lover of purity, the disinterested and simple and clean, the man of insight.

246, 247. The murderer, the liar, the thief, the adulterer, and the drunkard—these even in this world uproot themselves.

256, 257. Hasty judgment shows no man just. He is called just who discriminates between right and wrong, who judges others not hastily, but with righteous and calm judgment, a wise guardian of the law.

258. Neither is a man wise by much speaking: he is called wise who is forgiving, kindly, and fearless.

268, 269. Not by silence (mona) is a man a sage (muni) if he be ignorant and foolish: he who holds as it were the balance, taking the good and rejecting the bad, he is the sage: he who is sage for both worlds, he is the true sage.

270. A man is no warrior who worries living things: by not worrying is a man called warrior.

303. The faithful, upright man is endowed with (the true) fame and wealth, and is honoured wherever he goes.

304. Far off are seen the Holy Ones, like the Himalayas: the unholy pass unseen as arrows shot in the darkness.

305. Alone when eating, alone when sleeping, alone when walking, let a man strongly control himself and take his pleasure in the forest glade.

313. If a duty is to be done, do it with thy might: a careless recluse scatters contagion broadcast.

314. Better leave undone a bad deed; one day the doer will lament: good it is to do the good deed which brings no remorse.

315. As a fortress guarded within and without, so guard thyself. Leave no loophole for attack! They who fail at their post mourn here, and hereafter go to hell.

316. Some are ashamed at what is not shameful, and blush not at deeds of shame: these perverse ones go to hell.

317. They who see fear where there is no fear, and tremble not at fearful things: these perverse ones go to hell.

318. They who think evil where there is no evil, and make light of grievous sin: these perverse ones go to hell.

319. But whoso calls sin sin, and innocence innocence: these right-minded ones go to happiness.

327. Be ye zealous: guard your thoughts. As an elephant sunk in the mud extricate yourselves from the clutches of evil.

328. If you can find a dutiful friend to go with you, a righteous and prudent man not caring for hardships, go with him deliberately.

329. If you cannot find such a one, travel alone as a king leaving a conquered realm, or as the elephant in the jungle.

330. It is better to be alone; there is no companionship with a fool: travel alone and sin not, forgetting care as the elephant in the jungle.

331. Good are companions in time of need; contentment with thy lot is good; at the hour of death, merit is a good friend, and good is the leaving of all sorrow.

332. Good is reverence for mother and father: good, too, reverence for recluses and sages.

333. Good is lifelong righteousness; and rooted faith is good: good is the getting of wisdom, and good the avoiding of sin.

334. As the "maluwa" creeper, so spreads the desire of the sluggard. From birth to birth he leaps like a monkey seeking fruit.

335. Whoso is subdued by this sordid clinging desire, his sorrows wax more and more, like "birana" grass after rain.

336. But *his* sorrows drop off like water from the lotus leaf, who subdues this sordid, powerful desire.

372. There is no meditation apart from wisdom; there is no wisdom apart from meditation. Those in whom wisdom and meditation meet are not far from Nirvana.

373. Divine pleasure is his who enters into solitude, the Bhikkhu who is calmed and sees the law with the seeing eye:

374. Whenever he ponders the beginning and the end of the elements of being, he finds joy and bliss; nectar it is to those who know.

375. This is the beginning in my teaching for a wise Bhikkhu; self-mastery, contentment, and control by the precepts: to cultivate those who are noble, righteous, and zealous friends;

376. To be hospitable and courteous, this is to be glad and to make an end of sorrow.

377. As jasmine sheds its withered blossoms so, O Bhikkhus, do you put away lust and hatred.

378. He who is controlled in act, in speech, in thought, and altogether calmed, having purged away worldliness, that Bhikkhu is called calm.

379. Come, rouse thyself! Examine thine own heart. The Bhikkhu who is thus self-guarded and mindful will live in happiness.

380. Each man is his own helper, each his own host; therefore curb thyself as the merchant curbs a spirited horse.

381. The glad Bhikkhu who puts his trust in Buddha's Preaching goes to Nirvana, calm and blissful end of rebirth.

382. Let the young Bhikkhu apply himself to Buddha's Preaching: so will he light up the world as the moon escaped from the clouds.

390. It is no slight benefit to a Brahmin when he learns to hold his impulses in check; from whatever motive evil temper is controlled, by that control grief is truly soothed.

391. By whomsoever no evil is done in deed, or word, or thought, him I call a Brahmin who is guarded in these three.

392. As the Brahmin honours the burnt-sacrifice, so do thou honour him, from whomsoever is learnt the law of the true Buddha.

393. Not by matted locks, nor by lineage nor by caste is one a Brahmin; he is the Brahmin in whom are truth and righteousness and purity.

394. What boots your tangled hair, O fool, what avails your garment of skins? You have adorned the outer parts, within you are full of uncleaness.

395. A man clothed in cast-off rags, lean, with knotted veins, meditating alone in the forest, him I call a Brahmin.

396. Not him do I call Brahmin who is merely born of a Brahmin mother; men may give him salutation as a Brahmin, though he be not detached from the world: but him I call a Brahmin who has attachment to nothing.

397. Him I call a Brahmin who has cut the bonds, who does not thirst for pleasures, who has left behind the hindrances.

398. Whoso has cut the cable, and the rope and the chain with all its links, and has pushed aside the bolt, this wise one I call a Brahmin.

399. Whoever bears patiently abuse and injury and imprisonment, whose bodyguard is fortitude, he is the Brahmin.

400. He is the Brahmin who does not give way to anger, who is careful of religious duties, who is upright, pure, and controlled, who has reached his last birth.

401. He who clings not to pleasures as water clings not to the lotus leaf; nor mustard-seed to the needle-point, him I call Brahmin.

402. He is the Brahmin who in this very world knows the end of sorrow, who has laid the burden aside and is free.

403. Whoso is wise with deep wisdom, seeing the right way and the wrong, and has reached the goal, him I call Brahmin.

404. He is the Brahmin who is not entangled either with householders or with recluses, who has no home and few wants.

405. He who lays down the rod, who neither kills, nor causes the death of creatures, moving or fixed, he is the Brahmin.

406. Not opposing those who oppose, calm amidst the fighters, not grasping amidst men who grasp, he is the Brahmin.

407. He is the Brahmin from whom anger, and hatred, and pride, and slander have dropped away, as the mustard-seed from the needle-point.

Questions

(1) Compare/contrast the "Dhammapada" to "Apastamba" (Document 9–2); what similarities/differences can you discern?
(2) To what extent and in what manner is stress placed upon the "passive life"?
(3) Apart from passivity and resignation, what other notable themes recur in "Dhammapada"?

9–6

Kamo no Chomei: a Japanese monk looks back on his life.

In the year 1212, at the age of 59, Kamo no Chomei (1153–1216) wrote "An account of my hut" describing his early years and how he made a commitment to devote his remaining years to the Buddhist faith. His eyewitness accounts of the major disasters of his day, and of the inner tranquillity he was able to achieve by escaping from his former life, offer a particularly stark contrast between the dynamic historical world of Heiani-era Japan and the otherworldliness of the Japanese variant of Buddhism.

Source: Donald Keene, ed., *Anthology of Japanese Literature* (N.Y.: Grove Press, 1960), pp. 197–212.

The flow of the river is ceaseless and its water is never the same. The bubbles that float in the pools, now vanishing, now forming, are not of long duration: so in the world are man and his dwellings. It might be imagined that the houses, great and small, which vie roof against proud roof in the capital remain unchanged from one generation to the next, but when we examine whether this is true, how few are the houses that were there of old. Some were burnt last year and only since rebuilt; great houses have crumbled into hovels and those who dwell in them have fallen no less. The city is the same, the people are as numerous as ever, but of those I used to know, a bare one or two in twenty remain. They die in the morning, they are born in the evening, like foam on the water.

Whence does he come, where does he go, man that is born and dies? We know not. For whose benefit does he torment himself in building houses that last but a moment, for what reason is his eye delighted by them? This too we do not know. Which will be first to go, the master or his dwelling? One might just as well ask this of the dew on the morning-glory. The dew may fall and the flower remain—remain, only to be withered by the morning sun. The flower may fade before the dew evaporates, but though it does not evaporate, it waits not the evening.

THE GREAT FIRE

In the forty and more years that have passed since first I became aware of the meaning of things, I have witnessed many terrible sights. It was, I believe, the twenty-eighth day of the fourth month 1177, on a night when the wind blew fiercely without a moment of calm, that a fire broke out toward nine o'clock in the southeast of the capital and spread northwest. It finally reached the gates and buildings of the palace, and within the space of a single night all was reduced to ashes. The fire originated in a little hut where a sick man lodged.

The fire fanned out as the shifting wind spread it, first in one direction and then another. Houses far away from the conflagration were enveloped in the smoke, while the area nearby was a sea of flames. The ashes were blown up into the sky, which turned into a sheet of crimson from the reflected glare of the fire, and the flames relentlessly whipped by the wind, seemed to fly over two or three streets at a time. Those who were caught in the midst could not believe it was actually happening: some collapsed, suffocated by the smoke, others surrounded by flames died on the spot. Still others barely managed to escape with their lives, but could not rescue any of their property: all their treasures were turned into ashes. How much had been wasted on them!

Sixteen mansions belonging to the nobility were burnt, not to speak of innumerable other houses. In all, about a third of the capital was destroyed. Several thousand men and women lost their lives, as well as countless horses and oxen. Of all the follies of human endeavor, none is more pointless than expending treasures and spirit to build houses in so dangerous a place as the capital.

THE WHIRLWIND

Again, on the twenty-ninth day of the fourth moon of 1180, a great whirlwind sprang up in the northeast of the capital and violently raged as far south as the Sixth Ward. Every house, great or small, was destroyed within the area engulfed by the wind. Some were knocked completely flat, others were left with their bare framework standing. The tops of the gates were blown off and dropped four or five hundred yards away, and fences were swept down, making neighboring properties one. Innumerable treasures from within the houses were tossed into the sky; roofs of bark or thatch were driven like winter leaves in the wind. A smoke-like dust rose, blindingly thick, and so deafening was the roar that the sound of voices was lost in it. Even so must be the blasts of Hell, I thought.

Not only were many houses damaged or destroyed, but countless people were hurt or crippled while repairing them. The whirlwind moved off in a southwesterly direction, leaving behind many to bewail its passage. People said in wonder, "We have whirlwinds all the time, but never one like this. It is no common case—it must be a presage of terrible things to come."

THE MOVING OF THE CAPITAL

In the sixth month of the same year the capital was suddenly moved, a most unexpected occurrence. It had been hundreds of years since the reign of the Emperor Saga when the capital was fixed in Kyoto. The site of the capital was not a thing lightly to be changed without sufficient reason, and the people were excessively agitated and worried by the news.

However, complaints served no purpose and everyone moved, from the Emperor, his ministers, and the nobility on downward. Of all those who served the court, not a soul was left in the old capital. Those who had ambitions of office or favors to ask of the Emperor vied to be the first to make the move. Only those who, having lost their chances of success, were superfluous in the world and had nothing to hope for, remained behind, although with sorrow. The mansions whose roofs had rivaled one another fell with the passing days to rack and ruin. Houses were dismantled and floated down the Yodo River, and the capital turned into empty fields before one's eyes. People's ways changed completely—now horses were prized and oxcarts fell into disuse. Estates by the sea in the south or west were highly desired, and no one showed any liking for manors in the east or the north.

About this time I happened to have business which took me to the new capital. The site was so cramped that there was not even enough space to divide the city into the proper number of streets.To the north the land rose up high along a ridge of hills and to the south sloped down to the sea. The roar of the waves made a constant din, and the salt winds were of a terrible severity. The palace was in the mountains and, suggesting as it did the log construction of the ancient palaces, was not without its charms.

I wondered where they could have erected the houses that were daily dismantled and sent down the river so thick as to clog it. There were still many empty fields, and few houses standing. The old capital was now desolate but the new one had yet to be finished. Men all felt uncertain as drifting clouds. Those people who were natives of the place lamented the loss of their land, and those who now moved there complained over the difficulties of putting up houses. I could see on the roads men on horseback who should have been riding in carriages; instead of wearing court robes they were in simple service dress. The manners of the capital had suddenly changed and were now exactly like those of rustic soldiers.

Everywhere people could be heard wondering if future disorders were portended, and indeed, with the passage of the days, the country came to be torn by disturbances and unrest. The sufferings of the people were not, however, entirely in vain—in the winter of the same year the capital was returned to Kyoto. But what had happened to the dismantled houses? They could not all have been reerected in their former grandeur.

Some faint reports have reached my ears that in the wise reigns of former days the country was ruled with clemency. Then the Imperial palace was thatched with straw, and not even the eaves were aligned. When the Emperor saw that the smoke rising from the kitchen fires was thin, he went so far as to remit the taxes, although they were not excessive. That was because he loved his people and sought to help them. If we compare present conditions with those of ancient times, we may see how great is the difference.

THE FAMINE

Again, about 1181—it is so long ago that I cannot remember for certain—there was a famine in the country which lasted two years, a most terrible thing. A drought persisted through the spring and summer, while the autumn and winter brought storms and floods. One disaster followed another, and the grains failed to ripen. All in vain was the labor of tilling the soil in spring or planting in summer, for there was none of the joy of the autumn reaping or winter harvest. Some of the people as a result abandoned their lands and crossed into other provinces; some forgot their homes and went to live in the mountains. All manner of prayers were begun and extraordinary devotions performed, but without the slightest effect.

The capital had always depended on the countryside for its needs, and when supplies ceased to come it became quite impossible for people to maintain their composure. They tried in their desperation to barter for food one after another of their possessions, however cheaply, but no one desired them. The rare person who was willing to trade had contempt for money and set a high value on his grain. Many beggars lined the roads, and their doleful cries filled the air.

Thus the first year of the famine at last drew to a close. It was thought that the new year would see an improvement, but it brought instead the additional affliction of epidemics, and there was no sign of any amelioration. The people were starving, and with the passage of days approached the extremity, like fish gasping in insufficient water. Finally, people of quality, wearing hats and with their legs covered, were reduced to going from house to house desperately begging. 'Overwhelmed by misery, they would walk in a stupor, only presently to collapse. The number of those who died of starvation outside the gates or along the roads may not be reckoned. There being no one even to dispose of the bodies, a stench filled the whole world, and there were many sights of decomposing bodies too horrible to behold. Along the banks of the Kamo River there was not even room for horses and cattle to pass.

The lower classes and the woodcutters were also at the end of their strength, and as even firewood grew scarce those without other resources broke up their own houses and took the wood to sell in the market. The amount obtainable for all that a man could carry, however, was not enough to sustain life a single day. Strange to relate, among the sticks of firewood were some to which bits of vermilion or gold and silver leaf still adhered. This, I discovered came about because people with no other means of living were robbing the old temples of their holy images or breaking up the furnishings of the sacred halls for firewood. It was because I was born in a world of foulness and evil that I was forced to witness such heartbreaking sights.

There were other exceedingly unhappy occurrences. In the case of husbands and wives who refused to separate, the ones whose affections were the stronger were certain to die first. This was because whether man or woman, they thought of themselves second and gave to their beloved whatever food they occasionally managed to get. With parents and children it inevitably happened that the parents died first. Sometimes an infant, not realizing that its mother was dead, would lie beside her, sucking at her breast.

The Abbot Ryūgyō of the Ninnaji, grieving for the countless people who were dying, gathered together a number of priests who went about writing the letter A on the forehead of every corpse they saw, thus establishing communion with Buddha. In an attempt to determine how many people had died, they made a count during the fourth and fifth months, and found within the boundaries of the capital over 42,300 corpses lying in the streets. What would the total have been had it included all who died before or after that period, both within the city and in the suburbs? And what if all the provinces of Japan had been included?

I have heard that a similar disaster occurred in 1134, during the reign of the Emperor Sutoku, but I did not myself experience what happened then. Of all that has passed before my eyes, this famine was the strangest and saddest of all disasters.

THE EARTHQUAKE

Then there was the great earthquake of 1185, of an intensity not known before. Mountains crumbled and rivers were buried, the sea tilted over and immersed the land. The earth split and water gushed up; boulders were sundered and rolled into the valleys. Boats that rowed along the shores were swept out to sea. Horses walking along the roads lost their footing. It is needless to speak of the damage throughout the capital—not a single mansion, pagoda, or shrine was left whole. As some collapsed and others tumbled over, dust and ashes rose like voluminous smoke. The rumble of the earth shaking and the houses crashing was exactly like that of thunder. Those who were in their houses, fearing that they would presently be crushed to death, ran outside, only to meet with a new cracking of the earth. They could not soar into the sky, not having wings. They could not climb into the clouds, not being dragons. Of all the frightening things of the world, none is so frightful as an earthquake.

Among those who perished was the only child of a samurai family, a boy of five or six, who had made a little house under the overhanging part of a wall and was playing there innocently when the wall suddenly collapsed, burying him under it. His body was crushed flat, with only his two eyes protruding. His parents took him in their arms and wailed uncontrollably, so great was the sorrow they experienced. I realized that grief over a child can make even the bravest warrior forget shame—a pitiable but understandable fact.

The intense quaking stopped after a time, but the after-tremors continued for some while. Not a day passed without twenty or thirty tremors of a severity which would ordinarily have frightened people. After a week or two their frequency diminished, and there would be four or five, then two or three a day; then a day might be skipped, or there be only one tremor in two or three days. After-tremors continued for three months.

Of the four great elements, water, fire, and wind are continually causing disasters, but the earth does not normally afflict man. Long ago, during the great earthquake of the year 855, the head of the Buddha of the Tōdaiji fell off, a terrible misfortune, indeed, but not the equal of the present disaster. At the time everyone spoke of the vanity and meaninglessness of the world, and it seemed that the impurities in men's hearts had somewhat lessened, but with the passage of the months and the days and the coming of the new year people no longer even spoke in that vein.

HARDSHIPS OF LIFE IN THE WORLD

All is as I have described it—the things in the world which make life difficult to endure, our own helplessness and the undependability of our dwellings. And if to these were added the griefs that come from place or particular circumstances, their sum would be unreckonable.

When a man of no great standing happens to live next door to a powerful lord, however happy he may be he cannot celebrate too loudly; however grief-stricken, he cannot raise his voice in lamentations. He is uneasy no matter what he does; in his every action he trembles like a swallow approaching a falcon's nest. The poor man who is the neighbor of a wealthy family is always ashamed of his wretched appearance, and makes his entrances and exits in bursts of flattery. And when he sees how envious his wife and children and his servants are, or hears how the rich family despises him, his mind is incessantly torn by an agitation that leaves not a moment's peace. If a man's house stands in a crowded place and a fire breaks out in the neighborhood, he cannot escape the danger. If it stands in a remote situation, he must put up with the nuisance of going back and forth to the city, and there is always a danger of robbers.

Those who are powerful are filled with greed; and those who have no protectors are despised. Possessions bring many worries; in poverty there is sorrow. He who asks another's help becomes his slave; he who nurtures others is fettered by affection. He who complies with the ways of the world may be impoverished thereby; he who does not, appears deranged. Wherever one may live, whatever work one may do, is it possible even for a moment to find a haven for the body or peace for the mind?

RENUNCIATION OF THE WORLD

I inherited the house of my father's grandmother and for a long time lived there. Afterward I lost my position and fell on hard times. Many things led me to live in seclusion, and finally, unable longer to remain in my ancestral home, in my thirties I built after my own plans a little cottage. It was a bare tenth the size of the house in which I had lived, and being intended just as a place where I might stay it had no pretensions about it. An earthen wall was, it is true, raised around it, but I lacked the means to put up an ornamental gate. I also built a rough shed of bamboo posts for my carriage. I must confess that when the snow fell or gales blew, I could not but feel alarmed; and since the house was near the Kamo River, there was considerable danger of flooding as well as the threat of bandits.

For over thirty years I had tormented myself by putting up with all the things of this unhappy world. During this time each stroke f misfortune had naturally made me realize the fragility of my life. In my fiftieth year, then, I became a priest and turned my back on the world. Not having any family, I had no ties that would make abandoning the world difficult. I had no rank or stipend—what was there for me to cling to? How many years had I vainly spent among the cloud-covered hills of Ohara?

THE HUT TEN FEET SQUARE

Now that I have reached the age of sixty, and my life seems about to evaporate like the dew, I have fashioned a lodging for the last leaves of my years. It is a hut where, perhaps, a traveler might spend a single night; it is like the cocoon spun by an aged silkworm. This hut is not even a hundredth the size of the cottage where I spent my middle years.

Before I was aware, I had become heavy with years, and with each remove my dwelling grew smaller. The present hut is of no ordinary appearance. It is a bare ten feet square and less than seven feet high. I did not choose this particular spot rather than another, and I built my house without consulting any diviners. I laid a foundation and roughly thatched a roof. I fastened hinges to the joints of the beams, the easier to move elsewhere should anything displease me. What difficulty would there be in changing my dwelling? A bare two carts would suffice to carry off the whole house, and except for the carter's fee there would be no expenses at all.

Since first I hid my traces here in the heart of Mount Hino, I have added a lean-to on the south and a porch of bamboo. On the west I have built a shelf for holy water, and inside the hut, along the west wall, I have installed an image of Amida. The light of the setting sun shines between its eyebrows. On the doors of the reliquary I have hung pictures of Fugen and Fudo. Above the sliding door that faces north I have built a little shelf on which I keep three or four black leather baskets that contain books of poetry and music and extracts from the sacred writings. Beside them stand a folding koto and a lute.

Along the east wall I have spread long fern fronds and mats of straw which serve as my bed for the night. I have cut open a window in the eastern wall, and beneath it have made a desk. Near my pillow is a square brazier in which I burn brushwood. To the north of the hut I have staked out a small plot of land which I have enclosed with a rough fence and made into a garden. I grow many species of herbs there.

This is what my temporary hut is like. I shall now attempt to describe its surroundings. To the south there is a hamhoo pipe which empties water into the rock pool I have laid. The woods come close to my house, and it is thus a simple matter for me to gather brushwood. The mountain is named Toyama. Creeping vines block the trails and the valleys are overgrown, but to the west is a clearing, and my surroundings thus do not leave me without spiritual comfort. In the spring I see waves of wistaria like purple clouds, bright in the west. In the summer I hear the cuckoo call, promising to guide me on the road of death. In the autumn the voice of the evening insects fills my ears with a sound of lamentation for this cracked husk of a world. In winter I look with deep emotion on the snow, piling up and melting away like sins and hindrances to salvation.

When I do not feel like reciting the *nembutsu* and cannot put my heart into reading the Sutras, no one will keep me from resting or being lazy, and there is no friend who will feel ashamed of me. Even though I make no special attempt to observe the discipline of silence, living alone automatically makes me refrain from the sins of speech; and though I do not necessarily try to obey the Commandments, here where there are no temptations what should induce me to break them?

On mornings when I feel myself short-lived as the white wake behind a boat, I go to the banks of the river and, gazing at the boats plying to and fro, compose verses in the style of the Priest Mansei. Or if of an evening the wind in the maples rustles the leaves, I recall the river at Jinyō, and play the lute in the manner of Minamoto no Tsunenobu. If still my mood does not desert me, I often tune my lute to the echoes in the pines, and play the "Song of the Autumn Wind," or pluck the notes of the "Melody ot the Flowing Stream," modulating the pitch to the sound of the water. I am but an indifferent performer, but I do not play to please others. Alone I play, alone I sing, and this brings joy to my heart.

At the foot of this mountain is a rough-hewn cottage where the guardian of the mountain lives. He has a son who sometimes comes to visit me. When I am bored with whatever I am doing, I often go for a walk with him as my companion. He is sixteen and I sixty: though our ages greatly differ we take pleasure in each other's company.

Sometimes I pick flowering reeds or the wild pear, or fill my basket with berries and cress. Sometimes I go to the rice fields at the foot of the mountain and weave wreaths of the fallen ears. Or, when the weather is fine, I climb the peak and look out toward Kyoto, my old home, far, far away. The view has no owner and nothing can interfere with my enjoyment.

When I feel energetic and ready for an ambitious journey, I follow along the peaks to worship at the Iwama or Ishiyama Temple. Or I push through the fields of Awazu to pay my respects to the remains of Semimaru's hut, and cross the Tanagami River to visit the tomb of Sarumaru. On the way back, according to the season, I admire the cherry blossoms or the autumn leaves, pick fern-shoots or fruit, both to offer to the Buddha and to use in my house.

If the evening is still, in the moonlight that fills the window I long for old friends or wet my sleeve with tears at the cries of the monkeys. Fireflies in the grass thickets might be mistaken for fishing-lights off the island of Maki; the dawn rains sound like autumn storms blowing through the leaves. And when I hear the pheasants' cries, I wonder if they call their father or their mother; when the wild deer of the mountain approach me unafraid, I realize how far I am from the world. And when sometimes, as is the wont of old age,

I waken in the middle of the night, I stir up the buried embers and make them companions in solitude.

It is not an awesome mountain, but its scenery gives me endless pleasure regardless of the season, even when I listen in wonder to the hooting of the owls. How much more even would the sights mean to someone of deeper thought and knowledge!

When I first began to live here I thought it would be for just a little while, but five years have already passed. My temporary retreat has become rather old as such houses go: withered leaves lie deep by the eaves and moss has spread over the floor. When, as chance has had it, news has come to me from the capital, I have learned how many of the great and mighty have died since I withdrew to this mountain. And how to reckon the numbers of lesser folk? How many houses have been destroyed by the numerous conflagrations? Only in a hut built for the moment can one live without fears. It is very small, but it holds a bed where I may lie at night and a seat for me in the day; it lacks nothing as a place for me to dwell. The hermit crab chooses to live in little shells because it well knows the size of its body. The osprey stays on deserted shores because it fears human beings. I am like them. Knowing myself and the world, I have no ambitions and do no mix in the world. I seek only tranquility; I rejoice in the absence of grief.

Most people do not build houses for their own sake. Some build for their families or their relatives; some for their friends and acquaintances. Some build for their masters or teachers, and some even to hold their possessions or beasts. I have built for myself and not for others. This is because in times like these, being in the position I am, I have no companion and no servant to help me. Supposing that I had built a spacious house, whom should I have lodged? Whom should I have had live there?

A man's friends esteem him for his wealth and show the greatest affection for those who do them favors. They do not necessarily have love for persons who bear them warm friendship or who are of an honest disposition. It is better to have as friends music and the sights of nature. A man's servants crave liberal presents and are deferential to those who treat them generously. But however great the care and affection bestowed on them, they do not care the slightest for their master's peace and happiness. It is best to be one's own servant.

If there is something which must be done, I naturally do it myself. I do sometimes weary of work, but I find it simpler to work than to employ a servant and look after him. If some errand requires walking, I do the walking myself. It is disagreeable at times, but it is preferable to worrying about horse-trappings or an oxcart. I divide my body and make two uses of it: my hands are my servants, my feet my vehicle, and they suit me well. When my mind or body is tired, I know

it at once and I rest. I employ my servants when they are strong. I say "employ," but I do not often overwork them. If I do not feel like working, it does not upset me. And is it not true that to be thus always walking and working is good for the body? What would be the point in idly doing nothing? It is a sin to cause physical or mental pain: how can we borrow the labor of others?

My clothing and food are as simple as my lodgings. I cover my nakedness with whatever clothes woven of wistaria fiber and quilts of hempen cloth come to hand, and I eke out my life with berries of the fields and nuts from the trees on the peaks. I need not feel ashamed of my appearance, for I do not mix in society and the very scantiness of the food gives it additional savor, simple though it is.

I do not prescribe my way of life to men enjoying happiness and wealth, but have related my experiences merely to show the differences between my former and present life. Ever since I fled the world and became a priest, I have known neither hatred nor fear. I leave my span of days for Heaven to determine, neither clinging to life nor begrudging its end. My body is like a drifting cloud—I ask for nothing, I want nothing. My greatest joy is a quiet nap; my only desire for this life is to see the beauties of the seasons.

The Three Worlds are joined by one mind. If the mind is not at peace, neither beasts of burden nor possessions are of service, neither palaces nor pavilions bring any cheer. This lonely house is but a tiny hut, but I somehow love it. I naturally feel ashamed when I go to the capital and must beg, but when I return and sit here I feel pity for those still attached to the world of dust. Should anyone doubt the truth of my words, let him look to the fishes and the birds. Fish do not weary of the water, but unless one is a fish one does not know why. Birds long for the woods, but unless one is a bird one does not know why. The joys of solitude are similar. Who could understand them without having lived here?

Now the moon of my life sinks in the sky and is close to the edge of the mountain. Soon I must head into the darkness of the Three Ways: why should I thus drone on about myself? The essence of the Buddha's teaching to man is that we must not have attachment for any object. It is a sin for me now to love my little hut, and my attachment to its solitude may also be a hindrance to salvation. Why should I waste more precious time in relating such trifling pleasures?

One calm dawning, as I thought over the reasons for this weakness of mine, I told myself that I had fled the world to live in a mountain forest in order to discipline my mind and practice the Way. "And yet, in spite of your monk's appearance, your heart is stained with impurity. Your hut may take after Jōmyō's, but you preserve the Law even worse than Handoku. If your low estate is a retribution for the sins of a previous existence, is it right that you afflict yourself over it? Or should you permit delusion to come and disturb you?" To these questions my mind could offer no reply. All I could do was to use my tongue to recite two or three times the *nembutsu,* however inacceptable from a defiled heart.

It is now the end of the third moon of 1212, and I am writing this at the hut on Toyama.

Questions

(1) How does Kamo use houses to underline the extent of the disasters he mentions and to underscore the fragile nature of human existence?

(2) What were the unsettling effects brought about by the change of capitol cities?

(3) Describe the impact of the famine; what did the Buddhist priests attempt to ascertain and what did they discover?

(4) For Kamo, in what way did his hut come to symbolize a new beginning? What is the most significant feature of this different life, and why?

CHAPTER 10

10-1
Messianic Scriptures: Israel's expectations of a Redeemer.

Messianic references occur in the Books of the Old Testament from at least the 7th century B.C.E., most notably in the prophetic Books, and this would continue into the 4th century B.C.E. The Messiah ("Anointed One") is variously described as a judge, teacher, Godly representative, or military/political leader descended from the royal House of David to save Israel and to establish a Universal Kingdom. Differences in interpretation over the precise nature and identity of the Messiah and his mission would ultimately engender divisions within the Jewish community—the largest dissident group branching out to form the Christian faith. During the years of Herodian and Roman domination, c. 40 B.C.E.–66 CE., hopes for a Messianic Coming were at fever pitch and prophetic passages such as those listed below (respectively: Jeremiah 23:1–6, Micah 5:1–4, Isaiah 9:6–7 & 11:1–12, and Zechariah 8:1–13 & 9:9–17) were painstakingly scrutinized.

Source: James Moffatt, trans., *The Old Testament*, Vol. II (N.Y.: George H. Doran Co., 1924), pp. 749, 752–753, 843, 1004, 1023–1024.

JEREMIAH XXIII

...
Woe to rulers who ruin and scatter
  the flock that was theirs to shepherd!
This therefore is the Eternal's sentence
  on the rulers who are over his flock:
"You scattered my flock and drove them away,
  you took no care of them;
so I will take care to punish you
  for the evil you have done.
I will gather all that is left of my flock
  from every land where I have driven them;
I will bring them back to their folds,
  and they shall be fruitful and multiply;
over them I will put rulers,
  to shepherd them,
and they shall be no longer scared
  or startled or dismayed.
The day comes, the Eternal promises,
  when I raise up a true scion of David,
to reign both royally and skillfully,
  to enforce law and justice in the land;
under him Judah shall be safe,
  and Israel live secure,
and this shall be his title,
  'The Eternal our Champion.'...

MICAH VI

...
O Bethlehem Ephrathah,
tiniest of townships in all Judah,
out of you a king shall come
to govern Israel,
one whose origin is of old,
of long descent
  [[The Eternal leaves them to
themselves, until his mother gives birth to him; and
then the survivors of his family shall rejoin Israel;
return they shall, for by that time his power shall
extend to the ends of the earth]], one who stands firm
and rules with the strength of the Eternal, with high
authority from his
  God the Eternal....

ISAIAH IX

...
For a child has been born to us,
  a son has been given to us;
the royal dignity he wears,
  and this the title that he bears—
"A wonder of a counsellor,
  a divine hero,
a father for all time,
  a peaceful prince!"
Great is his authority,
  endless his peace,
over David's throne
  and his dominion,
to base it firm and stable
  on justice and good order....

ISAIAH XI

...

From the stump of Jesse a shoot shall rise,
  and a scion from his roots shall flourish;
on him shall rest the spirit of the Eternal,
  the spirit of wisdom and insight,
the spirit of counsel and strength,
  the spirit that knows and reverences the Eternal.
He will not judge by appearances,
  nor decide by hearsay.
but act with justice to the helpless
  and decide fairly for the humble;
he will strike down the ruthless with his verdicts,
  and slay the unjust with his sentences.
Justice shall gird him up for action,
  he shall be belted with trustworthiness.
The wolf shall couch then with the lamb,
  the leopard's lair shall be the kid's;
the lion shall eat straw like any ox,
  wolf and lion shall graze side by side,
  herded by a little child;
the cow and the bear shall be friends,
  and their young lie down together;
the infant shall play at the hole of an asp,
  and the baby's feet at the nest of a viper.
None shall injure, none shall kill.
  anywhere on my sacred hill;
for the land shall be as full of the knowledge of the
Eternal as the ocean-bed is fill of water. And the
Scion of Jesse who is to rally the peoples....

ISAIAH XIII

...him shall the nations then consult,
  and his seat shall be famous.
  And then will the Lord put
out his hand again to recover any of his people who are
left over, in Assyria and Egypt and Pathros and Kush
and Elam and Shinar and Hamath and the sea-coasts.
He will give the signal to the nations,
  and gather the outcasts of Israel,
collecting the scattered of Judah
  from the four corners of the earth....

ZECHARIAH IX

...

Rejoice indeed, O maiden Sion,
shout aloud, dear Jerusalem.
Here comes your King,
triumphant and victorious,
riding humbly on an ass,
on the foal of an ass!
He banishes all chariots from Ephraim,
war-horses from Jerusalem,
and battle-bows;
his words make peace for nations,
his sway extends from sea to sea,
from the Euphrates to the ends of the earth.

"And for the sake of your blood-bond with me
I set you captive exiles free
from their dungeon [[which has no water]].
Come back to your safe home,
poor prisoners, with your hopes;
I compensate you now twofold.
For I have bent Judah as my bow,
and fitted Ephraim like arrows to the string;
I will ply you like a hero's sword,
and urge your sons on, Sion,
against the sons of Greece.

Then shall the Eternal be seen above them.
speeding his shafts like lightening;
the Eternal blows a bugle blast
and marches from the south with whirlwinds.
Protected by the Lord of hosts, they shall prevail.
stamp on the sons of Greece,
drink up their blood like wine,
as full of it as altar bowls.
Their God the Eternal on that day
makes them victorious;
he sheperds them on his own land
[[like jewels for a crown]]
so fair, so fertile
[[Corn makes the young men flourish,
and new wine the maidens]]....

Questions

(1) What particular Messianic attribute is stressed in each of the separate passages?

(2) To what extent does each prophecy depict the Messiah politically, as opposed to religiously and vice-versa?

(3) How might foreigners who administered Israel have viewed these prophecies? What implications might they have derived from them?

10–2
The "Midrash": a legal commentary on the Torah with the "common touch."

Wisdom books and commentaries on the Jewish law contained within the Torah have long been favored literary forms within the various Hebrew communities. By a process similar to that which fostered the development of English Common Law, the sayings of the rabbis, pronouncements of Hebraic scholars, and tradition were set down into such religious works as the "Talmud," "Haggadah," "Mishnah," and "Gemaras." The "Midrash" is not generally held to as elevated a level as the above-mentioned works, probably because of the folklore that has been brought in and the impromptu, informal nature of the passages, which are more like rabbinic sermons than than studied legal interpretations.

Source: Lewis Brown, ed., *The Wisdom of Israel"* (N.Y.: Modern Library, 1945), pp. 244–251.

Rabbi Abbahu and Rabbi Hiyya ben Abba came to the same town at the same time. Rabbi Hiyya delivered a scholarly discourse on the Law, while Rabbi Abbahu delivered a Midrashic sermon. Thereupon all the people left Rabbi Hiyya and came to Abbahu.

Rabbi Hiyya was greatly discouraged, but his colleague said to him: "I will tell thee a parable. Two men once entered the same town, the one offering for sale precious stones and pearls, the other tinsel. To whom do you think people thronged? Was it not to him who sold the tinsel, seeing that that was what they could afford to buy?" *Sotah,* 40a

Let not the simple parable seem trivial in thine eyes, for through it thou acquirest an insight into the complex Law. *Shir ha-Shirim Rabbah,* l, 8

ON GOD

Rabbi Akiba said: "Do not act toward the Lord as other nations act toward their gods. They honor them solely when times are good, but when misfortune befalls them, they curse their gods. But you who belong to Israel should offer praise no matter whether the Lord brings you good times or evil." *Mekilta to Shemot,* 20: 30

The Emperor Hadrian, having returned from conquering the world, called his courtiers and said lo them, "Now I demand that you consider me God."

Hearing this, one of them said, "Be pleased then, Sire, to aid me in this hour of need."

"In what way?" asked the Emperor.

"I have a ship becalmed three miles out at sea, and it contains all I possess."

"Very well," Hadrian said. "I will send a fleet to rescue it."

"Why bother to do that?" asked the courtier. "Send merely a little puff of wind."

"But whence am I to get the wind?"

"If you do not know," the courtier retorted, "then how can you be God who created the wind?"

Hadrian went home highly displeased. *Tauhuma Bereshit,* 7:10

ON PRAYER

Rabbi Abbahu said in the name of Rabbi Johanan: "If a man seeks to praise God excessively, he is banished from the world, as it is said, 'Who can utter the mighty acts of the Lord, and show forth all His praise?'" (*Ps.* 106:2.) *Midrash Tehillim,* 29:1

It is said that Antoninus once asked Rabbi Judah ha-Nasi: "What is your opinion with respect to prayer at every hour?"

"It is forbidden," was the reply, "lest a man become accustomed to calling upon the Almighty falsely."

Antoninus did not appreciate the force of the answer until the Rabbi presented himself once every hour, beginning in the early morning, and greeted him nonchalantly, "Good morning, Emperor! Your good health, King!"

The Emperor became indignant: "How dare you treat royalty with such disrespect?" he demanded.

Rabbi Judah replied, "If you, a mere mortal king, object to being saluted every hour, how much more the King of Kings!" *Tanhuma Buber, Miketz,* 11

ON ISRAEL

Is then a Jew anywhere an alien? Wherever be goes, his God is with him. *Debarim Rabbah,* 2, 16

Why is Israel compared to a dove? All other birds, when tired, rest upon a rock or upon the branch of a tree. Not so the dove. When the dove tires, she does not cease flying; she rests one wing and flies with the other. *Bereshit Rabbah,* 39:10

Why is Israel like sand? As in the sand thou diggest a pit, and in the evening thou findest it filled up, so too is it with Israel. *Pesikta Buber,* 139

Israel is likened to file dust and the sand. As nothing can grow without the dust of the soil, so the nations exist without Israel, through whom they receive their blessing.

As sand mixed in bread injures the teeth, so those who persecute Israel suffer for it.

Pesikta Rabbati. 11:5

Israel is likened to sand. As sand is moved from place to place without a sound, so Israel is exiled from place to place without complaint.

Intro. to Tanhuma Buber, 134

As everyone treads on dust, so does every nation tread on Israel. But as dust lasts longer than metal, so shall Israel outlast all nations. *Bereshit Rabbah,* 41:9

As the myrtle is sweet to him who smells it, but bitter to him who bites into it, so Israel brings prosperity to the nation which grants it kindness, and depression to the people which afflicts it with evil.

Esther Rabbah, 6, 5

God said to Moses and Aaron: "My children are often obstinate, often angry, often tiresome. With this knowledge accept for yourselves My mission, but be prepared for curses and stones." *Shemot Rabbah,* 7

Rabbi said: "Great is peace, for even if the Israelites worship idols: 'I can do nothing to them.'"

Bereshit Rabbah, 38:6

"And they shall stumble, one man with his brother" (*Lev.* 26:37). This means that one man will stumble because of the sin his brother. Hence learn that every Israelite is surety for every other. *Siffra,* 112b

It is said (*Exod.* 32:9): "I have seen this people, mad behold, it is a stiff-necked folk." Commenting on this, Rabbi Johanan said: "There are three impudent creatures: among beasts, it is the dog; for birds, it is the cock; among people, it is Israel." But Rabbi Ammi added: "Do not suppose that this is said in blame. It is said in praise, for to be a Jew means a readiness to suffer crucifixion." *Shemot Rabbah,* 42:9

Rabbi Aha said: "When the Jew is reduced to eating the wretched fruit of the carob-tree, then he repents. Poverty suits the Jew as a red bridle suits a white horse.

Bamidbar Rabbah, 13:4

He who loveth My children will rejoice with My children. *Shemot Rabbah,* 18

When trouble comes into the world, Israel feels it first; when good comes, Israel feels it first.

Ekah Rabbah, 2, 3

When the Jews prosper, the Gentiles say: "We are your cousins." But when the Jews suffer tribulation, the Gentiles add to it. *Bereshit Rabbah,* 37

One empire cometh and another passeth away, but Israel abideth forever.

Derek Eretz Zuta, Perek ha-Shalom

The scourge that smites Israel will meet an evil end.

Mekilta Beshallah

Whatever robberies Gentiles commit against Jews, they do not consider to be crimes but acts of justice.

Bemidbar Rabbah, 10:2

ON GENTILES

The falling of rain is an event greater than the giving of the Law, since the Law is for Israel only, but rain is for the entire world. *Midrash Tehillim,* 117:1

The just among the Gentiles are priests of God.

Eliyahu Zuta, 20

He who acknowledges idols repudiates the whole Torah, but he who repudiates idolatry is like on who accepts the whole Torah.

Sitre Deuteronomy, Re'eh, 54:86b

A man cannot become a priest or a Levite, no matter how he might wish it, unless his father was one. But he can become righteous, even though he be a heathen, because righteousness does not depend on ancestry. To become righteous entails only thr resolve to do good and love God. *Midrash Tehillim,* 146:8

I call heaven and earth to witness that whether a person be Jew or Gentile, man or woman, manservant or maidservant, according to his acts does the Divine Spirit rest upon him. *Tana d'be Eliyahu,* 207

Israelites are enjoined to deal kindly with all whom they encounter. *Midrash Tehillim,* 52:6

The heathen is thy neighbor, thy brother; to wrong him is a sin. *Tana d'be Eliyahu,* 284.

If thou hast habituated thy tongue to speak evil of Gentiles, thou wilt end by speaking evil of Israelites.

Debarira Rabbah, 6:9

Simon ben Shetah was occupied with preparing flax. His disciples said to him, "Rabbi, desist. We will buy you an ass, and you will not have to work so hard."

They went and bought an ass from an Arab, and a pearl was found on it, whereupon they came to him and said, "From now on you need not work anymore."

"Why?" he asked.

They said, "We bought you an ass from an Arab, and a pearl was found on it."

He said to them, "Does its owner know of that?" They answered, "No."

He said to them, "Go and give the pearl back to him."

"But," they argued, "did not Rabbi Huma, in the name of Rab, say all the world agrees that if you find [not steal] something which belongs to a heathen, you may keep it?"

Their teacher said, "Do you think that Simon ben Shetah is a barbarian? He would prefer to hear the Arab say, 'Blessed be the God of the Jews,' than possess all the riches of the world...It is written, 'Thou shalt not oppress thy neighbor.' Now thy neighbor is as thy brother, and thy brother is as thy neighbor. Hence you learn that to rob a Gentile is robbery."

Tana d'be Eliyahu, 74

ON PROSELYTES

The Holy One loves the proselytes exceedingly. To what is the matter like? To a king who had a number of sheep and goats which went forth every morning to the pasture, and returned in the evening to the stable. One day a stag joined the flock and grazed with the sheep, and returned with them. Then the shepherd said to the king, "There is a stag which goes out with the sheep and grazes with them, and comes home with them."

The king loved the stag exceedingly. And he commanded the shepherd, saying, "Give heed unto this stag, that no man hurt it." He also ordered that when the sheep returned in the evening, the stag too should be given food and water.

Finally the shepherd said, "My Lord, thou hast many goats and sheep and kids, and thou givest us no directions concerning them. But concerning this stag thou givest us orders day by day."

Then the king replied: "It is the custom of the sheep to graze in the pasture, but the stags dwell in rise wilderness, and do not venture into cultivated places. Therefore it behooves us to be grateful to this stag for having left the great wilderness, where many stags and gazelles feed, to come to live among us."

Thus also spake the Holy One: "I owe great thanks to the stranger, in that he has left his family and his father's house, and has come to dwell among us. Therefore I declare in the Law: 'Love ye the stranger.'"

Numbers Rabbah, Naso, 8:2

God commanded the Israelites to do good to proselytes and treat them with gentleness.

Sifre Numbers, 78: f. 21a

Dearer to God is the proselyte who has come of his own accord than all the crowds of Israelites who stood around Mount Sinai. For had the Israelites not witnessed the thunder and lightning, the quaking mountain and sounding trumpets, they would not have accepted the Torah. But the proselyte, who saw not one of these things, came and surrendered himself to the Holy One, blessed be He, and took the yoke of heaven upon himself. Can anyone be dearer to God than this man?

Tanh. Buber, 6, f. 32a

ON THE CHIEF COMMANDMENT

It is related that an ass-driver came to Rabbi Akiba and said to him, "Rabbi, teach me the whole Torah all at once."

Akiba replied, "My son, Moses our teacher stayed on the Mount forty days and forty nights before he learned it, and you want me to teach you the whole Torah at once! Still, my son, this is its basic principle: What is hateful to yourself, do not to your fellowman. If you wish that nobody should harm you in connection with what belongs to you, you must not harm him in that way; if you wish that nobody should take away from you what is yours, do not take away from another what is his."

The man rejoined his companions, and they journeyed until they came to a field full of seed-pods. His companions each took two, but he took none. They continued their journey, and came to a field full of cabbages. Again each took two, but he took none. They asked him why he refrained, and he replied: "Thus did Akiba teach me: What is hateful to yourself, do not to fellowman. If you wish that nobody should take from you what is yours, do not take from another what is his."

Abot d'R. Nathan (vers. II), 26, i. 27a

Questions

(1) Do the "Midrash" passages contain or indicate conflict between scholarly legalism and popular faith? Explain.

(2) What distinction does Rabbi Akiba make between the worship of the One God, and of Pagan deities?

(3) What indications are there in the "Midrash" as to the nature of Israel's role in the overall scheme of existence?

(4) What attitude does the "Midrash" take regarding Gentiles? Explain.

10–3

Maimonides: the culmination of medieval Hebraic thought.

The most profound scholar of the medieval Jewish Diaspora was Moses Ben-Maimon, or Maimonides (1135—1204), who grew up in Moorish Spain and had become a rabbi before being forced to immigrate to Egypt, where he became Saladin's personal physician. He wrote extensively on rabbinic teaching and scriptural interpretation; his "A Guide for the Perplexed" is considered to be the ultimate medieval expression of Jewish piety; and the effective synthesis of philosophy and religion to come out of the Diaspora.

Source: Rev. A. Cohen, *The Teaching of Maimonides* (London: Shapiro, Vallentine & Co., 1927) Quoted in Lewis Brown, ed., *The Wisdom of Israel* (N.Y.: Modern Library, 1945), pp.405-415.

ON THE EXISTENCE OF EVIL

Men frequently think that the evils in the world are more numerous than the good things; many sayings and songs of the nations dwell on this belief. They say that a good thing is found only exceptionally, whilst evil things are numerous and enduring. Not only common people make this mistake, but even many who imagine they are wise…. The origin of the error is to be found in the circumstance that people judge the whole Universe on the basis of what happens to one particular individual. An ignorant man is prone to believe that the whole Universe only exists for him, and therefore if any disappointment comes to him, he immediately concludes that the whole Universe is evil. If, however, he would take the whole Universe into consideration, and realize how small a part of it he is, then he would know the real truth….

The numerous evils to which individual persons are exposed are due to the defects existing in the persons themselves. We complain and seek relief from our own faults; we suffer from the evils which we, by our own free will, inflict on ourselves. Why then ascribe them to God, who has no part in them?…

The evils which befall men are of three kinds:

The first kind of evil is that which comes to man because he is subject to birth and death, being possessed of a physical body….Now, it is in accordance with the divine wisdom that there can be no birth without death, for unless the individuals die, how can the species continue? Thus the true beneficence of God is proved. Whoever thinks he can have flesh and bones without being subject to external influences—to physical accidents, and so forth—unconsciously wishes to reconcile two opposites: viz., to be at the same time subject and not subject to change. If man were never subject to change, there could he no generation; there would be one single being, but no individuals forming a species….

The second class of evils comprises such as people cause to each other: e.g., when some of them use their strength against others. These evils are more numerous than those of the first kind, and originate in ourselves rather than in the outside elements. Nevertheless, against

them too the individual is helpless….

The third class of evils, however, comprises those which a man causes to himself by his own action. This is the largest class, and…originates in man's vices, such as excessive desire for eating, drinking, and love. Indulgence in these things in undue measure or in improper manner, brings disease and affliction to body and soul alike.

The sufferings brought to the body are familiar. The sufferings of the soul are twofold: First, those directly due to the afflictions of the body, since the properties of the soul depend on the condition of the body. Secondly, the soul, when accustomed to superfluous things, acquires a strong habit of desiring things which are neither necessary for the preservation of the individual nor for that of the species. This desire is without a limit, whilst things which are necessary are few in number and restricted with certain limits. For example, you desire to have your vessels of silver, but golden vessels are still better; others have even vessels of sapphire, or perhaps they can be made of emeralds or rubies, or any other substance that might be suggested. Those who are ignorant and perverse in their thought are therefore constantly in trouble and pain, because they cannot get as much of superfluous things as others possess. They are wont to expose themselves to great dangers—e.g., by sea-voyage, or service of kings—and all this for the purpose of obtaining that which is superfluous and not necessary. And when they incur the consequences of their folly, they blame the decrees and judgments of God!…

How many trials and tribulations are due to the lust for superfluous things! In our frantic search for them, we lose even those which are indispensable. For the more we strive after that which is superfluous, the less strength have we left to grasp that which is truly needed.

Observe how Nature proves the correctness of this assertion. The more necessary a thing is for living beings, the more easily it is found and the cheaper it is; the less necessary it is, the rarer and dearer it is. For example, air, water, and food are indispensable to man. Air is most necessary, for if man is without air a short time he dies, whilst he can be without water a day or two. And is not air more abundant and easily obtained than water? Again, water is more necessary than food, for some people can be four or five days without food, provided they have water. And is not water more abundant everywhere, and cheaper, than food? The same proportion can be noticed in the different kinds of food: that which is more necessary in a certain place exists there in larger quantities and is cheaper than that which is less necessary. No intelligent person, I think, considers musk, amber, rubies, and emeralds as very necessary for man except perhaps as medicines; and they, as well as other like substances, can be replaced for this purpose by herbs and minerals. This shows the kindness of God to his creatures, even to us weak beings....

Guide III, 12

ALL THAT GOD MADE IS GOOD

I contend thatt no intelligent person can assume that any of the actions of God can be in vain, purposeless, or unimportant. According to our view and the view of all who follow the Torah of Moses, all actions of God are "exceedingly good." Thus Scripture says, "And God saw everything that He had made, and behold, it was very good" (*Gen.* 1:31). And that which God made for a certain thing is necessary, or at least very useful, for the existence of that thing. Thus food is necessary for the existence of living beings; the possession of eyes is very useful to man during his life....This is assumed also by the philosophers, for they declare that nothing in nature is purposeless.   *Guide* III, 25

WAS THE UNIVERSE CREATED FOR MAN?

Some people assume that the Universe was created solely for the sake of man's existence, that he might serve God. Everything that is done they believe is done for man's sake; even the Spheres move only for his benefit, in order that his wants might be supplied....

On examining this opinion, as intelligent persons ought to examine all different opinions, we will discover that it is erroneous. Those who maintain it may be asked whether God could have created man without those previous creations, or whether man could only have come into existence after the creation of all other things. If they answer in the affirmative, insisting that man could have been created even if, for example, the heavens did not exist, then they must be asked what is the object of all these other things, since they do not exist for their own sake, but for the sake of something that could exist without them? Even if the Universe existed for man's sake and man existed for the purpose of serving God, one must still ask: What is the end of serving God? He does not become more perfect if all His creatures serve Him. Nor would he lose anything if nothing existed beside him.

It might perhaps be replied that the service of God is not intended for God's perfection, but for our own. Then, however, the question arises: What is the object of our being perfect?

Pressing the inquiry as to the purpose of the Creation, we must at last arrive at the answer: It was the will of God. And this is the correct answer....Logic as well as tradition proves clearly that the Universe does not exist for man's sake, but that all things in it exist each for its own sake.   *Guide* III, 13

CONCERNING GENTILES

The teachers of truth, our Rabbis, declared, "The pious of the Gentiles have a portion in the World to-Come," if they have attained what is due from them to attain relative to a knowledge of the Creator, and corrected their soul with the virtues. And there is no doubt about the matter that whoever corrects his soul with purity of morals and purity of knowledge in the faith of the Creator will assuredly be of the children of the World-to-Come. On that account our Rabbis stated, "Even the Gentile who occupies himself with the Torah of Moses is equal to the High Priest."

Responsa 11, 23d et seq.

CONCERNING ASTROLOGY

Do not believe the absurd ideas of astrologers, who falsely assert that the constellation at the time of one's birth determines whether one is to be virtuous or vicious, the individual being thus necessarily compelled to follow out a certain line of conduct.

C. M., Eight Chapters VIII

I know that nearly all men are led far astray in matters of [astrology], and think there is some reality in them. There are even good and pious men of our own faith who think there is sense in these practices, and refrain from them only because they are forbidden by the Torah. They do not understand that these things are hollow frauds, and that the Torah forbids us to practice them precisely as it forbids us to indulge in falsehood.

C. M, Abod. Zar. 4:7

Know, my masters, that the whole subject of astrology, whereby people say so and so will happen or not happen, and the constellation at a man's birth determines that he should be such and such, and this will befall him and not that—all these things are not obtained by study. Although the faculty is common to the whole race, yet it is not fully developed in each individual, either on account of the individual's defective constitution, or on account of some other external cause....Accordingly, it is impossible that an ignorant person should be a Prophet; or that a person being no Prophet in the evening should, unexpectedly on the following morning, discover himself to be a Prophet. But if a person, perfect in his intellectual and moral faculties, and also perfect, as far as possible, in his imaginative faculty, prepares himself in the manner which will be described, he must become a

Prophet; since Prophecy is a natural faculty of man. It is impossible that a man who has the capacity for Prophecy should prepare himself for it without attaining it, just as it is impossible that a person with a healthy constitution should he fed well and yet not properly assimilate his food.

But there is a third view taught in Scripture, and this forms one of the principles of our faith. It coincides with the opinion of the philosophers in all points except one. For we believe that, even if one has the capacity for Prophecy and has duly prepared himself, it may yet happen that he does not actually prophesy. In that case the will of God keeps him from the use of the faculty. (In my own opinion, however, such a case would be as exceptional as any other miracle, since the laws of Nature demand that whoever has a proper pbysical constitution, and has been duly prepared as regards education and training, can be a Prophet.) *Guide* II, 32

PROPHETS VS. SCIENTISTS

In the realm of science the Prophet is like the rest of men. If a Prophet expresses an opinion in this realm, and a non-prophet likewise expresses an opinion, and should the former declare, "The Holy One, blessed be He, has informed me that my view is correct" do not believe him. If a thousand Prophets, all of the status of Elijah and Elisha, were to entertain an opinion and a thousand plus one Sages held the opposite, we must abide by the majority and reject the view of file thousand distinguished Prophets.   *C. M., Introduction*

THE PURPOSES OF THE TORAH

The general aim of the Torah is twofold: the well-being of the soul and the well-being of the body. The well-being of the soul is promoted by correct opinions communicated to the people according to their capacity. Some of these opinions are therefore imparted in a plain form, others allegorically, since certain opinions, if given in their plain form, would be too burdensome for the capacity of the common people. The well-being of the body is established by a proper management of our conduct ourselves toward one another.

The latter object is required first and is dealt with in the Torah most carefully and minutely, since the well-being of the soul is obtainable only after that of the body has been secured.... First, therefore, a man must have all his wants supplied as they arise—i.e., food and other things for his body, e.g., shelter, sanitation, and the like. But no one man can procure all this by himself. The physical wants can be procured only through collective effort, since man, as is well-known, is by nature gregarious.

The spiritual perfection of man consists in his becoming an actually intelligent being; i.e., he knows all that a person is capable of knowing. Such knowledge can be obtained not by mere virtue and rIghteous conduct, But through philosophical inquiry and scientific research....

The true Torah—which is of course the Torah of our teacher Moses—aims first to foster good mutual relations among men by removing injustice and creating the noblest feelings, and secondly, to train us in faith, and to impart correct and true opinions when the intellect is sufficiently developed.   *Guide* III, 27

It is also the object of the perfect Torah to make man despise, reject, and reduce his desires as much as is in his power. He should give way to them only in so far as is absolutely necessary. Intemperance in eating, drinking, and sexual intercourse is what people most crave and indulge in; and these are the very things that do most to injure the well-being of the individual and disturb the social order of the country. For by yielding entirely to the domination of lust, as is the way of fools, man loses his inteltectual energy, wrecks his body, and perishes before his natural time. Sighs and cares multiply, and there is an increase of envy, hatred, and warfare for the purpose of taking what another possesses, Fools, being steeped in ignorance, consider physical enjoyment an object to be sought for its own sake. God in his wisdom has therefore given us such commandments as would counteract that idea by keeping us...from everything that leads to excessive desire and lust. This is an important thing included in the obiects of our Torah.   *Guide* III, 33

The ordinances of the Torah are not a burden, but a means of ensuring mercy, kindness, and peace in the world.   *Yad, Shahbat* II, 3

Every narrative in the Torah serves a certain purpose in connection with religious teaching. It either helps to establish a principle of faith, or to regulate our actions, and to prevent wrong and injustice among men.   *Guide.* III, 50

WHY THE DIETARY LAWS?

I maintain that the food which is forbidden by the Torah is unwholesome....The principal reason why the Torah forbids swine's flesh is to be found in the circumstance that the swine's habits and food are very dirty and loathsome. It has already been pointed out how emphatically the Torah enjoins the removal of the sight of loathsome objects, even in the field and in the camp; how much more objectionable is such a sight in towns. But if the eating of swine's flesh were permitted, the streets and houses would be dirtier than any cesspool, as may be seen at present in the country of the Franks. A saying of our Sages declares, "The mouth of a swine is as dirty as dung itself."

The fat of the intestines makes us full, interrupts

our digestion, and produces cold and thick blood; it is more fit for fuel than for human food.

Blood (*Lev.* 17:12.) and also the flesh of a diseased animal (*Exod.* 22:30), or of an animal that died of itself (*Deut.* 14:21), are indigestible and injurious as food.

The characteristics given in the Torah (*Lev.* 11 and *Deut.* 14) of the permitted animals viz., cud-chewing and divided hoofs for cattle, fins and scales for fish—are in themselves neither the cause of the permission when they are present, nor of the prohibition when they are absent. They are merely signs by which the recommended species of animals can be discerned from those that are forbidden....

It is prohibited to cut off a limb of a living animal and eat it, because such an act would be cruel and would encourage cruelty. Besides, the heathens used to do that, for it was a form of idolatrous worshipto cut a certain limb off a living animal and eat it.

Meat boiled in milk is undoubtably gross food and makes overfull; but I think that most probably, it is also prohibited because it is somehow connected with idolatry, forming perhaps part of the service, or being used during some heathen festival....

Questions

(1) Into what error do most individuals fall regarding evil, and what does Maimonides consider to be the actual cause of an individual's misfortune?

(2) What arguments does Maimonides employ to debunk astrology?

(3) What ideas does Maimonides present regarding the salvation of Gentiles? Regarding scientific research?

(4) What (medieval) scientific justification does Maimonides employ in favor of Jewish dietary laws?

10–4
Luke and Acts: foundations for a new faith.

One of the most detailed, evocative descriptions of the early years of the Christian Church occurs in the Book of Luke (one of the four Gospels recounting the life of Jesus), and in the continuation Book of Acts. Both are ascribed to the physician Luke, a Christian disciple. The date of writing for both is probably around 60–63 C.E. The final passage in Luke (24: 36–53) describes an appearance of the risen Christ to his disciples, and the first two chapters of Acts relates the circumstances behind the establishment of the first Christian community in Jerusalem.

The New Testament (King James Version) (South Holland, Il.: The Bible League), pp. 109–110, 141–144.

36 ¶ And as they thus spake, Jesus himself stood in the midst of them, and saith unto them, Peace be unto you.

37 But they were terrified and afrighted, and supposed that they had seen a spirit.

38 And he said unto them Why are ye troubled? and why do thoughts arise in your hearts?

39 Behold my hands and my feet that it is I myself: handle me and see; for spirit hath not flesh and bones, as ye see me have.

40 And when he had thus spoken,he shewed them his hands and his feet.

41 And while they yet believed not for joy, and wondered, he said unto them, Have ye here any meat?

42 And they gave him a piece of a broiled fish, and of an honeycomb.

43 And he took it, and did eat before them.

44 And he said unto them, These are the words which I spake unto you, while I was yet with you, that all things must be fulfilled, which were written in the law of Moses, and in the prophets, and in the psalms, concerning me.

45 Then opened he their understanding, that they might understand the scriptures,

46 And said unto them Thus it is written, and thus it behoved Christ to suffer, and to rise from the dead the third day:

47 And that repentance and remission of sins should be preached in his name among all nations, beginning at Jerusalem.

48 And ye are witnesses of these things.

49 ¶ And, behold, I send the promise of my Father upon you: but tarry ye in the city of Jerusalem, until ye be endued with power from on high.

50 ¶ And he led them out as far as to Bethany, and he lifted up his hands, and blessed them.

51 And it came to pass, while he blessed them, he was parted from them, and carried up into heaven.

52 And they worshipped him, and returned to Jerusalem with great joy:

53 And were continually in the temple, praising and blessing God. Amen.

***

CHAPTER 1

THE former treatise have I made, O Thē-ŏph´-ĭ-lŭs, of all that Jesus began both to do and teach,

2 Until the day in which he was taken up after that he through the Holy Ghost had given commandments unto the apostles whom he had chosen:

3 To whom also he shewed himself alive after his passion by many infallible proofs, being seen of them forty days and speaking of the things pertaining to the kingdom of God:

4 And, being assembled together with them commanded them that they should not depart from Jerusasalem, but wait for the promise of the Father, which, saith he, ye have heard of me.

5 For John truly baptized with water; but ye shall be baptized with the Holy Ghost not many days hence.

6 When they therefore were come together, they asked of him, saying, Lord, wilt thou at this time restore again the kingdom to Israel?

7 And he said unto them, It is not for you to know the times or the seasons, which the Father hath put in his own power.

8 But ye shall receive power, after that the Holy Ghost is come upon you: and ye shall be witnesses unto me both in Jerusalem, and in all Judea, and in Samaria, and unto the he uttermost part of the earth.

9 And when he had spoken these things, while they beheld, he was taken up; and a cloud received him out of their sight.

10 And while they looked stedfastly toward heaven as he went up, behold, two men stood by them in white apparel;

12 Which also said Ye men of Galilee, why stand ye gazing up into heaven? this same Jesus, which is taken up from you into heaven, shall so come in like manner as ye have seen him go into heaven.

12 Then returned they unto Jerusalem from the mount called Ōl-ĭ´-vĕt, which is from Jerusalem a sabbath day's journey.

13 And when they were come in, they went up into an upper room, where abode both Peter, and James, and John, and Andrew, Philip, and Thomas, Bartholomew, and Matthew, James the son of Al-phāe´-ŭs, and Simon Zē-lō´-tēs, and Judas the brother of James.

14 These all continued with one accord in prayer and supplication, with the women and Mary the mother of Jesus, and with his brethren.

15 ¶ And in those days Peter stood up in the midst of the disciples, and said, (the number of names togeth-er were about all hundred and twenty,)

16 Men and brethren, this scripture must needs have been fulfilled, which the Holy Ghost by the mouth of David spake before concerning Judas, which was guide to them that took Jesus.

17 For he was numbered with us, and had obtained part of this ministry.

18 Now this man purchased a field with the reward of iniquity; and falling headlong, he burst asunder in the midst, and all his bowels gushed out.

19 And it was known unto all the dwellers at Jerusalem; insomuch as that field is called in their proper tongue, A-cĕl´-dă-mă, that is to say, The field of blood.

20 For it is writtern in the book of Psalms, Let his habitation be desolate, and let no man dwell therein: and his bishoprick let another take.

21 Wherefore of these men which have companied with us all the time that the Lord Jesus went in and out among us,

22 Beginning from the baptism of John, unto that same day that he was taken up from us, must one be ordained to be a witness with us of his resurrection.

23 And they appointed two, Joseph called Bär´-să-băs, who was named Justus, and Matthias.

24 And they prayed, and said, Thou, Lord, which knowest the hearts of all men, shew whether of these two thou hast chosen,

25 That he may take part of this ministry and apostleship, from which Judas by transgression fell, that he might go to his own place.

26 And they gave forth their lots; and the lot fell upon Matthias; and he was numbered with the eleven apostles.

CHAPTER 2

AND when the day of Pentecost was fully come they were all with one accord in one place.

2 And suddenly there came a sound from heaven as of a rushing mighty wind and it filled all the house where they were sitting.

3 And there appeared unto them cloven tongues like as of fire, and it sat upon each of them.

4 And they were all filled with the Holy Ghost, and began to speak with other tongues, as the Spirit gave them utterance.

5 And there were dwelling at Jerusalem Jews, devout men, out of every nation under heaven.

6 Now when this was noised abroad, the multitude came together, and were confounded because that every man heard them speak in his own language.

7 And they were all amazed and marvelled saying one to another, Behold, are not all these which speak Galileans?

8 And how hear we every man in our own tongue, wherein we were born?

9 Pär-thĭ-ăns and Medes, and Elamites, and the dwellers in Mĕs-o-pŏ-tă´-mĭ-ă, and in Judaea, and Căp-pă-dō´-cĭ-ă, in Pontus and Asia,

10 Phrygia, and Păm-phyl´-ĭ-ă in Egypt, and in the parts of Libya about Cy-rē´-nē, and strangers of Rome, Jews and proselytes,

11 Cretes and Arabians, we do hear them speak in our tongues the wonderful works of God.

12 And they were all amazed, and were in doubt, saying one to another, What meaneth this?

13 Others mocking said, These men are full of new wine.

14 But Peter, standing up with the eleven, lifted up his voice,and said unto them Ye men of Judea, and all ye that dwelt at Jerusalem, be this known unto you, and hearken to my words:

15 ¶ For these are not drunken, as ye suppose, seeing it is but the third hour of the day.

16 But this is that which was spoken by the prophet Joel;

17 And it shall come to pass in the last days, saith God, I will pour out my Spirit upon all flesh: and your sons and your daughters shall prophesy, and your young men shall see visions, and your old men shall dream dreams;

18 And on my servants and on my handmaidens I will pour out in the days of my Spirit; and they shall prophesy:

19 And I will shew wonders in heaven above, and signs in the earth beneath; blood, and fire, and vapour of smoke:

20 The sun shall be turned into darkness, and the moon into blood, before that great and notable day of the Lord come:

21 And it shall come to pass, that whosoever shall call on the name of the Lord shall be saved.

22 Ye men of Israel, hear these words; Jesus of Nazareth, a man approved of God among you by miracles and wonders and signs, which God did by him in the midst of you, as ye yourselves also know:

23 Him, being delivered by the determinate counsel and foreknowledge of God,ye have taken, and by wicked hands have crucified and slain:

24 Whom God hath raised up, having loosed the pains of death: because it was not possible that he should be holden of it.

25 For David speaketh concerning him, I foresaw the Lord always before my face, for he is on my right hand, that I should not be moved:

26 Therefore did my heart rejoice, and my tongue was glad; moreover also my flesh shall rest in hope:

27 Because thou wilt not leave my soul in hell, neither wilt thou suffer thine Holy One to see corruption.

28 Thou hast made known to me the ways of life;

thou shalt make me full of joy with thy countenance.

29 Men and brethren, let me freely speak unto you of the patriarch David, that he is both dead and buried, and his sepulchre is with us unto this day.

30 Therefore being a prophet and knowing that God had sworn with an oath to him, that of the fruit of his loins, according to the flesh, he would raise up Christ to sit on his throne;

31 He seeing this before spake of the resurrection of Christ, that his soul was not left in hell, neither his flesh did see corruption.

32 This Jesus hath God raised up, whereof we all are witnesses.

33 Therefore being by the right hand of God exalted, and having received of the Father the promise of the Holy Ghost, he hath shed forth this, which ye now see and hear.

34 For David is not ascended into the heavens: but he saith himself The LORD said unto my Lord, Sit thou on my right hand,

35 Until I make thy foes thy footstool.

36 Therefore let all the house of Israel know assuredly, that God hath made that same Jesus, whom ye have crucified, both Lord and Christ.

37 ¶ Now when they heard this, they were pricked in their heart, and said unto Peter and to the rest of the apostles, Men and brethren, what shall we do?

38 Then Peter said unto them, Repent and be baptized every one of you in the name of Jesus Christ for the remission of sins, and ye shall receive the gift of the Holy Ghost.

39 For the promise is unto you, and to your children, and to all that are afar off, even as many as the Lord our God shall call.

40 And with many other words did he testify and exhort, saying, Save yourselves from this untoward generation.

41 ¶ Then they that gladly received his word were baptized: and the same day there were added unto them about three thousand souls.

42 And they continued stedfastly in the apostles' doctrine and fellowship and in breaking of bread and in prayers.

43 And fear came upon every soul: and many wonders and signs were done by the apostles.

44 And all that believed were together, and had all things common;

45 And sold their possessions and goods, and parted them to all men, as every man had need.

46 And they, continuing daily with one accord in the temple, and breaking bread from house to house, did eat their meat with gladness and singleness of heart,

47 Praising God, and having favour with all the people. And the Lord added to the church daily such as should be saved.

Questions

(1) What specific mission does Jesus enjoin upon the disciples? What instructions are they given?

(2) What evidence is offered in support of claims of Jesus being the Messiah?

(3) How does Peter employ Old Testament scripture in his sermon?

(4) What actions are taken by newly-converted Christians?

10–5

Eusebius of Caesarea: witness to persecution and deliverance.

Eusebius (260?–340? C.E.) was a Christian clergyman who survived the most horrific of the official persecutions, that of the Emperor Diocletian (286–305). An admirer and confidant of Constantine I (311–337) Eusebius was named bishop of Caesarea in 314 and subsequently became noted as a church scholar, writing "History of the Church from Christ to Constantine." The following selection gives Eusebius' account of the persecutions, and a copy of Constantine's Edict of Milan which affirmed the legality of Christian worship.

Source: G. A. Williams trans., *Eusebius: The History of the Church from Christ to Constantine* (Harmondsworth, England: Penguin, 1965), pp. 327–332, 401–403.

HAVING dealt fully with the apostolic succession in seven books, in this eighth section it is surely a matter of the highest importance that for the enlightenment of future generations I should set down the events of my own day, calling as they do for a most careful record. That shall be the starting-point for my account.

EVENTS BEFORE THE PERSECUTION OF MY TIME

I. How great, how unique were the honour, and liberty too, which before the persecution of my time were granted by all men, Greeks and non-Greeks alike, to the message given through Christ to the world, of true reverence for the God of the universe! It is beyond me to describe it as it deserves. Witness the goodwill so often shown by potentates to our people; they even put into their hands the government of the provinces, releasing them from the agonizing question of sacrificing, in view of the friendliness with which they regarded their teaching. What need I say about those in the imperial palaces and about the supreme rulers? Did they not permit the members of their households—consorts, children, and servants—to embrace boldly before their eyes the divine message and way of life, hardly minding even if they boasted of the liberty granted to the Faith? Did they not hold them in special esteem, and favour them more than their fellow servants? I might instance the famous Dorotheus, the most devoted and loyal of their servants, and on that account much more honoured than the holders of offices and governorships. With him I couple the celebrated Gorgonius, and all who because of God's word were held in the same honour as these two. And what

approbation the rulers in every church unmistakeably won from all procurators and governors! How could one describe those mass meetings, the enormous gatherings in every city, and the remarkable congregations in places of worship? No longer satisfied with the old buildings, they raised from the foundations in all the cities churches spacious in plan. These things went forward with the times and expanded at a daily increasing rate, so that no envy stopped them nor could any evil spirit bewitch them or check them by means of human schemes, as long as the divine and heavenly hand sheltered and protected its own people, as being worthy.

But increasing freedom transformed our character to arrogance and sloth; we began envying and abusing each other, cutting our own throats, as occasion offered, with weapons of sharp-edged words; rulers hurled themselves at rulers and laymen waged party fights against laymen, and unspeakable hypocrisy and dissimulation were carried to the limit of wickedness. At last, while the gatherings were still crowded, divine judgement, with its wonted mercy, gently and gradually began to order things its own way, and with the Christians in the army the persecution began. But alas! realizing nothing, we made not the slightest effort to render the Deity kindly and propitious; and as if we had been a lot of atheists, we imagined that our doings went unnoticed and unregarded, and went from wickedness to wickedness. Those of us who were supposed to be pastors cast off the restraining influence of the fear of God and quarelled heatedly with each other, engaged solely in swelling the disputes, threats, envy, and mutual hostility and hate, frantically demanding the despotic power they coveted. Then, then it was that in accordance with the words of Jeremiah, the Lord in

His anger covered the daughter of Zion with a cloud, and cast down from heaven the glory of Israel; He remebered not the footstool of His feet in the day of His anger, but the Lord also drowned in the sea all the beauty of Israel, and broke down all his fences. So also, as foretold in the Psalms, He overthrew the covenant of His bondservant and profaned to the ground (through the destruction of the churches) his sanctuary and broke down all his fences; He made his strongholds cowardice. All that passed by the way despoiled the multitudes of the people; moreover, he became a reproach to his neighbours. For He exalted the right hand of his enemies, and turned back the aid of his sword and did not assist him in the war. But He also cut him off from cleansing and threw down his throne to the ground, and shortened the days of his time, and finally covered him with shame.

THE DESTRUCTION OF THE CHURCHES

2. Everything indeed has been fulfilled in my time; I saw with my own eyes the places of worship thrown down from top to bottom, to the very foundations, the inspired holy Scriptures committed to the flames in the middle of the public squares, and the pastors of the churches hiding disgracefully in one place or another, while others suffered the indignity of being held up to ridicule by their enemies—a reminder of another prophetic saying: for contempt was poured on rulers, and He made them wander in a trackless land where there was no road. But it is not for me to describe their wretched misfortunes in the event: nor is it my business to leave on record their quarrels and inhumanity to each other before. the persecutions, so I have made up my mind to relate no more about them than enough to justify the divine judgement. I am determined therefore to say nothing even about those who have been tempted by persecution or have made complete shipwreck of their salvation and of their own accord flung themselves into the depths of the stormy sea; I shall include in my overall account only those things by which first we ourselves, then later generations, may benefit. Let me therefore proceed from this point to describe in outline the hallowed ordeals of martyrs of God's word.

It was the nineteenth year of Diocletian's reign and the month Dystrus, called March by the Romans, and the festival of the Saviour's Passion was approaching, when an imperial decree was published everywhere, ordering the churches to be razed to the ground and the Scriptures destroyed by fire, and giving notice that those in places of honour would lose their places, and domestic staff, if they continued to profess Christianity, would be deprived of their liberty. Such was the first edict against us. Soon afterwards other decrees arrived in rapid succession, ordering that the presidents of the churches in every place should all be first committed to prison and then coerced by every possible means into offering sacrifice.

ORDEALS ENDURED IN THE PERSECUTION: GOD'S GLORIOUS MARTYRS

3. Then, then it was that many rulers of the churches bore up heroically under horrible torments, an object lesson in the endurance of fearful ordeals; while countless others, their souls already numbed with cowardice, promptly succumbed to the first onslaught. Of the rest, each was subjected to a series of different tortures, one flogged unmercifully with the whip, another racked and scraped beyond endurance, so that the lives of some came to a most miserable end. But different people came through the ordeal very differently: one man would be forcibly propelled by others and brought to the disgusting, unholy sacrifices, and dismissed as if he had sacrificed, even if he had done no such thing; another, who had not even approached any abomination, much less touched it, but was said by others to have sacrificed, would go away without attempting to repudiate the baseless charge. Another would be picked up half dead, and thrown away as if already a corpse; and again a man lying on the ground might be dragged a long way by his feet, though included among the willing sacrificers. One man would announce at the top of his voice his determination not to sacrifice, another would shout that he was a Christian, exulting in the confession of the Saviour's Name, while yet another insisted that he had never sacrificed and never would. These were struck on the mouth and silenced by a formidable body of soldiers lined up for the purpose: their faces and cheeks were battered and they were forcibly removed. It was one object in life of the enemies of true religion to gain credit for having finished the job.

But no such methods could enable them to dispose of the holy martyrs. What could I say that would do full justice to them? 4. I could tell of thousands who showed magnificent enthusiasm for the worship of God of the universe, not only from the beginning of the general persecution, but much earlier when peace was still secure. For at along last the one who had received the authority was as it were awaking from the deepest sleep, after making attempts—as yet secret and surrepticious—against the churches, in the interval that followed Decius and Valerian. He did not make his preparations all at once for the war against us, but for the time being took action only against the members of the legions. In this way he thought that the rest would easily mastered if he joined battle with these and emerged victorious. Now could be seen large numbers of serving soldiers most happy to embrace civil life, in order to avoid having to repudiate their loyalty to the Architect of the universe. The commander-in-chief, whoever he was, was now first setting about persecuting the soldiery, classifying and sorting those serving in the legions, and allowing them to choose either to obey orders and retain their present rank, or alternatively to be stripped of it if they disobeyed the enactment. But a great many soldiers of Christ's kingdom without hesitation or question chose to confess Him rather than cling to the outward glory and prosperity they enjoyed. Already here and there one or two of them were suffering not only loss of position but even death as the reward of their unshakable devotion: for the time being the man behind the plot was acting cautiously and going as far as bloodshed in a few cases only; he was apparently afraid of the number of believers, and shrank from launching out into war with them all at once. But when he stripped more thoroughly for battle, words are inadequate to depict the host of God's noble martyrs whom the people of every city and every region were privileged to see with their own eyes.

COPIES OF IMPERIAL LAWS

At this point it would be well to reproduce also the imperial ordinances of Constantine and Licinius in translations from the Latin.

Copy of Imperial Ordinances, Translated from Latin

For a long time past we have made it our aim that freedom of worship should not be denied, but that every man, according to his own inclination and wish, should be given permission to practise his religion as he chose. We had therefore given command that Christians and non-Christians alike should be allowed to keep the faith of their own religious beliefs and worship. But in view of the fact that numerous conditions of different kinds had evidently been attached to that rescript, in which such a right was granted to those very persons, it is possible that some of them were soon afterwards deterred from such observance.

When with happy auspices I, Constantinus Augustus, and I, Licinius Augustus, had arrived at Milan, and were enquiring into all matters that concerned the advantage and benefit of the public, among the other measures directed to the general good, or rather as questions of highest priority, we decided to establish rules by which respect and reverence for the Deity would be secured, i.e. to give the Christians and all others liberty to follow whatever form of worship they chose, so that whatsoever divine and heavenly powers exist might be enabled to show favour to us and to all who live under our authority. This therefore is the decision that we reached by sound and careful reasoning: no one whatever was to be denied the right to follow and choose the Christian observance or form of worship; and everyone was to have permission to give his mind to that form worship which he feels to be adapted to his needs, so that the Deity might be enabled to show us in all things His customary care and generosity. It was desirable to send a rescript stating that this was our pleasure, in order that after the complete cancellation of the conditions contained in the earlier letters which we sent to Your Dedicatedness about the Christians, the procedure that seemed quite unjustified and alien to our clemency

should also be cancelled, and that now every individual still desirous of observing the Christian form of worship should without any interference be allowed to do so. All this, we have decided to explain very fully to Your Diligence, that you may know that we have given the said Christians free and absolute permission to practise their own form of worship. When you observe that this permission has been granted by us absolutely, Your Dedicatedness will understand that permission has been given to any others who may wish to follow their own observance or form of worship—a privilege obviously consonant with the tranquillity of our times—so that every man may have permission to choose and practise whatever religion he wishes. This we have done to make it plain that we are not belittling any rite or form of worship.

With regard to the Christians, we also give this further ruling. In the letter sent earlier to Your Dedicatedness precise instructions were laid down at an earlier date with reference to their places where earlier on it was their habit to meet. We now decree that if it should appear that any persons have bought these places either from our treasury or from some other source, they must restore them to these same Christians without payment and without any demand for compensation, and there must be no negligence or hesitation. If any persons happen to have received them as a gift, they must restore the said places to the said Christians without loss of time; provided that if either those who have bought these same places or those who have received them as a gift wish to appeal to our generosity, they may apply to the prefect and judge of the region, in order that they also may benefit by our liberality. All this property is to be handed over to the Christian body immediately, by energetic action on your part, without any delay.

And since the aforesaid Christians not only possessed those places where it was their habit to meet, but are known to have possessed other places also, belonging not to individuals but to the legal estate of the whole body, i.e. of the Christians, all this property, in accordance with the law set forth above, you will order to be restored without any argument whatever to the aforesaid Christians, i.e. to their body and local associations, the provision mentioned above being of course observed, namely, that those persons who restore the same without seeking compensation, as we mentioned above, may expect to recoup their personal losses from our generosity.

In all these matters you must put all the energy you possess at the service of the aforesaid Christian body, in order that our command may be carried out with all possible speed, so that in this also our liberality may further the common and public tranquillity. For by this provision, as was mentioned above, the divine care for us of which we have been aware on many earlier occasions will remain with us unalterably for ever. And in order that the pattern of this our enactment and of our generosity may be brought to the notice of all, it is desirable that what we have written should be set forth by an edict of your own and everywhere published and brought to the notice of all, so that the enactment giving effect to this our generosity may be known to every citizen.

Questions

(1) To what cause does Eusebius attribute the coming of Diocletian's persecution? How does he characterize the overall attitude of the Christian community prior to its outbreak?

(2) With what measures did Diocletian implement the persecution?

(3) How were those who morally professed Christianity dealt with?

(4) What is Constantine's ruling on the issue of confiscated church property?

10–6
Bishop Synesius of Cyrene: a lukewarm churchman.

In contrast with the steadfast conduct of the martyrs as described by Eusebius, there were some Christians who would not have carried their zeal for the faith to such lengths. Synesius (365?–414), who was born in North Africa, was a worldly-wise, skeptical man who was versed in hermetic studies through the school of Hypatia of Alexandria, and in Neoplatonic philosophy. Though he was named Bishop of Cyrene in 410, he was never that zealous in his faith, as evidenced from this letter to his brother.

Source: Finley Cooper & Matthew Schwartz, eds., *Roman letters: History from a Personal Point of View* (Detroit: Wayne State University, 1991), pp. 264–267.

I should be altogether lacking in sense, if I did not show myself very grateful to the inhabitants of Ptokmais, who consider me worthy of an honour to which I should never have dared to aspire. At the same time I ought to examine, not the importance of the duties with which they desire to entrust me, but merely my own capacity for fulfillng them. To see oneself called to a vocation which is almost divine, when after all one is only a man, is a great source of ioy, if one really deserves it. But if, on the other hand, one is very unworthy of it, the prospects of the future are sombre. It is by no means a recent fear of mine, but a very old one, the fear of winning honour from men at the price of sinning against God.

When I examine myself, I fail to find the capacity necessary to raise me to the sanctity of such a priesthood as this. I will now speak to you of the emotions of my soul: for I cannot speak to any one in preference to you who are so dear to me, and have been brought up with me. It is quite natural that you should share my anxieties, that you should watch with me during the night, and that by day we should search together whatever may bring me joy or turn sorrow away from me. Let me tell you, then, how my circumstances are, ahhough you know in advance most of what I am going to say to you.

I took up a light burden, and up to this moment I think I have borne it well. It is, in a word, philosophy Inasmuch as I have never fallen too far below the level of the duties which it imposed upon me, people have praised me for my work. And I am regarded as capable of better things still, by those who do not know how to estimate in what directions my talents lie. Now, if I

frivolously accept the dignity of the position which has been offered to me, I fear I may fail in both causes, slighting the one, without at the same time raising myself to the high level of the other. Consider the situation. All my days are divided between study and recreation. In my hours of work, above all when I am occupied with divine matters, I withdraw into myself. In my leisure hours I give myself up to my friends. For you know that when I look up from my books, I like to enter into every sort of sport. I do not share in the political turn of mind, either by nature or in my pursuits. [That statement seems to be at variance with his own actions, however.] But the priest should be a man above human weaknesses. He should be a stranger to every sort of diversion, even as God Himself. All eyes are keeping watch on him to see that he justifies his mission. He is of little or no use unless he has made himself austere and unyielding towards any pleasure. In carrying out his holy office he should belong no longer to himself, but to all men. He is a teacher of the law, and must utter that which is approved by law. In addition to all this, he has as many calls upon him as all the rest of the world put together, for the affairs of all he alone must attend to, or incur the reproaches of all.

Now, unless he has a great and noble soul, how can he sustain the weight of so many cares without his intellect being submerged? How can he keep the divine flame alive within him when such varied duties claim him on every side? I know well that there are such men I have every admiration for their character, and I regard them as really divine men, whom intercourse with man's affairs does not separate from God. But I know myself also. I go down to the town, and from the town I come up again, always enveloped in thoughts that drag me down to earth, and covered with more stains than anybody could imagine. In a word, I have so many personal defilements of old date, that the slightest addition fills up my measure. My strength fails me I have no strength and there is no health in me. I am not equal to confronting what is without me, and I am far from being able to bear the distress of my own conscience. If anybody asks me what my idea of a bishop is, I have no hesitation in saying explicitly that he ought to be spotless, more than spotless, in all things, he to whom is allotted the purification of others.

In writing to you, my brother, l have still another thing to say You will not be by any means the only one to read this letter. In addressing it to you, I wish above all things to make known to every one what I feel, so that whatever happens hereafter, no one will have a right to accuse me before God or before man, nor, above all, before the venerable Theophilus [the bishop of Alexandria]. In publishing my thoughts, and in giving myself up entirely to his decision, how can I be in the wrong? God himself, the law of the land, and the blessed hand of Theophilus himself have given me a wife. I, therefore, proclaim to all and call them to witness once for all that I will not be separated from her, nor shall I associate with her surrepticiously like an adulterer; for of these two acts, the one is impious, and the other is unlawful. I shall desire and pray to have many virtuous children. This is what I must inform the man upon whom depends my consecration. Let him learn this from his comrades Paul and Dionysius, for I understand that they have become his deputies by the will of the people.

There is one point, however, which is not new to Theophilus, but of which I must remind him. I must press my point here a little more, for beside his difficulty all the others are as nothing. It is difficult, if not quite impossible, that convictions should be shaken, which have entered the soul through knowledge to the point of demonstration. Now you know that philosophy rejects many of those convictions which are cherished by the common people. For my own part, I can never persuade myself that the soul is of more recent origin than the body. Never would l admit that the world and the parts which make it up must perish. This resurrection, which is an object of common belief, is nothing for me but a sacred and mysterious allegory, and I am far from sharing the views of the vulgar crowd thereon. The philosophic mind, albeit the discerner of truth, admits the employment of falsehood, for light is to truth what the eye is to the mind. Just as the eye would be injured by excess of light, and just as darkness is more helpful to those of weak eyesight, even so do I consider that the false may be beneficial to the populace, and the truth injurious to those not strong enough to gaze steadfastly on the radiance of

real being. If the laws of the priesthood that obtain with us permit these views to me, I can take over the holy office on condition that I may prosecute philosophy at home and spread legends abroad, so that if I teach no doctrine, at all events I undo no teaching, and allow men to remain in their already acquired convictions. But if anybody says to me that he must be under this influence, that the bishop must belong to the people in his opinions, I shall betray mysetf very quickly. What can there be in common between the ordinary man and philosophy? Divine truth should remain hidden, but the vulgar need a different system. I shall never cease repeating that I think the wise man, to the extent that necessity allows, should not force his opinions upon others, nor allow others to force theirs upon him.

No, if I am called to the priesthood, I declare before God and man that I refuse to preach dogmas in which I do not believe. Truth is an attribute of God, and I wish in all things to be blameless before Him. This one thing I will not dissimulate. I feel that I have a good deal of inclination for amusements. Even as a child, I was charged with a mania for arms and horses. I shall be grieved, indeed greatly shall I suffer at seeing my beloved dogs deprived of their hunting, and my bow eaten up by worms. Nevertheless I shall resign myself to this, if it is the will of God. Again, I hate all care; nevertheless, whatever it costs, I will endure lawsuits and quarrels, so long as I can fulfil this mission, heavy though it he, according to God's will; but never will I consent to conceal my beliefs, nor shall my opinions be at war with my tongue. l believe that I am pleasing God in thinking and speaking thus. I do not wish to give any one the opportunity of saying that I, an unknown man, grasped at the appointment. But let the beloved of God, the right reverend Theophilus, knowing the situation and giving me clear evidence that he understands it, decide on this issue concerning me. He will then either leave me to myself to lead my own life, and to philosophize, or he will not leave himself any grounds on which hereafter to sit in judgment over me, and to turn me out of the ranks of the priesthood. In comparison with these truths, every opinion is insignificant, for I know well that Truth is dearest to God. I swear it by your sacred head, nay, better still, I swear by God the guardian of Truth that I suffer. How can I fail to suffer, when I must, as it were, remove from one life to another? But if after those things have been made clear which I least desire to conceal, if the man who holds this power from Heaven persists in putting me in the hierarchy of bishops I will submit to the inevitable, and I will accept the token as divine. For I reason thus, that if the emperor or some ill-fated Augustal had given an order, I should have been punished if I disobeyed, but that one must obey God with a willing heart. But even at the expense of God's not admitting me to this service, I must nevertheless place first my love for Truth, the most divine thing of all. And I must not slip into His service through ways most opposed to it—such as falsehood. See then that the scholasti [We would say intellectuals of Alexandria] know well my sentiments, and that they inform Theophilus. (105)

Questions

(1) In what ways does Synesius believe that he falls short of the priestly requirements?

(2) What important dogmas of church belief does Synesius doubt? And how so?

(3) What does Synesius assert that he will not do if he becomes a bishop?

(4) What individual is dominant in this letter: Synesius the philosopher or Synesius the Christian? Explain.

10–7
Leo I: the man who laid the foundations for the medieval Papacy.

There is no evidence that, during the Church's early years, the Bishop of Rome was held in any greater esteem than his colleagues who shepherded the major cities of the time: Antioch, Alexandria, or Jerusalem. It was only after four centuries had elapsed that the leadership claims of the Bishop of Rome (who assumed the title of "Pope), on the basis of Apostolic Succession to St. Peter, and an interpretation of Matthew 16:13–19, were solidified into the Petrine Theory. It was Pope Leo I (440–461) who most effectively asserted these claims of supremacy as representative of Christ on earth. In the following instance, he states some of these claims while attacking an opponent, Bishop Hilary of Aries.

Source: Filey Cooper and Matthew Schwartz. eds., *Roman letters: History from a Personal Point of View* (Detroit: Wayne State University, 1991), pp. 291–292.

Our Lord Jesus Christ, Saviour of the human race, desired to have the observance of divine religion shine out through God's grace unto all nations and races. He established it in such a way that truth, previously contained only in proclamations of the Law and the Prophets, might proceed from the Apostles' trumpet for the salvation of all, as it is written: "Their sound has gone forth unto all the earth: and their words unto the ends of the world." Now, the Lord desired that the dispensing of this gift should be shared as a task by all the Apostles, but in such a way that He put the principal charge on the most blessed Peter, the highest of all the Apostles. He wanted His gifts to flow into the entire body from Peter himself, as it were from the head…But the man who attempts to infringe on its power by furthering his own desires and not following practices received from antiquity is trying with absolutely blasphemous presumption, to destroy this most sacred solidity of that rock, established with God as the builder, as we mentioned. For he believes that he is subject to no law, that he is not restrained by any regulations that the Lord ordained. Being intent on novel assumption of power, he departs from what you and we are accustomed to; he presumes to do what is illegal and neglects traditions that he ought to have maintained…Your Fraternities should, of course, realize with us that the Apostolic See (out of reverence for it) has countless times been reported to in consulta-tion by bishops even in your province. And through the appeal of various cases to it, decisions already made have been either rescinded or confirmed, as dictated by long-standing custom. As a result, with "unity of spirit in the bond of peace" being preserved, with letters being sent and received, what was done in a holy manner has been conducive to abiding charity. For our solicitude, which seeks not its own interests but those of Christ, does not detract from the dignity given by God to the churches and the bishops of the churches. This was the procedure always well observed and profitably maintained by our predecessors. But Hilary has departed from it, aiming to disturb the status of the churches and harmony among the bishops by his novel usurpations of power. He seeks to subject you to his authority while not allowing himself to be under the Jurisdiction of the blessed Apostle Peter. He claims for himself the right to consecrate in all the churches of Gaul and takes as his own the dignity which belongs to the metropolitan bishops. He even lessens the reverence due to the most blessed Peter himself by his quite arrogant statements. And although the power to bind and loose was given to Peter before the others, still, in an even more special way, the pasturing ot the sheep was entrusted to him. Anyone who thinks that the prima-cy should be denied to Peter cannot in any way lessen the Apostle's dignity: inflated with the wind of his own pride, he buries himself in hell.

Questions

(1) Of what does Leo accuse Bishop Hilary?

(2) How does Leo explain his ideas as to why Christ would have placed the Apostle Peter in the position of leadership?

(3) What consequences does Leo forsee for what he views as Hilary's insubordinate actions?

CHAPTER 11

11–1
The "Q'uran": the Divine recitation of the Prophet.

The "Q'uran" (or "Koran"), the holiest book of the Islamic faith, literally means "Recitation." The book is composed of verses ("suras") which were transcribed during Muhammad's lifetime as the words of Allah that the Angel Gabriel had commanded the Prophet to recite, and which had already been enscribed on tablets in Heaven. The first of these recitations occurred c. 610 C.E. Subsequent recitations were recorded through various media until they were organized into the "Q'uran" during the reign of the third Caliph, Omar (634-644).

Source: N.J. Dawood, trans., *The Koran* (Harmondsworth, England: Penguin, 1974), pp. 21–22,187–192.

ADORATION

In the Name of Allah, the Compassionate, the Merciful

ALIF *lam mim.* This Book is beyond doubt revealed by the Lord of the Creation.

Do they say: 'He[1] has invented it himself?'

It is the truth from your Lord, which He has bestowed upon you so that you may forewarn a nation, whom none has warned before you, and that they may be rightly guided.

It was Allah who in six days created the heavens and the earth and all that lies between them, and then ascended His throne. You have no guardian or intercessor besides Him. Will you not take heed?

He governs the creation from heaven to earth. And in the end it will ascend to Him in one day, a day whose space is a thousand years by your reckoning.

He knows the visible and the unseen. He is the Mighty One, the Merciful, who excelled in the making of all things. He first created man from clay, then bred his offspring from a drop of paltry fluid. He moulded him and breathed into him of His spirit. He gave you eyes and ears and hearts: yet you are seldom thankful.

They say: 'When we are once lost into the earth, shall we be restored to life?' Indeed, they deny that they will ever meet their Lord.

Say: 'The angel of death, who has been given charge of you, will carry off your souls. Then to your Lord you shall all return.'

Would that you could see the wrongdoers when they hang their heads before their Lord! They will say: 'Lord, we now see and hear. Send us back and we will never do wrong again. We are firm believers.'

Had it been Our Will, We could have guided every soul. But My word shall be fulfilled: 'I will fill the pit of Hell with jinn and men.'

We shall say to them: 'Taste Our punishment, for you forgot this day. We, too, will forget you. Taste Our eternal scourge, which you have earned by your misdeeds.'

None believes in Our revelations save those who, when reminded of them, prostrate themselves in adoration and give glory to their Lord in all humility; who forsake their beds to pray to their Lord in fear and hope; who give in charity of that which We have bestowed on them. No mortal knows what bliss is in store for these as a reward for their labours.

Can he, then, who is a true believer, be compared to him who is an evil-doer? Surely they are not alike.

Those that have faith and do good works shall be received in the gardens of Paradise, as a reward for that which they have done. But those that do evil shall be cast into the Fire. Whenever they try to get out of Hell they shall be driven hack, and a voice will say to them: 'Taste the torment of Hell-fire, which you have persistently denied.'

But We will inflict on them the lighter punishment of this world before the supreme punishment of the world to come, so that they may return to the right path. And who is more wicked than the man who gives no heed to the revelations of his Lord when he is reminded of them? We will surely take vengeance on the evil-doers.

We gave the Scriptures to Moses (never doubt that you will meet him) and made it a guide for the Israelites. And when they grew steadfast and firmly believed in Our revelations, We appointed leaders from among them who gave guidance at Our bidding. On the Day of Resurrection your Lord will resolve for them their differences.

Do they not know how many generations We have destroyed before them? They walk among their ruined dwellings. Surely in this there are veritable signs. Have they no ears to hear with?

Do they not see how We drive the rain to the parched lands and bring forth crops of which they and their cattle eat? Have they no eyes to see with?

They ask: 'When will this judgment come, if what you say be true?

Say: 'On the Day of Judgement the unbelievers will gain in nothing from their faith (for then they will surely-

1. Mohammed

believe) nor shall they be respited.'

Therefore give no heed to them, and wait as they are waiting.

LUQMAN

In the Name of Allah, the Compassionate, the Merciful

ALIF *lam mim.* These are the revelations of the Wise Book, a guide and a blessing to the righteous, who attend to their prayers, pay the alms-tax, and firmly believe in the life to come. These are rightly guided by their Lord and will surely prosper.

Some there are who would gladly pay for a frivolous tale, so that in their ignorance they may mislead others from the path of Allah and make fun of it. For these We have prepared a shameful punishment.

When Our revelations are recited to them, they turn their backs in scorn, as though they never heard them: as though their ears were sealed. To these proclaim a woeful scourge.

But those that have faith and do good works shall enter the gardens of delight, where they shall dwell for ever. Allah's promise shall be fulfilled: He is the Mighty, the Wise One.

He raised the heavens without visible Pillars and set immovable mountains on the earth lest it should shake with you. He dispersed upon it all manner of beasts, and sent down water from the Sky with which He caused all kinds of goodly plants to grow.

Such is Allah's creation: now show me what your other gods created. Truly, the unbelievers are in the grossest error.

We bestowed wisdom on Luqman, saying: 'Give thanks to Allah. He that gives thanks to Him has much to gain, but if any one denies His favours, Allah is self-sufficient and glorious.'

Luqman admonished his son. 'My son,' he said, 'serve no other god instead of Allah, for idolatry is an abominable sin.'

(We enjoined man to show kindness to his parents, for with much pain his mother bears him and he is not weaned before he is two years of age. We said: 'Give thanks to Me and to your parents. To Me shall all things return. But if they press you to serve, besides Me, what you know nothing of do not obey them. Be kind to them in this world, and turn to Me with all devotion. To Me you shall all return, and I will declare to you all that you have done.')

'My son, Allah will bring all things to light, be they as small as a grain of mustard seed, be they hidden inside a rock or in heaven or earth. Allah is wise and all-knowing.

'My son, be steadfast in prayer, enjoin justice, and forbid evil. Endure with fortitude whatever befalls you. That is a duty incumbent on all.

'Do not treat men with scorn, nor walk proudly on the earth: Allah does not love the arrogant and the vainglorious. Rather let your gait be modest and your voice low: the harshest of voices is the braying of the ass.'

Do you not see how Allah has subjected to you all that the heavens and the earth contain and lavished on you both His visible and unseen favours? Yet some would argue about Allah without knowledge or guidance or illuminating scriptures.

When it is said to them: 'Follow what Allah has revealed,' they reply: 'We will follow nothing but the faith of our fathers.' Yes, even though Satan is inviting them to the scourge of Hell.

He that surrenders himself to Allah and leads a righteous life stands on the firmest ground. To Allah shall all things shall return. As for those that disbelieve, let their unbelief not vex you. To Allah they shall return and He will declare to them all that they have done. Allah has knowledge of their inmost thoughts.

We suffer them to take their ease awhile, and then will sternly punish them.

If you ask them: 'Who has created the heavens and the earth?' they will reply: 'Allah.' Say: 'Praise, then, be to Allah!' But most of them are ignorant men.

His is what the heavens and the earth contain. He is self-sufficient and worthy of praise.

If all the trees in the earth Were pens, and the sea, with seven more seas to replenish it, were ink, the writing Of Allah's words could never be finished. Mighty is Allah and wise.

He created you as one soul, and as one soul He will bring you back to life. Allah hears all and observes all.

Do you not see how Allah causes the night to pass into the day and the day into the night? He has forced the sun and the moon into His service, each running for an appointed term. Allah is cognizant of all your actions, for you must know that He is the truth, while that which they invoke besides Him is false. Allah is the Most High, the Supreme One.

Do you not see how the ships speed upon the ocean by Allah's grace, so that He may reveal to you His wonders? Surely there are signs in this for every steadfast, thankful man.

When the waves, like giant shadows, envelop them, they pray to Allah with all devotion. But no sooner does He bring them safe to land than some of them falter between faith and unbelief. Truly, only the treacherous and the ungrateful deny Our revelations.

Men, fear your Lord, and fear the day when no parent shall avail his child nor any child his parent. Allah's promise is surely true. Let the life of this world not deceive you, nor let the Dissembler trick you concerning Allah.

Allah alone has knowledge of the Hour of Doom. He sends down the rain and knows what every womb conceals.

No mortal knows what he will earn tomorrow; no mortal knows where he will breathe his last. Allah alone is wise and all-knowing.

NOAH

In the Name of Allah, the Compassionate, the Merciful

WE sent forth Noah to his people, saying: 'Give warning to your people before a woeful scourge overtakes them.'

He said: 'My people, I come to warn you plainly. Serve Allah and fear Him, and obey me. He will forgive you your sins and respite you till an appointed time. When Allah's time arrives, none shall put it back. Would that you understood this!'

'Lord,' said Noah, 'day and night' I have pleaded with my people, but my pleas have only added to their aversion. Each time I call on them to seek Your pardon, they thrust their fingers in their ears and draw their cloaks over their heads, persisting in sin and bearing themselves with insolent pride. I called out loud to them, and appealed to them in public and in private. "Seek forgiveness of your Lord," I said. "He is ever ready to forgive you. He sends down for you abundant water from the sky and bestows upon you wealth and children. He has provided you with gardens and with flowing rivers. Why do you deny the greatness of Allah when He has made you in gradual stages? Can you not see how He created the seven heavens one above the other, placing in them the moon for a light and the sun for a lantern? Allah has brought you forth from the earth like a plant, and to the earth He will restore you. Then He will bring you back afresh. He has made the earth a vast expanse for you, so that you may traverse its spacious paths."'

1. *Names of idols.*

And Noah said: 'Lord, my people disobey me and follow those whose wealth and offspring will only hasten their perdition. They have devised an outrageous plot, and said to each other: "Do not renounce your gods. Do not forsake Wad or Sows or Yaghuth or Ya'uq or Nasr."¹ They have led numerous men astray. You surely drive the wrongdoers to further error.'

And because of their sins they were overwhelmed by the Flood and cast into the Fire. They found none to help them besides Allah.

And Noah said: 'Lord, do not leave a single unbeliever in the land. If you spare them they will mislead Your servants and beget none but sinners and unbelievers. Forgive me, Lord, and forgive my parents and every true believer who seeks refuge in my house. Forgive all the faithful men and women, and hasten the destruction of the wrongdoers.'

THE WAR STEEDS

In the Name of Allah, the Compassionale, the merciful

BY the snorting war steeds, which strike fire with their hoofs as they gallop to the raid at dawn and with a trail of dust split the foe in two; man is ungrateful to his Lord! To this he himself shall bear witness.

He loves riches with all his heart. But is he not aware that when the dead are thrown out from their graves and men's hidden thoughts are laid open their Lord will on that day know all that they have done?

Questions

(1) In "Adoration," what is revealed as being one of the major functions of the "Q'uran" regarding nonbelievers? Of what significance is the "lighter punishment" in Allah's scheme of salvation?

(2) In "Luqman," what qualities are singled out as being especially pleasing to Allah?

(3) What lesson is brought forward in the version of the story of Noah presented in the "Q'uran"?

11–2
Al-Tabari: an early biography of Islam's Prophet.

Though the Q'uran itself provides hints about Muhammad's past and his personal life, biographies of the Prophet, which drew upon various (usually oral) accounts and recollections, came out shortly after his death in 632 C.E. One of the most revered of the early Muslim chroniclers was Al-Tabari, who made it a habit to cite his souces whenever possible. Here he has left us an account of a crucial event: the first call of Muhammad to prophesy (note: Aisha was Muhamad's second wife; Khadija his first).

Source: Arthur Jeffrey, trans., *Islam, Muhammad and His Religion* (N.Y.: Liberal Arts Press, 1958), pp. 15–17. Quoted in Mircea Eliade, *From Medicine Men to Muhammad* (N.Y.: Harper & Row, 1974), pp. 63–64.

Ahmad b. 'Uthman, who is known as Abu'l-jawza', has related to me on the authority of Wahb b. Jarir, who heard his father say that he had heard from an-Nu'man b. Rashid, on the authority of az-Zuhri from 'Urwa, from 'A'isha, who said: The way revelation (*wahy*) first began to come to the Apostle of Allah—on whom be Allah's blessing and peace—was by means of true dreams which would come like the morning dawn. Then he came to love solitude, so he used to go off to a cave in Hira where he would practise *tahannuth* certain nights before returning to his family. Then he would come back to his family and take provisions for the like number [of nights] until unexpectedly the truth came to him.

He (i.e., Gabriel) came to him saying: 'O Muhammad, thou art Allah's Apostle (rasūl).' Said the Apostle of Allah—upon whom be Allah's blessing and peace: 'Thereat I fell to my knees where I had been standing, and then with trembling limbs dragged myself along till I came in to Khadija, saying: "Wrap ye me up! Wrap ye me up!" till the terror passed from me. Then [on another occasion] he came to me again and said: "O Muhammad, thou art Allah's Apostle," [which so disturbed me] that I was about to cast myself down from some high mountain cliff. But he appeared before me as I was about to do this, and said: "O Muhammad, I am Gabriel, and thou art Allah's Apostle." Then he said to me: "Recite!"; but I answered: "What should I recite?"; whereat he seized me and grievously treated me three times, till he wore me out.

Then he said: "Recite, in the name of thy Lord who has created" (Sūra XCVI, 1). So I recited it and then went to Khadija, to whom I said: "I am worried about myself." Then I told her the whole story. She said: "Rejoice, for by Allah, Allah will never put thee to shame. By Allah, thou art mindful of thy kinsfolk, speakest truthfully, renderest what is given thee in trust, bearest burdens, art ever hospitable to the guest, and dost always uphold the right against any wrong." Then she took me to Waraqua b. Naufal b. Asad [to whom] she said: "Give ear to what the son of thy brother [has to report]." So he questioned me, and I told him [the whole] story. Said he: "This is the *nāmūs* which was sent down upon Moses the son of Amram. Would that I might be a stalwart youth [again to take part] in it. Would that I might still be alive when your people turn you out." "And will they turn me out?" I asked. "Yes," said he, "never yet has a man come with that with which you come but has been turned away. Should I be there when your day comes I willlend you mighty assistance."'

Questions

(1) How did Muhammad react to the first visitations from Gabriel?

(2) What role did Khadija play?

(3) What form of suffering does Muhammad's uncle foresee will occur to the Prophet on account of his visions?

11–3
Orations: The words of the Prophet through his speeches.

Muhammad was more than a religious leader; he was a political figure who had, by the time of his death, united most of the Arab peoples into a centralized government based on "Shariah" (Islamic law), and which encompassed both the secular and religious. Church-state separation is a concept that is foreign to Orthodox Islam: the two were originally viewed as inseparable. Collections of Muhammad's "Orations" reveal the Prophet in his role of charismatic messenger. The excerpt is Muhammad's last oration and was delivered, while he was ill, only five days prior to his death.

Source; Mohammad Ubaidul Akbar, *Orations of Muhammad, the Prophet of Islam* (New Delhi, India: Nusrat Ali Nasri for Kitab Bhanan, 1979), pp. 101–106.

He praised Allah, thanked Him, sought forgiveness for the martyrs of the battle of Uhad and prayed for them. Then he said: "O people, (draw near) to me." So they gathered round him.

Then he said: "Well, there is a man whose Lord has given him option between living in this world as long as he wishes to live and eating from this world as much as he likes to eat, or meeting his Lord."

(Hearing it) Abu Bakr wept and said: "Nay, may our fathers, mothers and properties be your ransom…"

Then the Apostle of Allah—may Allah send him bliss and peace!—said: "There is none more bountiful to us for his company and wealth than the son of Abu Quhāfa (Abu Bakr). Had I taken any intimate friend except my Lord, I would have taken the son of Abu Quhāfa as my intimate friend. But there is love and brotherhood of

Faith"—He said it twice or thrice).

"The fact is that your companion is the intimate friend of Allah. There should not remain in the mosque any door (open) except the door of Abu Bakr."

"O people, it has reached me that you are afraid of your Prophet's death. Has any previous prophet lived for ever among those to whom he was sent: so that I would live for ever among you?

"Behold, I am going to my Lord and you will be going to Him. I recommend you to do good to the First Emigrants and I recommend the Emigrants to do good among themselves.

"Lo, Allah, the Exalted, says: 'By the time, Man is in loss'—to the end of the Sura (ciii.).

"Verily the things run with the permission of Allah, the Exalted, and verily delay in a matter should not urge you on its hastening in demand. Allah,—the Mighty and the Great—does not hasten for the hastiness of anybody.

"He who contends with Allah, He overcomes him. He who tries to deceive Allah, He outwits him. In a near future if you get the authority then do no mischief on the earth and do not cut off your blood relations.

"I recommend you to do good to the Helpers. They are those who prepared the lodging and faith for you. So you should behave them well.

"Did they not divide with you their fruits equally? Did they not make space for you in their houses? Did they not prefer you to themselves while poverty was with them?'

"Lo, men will increase in number, but the Helpers will decrease to the extent that they will be among men as salt in food. They are my family with whom I took my shelter; they are my sandals; and they are my paunch in which I eat. So observe me in them.

"By Him in Whose hand is my life, verily I love you; verily the Helpers have done what was on them and there remains what is on you.

"So he who from among you gets power in any matter and becomes able to do harm to people therein or to do good to other therein, then he should appreciate one of them who does well and should overlook one of them who does bad. Lo, do not be selfish about them.

"Behold, I shall precede you; I will be your witness and you are to meet me. Lo, the 'Haud' is your meeting place. By Allah, just now, I see my 'Haud' from here.

"Beware, he who likes to come to it along with me tomorrow, should hold back his hand and tongue except from necessary matters."

"Lo, I have, indeed, been given the keys of the treasures of the earth. By Allah, I do not fear for you that you will turn polytheists after me. But I fear for you that you will be entangled in them, then you will fight one another and will perish like those who perished before you.

"O people, verily the sins spoil the blessings and change the lots. When the people are good, their rulers do good to them and when the people are bad, they oppress them."

"Then he said: "There may be some rights which I owe to you and I am nothing but a human being. So if there be any man whose honour I have injured a bit, here is my honour; he may retaliate.

"Whosoever he may be if I have wounded a bit of his skin, here is my skin; He may retaliate.

"Whosoever he may be, if I have taken anything from his property, here is my property; so he may take. Know that he, among you, is more loyal to me who has got such a thing and takes it or absolves me; then I meet my Lord while I am absolved.

"Nobody should say, I fear enmity and grudge of the Apostle of Allah. Verily these things are not in my nature and character. He whose passion has overcome him in aught, should seek help from me so that I may pray for him."

Questions

(1) In what ways does Muhammad foster solidarity amongst his followers?

(2) How does Muhammad attempt to encourage and comfort his people against the eventuality of his death?

(3) From this last oration, how does it appear that Muhammad wishes to be remembered?

11–4
Islam in the Prophet's absence: continuation under the Caliphate.

The sudden demise of Muhammad in 632 left his state in disarray; he had never specified procedures for designating a successor. How was the Muslim state he had forged to be governed? A debate ensued and its results had far-reaching implications, as related by the respective chroniclers Al-Tabari and Ibn Hisham.

Source: Bernard Lewis, ed., *Islam from the Prophet to the Capture of Constantinople*, Vol. I (N.Y.: Walker & Co.,1974), pp. 2–6.

THE FOUNDING OF THE CALIPHATE (632)

An account of what happened between the Emigrants and the Helpers concerning the leadership, in the porch of the Banu Sa'ida[1]

Hishām ibn Muhammad told me on the authority of Abū Mikhnaf, who said: 'Abdallāh ibn 'Abd al-Rahmān ibn Abī 'Umra, the Helper, told me:

When the Prophet of God, may God bless and save him, died, the Helpers assembled in the porch of the Banū Sā'ida and said, "Let us confer this authority, after Muhammad, upon him be peace, on Sa'd ibn 'Ubāda." Sa'd, who was ill, was brought to them, and when they assembled Sa'd said to his son or to one of his nephews, "I cannot, because of my sickness, speak so that all the people can hear my words. Therefore, hear what I say and then repeat it to them so that they may hear it." Then he spoke and the man memorized his words and raised his voice so that the others could hear.

He said, after praising God and lauding Him, "O company of the Helpers! You have precedence in religion and merit in Islam which no other Arab tribe has. Muhammad, upon him be peace, stayed for more than ten years amid his people, summoning them to worship the Merciful One and to abandon false gods and idols. But among his own people only a few men believed in him, and they were not able to protect the Prophet of God or to glorify his religion nor to defend themselves against the injustice which beset them. God therefore conferred merit on you and brought honor to you and singled you out for grace and vouchsafed to you faith in Him and in His Prophet and protection for Him and His companions and glorification to Him and His religion and holy war against His enemies. It was you who fought hardest against His enemy and weighed more heavily on His enemy than any other, until the Arabs obeyed the command of God willy-nilly and the distant ones gave obedience, humbly and meekly; until Almighty God, through you, made the world submit to His Prophet, and through your swords the Arabs drew near to him. And when God caused him to die, he was content with you and delighted with you. Therefore, keep this authority for yourselves alone, for it is yours against all others."

They all replied to him, "Your judgment is sound and your words are true. We shall not depart from what you say and we shall confer this authority on you. You satisfy us and you will satisfy the right believer."

Then they discussed it among themselves and some of them said, "What if the Emigrants of Quraysh refuse, and say: 'We are the Emigrants and the first Companions of the Prophet of God; we are his clan and his friends. Why therefore do you dispute the succession to his authority with us?'" Some of them said, "If so, we would reply to them, 'An amir from us and an amir from you! And we shall never be content with less than that.'" Sa'd ibn 'Ubāda, when he heard this, said, "This is the beginning of weakness."

News of this reached 'Umar, and he went to the house of the Prophet, may God bless and save him. He sent to Abū Bakr, who was in the Prophet's house with 'Alī ibn Abī Tālib, upon him be peace, preparing the body of the Prophet, may God bless and save him, for burial. He sent asking Abū Bakr to come to him, and Abū Bakr sent a message in reply saying that he was busy. Then 'Umar sent saying that something had happened which made his presence necessary, and he went to him and said, "Have you not heard that the Helpers have gathered in the porch of the Banu Sā'ida? They wish to confer this authority on Sa'd ibn 'Ubāda, and the best they say is, 'an amir from among

us and an amir from among Quraysh.'" They made haste toward them, and they met Abū 'Ubayda ibn al-Jarrāh. The three of them went on together, and they met 'Asim ibn 'Adī and 'Uwaym ibn Sā'ida, who both said to them: "Go back, for what you want will not happen." They said, "We shall not go back," and they came to the meeting.

'Umar ibn al-Khattāb said: We came to the meeting, and I had prepared a speech which I wished to make to them. We reached them, and I was about to begin my speech when Abū Bakr said to me, "Gently! Let me speak first, and then afterwards say whatever you wish." He spoke. 'Umar said, "He said all I wanted to say, and more."

'Abdallāh ibn 'Abd al-Rahmān said: Abū Bakr began. He praised and lauded God and then he said, "God sent Muhammad as a Prophet to His creatures and as a witness to His community that they might worship God and God alone, at a time when they were worshipping various gods beside Him and believed that they were intercessors for them with God and could be of help to them, though they were only of hewn stone and carved wood. Then he recited to them, 'And they worship apart from God those who could neither harm them nor help them, and they say these are our intercessors with God' [Qur'ān x, 19/18]. And they said, 'We worship them only so that they may bring us very near to God' [Qur'ān xxxix, 4/3]. It was a tremendous thing for the Arabs to abandon the religion of their fathers. God distinguished the first Emigrants of his people by allowing them to recognize the truth and believe in him and console him and suffer with him from the harsh persecution of his people when they gave them the lie and all were against them and reviled them. Yet they were not affrighted because their numbers were few and the people stared at them and their tribe was joined against them. They were the first in the land who worshipped God and who believed in God and the Prophet. They are his friends and his clan and the best entitled of all men to this authority after him. Only a wrongdoer would dispute this with them. And as for you, O company of the Helpers, no one can deny your merit in the faith or your great precedence in Islam. God was pleased to make you Helpers to His religion and His Prophet and caused him to migrate to you, and the honor of sheltering his wives and his Companions is still yours, and after the first Emigrants there is no one we hold of equal standing with you. We are the amirs and you are the viziers. We shall not act contrary to your advice and we shall not decide things without you."

Abu Bakr said, "Here is 'Umar and here is Abū 'Ubayda. Swear allegiance to whichever of them you choose." The two of them said, "No, by God, we shall not accept this authority above you, for you are the worthiest of the Emigrants and the second of the two who were in the cave and the deputy [khalīfa] of the Prophet of God in prayer, and prayer is the noblest part of the religion of the Muslims. Who then would be fit to take precedence of you or to accept this authority above you? Stretch out your hand so that we may swear allegiance to you."

And when they went forward to swear allegiance to

1. *The Emigrants (Muhājirūn) were the Qurayshī Muslims from Mecca who accompanied the Prophet on his migration to Medina; the Helpers (Ansār) were the Medinans who joined them. The Banū Sā'ida were a clan of Khazraj, one of the two main Arab tribes of Medina; the other was Aws.*

him, Bashīr ibn Sa'd went ahead of them and swore allegiance to him…and when the tribe of Aws saw what Bashīr ibn Sa'd had done…they came to him and swore allegiance to him.…

Hishām said on the authority of Abū Mikhnaf: 'Abdallāh ibn 'Abd al-Rahmān said: People came from every side to swear allegiance to Abū Bakr.

2. The Accession Speech of Abū Bakr (632)

Then Abū Bakr spoke and praised and lauded God as is fitting, and then he said: O people, I have been appointed to rule over you, though I am not the best among you. If I do well, help me, and if I do ill, correct me. Truth is loyalty and falsehood is treachery; the weak among you is strong in my eyes until I get justice for him, please God, and the strong among you is weak in my eyes until I exact justice from him, please God. If any people holds back from fighting the holy war for God, God strikes them with degradation. If weakness spreads among a people, God brings disaster upon all of them. Obey me as long as I obey God and His Prophet. And if I disobey God and His Prophet, you do not owe me obedience. Come to prayer, and may God have mercy on you.

Questions

(1) What was the nature of the split between the Helpers and the Emigrants after the Prophet's death?
(2) What was Abu Bakr's perspective on the difference in prestige and authority between the two?
(3) In his accession speech, how does Abu Bakr personally set limits on his own authority as Caliph?

11–5
Harun al-Rashid and the zenith of the Caliphate.

The Caliphate endured as a political entity until 1258. After the rule of the first four ("Orthodox") Caliphs, all of whom had been directly associated with Muhammad, the Ummayyad family assumed control and maintained a dynasty from 661–750. They were then overturned by the Abbasid clan, who claimed descent from the Prophet's uncle, Abbas. The Abbasids established the Islamic capital at Baghdad, and it was there, during the reign of Caliph Harun al-Rashid (786–809), that the Empire attained its peak of power and prestige.

Source: Bernard Lewis., ed., *Islam from the Prophet to the Capture of Constantinople,* vol. I (N.Y.: Walker & Co., 1974), pp. 27–30

A woman came to rule over the Romans because at the time she was the only one of their royal house who remained. She wrote to the Caliphs al-Mahdī and al-Hādī and to al-Rashīd at the beginning of his Caliphate with respect and deference and showered him with gifts. When her son [Constantine VI] grew up and came to the throne in her place, he brought trouble and disorder and provoked al-Rashīd. The empress, who knew al-Rashīd and feared his power, was afraid lest the kingdom of the Romans pass away and their country be ruined. She therefore overcame her son by cunning and put out his eyes so that the kingdom was taken from him and returned to her. But the people of their kingdom disapproved of this and hated her for it. Therefore Nikephoros, who was her secretary, rose against her, and they helped and supported him so that he seized power and became the ruler of the Romans.

When he was in full control of his kingdom, he wrote to al-Rashīd, "From Nikephoros, the king of Romans, to al-Rashīd, the king of the Arabs, as follows: That woman put you and your father and your brother in the place of kings and put herself in the place of a commoner. I put you in a different place and am preparing to invade your lands and attack your cities, unless you repay

me what that woman paid you. Farewell!"

When his letter reached al-Rashīd, he replied, "In the name of God, the Merciful and the Compassionate, from the servant of God, Hārūn, Commander of the Faithful, to Nikephoros, the dog of the Romans, as follows: I have understood your letter, and I have your answer. You will see it with your own eye, not hear it." Then he at once sent an army against the land of the Romans of a size the like of which was never heard before and with commanders unrivaled in courage and skill. When news of this reached Nikephoros, the earth became narrow before him and he took counsel. Al-Rashīd advanced relentlessly into the land of the Romans, killing, plundering, taking captives, destroying castles, and obliterating traces, until they came to the narrow roads before Constantinople, and when they reached there, they found that Nikephoros had already had trees cut down, thrown across these roads, and set on fire. The first who put on the garments of the naphtha-throwers was Muhammad ibn Yazīd ibn Mazyad. He plunged boldly through, and then the others followed him.

Nikephoros sent gifts to al-Rashīd and submitted to him very humbly and paid him the poll tax for himself as well as for his companions.

On this Abu'l-'Atāhiya said:

O Imam of God's guidance, you have become the guardian of religion, quenching the thirst of all who pray for rain.

You have two names drawn from righteousness [rashād] and guidance [hudā], for you are the one called Rashīd and Mahdī,

Whatever displeases you becomes loathsome; if any thing pleases you, the people are well pleased with it.

You have stretched out the hand of nobility to us, east and west, and bestowed bounty on both easterner and westerner.

You have adorned the face of the earth with generosity and munificence, and the face of the earth is adorned with generosity.

O, Commander of the Faithful, brave and pious, you have opened that part of benevolence which was closed!

God has destined that the kingdom should remain to Hārūn, and, God's destiny is binding on mankind.

The world submits to Hārūn, the favored of God, and Nikepharos has become the dhimmī of Hārūn.

Then al-Rashīd went back, because of what Nikephoros had given him, and got as far as Raqqa. When the snow fell and Nikephoros felt safe from attack, he took advantage of the respite and broke the agreement between himself and al-Rashīd and returned to his previous posture. Yahyā ibn Khālid [the vizier], let alone any other, did not dare to inform al-Rashīd of the treachery of Nikephoros. Instead, he and his sons offered money to the poets to recite poetry and thereby inform al-Rashīd of this. But they all held back and refrained, except for one poet from Jedda, called Abū Muhammad, who was very proficient, strong of heart and strong of poetry, distinguished in the days of al-Ma'mūn and of very high standing. He accepted the sum of 100,000 dirhams from Yahyā and his sons and then went before al-Rashīd and recited the following verses:

Nikephoros has broken the promise he gave you, and now death hovers above him.

I bring good tidings to the Commander of the Faithful, for Almighty God is bringing you a great victory.

Your subjects hail the messenger who brings the good news of his treachery

Your right hand craves to hasten to that battle which will assuage our souls and bring a memorable punishment.

He paid you his poll tax and bent his cheek in fear of sharp swords and in dread of destruction.

You protected him from the blow of swords which we brandished like blazing torches.

You brought all your armies back from him and he to whom you gave your protection was secure and happy.

Nikephoros! If you played false because the Imam was far from you, how ignorant and deluded you were!

Did you think you could play false and escape? May your mother mourn you! What you thought is delusion.

Your destiny will throw you into its brimming depths; seas will envelop you from the Imam.

The Imam has power to overwhelm you, whether your dwelling be near or far away.

Though we may be neglectful the Imam does not neglect that which he rules and governs with his strong will.

A king who goes in person to the holy war! His enemy is always conquered by him.

O you who seek God's approval by your striving, nothing in your inmost heart is hidden from God.

No counsel can avail him who deceives his Imam, but counsel from loyal counsellers deserves thanks.

Warning the Imam is a religious duty, an expiation and a cleansing for those who do it.

When he recited this, al-Rashīd asked, "Has he done that?" and he learned that the viziers had used this device to inform him of it. He then made war against Nikephoros while the snow still remained and conquered Heraclea at that time.

Questions
(1) Under what circumstances did Nikephoros become ruler of the (Byzantine) Romans, and how did his attitude to the Caliph differ from his predecessor's?
(2) What was Harun's response, and the consequences?
(3) Why did no one wish to inform Harun of Nikephoros' treachery and what device was ultimately employed to alert him?

11–6
The Caliphate in decline: Al-Matawwakil's murder.

In the years following Harun al-Rashid's death, conflicts surfaced and, in many respects, the ethical qualities of those who held the Caliphate deteriorated to the point that the ruler openly violated the strictures of the Q'uran—notably those against alcohol consumption—and increasingly relied on brutal methods to enforce their authority. The last effective Caliph was al-Mutawwakil (847–861), whose celebrated Mosque at Samarra is among the greatest masterpieces of Muslim architecture. His assassination, related here by Al-Tabari, was followed by the disintegration of the Empire, a lengthy period of decline, and the burning of Baghdad by the Mongols in 1258.

Source: Bernard Lewis, ed., *Islam from the Prophet to the Capture of Constantinople,* Vol. I (N.Y.: Walker & Co., 1974), pp. 30–34.

It is said that on the feast of 'Id al-Fitr [247/861], al-Mutawakkil rode on horseback between two lines of soldiers four miles long. Everybody walked on foot in front of him. He conducted the public prayer and then returned to his palace, where he took a handful of earth and put it on his head. They asked him why and he replied, "I have seen the immensity of this gathering, I have seen them subject to me, and it pleased me to humble myself before Almighty God." The day after the feast he did not send for any of his boon companions. The third day, Tuesday, 3 Shawwāl [December 10] he was lively, merry, and happy....

The singer Ibn al-Hafsi, who was present at the party, said: The Commander of the Faithful was never merrier than on that day. He began his party and summoned his boon companions and singers, who came. Qabīha, the mother of al-Mu'tazz, presented him with a square cape of green silk, so splendid that no one had ever seen its like. Al-Mutawakkil looked at it for a long time, praised it and admired it greatly and then ordered that it be cut in two and taken back to her, saying to her messenger, "She can remember me by it." Then he added, "My heart tells me that I shall not wear it, and I do not want anyone else to wear it after me; that is why I had it torn." We said to him, "Master, today is a day of joy. God preserve you, O Commander of the Faithful from such words." He began to drink and make merry, but he repeated, "By God, I shall soon leave you." However, he continued to amuse and enjoy himself until nightfall.

Some said that al-Mutawakkil had decided, together with al-Fath [ibn Khāqān], to call next day, Thursday 5th Shawwāh [December 12], on 'Abdallāh ibn 'Umar al-Baziyār to ask him to murder al-Muntasir and to kill Wasīf, Bughā, and other commanders and leaders of the Turks.

On the previous day, Tuesday, according to Ibn al-Hafsī, the Caliph subjected his son al-Muntasir to heavy horseplay, sometimes abusing him, sometimes forcing him to drink more than he could hold, sometimes having him slapped, and sometimes threatening him with death.

It is reported, on the authority of Hārūn ibn Muhammad ibn Sulaymān al-Hashīmī, who said that he had heard it from one of the women behind the curtain, that al-Mutawakkil turned toward al-Fath and said to him, "I shall renounce God and my kinship with the Prophet of God (may God bless and save him) if you don't slap him (that is, al-Muntasir)." Al-Fath rose and slapped the back of his neck twice. Then al-Mutawakkil said to those present, "Be witnesses, all of you, that I declare al-Musta'jil al-Muntasir—deprived of his rights to my succession." Then he turned to him and said, "I gave you the name of al-Muntasir [the triumphant] but people called you al-Muntazir [the expectant] because of your foolishness. Now you have become al-Musta'jil [the urgent]."

"O, Commander of the Faithful," replied al-Muntasir, "If you were to give the orders to behead me, it would be more bearable than what you are doing to me!"

"Give him a drink!" cried al-Mutawakkil and called for supper, which was brought. It was late at night. Al-Muntasir went out and ordered Bunan, the page of Ahmad ibn Yahyā, to follow him. When he had gone the table was placed before al-Mutawakkil who began to eat and gobble. He was drunk.

It is related on the authority of Ibn al-Hafsī that when al-Muntasir left to return to his own quarters, he took the hand of Zurāfa and asked him to accompany him. "But my Lord," said Zurāfa, "the Commander of the Faithful has not yet risen." "The Commander of the Faithful," said al-Muntasir, "is overcome by drink, and Bughā and the boon companions will soon leave. I would like to talk to you about your son. Utamish has asked me to marry his son to your daughter and your son to his daughter."

"We are your slaves, my lord," replied Zurāfa, "and at your orders." Al-Muntasir then took him by the hand and led him away. Zurāfa had earlier said to me, "Be calm, for the Commander of the Faithful is drunk and will soon recover. Tamra called me and asked me to ask you to go to him. Let us therefore go together to his quarters." "I shall go there ahead of you," I said, and Zurāfa left with al-Muntasir for his quarters.

Bunān, the page of Ahmād ibn Yahyā, related that al-Muntasir said to him, "I have united Zurāfa's son to Utamish's daughter and Utamish's son to Zurāfa's daughter."

"My lord," asked Bunān, "where are the confetti, for in that lies the beauty of such a union."

"Tomorrow, please God!" he said, "for today has already passed."

Zurāfa had gone to Tamra's quarters. He entered and called for food, which was brought to him, but he had hardly begun to eat when we heard a noise and shouting. We stood up. "It is only Zurāfa leaving Tamra's quarters," said Bunān. Suddenly Bughā appeared before al-Muntasir, who asked, "What is this noise?"

"Good tidings, O, Commander of the Faithful," said Bughā.

"What are you saying, wretch?" said al-Muntasir.

"May God give you a great reward in return for our master the Commander of the Faithful. He was God's slave. God called him, and he went."

Al-Muntasir held an audience and gave orders to close the door of the room in which al-Mutawakkil had been murdered, as well as that of the audience chamber. All the doors were closed. He then sent for Wasīf and ordered him to summon al-Mu'tazz and al-Mu'ayyad, in the name of al-Mutawakkil.

It is reported, on the authority of 'Ath'ath, that when al-Muntasir had risen and gone, taking Zurāfa with him, al-Mutawakkil had sent for his table. Bughā the younger, known as al-Sharābī, was standing by the curtain. On that day it was the turn of Bughā the elder to be on duty in the palace, but as he was in Sumaysāt at the time he had himself replaced by his son Mūsā, whose mother was al-Mutawakkil's maternal aunt. Bughā the younger entered the gathering and ordered the boon companions of the Caliph to return to their quarters.

"It is not yet time for them to go," al-Fath said to him, "the Commander of the Faithful has not yet risen."

"The Commander of the Faithful," said Bughā, "has ordered me to leave no one in the room after he has drunk seven pints [ratl], and he has already drunk fourteen." Al-Fath objected to their going, but Bughā said, "The Commander of the Faithful is drunk, and his women are behind this curtain. Get up and go!" They all went out, leaving only al-Fath, 'Ath'ath, and four of the Caliph's servants, Shafī, Faraj the younger, Mu'nis, and Abū 'Isā

Mārid al-Muhrizī. 'Ath'ath said: The cook placed the table in front of al-Mutawakkil, who began to eat and gobble, and invited Marid to eat with him. He was drunk, and after eating, he drank again.

'Ath'ath said that Abū Ahmād, the son of al-Mutawakkil and uterine brother of al-Mu'ayyad, who was present in the hall, came out to go to the lavatory. Bughā al-Sharābī had closed all the doors except that which opened to the river bank. It was by this door that those who had been appointed to murder the Caliph entered. Abū Ahmad saw them enter, and cried out, "What is this, villains?" Then suddenly they drew their swords. Leading the murderers were Baghlun the Turk, Baghir, Musa ibn Bughā, Hārūn ibn Suwārtagin, and Bughā al-Sharābī.

When al-Mutawakkil heard Abū Ahmad shout, he raised his head and saw them and asked, "What is it, Bughā?" And Bughā answered, "These are the men of the night watch, who will guard the gate of my lord, the Commander of the Faithful." When they heard al-Mutawakkil speak to Bughā, they turned back. Neither Wajin and his men nor the sons of Wasīf were with them. 'Ath'ath said: I heard Bughā say to them, "Villains! You are all dead men without escape; at least die with honor." They then came back into the hall, and Baghūn attacked first, giving the Caliph a blow which cut off his ear and struck his shoulder. "Ho!" cried al-Mutawakkil. Hārūn ran him through with his sword, and he throw himself at his attacker, who, however, fended him off with his arm, and Bāghir joined them.

"Wretches!" cried al-Fath, "this is the Commander of the Faithful!"

"Be quiet!" said Bughā, and al-Fath threw himself over al-Mutawakkil. Hārūn ran him through with his sword, and he screamed "Death!" Hārūn and Bughā ibn Mūsā, striking him in turn with their swords, killed him, and cut him to pieces. 'Ath'ath was wounded in the head. A young eunuch who was with al-Mutawakkil hid behind the curtain and was saved. The others fled.

Questions

(1) What conclusions can one draw as to al-Mutawwakil's character, and his relationship with his son?
(2) What role did Bugha and the Turks play in this story?
(3) Where was al-Muntasir and was he allegedly doing while his father was being murdered?

11–7
Shiism and Caliph Ali: controversy over the Prophetic succession.

Shiism, the most substantial dissenting denomination within the Islamic faith (as opposed to the Sunni majority), was born out of the issue over who should succeed Muhammad in his leadership over the Muslim world. Shiites demand that true authority must be vested in an Imam, who must be a physical descendent of the Prophet through his daughter Fatima and her husband (Muhammad's nephew), Ali. Within the Shiite community, Ali, who from 656–661 was the fourth successor to Muhammad, is mainly considered to have been the sole legitimate Caliph. The following document is excerpted from Ali's instructions to Malik al-Ashtar, whom he had just appointed governor of Egypt.

Source: William C. Chittick, ed., *A Shiite Anthology* (Albany, N.Y.: State University of New York Press, 1981, copyright: Muhammadi Trust of Great Britain and Northern Ireland), pp.68–72.

ᶜAlī wrote these instructions to al-Ashtar al-Nakhaᶜt when he appointed him governor of Egypt and its provinces at the time the rule of Muhammad ibn Abī Bakr was in turmoil. It is the longest set of instructions (in the *Nahj al-balāghah*). Among all his letters it embraces the largest number of good qualities.

PART ONE: INTRODUCTION

In the Name of God, the Merciful, the Compassionate

This is that with which ᶜAlī, the servant of God and Commander of the Faithful, charged Malik ibn al-Hārith al-Ashtar in his instructions to him when he appointed him governor of Egypt: to collect its land tax, to war against its enemies, to improve the condition of the people and to engender prosperity in its regions. He charged him to fear God, to prefer obedience to Him (over all else) and to follow what He has directed in His Book—both the acts He has made obligatory and those He recommends—for none attains felicity but he who follows His directions, and none is overcome by wretchedness but he who denies them and lets them slip by. (He charged him) to help God—glory be to Him—with his heart, his hand and his tongue, for He—majestic is His Name—has promised to help him who exalts Him. And he charged him to break the passions of his soul and restrain it in its recalcitrance, for the soul incites to evil, except inasmuch as God has mercy.

PART TWO: COMMANDS AND INSTRUCTIONS CONCERNING RIGHTEOUS ACTION IN THE AFFAIRS OF THE STATE

Know, O Mālik, that I am sending you to a land where governments, just and unjust, have existed before you. People will look upon your affairs in the same way that you were wont to look upon the affairs of the rulers before you. They will speak about you as you were wont to speak about those rulers. And the righteous are only known by that which God causes to pass concerning them on the tongues of His servants. So let the dearest of your treasuries be the treasury of righteous action. Control your desire and restrain your soul from what is not lawful to you, for restraint of the soul is for it to be equitous in what it likes and dislikes. Infuse your heart with mercy, love and kindness for your subjects. Be not in face of them a voracious animal, counting them as easy prey, for they are of two kinds: either they are your brothers in religion or your equals in creation. Error catches them unaware, deficiencies overcome them, (evil deeds) are committed by them intentionally and by mistake. So grant them your pardon and your forgiveness to the same extent that you hope God will grant you His pardon and His forgiveness. For you are above them, and he who appointed you is above you, and God is above him who appointed you. God has sought from you the fulfillment of their requirements and He is trying you with them.

Set yourself not up to war against God, for you have no power against His vengeance, nor are you able to dispense with His pardon and His mercy. Never be regretful of pardon or rejoice at punishment, and never hasten (to act) upon an impulse if you can find a better course. Never say, "I am invested with authority, I give orders and I am obeyed," for surely that is corruption in the heart, enfeeblement of the religion and an approach to changes (in fortune). If the authority you possess engender in you pride or arrogance, then reflect upon the tremendousness of the dominion of God above you and His power over you in that in which you yourself have no control. This will subdue your recalcitrance, restrain your violence and restore in you what has left you of the power of your reason. Beware of vying with God in His tremendousness and likening yourself to Him in His exclusive power, for God abases every tyrant and humiliates all who are proud.

See that justice is done towards God and justice is done towards the people by yourself, your own family and those whom you favor among your subjects. For if you do not do so, you have worked wrong. And as for him who wrongs the servants of God, God is his adversary, not to speak of His servants. God renders null and void the argument of whosoever contends with Him. Such a one will be God's enemy until he desists or repents. Nothing is more conducive to the removal of God's blessing and the hastening of His vengeance than to continue in wrongdoing, for God harkens to the call of the oppressed and He is ever on the watch against the wrongdoers.

Let the dearest of your affairs be those which are middlemost in rightfulness, most inclusive in justice and most comprehensive in (establishing) the content of the subjects. For the discontent of the common people invalidates the content of favorites, and the discontent of favorites is pardoned at (the achievement of) the content of the masses. Moreover, none of the subjects is more burdensome upon the ruler in ease and less of a help to him in trial than his favorites. (None are) more disgusted by equity, more importunate in demands, less grateful upon bestowal, slower to pardon (the ruler upon his) withholding (favor) and more deficient in patience at the misfortunes of time than the favorites. Whereas the support of religion, the solidarity of Muslims and preparedness in the face of the enemy lie only with the common people of the community, so let your inclination and affection be toward them.

Let the farthest of your subjects from you and the most hateful to you be he who most seeks out the faults of men. For men possess faults, which the ruler more than anyone else should conceal. So do not uncover those of them which are hidden from you, for it is only encumbent upon you to remedy what appears before you. God will judge what is hidden from you. So veil imperfection to the extent you are able; God will veil that of yourself which you would like to have veiled from your subjects. Loose from men the knot of every resentment, sever from yourself the cause of every animosity, and ignore all that which does not become your station. Never hasten to believe the slanderer, for the slanderer is a deceiver, even if he seems to be a sincere advisor.

Bring not into your consultation a miser, who might turn you away from liberality and promise you poverty; nor a coward, who might enfeeble you in your affairs; nor a greedy man, who might in his lust deck out oppression to you as something fair. Miserliness, cowardliness and greed are diverse temperaments which have in common distrust in God.

Truly the worst of your viziers are those who were the viziers of the evil (rulers) before you and shared with them in their sins. Let them not be among your retinue, for they are aides of the sinners and brothers of the wrongdoers. You will find the best of substitutes for them from among those who possess the like of their ideas and effectiveness but are not encumbranced by the like of their sins and crimes; who have not aided a wrongdoer in his wrongs nor a sinner in his sins. These will be a lighter burden upon you, a better aid, more inclined toward you in sympathy and less intimate with people other than you. So choose these men as your special companions in privacy and at assemblies. Then let the most influential among them be he who speaks most to you with the bitterness of the truth and supports you least in activities which God dislikes in His friends, however this strikes your pleasure. Cling to men of piety and veracity. Then accustom them not to lavish praise upon you nor to (try to) gladden you by (attributing to you) a vanity you did not do, for the lavishing of abundant praise causes arrogance and draws (one) close to pride.

Never let the good-doer and the evil-doer possess an equal station before you, for that would cause the good-doer to abstain from his good-doing and habituate the evil-doer to his evil-doing. Impose upon each of them what he has imposed upon himself.

Know that there is nothing more conducive to the ruler's trusting his subjects than that he be kind towards them, lighten their burdens and abandon coercing them in that in which they possess not the ability. So in this respect you should attain a situation in which you can confidently trust your subjects, for trusting (them) will sever from you lasting strain. And surely he who most deserves your trust is he who has done well when you have tested him, and he who most deserves your mistrust is he who has done badly when you have tested him.

Abolish no proper custom (sunnah) which has been acted upon by the leaders of this community, through which harmony has been strengthened and because of which the subjects have prospered. Create no new custom which might in any way prejudice the customs of the past,

lest their reward belong to him who originated them, and the burden be upon you to the extent that you have abolished them.

Study much with men of knowledge (ʿulamāʾ) and converse much with sages (hukanāʾ) concerning the consolidation of that which causes the state of your land to prosper and the establishment of that by which the people before you remained strong.

PART THREE: CONCERNING THE CLASSES OF MEN

Know that subjects are of various classes, none of which can be set aright without the others and none of which is independent from the others. Among them are (1.) the soldiers of God, (2.) secretaries for the common people and the people of distinction, executors of justice, and administrators of equity and kindness, (3.) payers of jizyah and land tax, namely the people of protective covenants~and the Muslims, (4.) merchants and craftsmen and (5.) the lowest class, the needy and wretched. For each of them God has designated a portion, and commensurate with each portion He has established obligatory acts (farīdah) in His Book and the Sunnah of His Prophet—may God bless him and his household and give them peace—as a covenant from Him maintained by us.

Now soldiers, by the leave of God, are the fortresses of the subjects, the adornment of rulers, the might of religion and the means to security. The subjects have no support but them, and the soldiers in their turn have no support but the land tax which God has extracted for them, (a tax) by which they are given the power to war against their enemy and upon which they depend for that which puts their situation in order and meets their needs. Then these two classes (soldiers and taxpayers) have no support but the third class, the judges, administrators and secretaries, for they draw up contracts, gather yields, and are entrusted with private and public affairs. And all of these have no support but the merchants and craftsmen, through the goods which they bring together and the markets which they set up. They provide for the needs (of the first three classes) by acquiring with their own hands those (goods) to which the resources of others do not attain. Then there is the lowest class, the needy and wretched, those who have the right to aid and assistance. With God there is plenty for each (of the classes). Each has a claim upon the ruler to the extent that will set it aright. But the ruler will not truly accomplish what God has enjoined upon him in this respect except by resolutely striving, by recourse to God's help, by reconciling himself to what the truth requires and by being patient in the face of it in what is easy for him or burdensome.

Questions

(1) What advice does Ali give the al-Ashtar about policy towards the proper customs of the subject peoples?

(2) What does Ali recommend as a cure for pride generated by power?

(3) What five classes does Ali designate whose well-being is essential for conducting a successful administration, and what claims do each of them have on those who govern them?

CHAPTER 12

12–1
Tenochtitlan: Diaz de Castillo's description of the metropolis of Mesoamerica.

The Aztec capital of Tenochtitlan, now the urban core for Mexico City, was an entrepot for trade link-ing all centers of Mexico and Central America, and those as far afield as the Caribbean and South America. The intruding Spaniards were amazed at the level of sophistication and abundance that they found there during their initial visit in 1519. The excerpt is from the recollections of Bernal Diaz de Castillo (1492–1581), one of the soldiers under the command of conquistador Hernan Cortez.

Source: J.M. Cohen, trans., *Bernal Diaz de Castillo; The Conquest of New Spain* (HarmondsWorth, England: Penguin, 1975), pp. 232–237.

...on reaching the marketplace, escorted by the many *Caciques* whom Montezuma had assigned to us, we were astounded at the great number of people and the quantities of merchandise, and at the orderliness and good arrangements that prevailed, for we had never seen such a thing before. The chieftains who accompa-nied us pointed everything out. Every kind of mer-chandise was kept separate and had its fixed place marked for it.

Let us begin with the dealers in gold, silver, and precious stones, feathers, cloaks, and embroidered goods, and male and female slaves who are also sold there. They bring as many slaves to be sold in that mar-ket as the Portuguese bring Negroes from Guinea. Some are brought there attached to long poles by means of collars round their necks to prevent them from escaping, but others are left loose. Next there were those who sold coarser cloth, and cotton goods and fabrics made of twisted thread, and there were chocolate merchants with their chocolate. In this way you could see every kind of merchandise to be found anywhere in New Spain, laid out in the same waygoods are laid out in my own district of Medina del Campo, a centre for fairs, where each line of stalls has its own particular sort. So it was in this great market. There were those who sold sisal cloth and ropes and the san-dals they wear on their feet, which are made from the same plant. All these were kept in one part of the mar-ket, in the place assigned to them, and in another part were skins of tigers and lions, otters, jackals, and deer, badgers, mountain cats, and other wild animals, some tanned and some untanned, and other classes of mer-chandise.

There were sellers of kidney-beans and sage and other vegetables and herbs in another place, and in yet another they were selling fowls, and birds with great dewlaps, also rabbits, hares, deer, young ducks, little dogs, and other such creatures. Then there were the fruiterers; and the women who sold cooked food, flour and honey cake, and tripe, had their part of the market. Then came pottery of all kinds, from big water-jars to little jugs, displayed in its own place, also honey, honey-paste, and other sweets like nougat. Elsewhere they sold timber too, boards, cradles, beams, blocks, and benches, all in a quarter of their own.

Then there were the sellers of pitch-pine for torches, and other things of that kind, and I must also mention. with all apologies, that they sold many canoe-loads of human excrement, which they kept in the creeks near the market. This was for the manufacture of salt and the curing of skins, which they say cannot be done without it. I know that many gentlemen will laugh at this, but I assure them it is true. I may add that on all the roads they have shelters made of reeds or straw or grass so that they can retire when they wish to do so, and purge their bowels unseen by passers-by, and also in order that their excrement shall not be lost.

But why waste so many words on the goods in their great market? If I describe everything in detail I shall never be done. Paper, which in Mexico they call *amal,* and some reeds that smell of liquidamber, and are full of tobacco, and yellow ointments and other such things, are sold in a separate part. Much cochineal is for sale too, under the arcades of that market, and there are many sellers of herbs and other such things. They have a building there also in which three judges sit, and there are officials like constables who examine the merchandise. I am forgetting the sellers of salt and the makers of flint knives, and how they split them off the stone itself, and the fisherwomen and the men who sell small cakes made from a sort of weed which they get out of, the great lake, which curdles and forms a kind of bread which tastes rather like cheese. They sell axes too, made of bronze and copper and tin, and gourds and brightly painted wooden jars.

We went on to the great *cue,* and as we approached its wide courts, before leaving the market-place itself, we saw many more merchants who, so I was told, brought gold to sell in grains, just as they extract it from the mines. This gold is placed in the thin quills of the large geese of that country, which are so white as to be transparent. They used to reckon their accounts with one another by the length and thickness of these little quills, how much so many cloaks or so many gourds of chocolate or so many slaves were worth, or anything else they were bartering.

Now let us leave the market, having given it a final glance, and come to the courts and enclosures in which their great cue stood. Before reaching it you passed through a series of large courts, bigger I think than the Plaza at Salamanca. These courts were surrounded by a double masonry wall and paved, like the whole place, with very large smooth white flagstones. Where these stones were absent everything was whitened and polished, indeed the whole place was so clean that there was not a straw or a grain of dust to be found there.

When we arrived near the great temple and before we had climbed a single step, the great Montezuma sent six *papas* and two chieftains down from the top, where he was making his sacrifices, to escort our Captain; and as he climbed the steps, of which there were one hundred and fourteen, they tried to take him by the arms to help him up in the same way as they helped Montezuma, thinking he might be tired, but he would not let them near him.

The top of the *cue* formed an open square on which stood something like a platform, and it was here that the great stones stood on which they placed the poor Indians for sacrifice. Here also was a massive image like a dragon, and other hideous figures, and a great deal of blood that had been spilled that day. Emerging in the company of two *papas* from the shrine which houses his accursed images, Montezuma made a deep bow to us all and said: 'My lord Malinche, you must be tired after climbing this great cue of ours.' And Cortes replied that none of us was ever exhausted by anything. Then Montezuma took him by the hand, and told him to look at his great city and all the other cities standing in the water, and the many others on the land round the lake; and he said that if Cortes had not had a good view of the great market-place he could see it better from where he now was. So we stood there looking, because that huge accursed *cue* stood so high that it dominated everything. We saw the three causeways that led into Mexico: the causeway of Iztapalapa by which we had entered four days before, and that of Tacuba along which we were afterwards to flee on the night of our great defeat, when the new prince Cuitlahuac drove us outof the city (as I shall tell in due course), and that of Tepeaquilla. We saw the fresh water which came from Chapultepec to supply the city, and the bridges that were conctructed at intervals on the causeways so that the water could flow in and out from one part of the lake to another. We saw a great number of canoes, some coming with provisions and others returning with cargo and merchandise; and we saw too that one could not pass from one house to another of that great city and the other cities that were built on the water except over wooden drawbridges or by canoe. We saw *cues* and shrines in these cities that looked like gleaming white towers and castles: a marvellous sight. All the houses had flat roofs, and on the causeways were other small towers and shrines built like fortresses.

Having examined and considered all that we had seen, we turned back to the great market and the swarm of people buying and selling. The mere murmur of their voices talking was loud enough to be heard more than three miles away. Some of our soldiers who had been in many parts of the world, in Constantinople, in Rome, and all over Italy, said that they had never seen a market so well laid out, so large, so orderly, and so full of people.

But to return to our Captain, he observed to Father Bartolome de Olmedo, whom I have often mentioned and who happened to be standing near him: 'It would be a good thing, I think, Father, if we were to sound Montezuma as to whether he would let us build our church here.' Father Bartolome answered that it would be a good thing if it were successful, but he did not think this a proper time to speak of it, for Montezuma did not look as if he would allow such a thing.

Cortes, however, addressed Montezuma through Doña Marina: 'Your lordship is a great prince and worthy of even greater things. We have enjoyed the sight of your cities, and since we are now here in your temple, I beg of you to show us your gods and *Teules.*' Montezuma answered that first he would consult his chief *papas*; and when he had spoken to them, he said that we might enter a small tower, an apartment like a sort of hall, in which there were two altars with very rich wooden carvings over the roof. On each altar was a giant figure, very tall and very fat. They said that the one on the right was Hulchilobos, their war-god. He had a very broad face and huge terrible eyes. And there were so many precious stones, so much gold, so many pearls and seed-pearls stuck to him with a paste which the natives made from a sort of root, that his whole body and head were covered with them. He was girdled with huge snakes made of gold and precious stones, and in one hand he held a bow, in the other some arrows. Another smaller idol beside him, which they said was his page, carried a short lance and a very rich shield of gold and precious stones. Around Huichilobos' neck hung some Indian faces and other objects in the shape of hearts, the former made of gold and the latter of silver, with many precious blue stones.

There were some smoking braziers of their incense, which they call copal, in which they were burning the hearts of three Indians whom they had sacrificed that day; and all the walls of that shrine were so splashed and caked with blood that they and the floor too were black. Indeed, the whole place stank abominably. We then looked to the left and saw another great image of the same height as Huichilobos, with a face like a bear and eyes that glittered, being made of their mirror-glass, which they call *tezcat*. Its body, like that of Huichilobos, was encrusted with precious stones, for they said that the two were brothers. This Tezcatlipoca, the god of hell, had charge of the Mexicans' souls, and his body was surrounded by figures of little devils with snakes' tails. The walls of this shrine also were so caked with blood and the floor so bathed in it that the stench was worse than that of any slaughter-house in Spain. They had offered that idol five hearts from the day's sacrifices.

At the very top of the *cue* there was another alcove, the woodwork of which was very finely carved, and here there was another image, half man and half lizard, encrusted with precious stones, with half its body covered in a cloak. They said that the body of this creature contained all the seeds in the world, and that he was the god of seedtime and harvest. I do not remember his name. Here too all was covered with blood, both walls and altar, and the stench was such that we could hardly wait to get out, They kept, a very large drum there, and when they beat it the sound was most dismal, like some music from the infernal regions, as you might say, and it could be heard six miles away. This drum was said to be covered with the skins of huge serpents. In that small platform were many more diabolical objects, trumpets

great and small, and large knives, and many hearts that had been burnt with incense before their idols; and everything was caked with blood. The stench here too was like a slaughter-house, and we could scarcely stay in the place.

Our Captain said to Montezuma, through our interpreters with something like a laugh: 'Lord Montezuma, I cannot imagine how a prince as great and wise as your Majesty can have failed to realize that these idols of yours are not gods but evil things, the proper name for which is devils. But so that I may prove this to you, and make it clear to all your *papas,* grant me one favour. Allow us to erect a cross here on the top of this tower, and let us divide off a part of this sanctuary where your Huichilobos and Tezcatlipoca stand, as a place where we can put an image of Our Lady'—which image Montezuma had already seen—'and then you will see, by the fear that your idols have of her, how grievously they have deceived you.'

Montezuma, however, replied in some temper (and the two *papas* beside him showed real anger: 'Lord Malinche, if I had known that you were going to utter these insults I should not have shown you my gods. We hold them to be very good. They give us health and rain and crops and weather, and all the victories we desire. So we are bound to worship them and sacrifice to them, and I beg you to say nothing more against them.'

Questions

(1) What conclusions can be made about Aztec civilization and economic life from Diaz de Castillo's description of the Tenochtitlan's market?
(2) What means of regulation are there stated to be on the market?
(3) What impression did the Spaniards have upon viewing the Aztec gods?
(4) What was the reaction of the Aztecs to Cortez's suggestion regarding their temple?

12–2
Mansa Musa: the "king who sits on a mountain of gold."

Control of the Trans-Saharan trade from the cities of the Sahel to the North African ports was a certain guarantee to enormous wealth. During the medieval period, three great empires: Ghana, Mali, and Songhay, dominated this traffic in gold, salt, slaves, and ivory. The most fabulous of the West African emperors was Mansa Musa of Mall (1312–1337), whose lavish display and largess while on a his pilgrimmage to Mecca drew international attention. The following description is from Al' Umari, an Arab traveller.

Source: N. Levtzion & J. F. P. Hopkins, eds., *Corpus of Early Arabic Sources for West African History* (Cambridge, England: Cambridge University Press, 1981), pp. 267–272.

The king of this country imports Arab horses and pays high prices for them. His army numbers about 100,000, of whom about 10,000 are cavalry mounted on horses and the remainder infantry without horses or other mounts. They have camels but do not know how to ride them with saddles.

Barley is quite lacking; it does not grow there at all.

The emirs and soldiers of this king have fiefs (*iqtā'at*) and benefices (*in'āmāt*). Among their chiefs are some whose wealth derived from the king reaches 50,000 mithqāls of gold every year, besides which he keeps them in horses and clothes. His whole ambition is to give them fine clothes and to make his towns into cities. Nobody may enter the abode of this king save barefooted, whoever he may be. Anyone who does not remove his shoes, inadvertently or purposely, is put to death without mercy. Whenever one of the emirs or another comes into the presence of this king he keeps him standing before him for a time. Then the newcomer makes a gesture with his right hand like one who beats the drum of honour (*jūk*) in the lands of Tūrān and Irān. If the king bestows a favour upon a person or makes him a fair promise or thanks him for some deed the person who has received the favour grovels before him from one end of the room to the other. When he reaches there the slaves of the recipient of the favour or some of his friends take some of the ashes which are always kept ready at the far end of the king's audience chamber for the purpose and scatter it over the head of the favoured one, who then returns grovelling until he arrives before the king. Then he makes the drumming gesture as before and rises.

As for this gesture likened to beating the *jūk,* it is like this. The man raises his right hand to near his ear. There he places it, it being held up straight, and places it in contact with his left hand upon his thigh. The left hand has the palm extended so as to receive the right elbow. The right hand too has the palm extended with the fingers held close beside each other like a comb and touching the lobe of the ear.

The people of this kingdom ride with Arab saddles and in respect of most features of their horsemanship resemble the Arabs, but they mount their horses with the right foot, contrary to everybody else.

It is their custom not to bury their dead unless they be people of rank and status. Otherwise those without rank and the poor and strangers are thrown into the bush like other dead creatures.

It is a country where provisions go bad quickly, especially [clarified] butter (*samn*), which is rotten and stinks after two days. This is not to be wondered at, for their sheep go scavenging over the garbage heaps and the country is very hot, which hastens decomposition.

When the king of this kingdom comes in from a journey a parasol (*jitr*) and a standard are held over his head as he rides, and drums are beaten and guitars (*tunbūr*) and trumpets well made of horn are played in front of him. And it is a custom of theirs that when one whom the king has charged with a task or assignment returns to him he questions him in detail about everything which has happened to him from the moment of his departure until his return. Complaints and appeals against administrative oppression (*mazālim*) are placed before this king and he delivers judgement on them himself. As a rule nothing is written down; his commands are given verbally. He has judges, scribes, and government offices (*dīwān*). This is what al-Dukkālī related to me.

The emir Abū 'l-Hasan 'Alī b. Amīr Hājib told me that he was often in the company of sultan Mūsā the king of this country when he came to Egypt on the Pilgrimage. He was staying in [the] Qarāfa [district of Cairo] and Ibn Amīr Hājib was governor of Old Cairo and Qarāta at that time. A friendship grew up between them and this sultan Mūsā told him a great deal about himself and his country and the people of the Sūdān who were his neighbours. One of the things which he told him was that his country was very extensive and contiguous with the Ocean. By his sword and his armies he had conquered 24 cities each with its surrounding district with villages and estates. It is a country rich in livestock—cattle, sheep, goats, horses, mules—and different kinds of poultry—geese, doves, chickens. The inhabitants of his country are numerous, a vast concourse, but compared with the peoples of the Sūdān who are their neighbours and penetrate far to the south they are like a white birthmark on a black cow. He has a truce with the gold-plant people, who pay him tribute.

Ibn Amīr Hājib said that he asked him about the gold-plant, and he said: "It is found in two forms. One is found in the spring and blossoms after the rains in open country (*sahara*). It has leaves like the *najīl* grass and its roots are gold (*tibr*). The other kind is found all the year round at known sites on the banks of the Nīl and is dug up. There are holes there and roots of gold are found like stones or gravel and gathered up. Both kinds are known as *tibr* but the first is of superior fineness (*afhal fī 'l-'iyār*) and worth more." Sultan Mūsā told Ibn Amīr Hājib that gold was his prerogative and he collected the crop as a tribute except for what the people of that country took by theft.

But what al-Dukkālī says is that in fact he is given only a part of it as a present by way of gaining his favour, and he makes a profit on the sale of it, for they have none in their country; and what Dukkālī says is more reliable.

Ibn Amīr Hājib said also that the blazon (*shi'ār*) of this king is yellow on a red ground. Standards ('*alam*) are unfurled over him wherever he rides on horseback; they are very big flags (*liwā'*). The ceremonial for him who presents himself to the king or who receives a favour is that he bares the front of his head and makes the *jūk*-beating gesture towards the ground with his right hand as the Tatars do; if a more profound obeisance is required he grovels before the king. "I have seen this (says Ibn Amīr Hājib) with my own eyes." A custom of this sultan is that he does not eat in the presence of anybody, be he who he may, but eats always alone. And it is a custom of his people that if one of them should have reared a beautiful daughter he offers her to the king as a concubine (*ama mawtū' a*) and he possesses her without a marriage ceremony as slaves are possessed, and this in spite of the fact that Islam has triumphed among them and that they follow the Malikite school and that this sultan Mūsā was pious and assiduous in prayer, Koran reading, and mentioning God [*dhikr*].

"I said to him (said Ibn Amīr Ḥājib) that this was not permissible for a Muslim, whether in law (*shar'*) or reason (*'aql*), and he said: 'Not even for kings?' and I replied: 'No! not even for kings! Ask the scholars!' He said: 'By God, I did not know that. I hereby leave it and abandon it utterly!'

"I saw that this sultan Mūsā loved virtue and people of virtue. He left his kingdom and appointed as his deputy there his son Muhammad and emigrated to God and His Messenger. He accomplished the obligations of the Pilgrimage, visited [the tomb of] the Prophet [at Medina] (God's blessing and peace be upon him!) and returned to his country with the intention of handing over his sovereignty to his son and abandoning it entirely to him and returning to Mecca the Venerated to remain there as a dweller near the sanctuary (*mujāwir*); but death overtook him, may God (who is great) have mercy upon him.

"I asked him if he had enemies with whom he fought wars and he said: 'Yes, we have a violent enemy who is to the Sūdān as the Tatars are to you. They have an analogy with the Tatars in various respects. They are wide in the face and flat-nosed. They shoot well with [bow and] arrows (*nushshāb*). Their horses are cross-bred (*kadīsh*) with slit noses. Battles take place between us and they are formidable because of their accurate shooting. War between us has its ups and downs.'"

(Ibn Sa'īd, in the Mughrib, mentions the Damādim tribe who burst upon various peoples of the Sūdān and destroyed their countries and who resemble the Tatars. The two groups appeared upon the scene at the same moment.)

Ibn Amīr Ḥājib continued: "I asked sultan Mūsā how the kingdom fell to him, and he said: 'We belong to a house which hands on the kingship by inheritance. The king who was my predecessor~ did not believe that it was impossible to discover the furthest limit of the Atlantic Ocean and wished vehemently to do so. So he equipped 200 ships filled with men and the same number equipped with gold, water, and provisions enough to last them for years, and said to the man deputed to lead them: "Do no return until you reach the end of it or your provisions and water give out." They departed and a long time passed before anyone came back. Then one ship returned and we asked the captain what news they brought. He said: "Yes, O Sultan, we travelled for a long time until there appeared in the open sea [as it were] a river with a powerful current. Mine was the last of those ships. The [other] ships went on ahead but when they reached that place they did not return and no more was seen of them and we do not know what became of them. As for me, I went about at once and did not enter that river." But the sultan disbelieved him.

"'Then that sultan got ready 2,000 ships, 1,000 for himself and the men whom he took with him and 1,000 for water and provisions. He left me to deputize for him and embarked on the Atlantic Ocean with his men. That was the last we saw of him and all those who were with him, and so I became king in my own right.'

"This sultan Mūsā, during his stay in Egypt both before and after his journey to the Noble Hijāz, maintained a uniform attitude of worship and turning towards God. It was as though he were standing before Him because of His continual presence in his mind. He and all those with him behaved in the same manner and were well-dressed, grave, and dignified. He was noble and generous and performed many acts of charity and kindness. He had left his country with 100 loads of gold which he spent during his Pilgrimage on the tribes who lay along his route from his country to Egypt, while he was in Egypt, and again from Egypt to the Noble Hijāz and back. As a consequence he needed to borrow money in Egypt and pledged his credit with the merchants at a very high rate of gain so that they made 700 dinars profit on 300. Later he paid them back amply (*?: bi-'l-rājih*). He sent to me 500 mithqals of gold by way of honorarium.

"The currency in the land of Takrūr consists of cowries and the merchants, whose principal import these are, make big profits on them." Here ends what Ibn Amīr Ḥājib said.

From the beginning of my coming to stay in Egypt I heard talk of the arrival of this sultan Mūsā on his Pilgrimage and found the Cairenes eager to recount what they had seen of the Africans' prodigal spending. I asked the emir Abū 'l-'Abbās Ahmad b. al-Ḥāk the *mihmandar* and he told me of the opulence, manly virtues, and piety of this sultan. "When I went out to meet him (he said), that is, on behalf of the mighty sultan al-Malik al-Nāsir, he did me extreme honour and treated me with the greatest courtesy. He addressed me, however, only through an interpreter despite his perfect ability to speak in the Arabic tongue. Then he forwarded to the royal treasury many loads of unworked native gold and other valuables. I tried to persuade him to go up to the Citadel to meet the sultan, but he refused persistently, saying: 'I came for the Pilgrimage and nothing else. I do not wish to mix anything else with my Pilgrimage.' He had begun to use this argument but I realized that the audience was repugnant to him because he would be obliged to kiss the ground and the sultan's hand. I continued to cajole him and he continued to make excuses but the sultan's protocol demanded that I should bring him into the royal presence, so I kept on at him till he agreed.

"When we came in the sultan's presence we said to him: 'Kiss the ground!' but he refused outright saying: 'How may this be?' Then an intelligent man who was with him whispered to him something we could not understand and he said: 'I make obeisance to God who created me!' then he prostrated himself and went forward to the sultan. The sultan half rose to greet him and sat him by his side. They conversed together for a long time, then sultan Mūsā went out. The sultan sent to him several complete suits of honour for himself, his courtiers, and all those who had come with him, and saddled and bridled horses for himself and his chief courtiers. His robe of honour consisted of an Alexandrian open-fronted cloak (muftaraj) embellished with tard wahsh cloth containing much gold thread and miniver fur, bordered with beaver fur and embroidered with metallic thread, along with golden fastenings, a silken skull-cap with caliphal emblems, a gold-inlaid belt, a damascened sword, a kerchief [embroidered] with pure gold, standards, and two horses saddled and bridled and equipped with decorated mule[-type] saddles. He also furnished him with accommodation and abundant supplies during his stay.

"When the time to leave for the Pilgrimage came round the sultan sent to him a large sum of money with ordinary and thoroughbred camels complete with saddles and equipment to serve as mounts for him, and purchased abundant supplies for his entourage and others who had come with him. He arranged for deposits of fodder to be placed along the road and ordered the caravan commanders to treat him with honour and respect.

"On his return I received him and supervised his accommodation. The sultan continued to supply him with provisions and lodgings and he sent gifts from the Noble Hijāz to the sultan as a blessing. The sultan accepted them and sent in exchange complete suits of honour for him and his courtiers together with other gifts, various kinds of Alexandrian cloth, and other precious objects. Then he returned to his country.

"This man flooded Cairo with his benefactions. He left no court amīr (amir muqarrab) nor holder of a royal office without the gift of a load of gold. The Cairenes made incalculable profits out of him and his suite in buying and selling and giving and taking. They exchanged gold until they depressed its value in Egypt and caused its price to fall."

The mihmandār spoke the truth, for more than one has told this story. When the mihmandār died the' tax office (dīwān) found among the property which he left thousands of dinars' worth of native gold (al-dhahab al-maʿdinī) which he had given to him, still just as it had been in the earth (fī turābih), never having been worked.

Merchants of Misr and Cairo have told me of the profits which they made from the Africans, saying that one of them might buy a shirt or cloak (thawb) or robe (izār) or other garment for five dinars when it was not worth one. Such was their simplicity and trustfulness that it was possible to practice any deception on them. They greeted anything that was said to them with credulous acceptance. But later they formed the very poorest opinion of the Egyptians because of the obvious falseness of everything they said to them and their outrageous behaviour in fixing the prices of the provisions and other goods which were sold to them, so much so that were they to encounter today the most learned doctor of religious science and he were to say that he was Egyptian they would be rude to him and view him with disfavour because of the ill treatment which they had experienced at their hands.

Muhanna' b. ʿAbd al-Bāqī al-ʿUjrumī the guide informed me that he accompanied sultan Mūsā when he made the Pilgrimage and that the sultan was very open-handed towards the pilgrims and the inhabitants of the Holy Places. He and his companions maintained great pomp and dressed magnificently during the journey. He gave away much wealth in alms. "About 200 mithqals of gold fell to me" said Muhanna' "and he gave other sums to my companions.'" Muhanna' waxed eloquent in describing the sultan's generosity, magnanimity, and opulence.

Gold was at a high price in Egypt until they came in that year. The mithqal did not go below 25 dirharns and was generally above, but from that time its value fell and it cheapened in price and has remained cheap till now. The mithqal does not exceed 22 dirhams or less. This has been the state of affairs for about twelve years until this day~ by reason of the large amount of gold which they brought into Egypt and spent there.

A letter came from this sultan to the court of the sultan in Cairo. It was written in the Maghribī style of handwriting on paper with wide lines. In it he follows his own rules of composition although observing the demands of propriety (yumsik fīh nāmūsan li-nafsih maʿa murāʿāt qawānīn al-adab). It was written by the hand of one of his courtiers who had come on the Pilgrimage. Its contents comprised greetings and a recommendation for the bearer. With it he sent 5,000 mithqals of gold by way of a gift.

The countries of Mālī and Ghāna and their neighbours are reached from the west side of Upper Egypt. The route passes by way of the Oases (Wāhāt) through desert country inhabited by Arab and then Berber communities (tawāʾif) until cultivated country is reached by way of which the traveller arrives at Mālī and Ghāna. These are on the same meridian as the mountains of the Berbers to the south of Marrakech and are joined to them by long stretches of wilderness and extensive desolate deserts.

The learned faqih Abi ʾl-Rūb ʾlsā al-Zawāwī informed me that sultan Mūsā Mansā told him that the length of his kingdom was about a year's journey, and Ibn Amīr Hājib told me the same. AI-Dukkālī's version, already mentioned, is that it is four months' journey long by the same in breadth. What al-Dukkālī says is more to be relied on, for Mūsā Mansā possibly exaggerated the importance of his realm.

Al-Zāwāwī also said: "This sultan Mūsā told me

that at a town called ZKRY he has a copper mine from which ingots are brought to BYTY. "There is nothing in my kingdom (he said) on which a duty is levied (*shay' mumakkas*) except this crude copper which is brought in. Duty is collected on this and on nothing else. We send it to the land of the pagan Sūdān and sell it for two-thirds of its weight in gold, so that we sell 100 mithqals of this copper for 66²/₃ mithqals of gold." He also stated that there are pagan nations (*umam*) in his kingdom from whom he does not collect the tribute (*jizya*) but whom he simply employs in extracting the gold from its deposits. The gold is extracted by digging pits about a man's height in depth and the gold is found embedded in the sides of the pits or sometimes collected at the bottom of them.

The king of this country wages a permanently Holy War on the pagans of the Sūdān who are his neighhours. They are more numerous than could ever be counted.

Questions

(1) What light does Al' Umari's account shed on the Malian army? On the treatment of the corpses of the dead?

(2) In what way was Musa's conduct found to be contrary to Muslim law, and how did the Emperor react upon being informed of this?

(3) According to Musa, what happened to his predecessor, and under what circumstances did Musa himself come to the throne?

(4) What economic and/or other effects did Musa's pilgrimmage have in Egypt?

12–3
The cities of the Zanj and the Indian Ocean trade.

The Indian Ocean was, long before the Atlantic was opened by European navigators, one of the world's major maritime commercial arteries. The east coast of Africa was a prime component of this trade, and ships from Egypt, Arabia, India, and as far afield as China plied their way to the Swahili Cities of the Zanj (Africans). These cities, chief among them: Kilwa; Mogadishu; Mombasa; Tanga; Malindi; Sofala, and Zanzibar, developed the language from whose name they are collectively known (Swahili was originally concieved as a commercial language). The cities were known to travellers of varied backgrounds, as evidenced in the following selections.

Source: G. S. P. Freeman-Grenvillem, *The East African Coast: Selected Documents from the 1st to the 19th Century* (London: Rex Collins, 1975), pp. 19–24.

AL-IDRISI: THE FIRST WESTERN NOTICE OF EAST AFRICA

The Zanj of the East African coast have no ships to voyage in, but use vessels from Oman and other. countries which sail to the islands of Zanj which depend on the Indies. These foreigners sell their goods there, and buy the produce of the country. The people of the Djawaga islands go to Zanzibar in large and small ships, and use them for trading their goods, for they understand each others' language. Opposite the Zanj coasts are the Djawaga islands; they are numerous and vast; their inhabitants are very dark in colour, and everything that is cultivated there, fruit, sorghum, sugar-cane and camphor trees, is black in colour. Among the number of the islands is Sribuza, which is said to be 1,200 miles round; and pearl fisheries and various kinds of aromatic plants and perfumes are to be found there, which attract the merchants.

Among the islands of Djawaga included in the present section is Andjuba [Anjouan-Johanna], whose principal town is called Unguja in the language of Zanzibar, and whose people, although mixed, are actually mostly Muslims. The distance from it to Banas on the Zanj coast is 100 miles. The island is 400 miles round; bananas are the chief food. There are five kinds, as follows: the bananas called kundi; fill whose weight is sometimes twelve ounces; omani, muriani, sukari. It is a healthy, sweet, and pleasant food. The island is traversed by a mountain called Wabra. The vagabonds who are expelled from the town flee there, and form a brave and numerous company which frequently infests the surroundings of the town, and which lives at the top of the mountain in a state of defence against the ruler of the island. They are courageous, and feared for their arms and their number. The island is very populous; there are many villages and cattle. They grow rice. There is a great trade in it, and each year various products and goods are brought for exchange and consumption.

From Medouna [on the Somali coast] to Malindi, a town of the Zanj, one follows the coast for three days and three nights by sea. Malindi lies on the shore, at the mouth of a river of sweet water. It is a large town, whose people engage in hunting and fishing. On land they hunt the tiger [sic] and other wild beasts. They obtain various kinds of fish from the sea, which they cure and sell.

They own and exploit iron mines; for them iron is an article of trade and the source of their largest profits. They pretend to know how to bewitch the most poisonous snakes so as to make them harmless to everyone except those for whom they wish evil or on whom they wish to take vengeance. They also pretend that by means of these enchantments the tigers and lions cannot hurt them. These wizards are called *al-Musnafu* in the language of the people.

It is two days' journey along the coast to Mombasa. This is a small place and a dependency of the Zanj. Its inhabitants work in the iron mines and hunt tigers. They have red coloured dogs which fight every kind of wild beast and even lions. This town lies on the sea shore near a large gulf up which ships travel two days' journey; its banks are uninhabited because of the wild beasts that live in the forests where the Zanj go and hunt, as we have already said. In this town lives the King of Zanzibar. His guards go on foot because they have no mounts: horses cannot live there.

CHAO JU-KUA: ZANZIBAR AND SOMALIA IN THE THIRTEENTH CENTURY

Zanguebar (Ts'ong-Pa)

The Ts'ong-pa country is an island of the sea south of Hu-ch'a-la. To the west it reaches a great mountain. The inhabitants are of Ta-shi [Arab] stock and follow the Ta-shi religion. They wrap themselves in blue foreign cotton stuffs and wear red leather shoes. Their daily food consists of meal, baked cakes and mutton.

There are many villages, and a succession of wooded hills and terraced rocks. The climate is warm, and there is no cold season. The products of the country consist of elephants' tusks, native gold, amber-gris and yellow sandal-wood.

Every year Hu-ch'a-la and the Ta-shi localities along the sea-coast send ships to this country with white cotton cloth, porcelain, copper and red cotton to trade.

BERBERA COAST (PI-P'A-LO)

The country of Pi-p'a-lo contains four cities; the other places are all villages which are constantly at feud and fighting with each other. The inhabitants pray to Heaven and not to the Buddha. The land produces many camels and sheep, and the people feed themselves with the flesh and milk of camels and with baked cakes.

The other products are ambergris, big elephants' tusks and big rhinoceros' horns. There are elephants' tusks which weigh over 100 carries and rhinoceros' horns of over ten catties weight. The land is also rich in putchuk, liquid storax gum, myrrh, and tortoise-shell of extraordinary thickness, for which there is great demand in other countries. The country also brings forth the so-called 'camel-crane' [ostrich], which measures from the ground to its crown from six to seven feet. It has wings and can fly, but not to any great height.

There is also in this country a wild animal called tsu-la [giraffe]; it resembles a camel in shape, an ox in size, and is of a yellow colour. Its fore legs are five feet long, its hind legs only three feet. Its head is high up and turned upwards. Its skin is an inch thick.

There is also in this country a kind of mule [zebra] with brown, white, and black stripes around its body. These animals wander about in mountain wilds; they are a variety of camel. The inhabitants of this country, who are great huntsman, hunt these animals with poisoned arrows.

ABU-AL-FIDA: MALINDI, MOMBASA, AND SOFALA

Malindi is a town of the land of the Zanj, $81\frac{1}{2}°$ long., 2° 50' lat. West of the town is a great gulf into which flows a river which comes down from the mountain of Komr. On the banks of this gulf are very large dwellings belonging to the Zanj; the houses of the people of Komr are on the south side. East of Malindi is al-Kerany, the name of a mountain very famous among travellers; this mountain runs out into the sea fora distance of about 100 miles in a north-east direction; at the same time it extends along the continent in a straight line north for a distance of about fifty miles. Among other things which we might say about this mountain are the iron mine which is on the continental side and the lodestone in the part which is in the sea, which attracts iron.

At Malindi is the tree of zendj (the ginger tree) (or at Mallndi there are many Zanjian sorcerers). The King of the Zanj lives at Malindi. Between Mombasa and Mnllndi is about a degree. Mombasa is on the coast. On the west is a gulf along which buildings stand as far as 300 miles. Nearby to the east is the desert which separates the land of the Zanj from Sofaia.

Among the towns of the country of Sofala is Batyna (*or* Banyna). It is situated at the end of a great gulf, away from the equinoctial line, under $2\frac{1}{2}°$ lat., 87° long. According to Ibn Said, on the West of Batyna is Adjued, the name of a mountain which projects into the sea towards the north-east for a distance of 100 miles. The waves of the sea make a great noise here. The people of Sofala live to the east of this mountain: their capital is Seruna, under 99° long., 2½ lat. [south]. The town is built on a large estuary where a river, which rises in the mountain of Komr, flows out. There the King of Sofala resides.

Then one arrives at the town of Leirana. Ibn Fathuma, who visited the town, said that it was a seaport where ships put in and whence they set out. The inhabitants profess Islam. Leirana is on long. 102°, lat. 0° 30' [south]. It is on a great gulf.

The town of Daghuta is the last one of the country of Sofala and the furthest of the inhabited part of the continent towards the south. It is on long. 109°, lat. 12°, south of the equator.

Sofala. According to the Canon it is on 50° 3' long., 2° lat., south of the equator. Sofala is in the land of the Zanj. According to the author of the Canon, the inhabitants are Muslims. Ibn Said says that their chief means of existence are mining gold and iron, and that they dress in leopard skins. According to Masudi, horses do not reproduce in the land of the Zanj, so that the warriors go on foot or fight from the backs of oxen.

Questions

(1) Do the three accounts agree on any one (or more) points? Explain.

(2) How do the three accounts shed light on the religious life of the Eastern Africans?

(3) What are the chief products for trade and consumption?

12–4
The Mongol Khan's ultimatum to the nations of Europe.

Contact between the Mongol Empire of Genghis Khan and his successors and Western Europeans was slight, although detachments of the Mongol forces had stationed themselves in Russia at the doorstep of Eastern European states and had gone so far as to raid and devastate parts of Poland and Hungary. These Tartars (as the Mongols were often called) would maintain a lengthy presence in Russia under the designation of "The Golden Horde." From time to time popes would dispatch emissaries with letters to the Khan. That the Khan was not particularly impressed is made clear in his imperious reply.

Source: Christopher Dawson, ed., *Mission to Asia* (Toronto: University of Toronto Press, for the Medieval Academy of America, 1980), pp. 83–84. (First published by Sheed & Ward, London, 1955, as *The Mongol Mission*; reprinted by Harper & Row 1966).

The Strength of God, the Emperor of all men, to the Great Pope, Authentic and True Letters

Having taken counsel for making peace with us, You Pope and all Christians have sent an envoy to us, as we have heard from him and as your letters declare. Wherefore, if you wish to have peace with us, You Pope and all kings and potentates, in no way delay to come to me to make terms of peace and then you shall hear alike our answer and our will. The contents of your letters stated that we ought to be baptized and become Christians. To this we answer briefly that we do not understand in what way we ought to do this. To the rest of the contents of your letters, viz: that you wonder at so great a slaughter of men, especially of Christians and in particular Poles, Moravians and Hungarians, we reply likewise that this also we do not understand. However, lest we may seem to pass it over in silence altogether, we give you this for our answer.

Because they did not obey the word of God and the command of Chingis Chan and the Chan, but took council to slay our envoys, therefore God ordered us to destroy them and gave them up into our hands. For otherwise if God had not done this, what could man do to man? But you men of the West believe that you alone are Christians and despise others. But how can you know to whom God deigns to confer His grace? But we worshipping God have destroyed the whole earth from the East to the West in the power of God. And if this were not the power of God, what could men have done? Therefore if you accept peace and are willing to surrender your fortresses to us, You Pope and Christian princes, in no way delay coming to me to conclude peace and then we shall know that you wish to have peace with us. But if you should not believe our letters and the command of God nor hearken to our counsel then we shall know for certain that you wish to have war. After that we do not know what will happen, God alone knows.

Chingis Chan, first Emperor, second Ochoday Chan, third Cuiuch Chan.

Questions
(1) What is the Khan's response to requests that he be baptized?
(2) How does the Khan justify the slaying and seizure of the land of Eastern European Christians?
(3) What is the letter's general tone? What does the Khan command and what consequences does he state could arise from noncompliance?

12–5
William of Rubruck: impressions of the medieval Mongols.

One of the mere handful of Europeans who did willingly take the trek into the Mongolian ("Tartar") heartland was the monk, William of Rubruck. William was dispatched on a diplomatic Church mission to see the Great Khan Mongke (1251–1259), grandson of Ghengis Khan. Though this attempt proved to be just as fruitless as similar expeditons from the diplomatic and religious points of view, William's descriptions of the Mongol peoples and their culture has proven to be an invaluable resource for scholars of this period.

Source: Christopher Dawson, ed., *Mission to Asia* (Toronto: University of Toronto Press, for the Medieval Academy of America, 1980), pp. 93-104. (First published by Sheed & Ward, London, 1955 as *The Mongol Mission*; reprinted by Harper & Row, 1966.)

THE TARTARS AND THEIR DWELLINGS

THE Tartars have no abiding city nor do they know of the one that is to come. They have divided among themselves Scythia, which stretches from the Danube as far as the rising of the sun. Each captain, according to whether he has more or fewer men under him, knows the limits of his pasturage and where to feed his flocks in winter, summer, spring and autumn, for in winter they come down to the warmer districts in the south, in summer they go up to the cooler ones in the north. They drive their cattle to graze on the pasture lands without water in winter when there is snow there, for the snow provides them with water.

The dwelling in which they sleep has as its base a circle of interlaced sticks, and it is made of the same material; these sticks converge into a little circle at the top and from this a neck juts up like a chimney; they cover it with white felt and quite often they also coat the felt with lime or white clay and powdered bone to make it a more gleaming white, and sometimes they make it black. The felt round the neck at the top they decorate with lovely and varied paintings. Before the doorway they also hang felt worked in multicoloured designs; they sew coloured felt on to the other, making vines and trees, birds and animals. They make these houses so large that sometimes they are thirty feet across; for I myself once measured the width between the wheel tracks of a cart, and it was twenty feet, and when the house was on the cart it stuck out at least five feet beyond the wheels on each side. I have counted to one cart twenty-two oxen drawing one house, eleven in a row across the width of the cart, and the other eleven in front of them. The axle of the cart was as big as the mast of a ship, and a man stood at the door of the house on the cart, driving the oxen.

In addition they make squares to the size of a large coffer out of slender split twigs; then over it, from one end to the other, they build up a rounded roof out of similar twigs and they make a little entrance at the front end; after that they cover this box or little house with black felt soaked in tallow or ewes' milk so that it is rain-proof, and this they decorate in the same way with multi-coloured handwork. Into these chests they put all their bedding and valuables; they bind them onto high carts which are drawn by camels so that they can cross rivers. These chests are never removed from the carts. When they take down their dwelling houses, they always put the door facing the south; then afterwards they draw up the carts with the chests on each side, half a stone's throw from the house, so that it stands between two rows of carts, as it were between two walls.

The married women make for themselves really beautiful carts which I would not know how to describe for you except by a picture; in fact I would have done you paintings of everything if I only knew how to paint. A wealthy Mongol or Tartar may well have a hundred or two hundred such carts with chests. Baatu has twenty-six wives and each of these has a large house, not counting the other small ones which are placed behind the large one and which are, as it were, chambers in which their attendants live; belonging to each of these houses are a good two hundred carts. When they pitch their houses the chief wife places her dwelling at the extreme west end and after her the others according to their rank, so that the last wife will be at the far east end, and there will bc the space of a stone's throw between the establishment of one wife and that of another. And so the orda of a rich Mongol will look like a large town and yet there will be very few men in it.

One woman will drive twenty or thirty carts, for the country is flat. They tie together the carts, which are drawn by oxen or camels, one after the other, and the woman will sit on the front one driving the ox while all the others follow in step. If they happen to come on a bad bit of track they loose them and lead them across it one by one. They go at a very slow pace, as a sheep or an ox might walk.

When they have pitched their houses with the door facing south, they arrange the master's couch at the northern end. The women's place is always on the east side, that is, on the left of the master of the house when he is sitting on his couch looking towards the south; the men's place is on the west side, that is, to his right.

On entering a house the men would by no means hang up their quiver in the women's section. Over the head of the master there is always an idol like a doll or little image of felt which they call the master's brother, and a similar one over the head of the mistress, and this they call the mistress's brother; they are fastened on to the wall. Higher up between these two is a thin little one which is, as it were, the guardian of the whole house. The mistress of the house places on her right side, at the foot of the couch, in a prominent position, a goat-skin stuffed with wool or other material, and next to it a tiny image turned towards her attendants and the women. By the entrance on the women's side is still another idol with a cow's udder for the women who milk the cows, for this is the women's job. On the other side of the door towards the men is another image with a mare's udder for the men who milk the mares.

When they have foregathered for a drink they first sprinkle with the drink the idol over the master's head, then all the other idols in turn; after this an attendant goes out of the house with a cup and some drinks; he sprinkles thrice towards the south, genuflecting each time; this is in honour of fire; next towards the east in honour of the air, and after that to the west in honour of water; they cast it to the north for the dead. When the master is holding his cup in his hand and is about to drink, before he does so he first pours some out on the earth as its share. If he drinks while seated on a horse, before he drinks he pours some over the neck or mane of the horse. And so when the attendant has sprinkled towards the four quarters of the earth he returns into the house; two servants with two cups and as many plates are ready to carry the drink to the master and the wife sitting beside him upon his couch. If he has several wives, she with whom he sleeps at night sits next to him during the day, and on that day all the others have to come to her dwelling to drink, and the court is held there, and the gifts which are presented to the master are placed in the treasury of that wife. Standing in the entrance is a bench with a skin of milk or some other drink and some cups.

In the winter they make an excellent drink from rice, millet, wheat and honey, which is clear like wine. Wine, too, is conveyed to them from distant regions. In the summer they do not bother about anything except cosmos. Cosmos [koumiss] is always to be found inside the house before the entrance door, and near it stands a musician with his instrument. Our lutes and viols I did not see there but many other instruments such as are not known among us. When the master begins to drink, then one of the attendants cries out in a loud voice "Ha!" and the musician strikes his instrument. And when it is a big feast they are holding, they all clap their hands and also dance to the sound of the instrument, the men before the master and the women before the mistress. After the master has drunk, then the attendant cries out as before and the instrument-player breaks off. Then they drink all round, the men and the women, and sometimes vie with each other in drinking in a really disgusting and gluttonous manner.

When they want to incite anyone to drink they seize him by the ears and pull them vigorously to make his gullet open, and they clap and dance in front of him. Likewise when they want to make a great feast and entertainment for anyone, one man takes a full cup and two others stand, one on his right and one on his left, and in this manner the three, singing and dancing, advance right up to him to whom they are to offer the cup, and they sing and dance before him; when he stretches out his hand to take the cup they suddenly leap back, and then they advance again as before; and in this way they make fun of him, drawing back the cup three or four times until he is in a really lively mood and wants it: then they give him the cup and sing and clap their hands and stamp with their feet while he drinks.

THE FOOD OF THE TARTARS

As for their food and victuals I must tell you they eat all dead animals indiscriminately and with so many flocks and herds you can be sure a great many animals do die. However, in the summer as long as they have any cosmos, that is mare's milk, they do not care about any other food. If during that time an ox or a horse happens to die, they dry the flesh by cutting it into thin strips and hanging it in the sun and the wind, and it dries immediately without salt and without any unpleasant smell. Out of the intestines of horses they make sausages which are better than pork sausages and they eat these fresh; the rest of the meat they keep for the winter. From the hide of oxen they make large jars which they dry in a wonderful way in the smoke. From the hind part of horses' hide they make very nice shoes.

They feed fifty or a hundred men with the flesh of a single sheep, for they cut it up in little bits in a dish with salt and water, making no other sauce; then with the point of a knife or a fork especially made for this purpose—like those with which we are accustomed to eat pears and apples cooked in wine—they offer to each of those standing round one or two mouthfuls, according to the number of guests. Before the flesh of the sheep is served, the master first takes what pleases him; and also if he gives anyone a special portion then the one receiving it has to eat it himself and may give it to no one else. But if he cannot eat it all he may take it away with him or give it to his servant, if he is there to keep for him; otherwise he may put it away in his *captargac,* that is, a square bag which they carry to put all such things in: in this they also keep bones when they have not the time to give them a good gnaw, so that later they may gnaw them and no food be wasted.

HOW THEY MAKE COSMOS

COSMOS, that is mare's milk, is made in this way: they stretch along the ground a long rope attached to two stakes stuck into the earth, and at about nine o'clock they tie to this rope the foals of the mares they want to milk. Then the mothers stand near their foals and let themselves be peacefully milked; if any one of them is too restless, then a man takes the foal and, placing it under her, lets it suck a little, and he takes it away again and the milker takes its place.

And so, when they have collected a great quantity of milk, which is as sweet as cow's milk when it is fresh, they pour it into a large skin or bag and they begin churning it with a specially made stick which is as big as a man's head at its lower end, and hollowed out; and when they beat it quickly it begins to bubble like new wine and to turn sour and ferment, and they churn it until they can extract the butter. Then they taste it and when it is fairly pungent they drink it. As long as one is drinking, it bites the tongue like vinegar; when one stops, it leaves on the tongue the taste of milk of almonds and greatly delights the inner man; it even intoxicates those who have not a very good head. It also greatly provokes urine.

For use of the great lords they also make caracosmos, that is black cosmos, in this wise. Mare's milk does not curdle. Now it is a general rule that the milk of any animal, in the stomach of whose young rennet is not found, does not curdle; it is not found in the stomach of a young horse, hence the milk of a mare does not curdle. And so they churn the milk until everything that is solid in it sinks right to the bottom like the lees of wine, and what is pure remains on top and is like whey or white must. The dregs are very white and are given to the slaves and have a most soporific effect. The clear liquid the masters drink and it is certainly a very pleasant drink and really potent.

Baatu has thirty men within a day's journey of his camp, each one of whom provides him every day with such milk from a hundred mares—that is to say, the milk of three thousand mares every day, not counting the other white milk which other men bring. For, just as

in Syria the peasants give a third part of their produce, so these men have to bring to the orda of their lords the mare's milk of every third day.

From cow's milk they first extract the butter and this they boil until it is completely boiled down; then they store it in sheep's paunches which they keep for this purpose; they do not put salt into the butter; however it does not go bad owing to the long boiling. They keep it against the winter. The rest of the milk which is left after the butter has been extracted they allow to turn until it is as sour as it can be, and they boil it, and in boiling, it curdles; they dry the curd in the sun and it becomes as hard as iron slag, and this they keep in bags against the winter. During the winter months when there is a scarcity of milk, they put this sour curd, which they call grut, into a skin and pour hot water on top of it and beat it vigorously until it melts in the water, which, as a result, becomes completely sour, and this water they drink instead of milk. They take the greatest care never to drink plain water.

THE ANIMALS THEY EAT, THEIR CLOTHES, AND THEIR HUNTING

THE great lords have villages in the south from which millet and flour are brought to them for the winter; the poor provide for themselves by trading sheep and skins; and the slaves fill their bellies with dirty water and are content with this. They also catch mice, of which many kinds abound there; mice with long tails they do not eat but give to their bards; they eat dormice and all kinds of mice with short tails. There are also many marmots there which they call *sogur* and these congregate in one burrow in the winter, twenty or thirty of them together, and they sleep for six months; these they catch in great quantities.

Also to be found there are comes with a long tail like a cat and having at the tip of the tail black and white hairs. They have many other little animals as well which are good to eat, and they are very clever at knowing the difference. I saw no deer there, I saw few hares, many gazelles; wild asses I saw in great quantifies and these are like mules. I also saw another kind of animal which is called *arcali* and which has a body just like a ram's and horns twisted like a ram's but of such a size that I could scarce lift the two horns with one hand; and they make large cups out of these horns.

They have hawks, gerfalcons and peregrine falcons in great numbers and these they carry on their right hand, and they always put a little thong round the hawk's neck. This thong hangs down the middle of its breast and by it they pull down with the left hand the head and breast of the hawk when they cast it at its prey, so that it is not beaten back by the wind or carried upwards. They procure a large part of their food by the chase.

When they want to hunt wild animals they gather

together in a great crowd and surround the district in which they know the animals to be, and gradually they close in until between them they shut in the animals in a circle and then they shoot at them with their arrows.

I will tell you about their garments and their clothing. From Cathay and other countries to the east, and also from Persia and other districts of the south, come cloths of silk and gold and cotton materials which they wear in the summer. From Russia, Moxel, Great Bulgaria and Pascatu, which is Greater Hungarys and Kerkis, which are all districts towards the north, and full of forests, and from many other regions in the north which are subject to them, valuable furs of many kinds are brought for them, such as I have never seen in our part of the world; and these they wear in winter. In the winter they always make at least two fur garments, one with the fur against the body, the other with the fur outside to the wind and snow, and these are usually of the skins of wolves or foxes or monkeys, and when they sitting in their dwelling they have another softer one. The poor make their outer ones of dog and goat.

They also make trousers out of skins. Moreover, the rich line their garments with silk stuffing which is extraordinarily soft and light and warm. The poor line their clothes with cotton material and with the softer wool which they are able to pick out from the coarser. With the coarse they make felt to cover their dwellings and coffers and also for making bedding. Also with wool mixed with a third part horse-hair they make their ropes. From felt they make saddle pads, saddle cloths and rain cloaks, which means they use a great deal of wool. You have seen the men's costume.

HOW THE MEN SHAVE AND THE WOMEN ADORN THEMSELVES

THE men shave a square on the top of their heads and from the front corners of this they continue the shaving in strips along the sides of the head as far as the temples. They also shave their temples and neck to the top of the cervical cavity and their forehead in front to the top of the frontal bone, where they leave a tuft of hair which hangs down as far as the eyebrows. At the sides and the back of the head they leave the hair, which they make into plaits, and these they braid round the head to the ears.

The costume of the girls is no different from that of the men except that it is somewhat longer. But on the day after she is married a woman shaves from the middle of her head to her forehead, and she has a tunic as wide as a nun's cowl, and in every respect wider and longer, and open in front, and this they tie on the right side. Now in this matter the Tartars differ from the Turks, for the Turks tie their tunics on the left, but the Tartars always on the right.

They also have a head-dress which they call

bocca, which is made out of the bark of a tree or of any other fairly light material which they can find; it is large and circular and as big as two hands can span around, a cubit and more high and square at the top like the capital of a column. This *bocca* they cover with costly silk material, and it is hollow inside, and on the capital in the middle or on the side they put a rod of quills or slender canes, likewise a cubit and more in length; and they decorate this rod at the top with peacock feathers and throughout its length all round with little feathers from the mallard's tail and also with precious stones. The wealthy ladies wear such an ornament on the top of their head and fasten it down firmly with a hood which has a hole in the top for this purpose, and in it they stuff their hair, gathering it up from the back on to the top of the head in a kind of knot and putting over it the *bocca* which they then tie firmly under the chin. So when several ladles ride together and are seen from a distance, they give the appearance of soldiers with helmets on their heads and raised lances; for the *bocca* looks like a helmet and the rod on top like a lance.

All the women sit on their horses like men, astride, and they tie their cowls with a piece of sky-blue silk round the waist, and with another strip they bind their breasts, and they fasten a piece of white stuff below their eyes which hangs down to the breast.

The women are wondrous fat and the less nose they have the more beautiful they are considered. They disfigure themselves hideously by painting their faces. They never lie down on a bed to give birth to their children.

THE DUTIES OF THE WOMEN AND THEIR WORK

IT is the duty of the women to drive the carts, to load the houses on to them and to unload them to milk the cows, to make the butter and *grut,* to dress the skins and to sew them, which they do with thread made out of tendons. They split the tendons into very thin threads and then twist these into one long thread. They also sew shoes and socks and other garments. They never wash their clothes, for they say that that makes God angry and that it would thunder if they hung them out to dry; they even beat those who do wash them and take them away from them. They are extraordinarily afraid of thunder. At such a time they turn all strangers out of their dwellings and wrap themselves in black felt in which they hide until it has passed over. They never wash their dishes, but when the meat is cooked, they wash out the bowl in which they are going to put it with some boiling broth from the cauldron which they afterwards pour back. The women also make the felt and cover the houses.

The men make bows and arrows, manufacture stirrups and bits and make saddles; they build the houses and carts, they look after the horses and milk the mares, churn the cosmos, that is the mares' milk, and make the skins in which it is kept, and they also look after the camels and load them. Both sexes look after the sheep and goats, and sometimes the men, sometimes the women, milk them. They dress skins with the sour milk of ewes, thickened and salted.

When they want to wash their hands or their head, they fill their mouth with water and, pouring this little by little from their mouth into their hands, with it they wet their hair and wash their head.

As for their marriages, you must know that no one there has a wife unless he buys her, which means that sometimes girls are quite grown up before they marry, for their parents always keep them until they sell them. They observe the first and second degrees of consanguinity, but observe no degrees of affinity; they have two sisters at the same time or one after the other. No widow among them marries, the reason being that they believe that all those who serve them

in this life will serve them in the next, and so of a widow they believe that she will always return after death to her first husband. This gives rise to a shameful custom among them whereby a son sometimes takes to wife all his father's wives, except his own mother; for the orda of a father and mother always falls to the youngest son and so he himself has to provide for all his father's wives who come to him with his father's effects; and then, if he so wishes, he uses them as wives, for he does not consider an injury has been done to him if they return to his father after death.

And so when anyone has made an agreement with another to take his daughter, the father of the girl arranges a feast and she takes flight to relations where she lies hid. Then the father declares: "Now my daughter is yours; take her wherever you find her." Then he searches for her with his friends until he finds her; then he has to take her by force and bring her, as though by violence, to his house.

Questions

(1) As described by William Rubruck, in a culture such as that of the Mongols, what items would have been held in the greatest value?

(2) What was cosmos, and what role did it play in Mongolian popular culture?

(3) Why did the Mongols not believe in washing clothes?

(4) What had to occur before a Mongol could take a wife? How was he expected to take her following the wedding feast?

12–6
Castiglione's "Courtier": prosperity makes a gentleman.

The increase in mercantile contact from Asia and Africa with Europe revitalized the latter's moribund markets, and helped generate the Renaissance, wherein Europe broke the bond of manorialism in favor of a capitalist economy. A rising standard of living, most pronounced among the noble and upper-middle classes, and increasing literacy levels and intellectual sophistication had, as one byproduct, the conceptualization of the courtly "gentleman." The new breed of noble, the courtier, was not expected to be one-dimensional as his predecessor, the feudal knight. While the courtly Renaissance noble still had a military function, he was expected to be versatile and as much at home with the arts of peace (music, art, letters, politics, etc.) as those of war. This new type of aristocrat is depicted in "The Book of the Courtier" by Baldassaro Castiglione (1478–1529), which was meant to serve as a handbook for genteel conduct.

Source: Friench Simpson, ed., *Baldassare Castiglione: The Book of the Courtier* (N.Y.: Frederick Ungar, 1959), pp. 34–40, 46–47.

41. The Courtier must be a man of virtue and integrity.

You can appreciate how contrary and fatal affectation is to the grace of every function not only of the body, but likewise of the mind, concerning which we have as yet said little, though we should not therefore pass it over. For as the mind is much more noble than the body, so also it deserves to be more cultivated and enriched. And as to how this should be accomplished in our Courtier, let us leave aside the precepts of so many wise philosophers

who write on this subject and define the powers of the mind and so subtly dispute about their worth, and let us, keeping to our subject, say in few words that it is enough he should be, as they say, a man of virtue and integrity; for in this are com- prehended the practical wisdom, justice, fortitude, and temperance of mind and all the other qualifies which attend upon so honored a name. And I feel that he alone is the true moral philosopher who wishes to be good; and for that purpose he needs few precepts other than that wish....

42–44. Next in importance to virtue comes knowledge of humane letters.

"But with the exception of goodness, the true and chief ornament of the mind in each of us is, I think, letters....

I desire that in letters [our Courtier] should be more than passably learned, at least in these studies which men call humanities, and that he be acquainted not only with Latin but also with Greek, for the sake of the numerous and varied works which have been superbly written in that language. Let him be versed in the poets, and no less in the orators and historians. Let him also be trained in the writing of verse and prose, especially in our vernacular tongue. For in addition to the private enjoyment which he will derive, he will, thanks to this, never find himself at a loss for pleasing pastime with women, who for the most part love such things.

"And if, either because of other employment or because of lack of study he does not arrive at such perfection that his compositions are worthy of much praise, let him take the precaution of concealing them in order not to make others laugh at him and let him show them only to a friend whom he can trust, because they will benefit him to this extent at least that through that training he will know how to judge the works of others, for indeed it rarely happens that a person not accustomed to writing, however learned he be, can ever fully appreciate the labor and ingenuity of writers or enjoy the sweetness and excellence of styles and those latent niceties which are often found in the ancients. And besides that, these studies make him fluent and, as Aristippus replied to that tyrant, bold enough to speak with confidence to everyone. I greatly desire furthermore that our Courtier hold fixed in his mind one precept, namely, that in this and in every other thing he always be attentive and cautious rather than daring, and that he guard against persuading himself mistakenly that he knows what he does not know; for we are all by nature much more eager for praise than we should be, and our ears love the melody of the words which sing our praises more than any other song or sound, however sweet; and yet often, like the Siren's voices, these words bring shipwreck to any man who does not stop his ears against music so deceiving. Recognizing this danger, some among the sages of antiquity have written books telling us how we may distinguish the true friend from the flatterer. But what benefit has come of this if many, nay innumerable, are those who clearly realize that they are being flattered and yet love the flatterer and loathe the man who tells them the truth? And often it appears to them that the man who praises is too niggardly in what he says; so they themselves come to his aid and say such things about themselves as make the most shameless flatterer blush.

"Let us leave these blind men in their error and see to it that our Courtier is so sound of judgment that he cannot be made to take black for white or think highly of himself except in such measure as he clearly knows to be just....On the contrary, in order not to err, even if he knows very well that the praises that are given him are just, let him not concur in them too openly or confirm them without some show of opposition, but rather let him modestly come near to denying them, always claiming and actually considering arms as his chief calling and all the other good attributes as ornaments of them. Let him observe this caution especially among soldiers, in order not to behave like those who in their studies wish to appear men of war and among men of war wish to appear men of letters. In this fashion and for the reasons which we have given, he will avoid affectation, and even the commonplace things that he does will appear very impressive."

45. Bembo objects that letters rather than arms ought to be the Courtier's chief glory.

At this point Messer Pietro Bembo said in reply: "I do not know, Count, why you should desire that this Courtier, accomplished in letters and possessed of so many other qualities, should consider everything an ornament of arms and not arms and the rest an ornament of letters, which in and for themselves are as much superior to arms in worth as the mind is to the body, since the pursuit of letters belongs properly to the mind, as that of arms does to the body."

The Count then replied:

"Rather, the pursuit of arms belongs to the mind and to the body. But I am not desirous of having you, Messer Pietro, as judge of this dispute, because you would be too suspect of bias in the eyes of one of the parties; and since this debate has long been carried on by the most learned men, there is no need to renew it. However, I consider it settled in favor of arms and I stipulate that our Courtier, since I can shape him according to my will, shall also consider the matter so. And if you are of contrary opinion, wait until you hear of a dispute over it in which those who defend the case for arms may as lawfully use arms as those who defend letters use those same letters in their defence. For if each can avail himself of his own instruments, you will see that the men of letters will lose...."

47. The Courtier should be an accomplished musician.

"My lords..., you must know that I am not satisfied with the Courtier if he is not also a musician and if besides understanding music and reading notes readily he does not know a variety of instruments; for if we consider the matter carefully, we can find no repose from toil or medicine for ailing minds more wholesome and commendable for leisure time than this; and especially at courts, where much is done not only to provide the relief from vexations that music offers all of us but also to please the women, whose delicate and impressionable spirits are easily penetrated by harmony and filled with sweetness. Therefore it is no wonder if in ancient and in modern times women have always been favorably disposed toward musicians and have found music a most welcome food for the spirit."

Thereupon Lord Gaspar said:

"Music, along with many other follies, I consider suitable indeed for women and perhaps also for some who possess the appearance of men, but not for those who truly are men and who ought not to unman their minds with pleasures and thus incline them to be afraid of death."

"Do not say such a thing," answered the Count; "for I will here set forth on a vast sea of praise of music, and I will recall to what a degree among the ancients it was always extolled and regarded as something holy and how widely the wisest philosophers held that the world is fashioned of music and that the heavens produce harmony as they move and, moreover, that our soul was formed according to the same principles and therefore awakens and, as it were, quickens its powers through music. For this reason it is recorded that Alexander was so warmly aroused by it on a certain occasion that almost against his will he was obliged to rise from the banquet and rush to arms; then, as the musician altered the quality of the tone, to grow mild and return from arms to banqueting…

"Have you not read that music was one of the first disciplines that the good old Chiron taught Achilles, when Achilles, whom he reared from the time of milk and cradle, was at a tender age; and the wise master desired that the hands which were to spill so much Trojan blood should be often busied with the music of the cithara? What soldier, pray, will there be who is ashamed to imitate Achilles, not to mention many other famous commanders whom I could name? Therefore do not be disposed to deprive our Courtier of music, which not only softens the minds of men but often makes the fierce become gentle; and one can be certain that if a man does not enjoy music his spirits are all out of tune."

48. Giuliano de' Medici wishes to know how the Courtier is to apply his attributes in actual practice.

Since the Count was silent for a little while at this point, the Magnifico Giuliano said: "I am not at all of Lord Gaspat's opinion; on the contrary I believe, for the reasons that you state and for many others, that music is not only an ornament but a necessity for the Courtier. I should greatly like you to declare in what way this and the other attributes which you assign to him are to be put into practice, both at what time and after what fashion. For many things which in themselves deserve praise frequently become highly unsuitable when done at the wrong time. And by way of contrast, some things

which appear of small weight are much valued when they are properly managed."

49. Before answering Giuliano the Count recommends that the Courtier be taught to draw and to understand painting.

Then the Count said:

"Before we enter into this subject I want to talk of another matter which, since I consider it of great importance, should, I think, by no means be left out by our Courtier. And this is knowing how to draw and possessing an understanding of the true art of painting. Do not marvel if I desire this skill which today perhaps is judged to be a craft and little fitting for a gentleman; for I recall having read that the ancients, especially through the whole of Greece, used to require that children of noblemen give attention to painting in school, as something wholesome and requisite; and that this subject was admitted into the first rank of the liberal arts and subsequently by public edict was forbidden to be taught to slaves. Among the Romans also it was held in the highest honor.…

"And to tell the truth I think that anyone who does not value this art is very much a stranger to reason; for the universe in its structure, with the wide heaven of bright stars surrounding it and in the middle the earth girdled by the seas, figured with mountains, valleys, and rivers, and embellished by trees of many different kinds and by lovely flowers and plants, one can call a noble and magnificent picture executed by the hand of nature and of God; and the man who can imitate it I consider worthy of great praise; nor can one succeed in this without the knowledge of many things, as anyone who tries it well knows.

BOOK THREE

The Attributes of the Court Lady and the Character of Women in General

The Court Lady as described by the Magnifico is to possess the same virtues as the Courtier and undergo the same training in letters, music, painting, dancing and other graces; also she should avoid affectation and cultivate *sprezzatura*. She is to avoid manly exercises and manners and preserve a feminine sweetness and delicacy. For example, she should not play on drums or trumpets, or take part in tennis or hunting. Above all she should acquire a pleasant affability in entertaining men, being neither too bashful nor too bold in company.

Gaspar Pallavicino declares such a woman impossible; women are imperfect creatures. The Magnifico answers this with the proposition that since two members of the same species have the same essential substance, one cannot be essentially less perfect than the other. Pallavicino counters with the claim that man is to woman as form is to matter; woman is imperfect without man. The argument follows these metaphysical lines for a while; then the Magnifico undertakes to show that for every great man there are equally admirable women to be cited, both in ancient and in modern times.

Lord Gaspar Pallavicino continues to insist that women are chaste only through fear of punishment, Cesare Gonzaga then takes up the defense of women, citing cases of women who defended their chastity to the death and describing the wiles which men use to overcome female chastity; then, passing on to the Courtly Love tradition, he asserts that all the refinements of life are cultivated in order to please women.

Finally the discussion turns to the way the Court Lady should respond to talk of love. The Magnitieo's opinion is that only unmarried women should allow themselves to fall in love, and then only when love is likely to end in marriage. All physical gratification outside marriage is forbidden. Federico Fregoso suggests that where there is no possibility of divorce a woman whose husband hates her should be permitted to bestow her love elsewhere. The Magnifico replies that she may bestow only spiritual love. Pallavicino denounces women because they love to drive a lover mad by refusing their favors for a very long while and then, when the lover's appetite is dulled by exasperation, at last bestowing favors that can no longer be fully enjoyed by him.

Questions
(1) For what reasons should a courtly man possess knowledge of the "humane letters" and what should he do if he has not had the time to acquire this knowledge?

(2) In what light should the courtier consider the noble ladies?

(3) Why should the courtier be versed in music and painting?

(4) What virtues, in and of herself, is the court lady expected to possess that differs from the expectations of a courtly gentleman?